Program Verification

INTERNATIONAL COMPUTER SCIENCE SERIES

Consulting editors **A D McGettrick** University of Strathclyde

J van Leeuwen University of Utrecht

SELECTED TITLES IN THE SERIES

Distributed Systems: Concepts and Design *G Coulouris and J Dollimore*

Software Prototyping, Formal Methods and VDM *S Hekmatpour and D Ince*

High-Level Languages and their Compilers *D Watson*

Elements of Functional Programming *C Reade*

Software Development with Modula-2 *D Budgen*

Interactive Computer Graphics: Functional, Procedural and Device-Level Methods *P Burger and D Gillies*

Program Derivation: The Development of Programs from Specifications *R G Dromey*

Program Design with Modula-2 *S Eisenbach and C Sadler*

Parallel Processing: Principles and Practice *E V Krishnamurthy*

Real Time Systems and their Programming Languages *A Burns and A Wellings*

Prolog Programming for Artificial Intelligence (2nd Edn) *I Bratko*

Introduction to Expert Systems (2nd Edn) *P Jackson*

Logic for Computer Science *S Reeves and M Clarke*

Computer Architecture *M De Blasi*

The Programming Process: an Introduction using VDM and Pascal *J T Latham, V J Bush and D Cottam*

Analysis of Algorithms and Data Structures *L Banachowski, A Kreczmar and W Rytter*

Handbook of Algorithms and Data Structures in Pascal and C (2nd Edn) *G Gonnet and R Baeza-Yates*

Algorithms and Data Structures *J H Kingston*

Principles of Expert Systems *P Lucas and L van der Gaag*

Discrete Mathematics for Computer Scientists *J K Truss*

Programming in Ada plus Language Reference Manual (3rd Edn) *J G P Barnes*

Software Engineering (4th Edn) *I Sommerville*

Software Development with Z: A Practical Approach to Formal Methods in Software Engineering *J B Wordsworth*

Program Verification

Nissim Francez

Technion – Israel Institute of Technology

ADDISON-WESLEY
PUBLISHING
COMPANY

Wokingham, England · Reading, Massachusetts · Menlo Park, California · New York
Don Mills, Ontario · Amsterdam · Bonn · Sydney · Singapore
Tokyo · Madrid · San Juan · Milan · Paris · Mexico City · Seoul · Taipei

Cover designed by Chris Eley, from an idea by Professor Alfred Bruckstein, and printed by The Riverside Printing Co. (Reading) Ltd. Typeset and printed in Great Britain by the University Press, Cambridge.

First printed 1992.

British Library Cataloguing in Publication Data
A catalogue record for this book is available from the British Library.

Library of Congress Cataloging in Publication Data
Francez, Nissim.
Program verification / Francez Nissim.
p. cm.
Includes bibliographical references and index.
ISBN 0-201-41608-5.
1. Computer software—Verification. I. Title.
QA76.76.V47F73 1992
005.1′4—dc20 92-25895
CIP

PREFACE

Aims and objectives

This book is based on lectures given in the Computer Science Department of the Technion, intended for final year undergraduate and graduate students. It aims to teach the fundamentals of program verification, drawing motivation from the practical problem of software correctness, but stressing the theory and, in particular, the meta-theory. In this aim, it is rather different from the (not too many) related books on the subject. On the one hand, it is not a discussion on the level of pure mathematics (or logic). Whenever possible, the discussion relates to actual phenomena occurring in programming, stressing the intuitive connection with the operational intuition the student has from his or her programming courses, without losing the rigorous mathematical and logical treatment. For example, the semantics of the languages used is always an **operational semantics**, defined in a formal way, in contrast to the use of **denotational semantics** by pure mathematically oriented presentations. On the other hand, it is not a recipe in the form of 'here are some rules, and many examples of their application in systematic ways'. I believe that neither of these extremes serves the goals of teaching the computer scientist to reason rigorously about programs and to become aware of the importance of correctness, as well as the fundamental role verification has in the foundations of computer science.

While there are some books that adhere to this intermediate approach, few of them extend their coverage to the recent developments in this field, covering nondeterminism and concurrency, discussing compositionality, and stressing soundness and completeness proofs. Until now, the lack of a textbook covering these later developments, which are no longer on the frontier of research in this area, forced the use of original research papers as source materials, which makes teaching much harder.

Pedagogical approach

The flavor of the book can be clearly seen from the kinds of exercises given. While other textbooks on verification have as their typical exercise something of the form 'prove the correctness of the following program w.r.t. the following specification', the exercises here relate to a variety of properties of the proof systems themselves, asking for alternate proof rules, for reduction of proofs in one method to proofs in another method, for resolving semantic issues in the minilanguages used, and similar questions. Many in-line exercises ask the student to complete technical details in proofs, which were left out for that purpose. The emphasis is on training the student in the finer details of the systems studied. I believe that only by mastering these details will the student be able to apply the theory successfully and judiciously in practical situations, not exactly similar to the ones considered explicitly. We may compare the situation with that of finding the right mathematical training for an engineer. One approach trains the student with recipes for differentiating and integrating, and numerous techniques of solving differential equations. As I see it, a better approach is to stress the study of abstract notions such as continuity and limit, dwelling on issues such as existence and uniqueness of solutions. Most important, the student should be trained in the mathematical approach of relying on definitions, proving claims made, paying attention to borderline cases, and so on. Once the student gains this deeper understanding, he or she is better equipped to solve equations or find integrals as they arise in practical engineering problems. It is my sincere hope that this book will contribute towards encouraging more computer science departments to include a similar program verification course in their standard curriculum.

Prerequisites

The assumption on the background of the student, in addition to the obvious background in programming and programming languages, is that he or she has a basic first year mathematical education and the ability to follow a mathematical presentation. Also, the student is assumed to have taken at least one introductory course in mathematical logic, and to be familiar with first-order predicate calculus, including its semantics and proof theory. A small number of subsections call for a deeper acquaintance with logic and computability theory, for example, familiarity with coding syntax using arithmetic and Gödel's incompleteness theorem.

Acknowledgements

I would like to thank the following colleagues for useful discussions, reading drafts and helping in many other ways: Krzysztof Apt, Shai Ben-David, Ran

Ever-Hadani, Limor Fix, Orna Grumberg, Michael Kaminski, Shmuel Katz, Amir Pnueli, Sara Porat, and Gadi Taubenfeld. Frank Stomp is thanked for a critical reading of the whole manuscript, and for many corrections and suggestions for improvements in presentation. I wish to thank Simon Plumtree, the editor in charge, for enduring the many obstacles I had in completing the manuscript on time, culminating in the attacks of Iraqi SCUD missiles on Haifa....

At the Technion, my work was funded by a grant from the Israeli Academy of Sciences (basic research), and by the fund for the promotion of research in the Technion.

Nissim Francez

Computer Science Department,
Technion 1992

To Tikva

my sound and complete love.

CONTENTS

Chapter 1
INTRODUCTION

Our main aim is in studying mathematical–logical methods for proving properties of programs (sometimes referred to as **program verification**), and also in studying properties of the proof methods themselves. Already in the early 1940s, with the development of more and more complicated programs, some dissatisfaction had been expressed with the then prevailing technique (still in use nowadays...) for validating one's programs: testing the performance of the program on some (finite, usually relatively small) number of 'test cases'. This technique received the nickname 'debugging'. A saying by E.W. Dijkstra is well known, that testing can reveal the presence of errors, not their absence.

Thus, there has been a continuous quest for an alternative methodology, one that would use more analytical methods, the latter having proved themselves effective in other disciplines of science and engineering. By such a methodology, one should be able to prove a theorem whose interpretation is that a given program is 'correct' (we shall return in the next chapter to the meaning of the 'correctness' in this context). In order to apply such a methodology, the following prerequisites should be satisfied, serving as its building blocks.

A formal specification method A **specification** of a program is a collection of criteria, which, if met by that program, would qualify it as **correct** (with respect to those criteria). For the formulation of such criteria, a **specification language** is needed, generically denoted here by SL, which has a rigorously defined semantics, amenable to formal manipulations. We would expect such a language to be close to a mathematical formalism with which we are familiar.

As such a language is intended for use by some person for the formulation of his or her requirements from a program to be designed, it would be preferable for a specification language to be as abstract as possible, that is, avoiding unnecessary details originating from the nature of a machine that would execute the resulting program. It is commonly agreed that a specification describes what is required, whereas a (correct) implementing program describes how the requirement is met, that is, how the intended effect is brought about. In particular, there is a tendency to avoid in a specification language any reference to dynamic aspects of computations, such as control structures, dynamic assignments, and concurrency. A general property of formal specifications is their enforcement of explicit statement of all assumptions employed, some of which are left implicit in many informal specifications. As a result, formal specifications tend to become tediously lengthy, though complete.

This building block of the sought methodology is the most complicated one, and until now there has been no universally accepted specification method and language. A whole variety of such methods and languages has emerged, each one appropriate for different properties of programs and for different levels of detail in the specification.

One of the hardest problems in this area is of a nonmathematical nature: how does one ensure that a certain formula in *SL* indeed corresponds to one's intuitive intention of what the problem to be solved really is? As the intention in the mind of the specifier is not a formal entity, no formal reasoning can be applied in order to establish the correspondence between intention and formal specification. One has to rely on intuition here. The methodology's point of departure here is that the given formula in *SL* is indeed the requirement to be met by the program. In the next chapter, we shall encounter several examples demonstrating the existence of this gap between the intuitive intention and its formal expression.

Formal semantics of the programming language Programming languages, abbreviated here as *PL*s, are usually perceived as languages for the description of dynamic, time-varying processes, closely related to a notion of execution by some machine (an electronic computer in real life, but more abstract machines for the ease of understanding). Therefore, programming languages abound with constructs such as iteration, recursion, parameter passing, concurrency, and interprocess communication. To each of those constructs an exact meaning has to be attributed in order to enable formal correctness proofs of programs using those constructs.

Having a rigorously defined semantics allows a program to be regarded as a mathematical object, whose properties can be indeed proved. To this end, several methods to provide such semantics of programming languages have been developed. Here too, no single method has been accepted as adequate for all purposes. We shall mainly use an abstract formulation of what is known as **operational semantics** which provides us with some abstract view of what a computation is.

Formal proof rules This component is the 'heart' of the methodology, and its task is to provide the means for establishing the required correspondence between a program and a specification. Our main concern is, for simple enough PL and SL, to find rules for the expression of this correspondence and to study their properties. Several subproblems can be identified in the context of relating PL to SL.

(1) *Synthesis:* Given a specification ϕ in some SL, construct a program (in a given PL) which satisfies ϕ.

Were we able to provide practical automatic solutions to this problem, the whole discipline of programming would disappear.... Until now, not much progress has been achieved towards solving this problem in its full generality. Considerable advance, however, has been made in some special cases of the problem, under some (rather strong) additional assumptions.

(2) *Analysis:* Given a program P in some programming language PL, construct its most 'adequate' specification (in some given specification language SL).

This problem is as hard as, but of much less applicability and importance than, the synthesis problem, and has not been very intensively studied.

(3) *Verification:* Given a program P in a given PL and a specification ϕ in a given SL, show that P satisfies ϕ (in other words, show the correctness of P w.r.t. ϕ).

This is the main problem with which we are concerned in this book, and it has considerable practical importance as well as great theoretical interest. Compared with the other problems, it also displays the highest scientific advance in its solution, at least on the theoretical level. As presented here, the problem is also known as the problem of **a posteriori verification** where one is asked to prove the satisfiability of ϕ by an already existing program P. A more practically useful variant of the problem, which has the potential of becoming industrially applied, is the construction of the program together with its proof. When the latter activity takes place, the final product does not need any further proof.

(4) *Equivalence and optimization:* Given a specification ϕ in some SL and a program P satisfying ϕ, find an equivalent program P', optimal under some given complexity measure.

The equivalence relation considered here is that of satisfying the same specification. Variants of such problems are imposed on what are known as 'optimizing compilers', which, however, work under the assumption of a much stronger equivalence relation among programs.

(5) *Correction:* Given a specification ϕ in some SL and a program P in some PL not satisfying ϕ, find a program P' 'close' to P (under some given proximity relation) which does satisfy ϕ.

This is the problem supposedly solved (repeatedly, usually...) while 'debugging'.

Following are some general comments on the methodology considered above.

(1) As is evident from the list of problems mentioned above, the main concept under investigation in this book is that of a program $P \in PL$ satisfying a specification $\phi \in SL$. Both directions of research, that of designing specification languages and that of formally defining programming languages, have developed into rich disciplines within computer science, known as **logics of programs** and **semantics of programming languages.** We shall dwell only briefly on each of them separately, with an emphasis on ways of establishing their correspondence.

(2) The discussion on applying the above-mentioned methodology did not relate to its automatic (that is, algorithmic) application. It is not hard to show that, in the interesting cases, all these problems are **undecidable**, that is there are no algorithms for solving them. Thus, we are interested in techniques for their solution that rely on the human understanding of the specification and the way this specification is implemented by the program.

However, there is a lot of interest in what is known as **automatic programming**, which seeks additional assumptions under which such problems can be algorithmically solved. For example, if the specification language is on the propositional level and if the programs considered are finite state, then all the above-listed problems have algorithmic solutions (usually of at least exponential complexity).

(3) It should be emphasized that we are not focusing here on any kind of efficiency in applying the methodology. Rather, we are interested in its logical possibility. The main problem regarding its effectiveness arises from the infinite number of the conditions that have to be shown to hold. For finite programs (that is, without any kind of circularity such as iteration or recursion), the problem is considered solved when an exhaustive procedure, that checks all possible executions, does exist, in spite of its combinatorial explosion.

(4) Our main mathematical tool is that of **induction**. We shall distinguish between two kinds of induction.

(a) *Computational induction:* Here, the induction is on the (dynamic) progress of the computation. By the kind of semantics we are going to use, a computation has the form of a (possibly infinite) sequence of some elementary transitions. Thus, in order to establish that some property holds at any point in a computation, the inductive property must be shown to hold at the beginning of a computation and to be preserved by every elementary transition. Such a property is known as an **invariant** of the computation.

(b) *Structural induction:* Here, the induction is on the structure of the objects on which the program operates. The property has to hold for the simplest, nondecomposable objects, and has to be preserved by every combination of objects, in order to hold for any object. This kind of induction generalizes the usual mathematical induction on natural numbers.

We shall return to these subjects in more detail in later chapters.

(5) In addition to our interest in proof methods that fit the above-mentioned methodology we shall be concerned also with properties of the proof methods themselves. For example, we might be interested in proving that under certain conditions no proof method of a certain type exists. Also, we shall discuss the comparative power of different proof methods, and their classification.

What is the merit of a formal methodology? Mainly, it replaces arguments about the behaviors of computations by a systematic application of formal rules. Especially in the realm of concurrent programs, which display a rich multitude of behaviors, it is hard to convince oneself that a given *ad hoc* reasoning is indeed correct. Have all computations been accounted for? Have all details of a given computation been considered? Many such problems are automatically taken care of when the suggested methodology is being applied, once the set of rules has been shown to be adequate (in a sense explained in the next chapter).

However, such merits distinguish the approach to be presented here from other approaches, which are based on direct appeals to semantic definitions, and which, while of a more operational nature, can still be rendered perfectly rigorous. Sometimes, the 'very idea' of program verification, using *any* mathematical or logical method, is criticized. The main argument is that, when programs are actually executed on electronic computers, the above-listed prerequisites for successful application cannot be assumed to hold. Computers, being physical devices, cannot be assumed to behave reliably. In addition, standard implementations at best approximate the formal definition of the semantics. Thus, no logical conclusion can be drawn about the real-life behavior of programs, no more than about any other natural phenomena, with absolute certainty.

Even if one accepts the above characteristics of computers (and for many these are mere truisms), formal methods have still a lot to achieve. Programs are still developed which violate their specifications even under the assumption that all the prerequisites do hold. Thus, even though the issue of absolute certainty might be one of philosophical debate, there is a lot to be desired in *relative* certainty, under the methodological assumptions mentioned, even if the latter are considered idealized. The latter relativization is certainly a necessary condition for a reliable program, even if its sufficiency is being criticized.

On different grounds, formal methods are claimed to be inadequate because of the shortcomings of their application by humans. The latter is conceived as a 'social process', subject to human fallibility. This criticism applies to mathematics as well, where there are known cases of erroneous 'proofs'. Here also, this kind of debate would be better postponed until programming achieves the rigor of mathematics.

There remain, of course, the real obstacles of applying such a methodology, owing to its inherent complication, complexity and limitation. We shall present some perspective in the concluding chapter, after all technical details of the underlying theory have been presented.

In addition to providing a successful methodology, research in formal program verification has had several additional beneficial side effects. We mention three of the main ones. It has increased the general conviction about the merits of advanced programming methodologies, for example that of structured programming, by showing that well-structured programs are easier to verify. Related to this issue, it has influenced the design of programming languages in such a way that their definition by proof rules became a design goal, and changes were introduced in several cases to fit this goal. Its notation has become an accepted way of providing documentation of programs, in addition to verbal comments.

While the above-stated methodology serves as the lighthouse directing the research in program verification, this book is mainly concerned with the theoretical and meta-theoretical background, which we regard as a necessary condition for a successful application of this methodology. Unfortunately, no sufficient conditions for such a success can be proposed. Thus, while the main methodological usage of the principles to be described is in development of *a priori* correct programs, the description here is focused on *a posteriori* verification of (already developed) programs. References to other texts, which stress the methodology, exemplified by many illuminating examples, but avoiding meta-theoretic considerations, are presented after the next chapter.

Thus, the study of formal approaches in general, and the logically oriented ones in particular, in addition to serving as a basis for a sound methodology, also provides a firm foundation to programming and programming languages. An awareness of foundational issues is indispensable for any science, computing science being no exception.

The general discussion will be presented in a natural order of increasing complexity. We shall start by considering a very simple programming language and some simple correctness criteria, expressed in a familiar specification language. In this setup, we shall develop verification techniques and study some of their properties. Then, we shall increase the complexity of the programming language constructs, and also the complexity of the properties to be proved and of the specification language for their expression. The text is naturally partitioned by the separation of verifying sequential programs from the verification of concurrent (or parallel) programs. It is this second half that has not been successfully covered in any text book hitherto, although a recently published book [169] by Apt and Olderog (1991) does treat concurrent programs. However, it has a more restricted scope than this book and less emphasis on meta-theory.

Bibliographic notes and suggestions for further reading

Suggestions for further reading Critical comments about the applicability of program verification to real-life, industrial programming may be found in [1] and [2]. The *Comm. ACM* issues of March–April 1989 contain, under the 'Technical Correspondence' sections, vivid arguments against and in favor of the pertinent use of program verification to real life. An excellent critical review of this ongoing debate, which happens to reflect quite closely my personal point of view, is presented by Jon Barwise [3]. A whole issue of the *ACM SIGSOFT Software Engineering Notes*, Volume 5, Number 3, July 1980, presents the minutes of a workshop on program verification, with many positive accounts of applying the formal methodology. More about positive views of the general methodology of formal methods may be found in [4], [5], and [6].

Chapter 2
ON SPECIFICATIONS

2.1 Introduction

In this book we consider the problem of proving properties of a family of programs, which may be thought of as **value transformers,** or more accurately as **state transformers**. Many of the programs the reader is familiar with fall under this category. These programs can be characterized as follows: the 'task' of the program is to compute, starting in some **initial state** (where a state is defined below), for some finite amount of time, and then to **terminate** by producing some **final state** or **outcome** of the computation, having some desirable properties. Examples of programs of this general kind are as follows.

- *Computing functions*: Given some initial values (arguments) $x_1, \ldots, x_n$, the program has to produce upon termination the value $f(x_1, \ldots, x_n)$, for some given function f. For instance, computing the square root of a number or computing the median of a list of numbers are examples of such tasks.
- *Sorting:* Given an initial array (or list) of numbers (or other elements taken from some ordered domain), provide upon termination an increasing arrangement of the same elements.
- *Compiling:* Given initially some source program in some high-level programming language (such as Pascal), provide upon termination an 'equivalent' program in the assembly language of a given computer. The definition of the required equivalence itself is a nontrivial task.

An operating system, for example, is not such a state transformer. When it happens to halt, the situation is called a 'crash' and considered a disastrous event.... An airline reservation system or a real-time plant control are other examples of programs which are not state transformers.

At a first stage of describing verification techniques, we shall assume further that we are dealing with **deterministic** programs, which for every initial state have exactly one computation (and, hence, at most one final outcome). In a later chapter we relax this assumption and extend the techniques to cover nondeterministic programs as well. Finally, concurrent and distributed programs are considered, too.

A natural way of specifying state transformer programs is by means of a pair of **assertions** about program states:

> A **precondition** (denoted by p) and a **postcondition** (denoted by q). Their roles are to characterize the admissible initial states and the corresponding acceptable (called also 'correct') final states, respectively. This specification is indeed abstract, in telling only some properties of the desired outcome, without giving any hint as to how to obtain these outcomes. Of course, for many complicated programs such as compilers, it is quite hard to formulate the appropriate assertions.

We shall use **operational semantics** to define the various programming minilanguages to be employed, with **computations** being the main semantic concept. As the specification language, we shall consider the familiar first-order logic with equality. Then, we define the **correctness assertions** (two of them to start with), and their **satisfiability** by (the computations of) a program. We shall see that there are two basic proof principles, essentially differing from each other, for the two different correctness assertions. All the proof methods will be exemplified, and transforming proofs in one of them into proofs in the other one will also be described. Finally, we discuss two properties of such methods, known as **soundness** and **completeness**.

As stressed in Chapter 1, our interest in this book is in confronting specifications with programs implementing them. However, there is another important aspect of specifications, namely their amenability to formal manipulation, which should not be neglected when different specification formalisms are compared and evaluated. Occasionally, one may be interested in deriving properties of the specified object from its specification, without necessarily implementing it. For example (due to Jayadev Misra), one may wish to show that a certain combination of a buffer of size n with a buffer of size m forms a buffer of size $m+n$. Here, however, we are not examining this property of specifications. We are only concerned with rigorously proving their satisfaction whenever this happens to be the case.

2.2 Programming languages and their definition

We shall deal with verification of various kinds of programs, each kind presenting its particular problems and issues. In order to focus on the issue at hand, each kind of program is studied via a specially 'tailored' programming minilanguage, providing constructs for the expression of the studied topic. Thereby, we are able to bypass irrelevant or orthogonal details. For each such language, a concise syntactic description is provided, and a semantic definition is presented. The way the semantics is defined is known as **structured operational semantics (sos)**.

Consider an arbitrary programming language *PL*. Its operational semantics is obtained by defining the notions of a **configuration** C, and associating with every program $P \in PL$ and (initial) configuration a **computation,** (or a set of computations in the nondeterministic case).

Typically, a configuration C specifies the following components.

- *A visible state:* The state σ usually assigns values to program variables. (*Note:* We will be liberal in the use of variables and use notation like x, y, z and indexed notation such as x_1, x_2. Occasionally we will also use mnemonic names like 'sum' and 'buffer' as is conventional in programming languages.) We use the notation $\sigma[\![x]\!]$ to denote the value of variable x in state σ. Similarly, for an expression e (over variables in the domain of state σ), we use $\sigma[\![e]\!]$ to denote the value of e in the state σ. The special brackets '$[\![$' and '$]\!]$' emphasize the fact that the entity enclosed between them (the expression e in this case) is of a syntactic nature. The state in an intermediate configuration of a computation represents the **current** values of the (visible) variables. The state in the last configuration of a terminating computation is the (visible) **outcome** of the computation. Correctness assertions (that is, specifications) relate to visible state variables.

  A useful concept that plays an important role in definitions of operational semantics is that of a **variant** (defined below), reflecting 'successive' changes in state.

  Definition: For a state σ, value a in the domain of computation, and variable x, the **variant** of σ (w.r.t. a and x), denoted by $\sigma[a \mid x]$, is defined by

  $$\sigma[a \mid x][\![\mathbf{v}]\!] \stackrel{df.}{=} \begin{cases} a & \text{if } \mathbf{v} \text{ is } x \\ \sigma[\![\mathbf{v}]\!] & \text{otherwise} \end{cases}$$

  □

  Thus, this is a state agreeing with σ on any variable other than x, and assigning the value a to x. This notation is naturally extended to $\sigma[\bar{a} \mid \bar{x}]$ for simultaneous state modifications.

It is convenient to extend the definition to expressions instead of values, by putting $\sigma[e \mid x] \stackrel{df.}{=} \sigma[\sigma[\![e]\!] \mid x]$.

- *A hidden state:* The hidden state assigns values to 'internal' variables, needed to control the computation, but not part of the outcome. In particular, correctness assertions do not relate to the values of such variables.
- *A syntactic continuation:* This is usually a program in the language, representing the 'rest' of the computation that still has to be executed. We stipulate (for facilitating the definition of the operational semantics) an **empty** continuation E (not a program in the language PL) satisfying the identities $S;E = E;S = S$ for every S where ';' denotes sequential composition (defined in Chapter 4).

The semantics is specified by providing a **transition** relation '$\rightarrow$' among configurations, denoted by $C \rightarrow C'$, and then letting a **computation** consist of a **maximal** (finite or infinite) sequence of configurations $C_0 \rightarrow C_1 \cdots \rightarrow C_i \rightarrow \cdots$. The transition relation is an abstract description of a computation **step**, and the appeal to it justifies the adjective 'operational' for this kind of semantic definition. We denote by '$\stackrel{*}{\rightarrow}$' the **reflexive–transitive** closure of '$\rightarrow$'. An infinite '$\rightarrow$'-sequence is always maximal. Finite maximal '$\rightarrow$'-sequences arise from the presence of **terminal** configurations, to be separately defined for each language studied.

For a deterministic program P and an (initial) state σ, the computation of P starting in an initial configuration C_0 having σ as its state component and P itself as the syntactic continuation is denoted by $\pi(P, \sigma)$. We abbreviate $\pi(P, \sigma)$ to π whenever P and σ are clear from the context. Similarly for a nondeterministic program, P, we let $\Pi(P, \sigma)$ denote the collection of all computations of P starting with $C_0 = \langle P, \sigma \rangle$.

Furthermore, if π is a finite sequence, where the induced sequence of states is

$$\sigma_0 \rightarrow \cdots \rightarrow \sigma_k$$

for some $k \geqslant 0$ (with an obvious abuse of notation in the use of transitions among states), we put $val(\pi) \stackrel{df.}{=} \sigma_k$. If π is infinite, we put $val(\pi) \stackrel{df.}{=} \bot$, where $\bot$ is a special symbol, indicating an **undefined** state. A state $\sigma \neq \bot$ is also referred to as **proper**. We associate with every language PL a **meaning function** $\mathbf{M}_{PL}$, mapping pairs of programs and initial states to final states, by

$$\mathbf{M}_{PL}[\![P]\!](\sigma) \stackrel{df.}{=} val(\pi(P, \sigma)) \quad \text{in the deterministic case and}$$

$$\mathbf{M}_{PL}[\![P]\!](\sigma) \stackrel{df.}{=} \{val(\pi(P, \sigma))/\pi \in \Pi(P, \sigma)\} \quad \text{in the nondeterministic case.}$$

Note again the special brackets encompassing the syntactic argument P, in contrast to the state argument which is a semantic entity and therefore is enclosed within regular parentheses. In the case that $\perp \in \mathbf{M}_{\mathrm{PL}}[\![P]\!](\sigma_0)$ (or $\perp = \mathbf{M}_{\mathrm{PL}}[\![P]\!](\sigma)$ in the deterministic case), we say that P **diverges** for σ_0; otherwise, it **terminates** for σ_0.

Thus, for every particular language studied, one has to define the exact form of configurations and the transition relation among configurations, all the rest being uniformly inherited from the above schematic definition. Note also, that all the semantic notions mentioned depend on the interpretation **I**, specifying the domain over which computations are carried out. For simplicity this dependence is only marked when needed.

A useful notion used in the sequel is that of *var* (P), the collection of all state variables occurring in P. This is usually defined by induction on the structure of P, given an inductive definition of the syntax of PL. Similarly, *change* (P) denotes the collection of state variables the value of which P possibly modifies (that is, if $x \notin$ *change* (P), then the value of the variable x definitely does not change by executing P). Obviously, *change* $(P) \subseteq$ *var* (P).

At this stage, one can raise some natural questions about this way of defining the meanings of programs. For this approach to be justified, there has to be a way to tie it up to any of the more standard notions of computability in some model of computation. By adherence to the generally accepted Church thesis, any of them forms the appropriate abstraction of 'real' computers. If one does not restrict sufficiently this way of defining semantics, no such correspondence need exist. Without more severe restrictions, one can obtain 'transition systems' and a notion of 'execution' for arbitrary logical statements, which we prefer to view as specifications (described in the next section) rather than as programs. Logic programming is one well-known example of an attempt to restrict the formalism so that its natural operational semantics (traditionally described somewhat differently) does correspond to effective computability.

Since (operational) semantics does not constitute the main topic of interest here, and is used only as the rigorous support for meta-theorems about properties of proof systems for correctness assertions (introduced in Section 2.3), we do not elaborate on these issues here. We do rely on the reader's intuitive understanding and general background in computing in order to fill in the needed missing connections.

2.3 Specifications and correctness assertions

We next consider specifications of programs in PL. Every choice of a specification method starts with a determination of **observables**, to the properties of which a specification may relate. As mentioned, a program is viewed here as a **state transformer**, that is taking (initial and final) states as the observables for our specification method. In other words, the 'purpose' of activating a program (in some initial state) is to obtain an intended final state.

States have been defined as assignments of values (taken from the domain of computation) to the variables of the program. Therefore, we may use state **predicates** as a means for describing the intended correspondence between initial and final states. Predicates can be thought about either **semantically**, as sets of states, or **syntactically**, expressed by formulas in some specification language *SL*. We reserve the name **predicate** for the semantically determined sets, while using **state assertions** to refer to their *SL*-expressions. At a first stage, we emphasize the semantical point of view, though in concrete examples we most often use the familiar first-order logic with equality (over the domain of standard integers $\mathbf{I}_0$) as *SL*. The syntactic expressibility becomes a more important issue when completeness properties are studied.

We next describe the way state assertions are used to construct specifications for programs.

> **Definition:** A **specification** ϕ is an ordered pair of state assertions $\langle p(\bar{x}), q(\bar{x})\rangle$.
>
> □

We refer to p as a **precondition** and to q as a **postcondition**. The free variables $\bar{x}$ are a finite list of program variables, assigned values by states. We use the notation $\sigma \models_{\mathbf{I}_0} p(\bar{x})$ for the usual notion of **satisfaction** of a state assertion $p(\bar{x})$ under the values assigned to the program variables $\bar{x}$ by the state† σ. Two special state assertions are

- *true* – expressing the predicate satisfied by *every* proper state, and
- *false* – expressing the predicate satisfied by *no* proper state.

> **Convention:** The undefined state $\perp$ satisfies no predicate (including *true*). We will always be careful and test for the appropriateness of a state before attributing any predicate to it.
>
> □

An **implementation** of a specification is a program (in the programming language considered) which realizes effectively the correspondence of states implied by the specification. The precondition characterizes admissible initial states. No claim whatsoever is made about computations of an implementation starting in an initial state not satisfying this precondition. Such computations are thus not restricted by the specification. Similarly, the postcondition is supposed to characterize the required final state resulting from computations on admissible initial states. The state assertion *true* is used whenever no restriction on states is intended. Note that though both the precondition and the postcondition refer to the same collection of state variables $\bar{x}$, these variables carry different meanings in the two state assertions.

† In logic, the term **valuation** is often used for states.

For the precondition, they refer to the values assigned to them by an initial state, whereas for the postcondition they refer to the values assigned to them by the corresponding final state, the outcome of the computation. When formulating proof rules, it is a common practice to leave the state variable implicit.

As we shall see, there are (at least) two natural ways of interpreting specifications; these will give rise to two corresponding correctness assertions, the validity of which has to be defined based on the assumed semantics of the programming language at hand. Each of those two kinds will be distinguished by calling for a different way of proving its satisfaction by a given program.

In most of the examples, we shall use as our domain of computation the integers $\mathbf{I}_0$, with their usual operations, as well as the **truth values** denoted by *tt*, *ff* with their usual operations. The theory of formally defining other domains of computations is beyond the scope of this book, and references for further reading are listed at the end of this chapter. Occasionally, though, we might use examples involving lists, trees, queues, and so on, relying on informal knowledge from programming experience. In such cases, their properties used in proofs will be explicitly listed. In some of the more logic-based treatment, we shall also consider *arbitrary* domains of computation.

We now consider some simple examples of specifications, which will be used also for explaining the notational conventions.

EXAMPLE (ordering):

We want to specify a program that for an arbitrary initial state with integer variables x and y will end up in a final state such that $x > y$ holds in it. This is expressed by the specification $\phi = \langle true, x > y \rangle$.

□

Remarks:

(1) From the above very simple example, one can see an important property of specifications, namely being nondeterministic. Clearly, there are many ways of satisfying the above specification, for example by assigning 10 to x and 7 to y, or by assigning 1 to x and -1 to y. We return to this issue in Chapter 5 on nondeterministic programs.

(2) In many cases, as in this example, a specification does not tell the 'whole truth' about a required program even in terms of its implied state transformation. Viewed differently, for a given program, sometimes it is required to prove a property which is not necessarily the strongest possible. Thus, even if the program given is the one assigning 10 to x and 7 to y, it may well be that the only property needed is $x > y$, even though the stronger property $x = 10 \wedge y = 7$, which logically implies $x > y$, is provable.

EXAMPLE (even outcome):

Suppose we want to specify a program with an integer state variable x, so that upon termination x has an even value. Here a question arises: what exactly are the primitive predicates available, and is *even*(x) one of them? If it is, then a specification would be $\langle true,\ even(x)\rangle$. However, suppose it is not one of the given primitive predicates. In such a case, it has to be *expressed* by means of a state assertion over the primitive predicates and the logical building blocks (such as connectives and quantifiers). For example, assuming that $x \times y$ denotes the multiplication operation (of integers), we may formulate the above specification as $\phi \overset{df.}{=} \langle true,\ \exists y{:}x = 2 \times y\rangle$. This shows the use of existentially quantified bound variables, which are not state variables in specifications.

□

In most cases, the discussion will leave unspecified the exact collection of primitive operations and predicates available, and leave it to context. An exception is made when **inexpressibility** is the issue, where it really makes a difference. There is also an implicit assumption connecting *PL* and *SL*, in that tests occurring in programs are quantifier-free Boolean combinations of the primitive predicates.

A. Specification variables

The above two examples were oversimplified in that the outcome state did not depend on the initial state. Most often, such a dependence is required. The following example shows what is needed in order to express it within the stated framework.

EXAMPLE (doubling):

Suppose we want to specify a program, using a state variable x, whose task is to end up in a state in which the value of x is twice its initial value. Thus, in the postcondition we would like to refer to the 'old' value of x in the initial state; however, we cannot use just x for that purpose, since the value of x is changed, and x refers to the value assigned to it by the final state. The way to overcome this difficulty is to introduce more free variables, that in some sense 'freeze' the values of the initial state. These variables are 'specification variables' (known also as **logical** variables), and are not state variables, that is they are *not* occurring in the specified program (neither being subject to change nor being accessed). Thus, specification variables are similar to the bound variable in the previous example, only that here they are left **free**, implicitly universally quantified. In our example, we have

$$\phi \overset{df.}{=} \langle x = X, x = 2 \times X \rangle$$

Here X represents the initial value of x, and clearly ϕ expresses our intended specification.

□

Note that the scope of the implicit universal quantification over X is the whole specification, that is X denotes the same value in the precondition and in the postcondition. This property is the justification of their name and is in contrast to state variables, which are state dependent and may denote different values in the pre- and postconditions. As a notational convention, we use the capitalized name of a variable as representing its initial value. In more general situations, the role of specification variables is not necessarily confined to 'freezing' initial values; rather, they may be used to connect arbitrarily the final states to the initial states. For example, $\langle x > Z, x > 2 \times Z \rangle$ is also an admissible specification. Specification variables will turn out to have a crucial importance in the treatment of recursive procedures (Chapter 6).

EXAMPLE (integer division):

Consider a program whose initial state contains two integer variables x_1 and x_2. Its task is to end in a state where, provided that x_1 is nonnegative and x_2 is positive, the value of a variable q is set to the quotient of the division of x_1 by x_2, whereas the variable r is set to the remainder of that division. The usual way of expressing such a requirement is

$$\phi \overset{df.}{=} \langle x_1 = X_1 \geqslant 0 \wedge x_2 = X_2 > 0, X_1 = q \cdot X_2 + r \wedge 0 \leqslant r < X_2 \rangle$$

Note that in this specification the postcondition does not restrict the final values of x_1 and x_2. Therefore, a correct program may modify them arbitrarily. If the specifier intends the program to preserve the initial values of these two variables, the condition $x_1 = X_1 \wedge x_2 = X_2$ should be added to the postcondition. This is an example of the kind of condition often overlooked in specifications, causing the formal statement to have a different meaning to the informal intention. We elaborate more on this issue in Section 2.4.

□

There is one important syntactic operation which we use quite often, namely substitution, which is now reviewed.

B. Substitutions

Substitution is a logical operation that modifies the syntactic structure of formulas or terms. We shall use it to capture the (dynamic) effect of the assignment operation, and, later, to capture the meaning of parameter passing to procedures. One has to beware of a logical fallacy associated with uncontrolled substitutions.

Definition: For a first-order formula p and term (or synonymously, an expression) e, p_e^x is obtained by replacing all *free* occurrences of x in p by e. By convention, $true_e^x \overset{df.}{=} true$ and $false_e^x \overset{df.}{=} false$.

For a finite and non-empty list of pairwise distinct variables $\bar{x} = (x_1, \ldots, x_n)$, $n \geqslant 1$, and a list $\bar{e}$ of expressions the same size $\bar{x}$, $p_{\bar{e}}^{\bar{x}}$ denotes the *simultaneous* substitution of e_i for all free occurrences of x_i, $1 \leqslant i \leqslant n$, in p.

□

EXERCISE:

Define p_e^x by induction on the structure of p, where p is an arbitrary first-order formula (this is standard definition in any logic book).

□

EXAMPLE:

Let p be $\exists z\colon x \neq z \wedge \forall x\colon \neg x > u$. Here the first occurrence of x in p is free and the second occurrence is bound. First, consider the case where the expression e is a variable, say y. Then $p_y^x = \exists z\colon y \neq z \wedge \forall x\colon \neg x > u$. Here it is clear that if σ and σ' are two states such that $\sigma[\![x]\!] = \sigma'[\![y]\!]$ and both states agree on all other variables, then $\sigma \models_{I_0} p \Leftrightarrow \sigma' \models_{I_0} p_y^x$. We would like to have this property in general. It is preserved also for e being $x+1$. We get $p_{x+1}^x = \exists z\colon x+1 \neq z \wedge \forall x\colon \neg x > u$, and if $\sigma[\![x+1]\!] = \sigma'[\![x]\!]$ and both states agree on every variable different from x, then $\sigma \models_{I_0} p \Leftrightarrow \sigma' \models_{I_0} p_{x+1}^x$. However, if we compute p_z^x naively we obtain a logical contradiction, namely, $\exists z\colon z \neq z \wedge \forall x\colon \neg x > u$, which is unsatisfiable (because $z = z$ always holds, of course).

The problem with the last substitution, known as **variable clashing**, is that a position of a free variable (x) became bound (z) because of the substitution. A usual way out is to **rename** the bound variables causing the problem, before performing the substitution. Such a renaming preserves equivalence. For example, we could modify p into $\exists w\colon x \neq w \wedge \forall x\colon \neg x > u$, which is equivalent to p, and now safely substitute z for x. In the sequel, it is assumed that all substitutions avoid variable clashing by a suitable renaming.

□

An important property, relating variants to substitutions, is expressed by the following theorem.

Theorem (substitution):

$\sigma[e \mid x] \models p$ iff $\sigma \models p^x_e$

Proof: Directly from the definitions.

□

This theorem will serve us in reasoning about assignment statements. In Chapter 4 we discuss an extension treating arrays too.

As noted in the short discussion of computability in the previous section, the kind of logical specification considered here is very **permissive**, in that it is not limited to specifications of effectively solvable problems. It is possible to specify a program that, for an input x which is (the code of) a Turing machine, will produce an output state with $y = true$ iff x halts on an empty tape, a problem known to have no effective solutions.

Since we are not concerned here with ways of converting logical specifications to programs satisfying them, we prefer to retain these kinds of permissive specification methods, which are better known and easier to handle. Since the technical content of this presentation is *a posteriori* program verification, that is establishing that a given program satisfies a correctness assertion (as described below), this permissiveness does not constitute an obstacle. It is an obstacle from the methodological point of view. Though in practice non-effective specifications rarely arise, one has to be aware of this possibility.

We now distinguish between two correctness assertions based on specifications. These correctness assertions represent two different properties of programs, which are proved using different proof methods.

A. Partial correctness

Definition: A program P is **partially correct** w.r.t. a specification $\phi = \langle p(\bar{x}), q(\bar{x}) \rangle$ in interpretation **I** iff for every computation $\pi(P, \sigma)$, where $\sigma \models_{\mathbf{I}} p(\bar{x})$, the following holds: if $val(\pi(P, \sigma)) \neq \bot$, then $val(\pi(P, \sigma)) \models_{\mathbf{I}} q(\bar{x})$.

We use the notation $\{p\} P \{q\}$ to denote this correctness assertion, and $\models_{\mathbf{I}} \{p\} P \{q\}$ for asserting its truth in the given interpretation **I**.

□

According to the definition above, a program is partially correct w.r.t. a specification iff for every computation starting in an initial state satisfying the precondition, *if* this computation terminates then its final state satisfies the postcondition. Thus, infinite computations do not ever violate any partial correctness assertion. The only way to violate such an assertion is by a terminating computation starting in an initial state that satisfies the precondition and ending in a final state that does not satisfy the postcondition.

It is important to notice that partial correctness is a conditional property and it does not require termination for any state. Also, nothing is claimed about computations starting in initial states not satisfying the precondition, which 'filters' admissible initial states for the specified program.

EXAMPLE (divergence):

The validity of the partial correctness assertion $\{true\}\ P\ \{false\}$ implies that no computation of P, from any initial state, ever terminates, since no state satisfies *false*.

□

EXERCISE:

Show that every program P satisfies the partial correctness assertion $\{true\}\ P\ \{true\}$.

□

B. Total Correctness

Definition: A program P is **totally correct** w.r.t. a specification $\phi = \langle p(\bar{x}), q(\bar{x})\rangle$ in interpretation **I** iff for every computation $\pi(P,\sigma)$, where $\sigma \models_{\mathbf{I}} p(\bar{x})$, we have $val(\pi(P,\sigma)) \not\models \bot$ and $val(\pi(P,\sigma)) \models_{\mathbf{I}} q(\bar{x})$.

We use the notation $\langle p\rangle\, P\, \langle q\rangle$ to denote this correctness assertion, and $\models_{\mathbf{I}} \langle p\rangle\, P\, \langle q\rangle$ for asserting its truth in **I**.

□

Thus, a program is totally correct w.r.t. a specification iff all its computations which start in initial states satisfying the precondition are finite and the respective final states satisfy the postcondition. Thus, termination is required by this correctness assertion. Once again, nothing is claimed about computations starting in initial states not satisfying the precondition. Note again, that all the free specification variables in a specification are implicitly universally quantified.

Trivially, total correctness of a program w.r.t. any specification implies the partial correctness of this program w.r.t. to the same specification. The converse, of course, is not true.

EXAMPLE (termination assertion):

Often one is only interested in claiming (and proving) the property of **termination,** of some program P regardless of any property of the final state. This property is expressible by the total correctness assertion $\langle p\rangle\, P\, \langle true\rangle$.

□

From the above definitions, we immediately obtain the following property:

Lemma (separation):

For every interpretation **I**, program P, and specification $\phi = \langle p, q\rangle$,

$\models_{\mathbf{I}} \langle p\rangle\, P\, \langle q\rangle$ iff both $\models_{\mathbf{I}} \{p\}\, P\, \{q\}$ and $\models_{\mathbf{I}} \langle p\rangle\, P\, \langle true\rangle$

□

This lemma means that total correctness can be decomposed into partial correctness and termination. As mentioned before, this is a useful decomposition, as partial and total correctness of programs are proved using different methods.

The presence of free specification variables in correctness assertions suggests a 'universal' proof rule, applicable to correctness assertions in any PL and SL, allowing for the **instantiation** of such correctness assertions to specific values for the specification variables. The reason for the need for such a rule in spite of its availability in most deduction systems for the predicate calculus is that the use of the predicate calculus in proof systems for correctness assertions is confined to state assertions (both pre- and post-condition). Note that the language of correctness assertions is *not* closed under logical combinations. Thus, neither $\neg\{p\}\, P\, \{q\}$ nor $\{p_1\}\, P_1\, \{q_1\} \Rightarrow \{p_2\}\, P_2\, \{q_2\}$ is a correctness assertion. More about this issue is said in Chapter 4 (and its exercises). We get the following instantiation rule.

Instantiation rule:

$$\frac{\mathbf{c}(X)}{\mathbf{c}(a)} \qquad \text{(INST)}$$

where $\mathbf{c}(X)$ is a correctness assertion having X as a free specification variable and where a is in the domain of X.

□

Appeals to this rule are occasionally not mentioned explicitly. We deliberately distinguish the notation for instantiation from that of substitution in state assertions. Note that one has to be careful not to instantiate freely by means of a term e, supposedly denoting the instant a. If X occurs free both in the precondition and in the postcondition, the expression e should not refer to program variables. This restriction on the variables in e is important, and ensures that indeed the same value is substituted for all occurrences of the free specification variable. To see this, suppose we have established, for some program P with state variable x, the partial correctness assertion $\{x = X\}\, P\, \{x = X + 1\}$ (that is, P increases the value of x by one). By means of an instantiation of X to x, violating the above restriction, we may derive $\{x = x\}\, P\, \{x = x + 1\}$, which certainly is not a valid consequence of the original correctness assertion, having a self-contradictory postcondition (in case P terminates). The discrepancy arises because the instantiation of the precondition uses the 'old' value of x, while that in the postcondition uses the 'new' value of x, which is different owing to the execution of P. The restriction imposed prohibits such discrepancies.

Comment:

One can consider a somewhat more general situation, where a computation may become 'stuck' because of some undefined local action, for example division by zero. Semantically, this possibility may be incorporated by adjoining special **error** states, and defining the transitions so that error states are always propagated (error strictness). Then, another correctness assertion can be formulated, asserting the absence of such local failures (but not committing to finiteness or infiniteness of the computation). A simple variant of the proof theory presented here can handle this situation, known also as **clean termination**. We shall not dwell on this issue here any further, and assume that expressions always have well-defined values in any state.

□

2.3.1 Soundness and completeness

As mentioned, our aim is to find **proof rules** for proving the above-mentioned correctness assertions. Suppose that **D** is such a deductive system. We use the notation $\vdash_{\mathbf{D}} \mathbf{c}$ for **provability** of the correctness assertion **c** using **D**. We will say more later about the structure of proofs. There are two main properties of interest in such systems. The first one, *soundness*, is always required for the proof system to be of use. The second one, namely *completeness*, is not always achievable but is very helpful when applicable.

The **soundness** of **D** means, informally, that every correctness assertion proved by applying **D** does hold semantically. Indeed, a proof system by which false properties can be proved is not very useful....

Definition: A proof system **D** is **sound** iff for every correctness assertion **c**, $\vdash_{\mathbf{D}} \mathbf{c}$ implies $\models_{\mathbf{I}_0} \mathbf{c}$.

□

Note that, in the absence of negations of correctness assertions in our formalism, one cannot refer to *inconsistent* deductive systems for correctness assertions. The latter are considered 'bad' deductive systems in logic.

EXERCISE:

What can you say about program P if both $\vdash_{\mathbf{D}} \{p\} P \{q\}$ and $\vdash_{\mathbf{D}} \{p\} P \{\neg q\}$, given that the deductive system **D** is sound?

□

In the other direction, a deductive system **D** is complete iff it is powerful enough to prove every semantically true correctness assertion.

Definition: A proof system **D** is **complete** iff for every correctness assertion **c**, $\models_{\mathbf{I}_0} \mathbf{c}$ implies $\vdash_{\mathbf{D}} \mathbf{c}$.

□

Note:

Here the semantic truth is taken over a given domain of computation, which is a (fixed) interpretation of *SL*, $\mathbf{I}_0$ in our case. One can speak about stronger versions of these two properties, where 'truth in a given interpretation' is replaced by **validity**, that is truth under *all* interpretations, or relativized to a family $\mathscr{F}$ of interpretations. We refer to the corresponding properties as **totally sound**, and **totally complete**, $\mathscr{F}$**-sound** and $\mathscr{F}$**-complete**, respectively. A particular case of interest and importance is when $\mathscr{F}$ is characterized axiomatically, and all the domain-dependent arguments are provable from the axioms.

□

An immediate consequence from the definition of the satisfaction of correctness assertions with free specification variables is the soundness of the instantiation rule.

Theorem (total soundness of INST):

For every interpretation **I**, if $\vdash_{\mathrm{D} \cup \{\mathrm{INST}\}} \{p\} P \{q\}$, then $\models_{\mathbf{I}} \{p\} P \{q\}$, where D is any sound proof system for partial correctness.

□

Another aspect of completeness is the distinction between several completeness properties, depending on whether we are interested in the specification of predicates in some formal specification language, or on whether we consider them on a semantic level as sets of states, and depending on the way proofs of claims about the domain are treated. We shall elaborate on this later.

In the next chapter we consider only simple variants of soundness and completeness, deferring the consideration of the more elaborate ones to Chapter 4, where a more suitable framework is introduced.

2.4 Specifications and intentions

Even though the main concern of this book is a systematic presentation of major parts of the theory and meta-theory of program verification, one has constantly to keep in mind the methodological applications of this theory, as presented in Chapter 1. A major obstacle from the methodological point of view is the gap between the intention of a specification and the formal statement of a specification. One example of a formal specification not reflecting the specifier's intention has already been mentioned in Section 2.3. This section considers this issue in more detail.

The crucial and most important observation about the above stated gap is that in *principle* it cannot be bridged in any absolute way. While formal specifications are mathematical entities amenable to formal reasoning (this being their *raison d'être*), intentions are mental objects, depending on the specifier's intuition. Hence, no formal arguments can establish any correspondence between them, let alone a perfect one. Thus, the best one can hope for is the design of specification methods that make the formalization of intention easier. As in many other similar problems, experience of formally stating requirements increases the degree of correspondence.

The ways in which this gap manifests itself can be broadly grouped into two classes:

(1) inexpressible intentions,

(2) erroneous expressions.

Examples that fall into the first class include requirements about efficiency and performance. In the kind of logical specification considered in this book, such requirements are not expressible, since they do not constitute a restriction on the initial state–final state correspondence, rather a restriction on ways of achieving such a correspondence. Expressing this kind of property requires a change in the choice of observables.

Similarly, requirements about bounded computer resources, the nature of the execution environment, portability, and so on do not fall under most formal specification methods.

However, such imperfections of a specification are less relevant to program verification, because it is easier to be aware of the absence of these requirements and not to fall into a trap of believing that the verification also established these requirements.

A more serious inexpressibility gap occurs as a result of genuine weakness of *SL*, even when dealing with observable entities. For example, it is known that the transitive closure of a relation is not expressible in first-order predicate logic. Another example is due to the confinement of state assertions to refer only to a finite number of free state variables. This creates problems in specifying programs with an unbounded number of outputs, without coding them into one value (or finitely many). For example, suppose we want to formulate a specification corresponding to the informally stated intention 'For $x \geqslant 2$, decompose x into its prime factors.' This specification requires coding all the prime factors of x into the value of one (or finitely many) state variables, since we cannot 'dedicate' a state variable for each prime factor, their number growing with x.

This brings us to the second kind of mismatch between intention and formal statement which is more dangerous from the methodological point of view, since one tends to believe that a successful verification of the satisfaction of the formal statement by a program guarantees also the satisfaction of one's intention by the same program.

A typical error occurring while formalizing an intention is the omission of a sufficiently tight range restriction of a variable, mainly when such a restriction is an implicit default at the intentional level. For example, suppose one intends to specify a program that should test whether the contents of a variable x satisfies a property $p(x)$. The result should be recorded as the value of y, where $y = 1$ means that x enjoys property p, while $y = 0$ means that x does not enjoy it. A common error is to define the postcondition for partial correctness as

$$q(y, x) \stackrel{df.}{=} [(y = 1 \Rightarrow p(x)) \wedge (y = 0 \Rightarrow \neg p(x))].$$

The specifier had an implicit assumption that the only values of y are 1 and 0. However, this is not implied by the above formal specification. Thus, an unintended, but formally correct solution is by means of the trivial program $y := 2$, assigning 2 to y. What is missing is a conjunct $0 \leqslant y \leqslant 1$. In many cases, such errors are caused by the lack of type information about the program in (one-sorted) first-order logic.

Yet another common error of specification is displayed by the above postcondition, namely the omission of value preservation. Suppose that the initial value of x is 7, but $p(5)$ holds. Then, the program $[x := 5; y := 1]$ (that is, assigning 5 to x and 1 to y) is a correct but unintended solution. To resolve this difficulty, one should use logical variables (as in the example in Section 2.3), by means of which modification of x can be excluded. A better specification might look like

$$\phi \stackrel{df.}{=} \langle (x = X), (0 \leqslant y \leqslant 1) \wedge [(y = 1 \Rightarrow p(X)) \wedge (y = 0 \Rightarrow \neg p(X))] \rangle$$

Even this specification allows for the modification of x while testing it, though without affecting the value of y, which this time is properly restricted. To enforce the preservation of the value of x to the final state, $x = X$ should be conjoined to the postcondition.

The most notorious occurrence of this type of omission is in specifications of sorting programs, where only the ordering requirement is stated, omitting the requirement that the output sequence is a permutation of the input sequence. This leads to an unintended, but correct solution of the form **for** $i = 1, n$ **do** $a[i] := i$. Such an omission usually results from the implicit assumption that only value-exchange operations are employed by the solution, the latter preserving permutations. Clearly, this assumption is not enforced by the specification.

The specification method employed here is not particularly suitable for the methodological requirements from a useful specification method. However, it relies on the well-known and well-understood discipline of logic, and it allows for a relatively concise exposition of much of the theory.

In the remainder of this book, we relate only to formal specifications and do not try to relate the latter to the intentions which they are supposed to formalize.

Bibliographic notes and suggestions for further reading

Bibliographic notes The **sos** method of defining operational semantics is due to Plotkin [7, 8]. The distinction between partial and total correctness is present in the earlier work on program verification, for example in [9] and [10]. The terms are from [11]. The relationship between specification and intention is analyzed in more detail in [12], together with more methodological difficulties in formal approaches to programming. Bibliographic notes on soundness and completeness are given after Chapter 4. The first usage of specification variables, whose range is a whole correctness assertion, to 'freeze' initial values of program variables seems to be [13]. An explicit discussion of this technique (overlooking [13]) appears, in the context of verification of procedures, in [14] (with a minor incorrect remark about universal quantification of proper state variables). There the instantiation of free logical variables is mentioned and used (again in the context of procedures), though it is not formulated as an explicit proof rule. The first explicit distinction between free specification variables (called there logical variables) and program variables, together with an instantiation rule, seems to be [15]. Another notational convention for 'freezing' initial values, also in the context of procedures, appears in [16]. Yet another framework is presented in [11], where there is a syntactic distinction between 'input variables', 'program variables', and 'output variables', where input variables are not subject to change by the program by definition.

Suggestions for further reading The denotational approach to defining the semantics of programming languages, which does not rely on transitions (or other computation steps) can be found in many text books, for example [17], [18], or [19]. A different formulation of logical specifications as well as the design and verification based on it may be found in [20]. A methodology relying on a different specification paradigm appears in [21]. An abstract treatment of the specification of programs is presented in [22]. Books that describe the verification of sequential programs, emphasizing methodological considerations but without much emphasis on meta-theory, are [23], [24], [25] and [26] (the latter having a small section on concurrency). Treatments similar to ours, but confined to sequential programs only and based on denotational semantics, are [17] and [19]. A major issue not covered by this book is the specification of more general domains of computation over which programs compute. The prevailing mathematical approach to this issue is **algebraic specifications** (of abstract data types). A recent survey appears in [27]. Another treatment of program verification of simple programs over classes of computation domains (interpretations), stressing exceptional error states and based on many-sorted logic, appears in [28]. The inclusion of error states is a possible way to cope with clean termination.

EXERCISES

2.1 Prove the separation lemma.

2.2 **Simultaneous compared with iterative substitution:** Show that for $\bar{x} = (x_1, x_2), \bar{e} = (e_1, e_2)$, $p^{\bar{x}}_{\bar{e}}$ is not logically equivalent to $(p^{x_1}_{e_1})^{x_2}_{e_2}$.

2.3 **Semantic invariance:** Formulate an assumption about the transition relation, such that for every interpretation **I** and programming language $PL, \models_{\mathbf{I}} \{p(y)\} P \{p(y)\}$ whenever $y \notin var(P)$. [Later discussions and exercises relate to the provability of this correctness assertion in the corresponding proof systems.]

2.4 **Integer square root:** Let the integer square root of a natural number n be defined as $\max\{m \mid m \geqslant 0 \wedge m^2 \leqslant n\}$. Formulate a specification for a program that, given a nonnegative x, computes in y the integer square root of x, preserving the value of x.

2.5 Prove that for any state $\sigma, \sigma[a \mid x][b \mid x] = \sigma[b \mid x]$.

2.6 **Termination in non-standard models:** Assuming some PL in which iteration (or recursion) is present, show a program S with a free variable x, such that

(1) $\models_{I_0} \langle x > 0 \rangle\ S\ \langle true \rangle$, but
(2) $\not\models \langle x > 0 \rangle\ S \langle true \rangle$
(that is, $\models_I \langle x > 0 \rangle\ S\ \langle true \rangle$ does not hold for every I)

What is the meaning of this observation? [This issue is covered in more detail in Chapter 4.]

2.7 What is the difference between an unsound proof system (for correctness assertions) and a (logically) inconsistent proof system?

2.8 Can you express by means of a partial correctness assertion the following properties of programs?

(1) The variable x is never assigned to during execution.
(2) The value of variable x is never modified during execution.

Comment on the use of such properties in program specification.

2.9 Consider the state property 'There are two state variables having the same value.'

(1) Can it serve as a precondition or as a postcondition in a partial correctness assertion?
(2) Will your answer to (1) change if you are given that, for the specified program P, it holds that $var(P) \subseteq V$, where V is some finite collection of state variables?

2.10 **Instantiation:** Show that if $var(e) \cap change(S) = \varnothing$, it is sound to apply the rule INST with the expression e.

2.11 **Combining specifications:** Consider a pair of partial correctness specifications $\{p_i\} S \{q_i\}$, $i = 1, 2$. Provide a **combined** partial correctness specification $\{p\} S \{q\}$ satisfied iff *both* of the given specifications are satisfied.

2.12 **Contrapositive correctness assertions [170]:** Show that the following is an equivalent reading of the partial correctness assertion $\{p\} P \{q\}$: for every computation of P, if it ends in a state not satisfying q, then it started in a state not satisfying p.

Chapter 3
VERIFYING DETERMINISTIC PROGRAMS

3.1 Introduction

In this chapter we consider verification of deterministic programs, presented in a simple minilanguage known as the language of **flow programs.** While this language is not recommended for the expression of solutions to actual programming problems, it serves well in order to introduce the basic ideas in the simplest way, focusing only on the verification problems. It is later contrasted with a more structured language, allowing us to focus on compositionality as an orthogonal, but central issue.

We consider proof methods for both types of correctness assertions introduced in the previous chapter, and show that they are based on two different approaches. For partial correctness, we consider a form of what is known as **computational induction**, represented here as induction on the lengths of paths in the graph of the flow program. The lack of a syntactic counterpart for this induction motivates the compositional approach, introduced in the next chapter. Thus, a program is viewed as a global entity, decomposed by the proof method to simpler units, which are not syntactic subparts of the program. For termination and total correctness, another kind of induction, known as **structural induction**, based on well-founded, partially ordered sets is used.

In both cases, what the proof methods really achieve is a reduction of claims about the program, presented as correctness assertions, to claims about the domain of computation (integers in most examples). Indeed, this is the essence of program verification in general.

Note that the validation of claims about the domain is taken as a 'solved problem', having nothing to do with programs. We also consider relations among different proof methods for the same kinds of correctness assertions.

We stress here the use of proof methods, as opposed to proof rules to be used in the next chapter. For a proof method, we are interested in the semantic view of predicates, namely the set of states satisfying them, independently of the expressibility of such sets in a given logic. The method will be a kind of a recipe to a number of steps, which if carried out successfully guarantee the correctness of the program. This will contrast with a proof based on proof rules, which has the more traditional syntactic appearance as a sequence of correctness assertions, each being either an axiom or derived from previous ones by a proof rule.

Finally, we open a small window to the issue of the verification of programs transcending the state transformers. For such programs, other means are needed for specifying properties that could serve as their correctness criteria. This issue emerges in its full significance in later chapters, dealing with concurrent and distributed programs.

3.2 Flow programs

In this section, we introduce the programming language *PLF*, to whose programs we refer as flow programs. This is a very simple language for the expression of deterministic, state transforming programs, which fits the informal intuition of 'flow of control' one has acquired from previous experience in programming.

Commands The language includes several forms of commands, which we list below, together with their informal interpretations. Then, a formal definition of a computation is presented in the framework considered in Section 2.2, namely a transition relation between configurations. Each command has a distinct **label** $l \in L_P$, where L_P is a finite, not further specified set of labels for the program P. The label is separated from the command by a colon.

- *Start:* This indicates the entry point, where the computation starts. In the examples, programs usually have a single entrance, though this is not an essential restriction.

- *Assignments:* These take the form $\bar{x} := \bar{e}$, where $\bar{x}$ is a list of pairwise distinct state variables, and $\bar{e}$ is a list (of the same length as $\bar{x}$) of expressions over state variables. This is actually a multiple assignment, where the current value of the expression e_i is assigned to the variable x_i, simultaneously for all i. For example, $(x_1, x_2) := (x_1 + 1, x_1 + x_2)$ assigns to x_1 the successor of its value and to x_2 the sum of the (old) values of

x_1 and x_2. In examples, mnemonic variable names are often used instead of x_i. We recall that it is assumed that all operations are total, and the values of $\bar{e}$ are always defined. As already mentioned, this restriction is not essential and can be easily relaxed. We do not further specify here the structure of expressions.

- *Tests:* These are Boolean expressions of the form $B(\bar{x})$ over the state variables, also assumed to be always defined, yielding a truth value in $\{tt, ff\}$. The computation branches according to the value of the test.
- *Halt:* This indicates an exit point of the program, ending the computation when reached. In the examples, programs usually have a single exit.

Definition: A flow program $P \in PLF$ is a (finite) directed graph with labeled commands as nodes, satisfying the following restrictions:

(1) A **start** node (also called **entry** node) has no predecessors and only one successor.

(2) A **halt** node (also called an **exit** node) has no successors.

(3) An **assignment** node has exactly one successor.

(4) A **test** node has two successors, with two labeled edges, one with *tt* and the other with *ff*.

(5) Every node resides on a directed path from a start node to a halt node.

(6) Different nodes have different labels. We shall refer to a node through its label.

For an assignment or start node labeled l, $suc(l)$ denotes its successor. For a test node labeled l, $suc^+(l)$, $suc^-(l)$ denote the two respective successors of l, the one labeled *tt* and the other labeled *ff*. □

Remark:

In such a graph, a node may have multiple entering edges. This will be represented as a **join** node, having no command associated with it, but possibly having a label.

An example of a program $P_{idiv} \in PLF$ is shown in Figure 3.1. Label l_4 is an example of the join nodes mentioned above, having a label but no command associated with it. We will return to this example and prove some properties of this program.

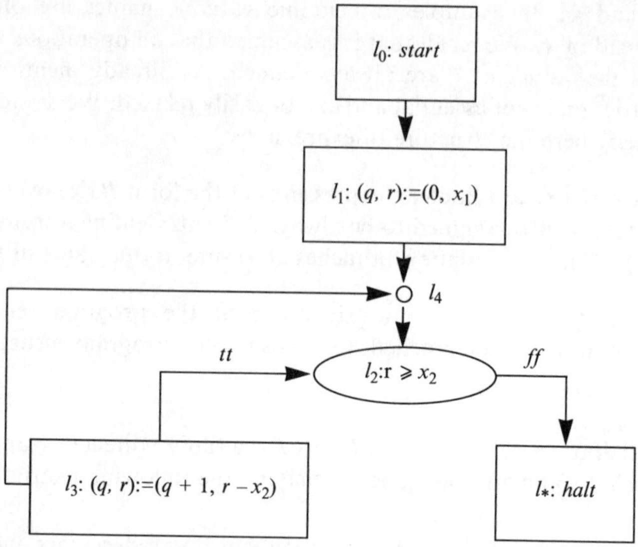

Figure 3.1 The flow program P_{idiv}.

Formal semantics We now turn to presenting a formal definition of the semantics of *PLF*. Throughout the rest of this chapter, we assume that the domain of computation is $\mathbf{I}_0$, and omit it as explicitly qualifying the satisfaction relation. A **configuration** of a flow program is a pair $C = \langle \sigma, \lambda \rangle$. The state σ assigns, as explained before, values to the variables $\bar{x}$, which are the program variables. The **location counter** λ, a hidden state component in a configuration, ranges over L_P. Its value is the (label of the) **current command** to be executed next. Most often we identify the current command with its label. Strictly speaking, the program P itself has to be part of the configuration, to determine the relationship between the value of λ and actual commands. Since this part does not change during transitions, we systematically omit it and leave its determination to context.

Convention: When a program P has a single start node, we agree that its label is l_0. Similarly, whenever there is a unique halt node, we agree that its label is l_*.

□

We next define the particular transition relation '$\rightarrow$' for configurations of *PLF* programs.

Definition: Let '$\rightarrow$' be the least relation among configurations satisfying the conditions below. Let $C = \langle \sigma, \lambda \rangle$ and $C' = \langle \sigma', \lambda' \rangle$ be two configurations (for the same program P). Then $C \rightarrow C'$ iff the following hold.

- If λ is the start, then $\lambda' = suc(\lambda)$ and $\sigma' = \sigma$.
- If λ is an assignment $\bar{x} := \bar{e}$, then $\lambda' = suc(\lambda)$ and $\sigma' = \sigma[\bar{e} \mid \bar{x}]$.
- If λ is a test $B(\bar{x})$ then $\sigma' = \sigma$, and either $\lambda' = suc^{+}(\lambda)$, in the case $\sigma \models B(\bar{x})$, or $\lambda' = suc^{-}(\lambda)$ in the case $\sigma \models \neg B(\bar{x})$.

An **initial** configuration has $\lambda = l_0$ denoting a start node, and in a **terminal** configuration λ denotes an exit node.

□

Recall that we inherit from Section 2.2 the general definitions of the accompanying notions of a computation, semantic function, and so on. We say that a computation π **visits** $l \in L_P$ iff π contains a configuration $C = \langle \sigma, \lambda \rangle$ with $\lambda = l$. In addition, for a sequence of transitions $C_i \to C_{i+1} \to \cdots \to C_{i+k}$, for some $k \geqslant 1$, such that the corresponding sequence of values of λ_i forms a path $\tau = l_{j_1} \to \cdots \to l_{j_{k+1}}$ in P, we say that the computation **traverses** the path τ. In particular, if $l_{j_1} = l_{j_{k+1}}$, we say that the computation traverses a **loop** in P. Note that by the definition of '$\to$', there is a unique computation of a program from any given initial configuration.

Thus, one sees that it is possible to define precisely the informal operational jargon often used, and to connect it to a rigorous treatment. To set the stage for the presentation of the verification techniques, we need a few more definitions and notations about finite segments of computations.

Let τ be a finite path in P. We associate with τ two semantic characteristics:

- *Reachability condition:* This condition (on states at the beginning of τ) guarantees that control will traverse τ. It is denoted by $R_\tau(\bar{x})$.
- *State transformation:* The final state obtained if control indeed traverses τ starting with $\bar{x}$. It is denoted by $T_\tau(\bar{x})$.

The definition of both is by induction on τ, and it employs a technique known as **backward substitution**.

Let $\tau = l_{i_0} \to \cdots \to l_{i_k}$ be a finite path in P of length $k+1$, for some natural number k. We first define $R_\tau^m(\bar{x})$ and $T_\tau^m(\bar{x})$, the corresponding characteristics of the suffix $l_{i_m} \to \cdots \to l_{i_k}$ of τ, by induction on m going down from k to 0.

Induction basis:

$$R_\tau^k(\bar{x}) \overset{df.}{=} true, \quad T_\tau^k(\bar{x}) \overset{df.}{=} \bar{x}$$

In other words, being at the end of τ implies an identically true reachability condition and an identity state transformation, as can be expected.

Induction assumption:
Suppose that $R_\tau^{m+1}(\bar{x})$, $T_\tau^{m+1}(\bar{x})$ have already been defined for $0 \leqslant m < k$.

Induction step:
We define $R_\tau^m(\bar{x})$, $T_\tau^m(\bar{x})$ according to the command at node l_{i_m}.

- *Assignment:* $R_\tau^m(\bar{x}) \stackrel{df.}{=} (R_\tau^{m+1}(\bar{x}))_{\bar{e}}^{\bar{x}}$, $T_\tau^m(\bar{x}) \stackrel{df.}{=} (T_\tau^{m+1}(\bar{x}))_{\bar{e}}^{\bar{x}}$. Thus, the effect of an assignment is captured by substitutions.
- *Positive test:* $R_\tau^m(\bar{x}) \stackrel{df.}{=} R_\tau^{m+1}(\bar{x}) \wedge B(\bar{x})$, $T_\tau^m(\bar{x}) \stackrel{df.}{=} T_\tau^{m+1}(\bar{x})$. Thus a test does not change the state and 'remembers' the condition.
- *Negative test:* $R_\tau^m(\bar{x}) \stackrel{df.}{=} R_\tau^{m+1}(\bar{x}) \wedge \neg B(\bar{x})$, $T_\tau^m(\bar{x}) \stackrel{df.}{=} T_\tau^{m+1}(\bar{x})$. This is similar to the positive case.

Finally, we define $R_\tau(\bar{x}) \stackrel{df.}{=} R_\tau^0(\bar{x})$, $T_\tau(\bar{x}) \stackrel{df.}{=} T_\tau^0(\bar{x})$.

EXERCISE:

Enter the right clause for 'start' and 'halt' nodes.

□

We now formulate a lemma, which attributes to R and to T their intended meaning, thereby justifying their names as 'semantic characteristics' of finite paths.

Lemma (semantic characterization of finite paths):

Let $\tau = l_{i_0} \rightarrow \cdots \rightarrow l_{i_k}$, $k \geqslant 0$, be a finite path in P, and $C = \langle \sigma, l_{i_0} \rangle$ a configuration.

(1) A (partial) computation starting in C traverses τ iff $\sigma \models R_\tau(\bar{x})$.

(2) If a (partial) computation starting in C traverses τ, ending in $C' = \langle \sigma', l_{i_k} \rangle$, then $\sigma' = \sigma[T_\tau(\bar{x}) | \bar{x}]$.

□

EXERCISE:

Prove the above lemma (by induction on the length of τ, using R^m, T^m from the inductive definition of R, T).

□

EXAMPLE:

In Figure 3.2, a simple path from the program P_{idiv} of Figure 3.1 is considered, and its characteristics are computed and displayed.

□

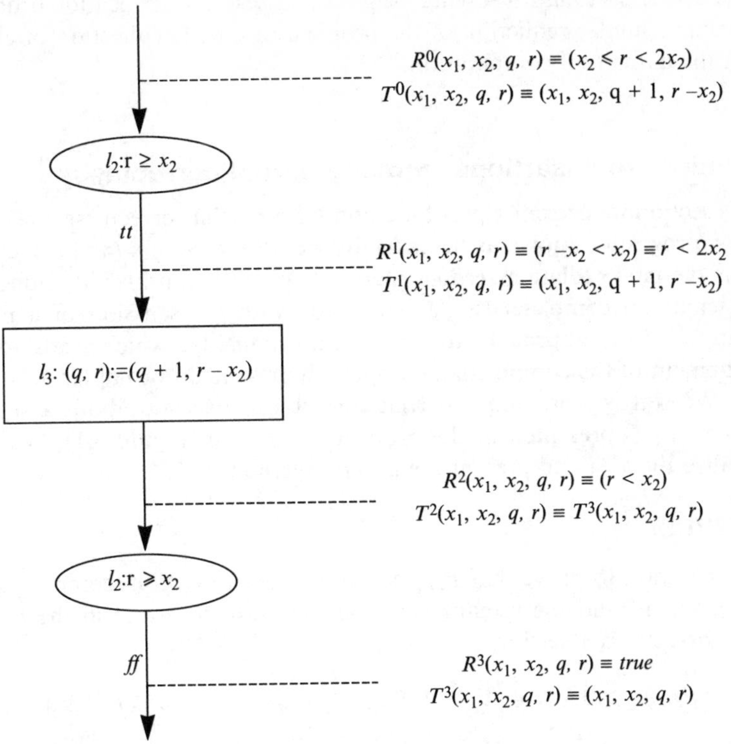

Figure 3.2 Semantic path characteristics.

A direct appeal to the semantic characterization of finite paths lemma actually solves the verification problem for **loop-free** flow programs, that is programs without any cycles in their underlying graphs. This is expressed by the following lemma, which follows immediately from the definitions. Call a finite path τ **complete** if l_{i_0} labels *start* and l_{i_k} labels *halt*.

Lemma (correctness of loop-free flow programs):

Let P be a loopless flow program and let $\phi = \langle p, q \rangle$ be a specification. Then, $\models \langle p \rangle P \langle q \rangle$ iff for every complete path τ in P,

$$\models \forall \bar{x}: [p(\bar{x}) \wedge R_\tau(\bar{x}) \Rightarrow q(T_\tau(\bar{x}))].$$

□

The proof of this lemma is left as an exercise. Note that a loop-free program has a finite number of complete paths. Therefore, verification by means of an exhaustive checking procedure is possible. By the correctness of loop-free programs lemma, the actual verification of such programs is reduced to a finite collection of claims about the domain of computation (one for each complete path). Our task in the next section is to use the same path characteristics as tools for solving the general case of the verification problem, obtaining a similar reduction of the problem to a finite collection of claims about the domain of computation.

3.3 Inductive assertions: proving partial correctness

In this section we present a proof method **F** for partial correctness assertions on flow programs, known as the **inductive assertions** method (and sometimes also as the **intermediate assertions** method). We also consider its soundness and (semantic) completeness. We conclude with a discussion of a major limitation of the approach, its non-compositionality, which leads to the development of the compositional approach presented in Chapter 4.

We start by proving a partial correctness assertion about a specific program, P_{idiv}, presented in the previous section (in Figure 3.1). We then generalize the idea and present the general method.

EXAMPLE:

We want to prove that P_{idiv} performs integer division (computing the quotient and the remainder). Thus we want to establish the partial correctness assertion

$$\{x_1 = X_1 \geqslant 0 \wedge x_2 = X_2 \geqslant 0\}\, P_{idiv}\, \{X_1 = q\cdot X_2 + r \wedge 0 \leqslant r < X_2\}$$

As we already know how to handle loop-free flow programs, we would like to reduce the correctness of the whole program to some finite collection of proofs about finite paths. Observe that all computations of the program repeatedly visit the node l_4 as they repeatedly traverse the loop. Thus, we may treat separately the segment of the computation between consecutive visits to l_4.

This leads to the following idea: let us find a state predicate that holds when control reaches l_4, which will serve as an induction assumption about properties of the state at l_4. Denote this state predicate by $I(\bar{x})$. Also, we associate the precondition with the entry point and the postcondition with the exit point.

What properties should the intermediate assertion $I(\bar{x})$ have, so that the right conclusions can be drawn from this association?

For the given case there are three properties, which we list below.

- *Establishment:* It should be the case that $I(\bar{x})$ holds when l_4 is reached for the first time. Since we know by assumption that the precondition holds at the entry point, we may use this to show that indeed $I(\bar{x})$ is established. We get

$$\forall \bar{x}: [(p(\bar{x}) \wedge R_{(l_0, l_4)}(\bar{x})) \Rightarrow I(T_{(l_0, l_4)}(\bar{x}))] \qquad \text{(ESTABLISH)}$$

- *Preservation:* Next, we have to show that $I(\bar{x})$ is preserved by a traversal of the loop. Here we use the characteristics of the simple path (l_4, l_4). We get

  $$\forall \bar{x}: [(I(\bar{x}) \wedge R_{(l_4,l_4)}(\bar{x})) \Rightarrow I(T_{(l_4,l_4)}(\bar{x}))] \qquad \text{(PRESERVE)}$$

- *Exit:* Finally, we have to show that if the exit condition is satisfied, this implies, together with the intermediate assertion, that the postcondition holds. We get

  $$\forall \bar{x}: [I(\bar{x}) \wedge R_{(l_4,l_*)}(\bar{x}) \Rightarrow q(\bar{x})] \qquad \text{(EXIT)}$$

Suppose for a moment that such a predicate $I(\bar{x})$, satisfying the three conditions, has been found. We now show that the partial correctness assertion is implied. Consider any computation starting from an initial state satisfying the precondition. It must reach l_4 (since $R_{(l_0,l_4)} \equiv true$), and, by (ESTABLISH), $I(\bar{x})$ is satisfied. By a simple inductive argument, using (PRESERVE), we obtain that $I(\bar{x})$ holds whenever l_4 is visited. We now distinguish between two possibilities:

(1) The first possibility is that the loop is never exited, that is the computation is infinite. This certainly does not violate the partial correctness claim.

(2) The second possibility is that the loop is eventually left. In that case, the path (l_4, l_*) is followed at some stage. However, because of the (EXIT) property, we get that $q(\bar{x})$ holds at the exit point, again not violating partial correctness.

What is left is to designate a state predicate $I(\bar{x})$ having the three required properties. An easy calculation shows that a candidate (not a unique one) is

$$I(x_1, x_2, q, r) \stackrel{df.}{=} (x_1 = X_1, \geqslant 0 \wedge x_2 = X_2 \geqslant 0 \wedge X_1 = q \cdot X_2 + r \wedge r \geqslant 0)$$

We give the detailed argument below.

(ESTABLISH) We have that $R_{(l_0,l_4)}(x_1, x_2, q, r) \equiv true$, $T_{(l_0,l_4)}(x_1, x_2, q, r) = (x_1, x_2, 0, x_1)$ and we have to show that

$$(x_1 = X_1 \geqslant 0 \wedge x_2 = X_2 \geqslant 0 \wedge true) \Rightarrow$$
$$(x_1 = X_1 \geqslant 0 \wedge x_2 = X_2 \geqslant 0 \wedge X_1 = 0 \cdot X_2 + x_1 \wedge x_1 \geqslant 0)$$

The condition on the values of x_1 and x_2 is the same in the antecedent and the consequent. The third conjunct in the consequent follows from an identity of arithmetic. The last conjunct in the consequent follows from the first conjunct in the antecedent.

(PRESERVE) We have that $R_{(l_4, l_4)}(x_1, x_2, q, r) \equiv r \geqslant X_2$, $T_{(l_4, l_4)}(x_1, x_2, q, r) = (x_1, x_2, q+1, r-x_2)$ and we have to show that

$$(x_1 = X_1 \geqslant 0 \wedge x_2 = X_2 \geqslant 0 \wedge X_1 = q \cdot X_2 + r \wedge r \geqslant 0 \wedge r \geqslant x_2) \Rightarrow$$
$$(x_1 = X_1 \geqslant 0 \wedge x_2 = X_2 \geqslant 0 \wedge x_1 = (q+1) \cdot X_2 + r - x_2 \wedge r - x_2 \geqslant 0)$$

The main conjunct of the consequent is shown by $X_1 = (q+1) \cdot X_2 + r - x_2 = q \cdot X_2 + X_2 + r - x_2 = q \cdot X_2 + r$, as $x_2 = X_2$. Also, $r - x_2 \geqslant 0$ in the consequent follows from $r \geqslant x_2$ in the antecedent.

(EXIT) We have that $R_{(l_4, l_*)}(x_1, x_2, q, r) \equiv \neg r \geqslant x_2$ (equivalent to $r < x_2$) and $T_{(l_4, l_*)}$ is the identity state transformation. All we have to show is that $x_1 = X_1 \geqslant 0 \wedge x_2 = X_2 \geqslant 0 \wedge X_1 = q \cdot X_2 + r \wedge r \geqslant 0 \wedge r < x_2$ implies the postcondition, which is trivial.

Thereby, we have derived the required partial correctness assertion.

Thus, we see how, in this example, the correctness of the given program is reduced once again to three simple arithmetic claims, that are program free (that is, do not refer to programs or computations).

□

EXERCISE:

How can the above proof be strengthened to establish also $x_1 = X_1 \wedge x_2 = X_2$ in its postcondition?

□

Our aim is now to generalize the ideas used in the example into a full proof method for the general case. The main idea is to break the global partial correctness assertion about the whole program into a finite collection of assertions about loop-free programs, known as **verification conditions**, for which the characteristics mentioned above solve the problem. The global partial correctness assertion will follow by an inductive argument on the number of times each finite section is executed. In general, the claims about the domain need not be (and most often are not) such immediate properties as in the example. However, we are not concerned here with the complexity of domain-dependent properties. Any reduction of correctness assertions to a finite number of claims about the domain achieves our goal.

The way to achieve this decomposition is to select a subset of control points in the program, which we call **cut points**, and to associate with each cut point a state predicate, referred to as an **inductive assertion** (or **intermediate**

To prove $\{p(\bar{x})\}\, P\, \{q(\bar{x})\}$:

Cut points: Find a set $\mathbf{C} \subseteq L_p$ such that

(1) $l_0, l_* \in \mathbf{C}$.

(2) Every cycle in (the graph of) P contains at least one cut point $l \in \mathbf{C}$.

A **basic path** (l, l') is a path between two cut points (without another cut point in between).

Inductive assertions: With each cut point $l \in \mathbf{C}$ associate a state predicate $I_l(\bar{x})$, with $I_{l_0} \overset{df.}{=} p$ (the precondition) and $I_{l_*} \overset{df.}{\Rightarrow} q$ (the post-condition).

Verification conditions: For each basic path $\alpha = (l, l')$, prove that $\forall \bar{x}: [I_l(\bar{x}) \wedge R_\alpha(\bar{x}) \Rightarrow \nwarrow_{='}(T_\alpha(\bar{x}))]$.

Figure 3.3 The method **F**.

---

assertion), characterizing the states at this cut point whenever it is reached. The basic property of these predicates, of holding in the (current) state whenever control visits that cut point, is the required generalization of the three specific properties in the example above. Note that even though the name inductive (state) assertion is used, at this stage we are interested really in predicates. The name anticipates the expression of these predicates as state assertions. A formal formulation of this method (for programs with a unique entry and a unique exit) is presented in Figure 3.3.

Note that for a given pair of cut points (l, l'), more than one simple path leading from the one to the other may exist. All of them generate verification conditions. We distinguish between different paths that share end points by including another intermediate label (not from $\mathbf{C}$).

At this stage, we do not impose any restriction as to how the verification conditions are proved. We may take advantage of any known mathematical properties of the integers. In other words, we are using an 'oracle' that knows all true statements about the integers. The meaning of the verification conditions is a correct behavior of basic paths: if the precondition of such a path, namely the inductive assertion of the source node, holds and if the condition for traversing the path is satisfied, then the postcondition, namely, the inductive assertion at the destination node, also holds for the resulting state. Thus, we were able to generalize the verification of loop-free programs considered before. We require basic paths in a general program to behave like complete paths in a loop-free program.

It is important to notice that the effect of a successful application of **F** is the reduction of a partial correctness assertion about programs to 'pure' arithmetical assertions which do not depend on programming languages or programs, but are amenable to the usual mathematical treatment. The number of such program-free assertions is finite, since the number of basic paths in the program is finite. In that, we again have a natural generalization of the similar reduction for loop-free programs.

> **Notation:** We use $\vdash_{\mathbf{F}}$ to indicate a successful application of the method. This notation is used for uniformity, in anticipation of its later use for its more traditional meaning of provability in a formal proof system. Note that at this stage we continue the systematic omission of the structure $\boldsymbol{I}$ in '$\models$' assertions, as well as the true arithmetic assertions used as assumptions in '$\vdash$' assertions.

We now turn to a justification of the claim that method **F** indeed solves the verification problem as claimed.

3.3.1 Soundness and completeness of F

In this section we turn our attention to properties of the method **F**, and formulate and prove two theorems stating the properties of soundness and (semantic) completeness. We return to another property at the end of the chapter.

Theorem (soundness of method F):

If $\vdash_{\mathbf{F}} \{p(\bar{x})\}\, P\, \{q(\bar{x})\}$ then $\models \{p(\bar{x})\}\, P\, \{q(\bar{x})\}$

Proof: As mentioned, the proof method is a generalization of the argument in the example. Therefore, we prove first a central lemma, stating that whenever a cut point is visited during a computation, the associated inductive assertion is satisfied by the corresponding state.

□

Lemma (preservation):

If $\vdash_{\mathbf{F}} \{p(\bar{x})\}\, P\, \{q(\bar{x})\}$, then for every computation π of P starting in a configuration $C_0 = \langle \sigma, start \rangle$ such that $\sigma \models p(\bar{x})$ the following holds: if the computation visits a cut point $l \in \mathbf{C}$ with state σ', then $\sigma' \models I_l(\bar{x})$.

Proof of the lemma: The proof is by induction on the number of visits to cut points.

Induction basis: By definition, $l_0 \in \mathbf{C}$ is always the first cut point visited. Also, by definition $I_{l_0} = p$ (the precondition), which is satisfied by the initial state σ by assumption.

Induction step: Suppose that the nth cut point visited is $l \in \mathbf{C}$, and that the corresponding state is σ'' satisfying $\sigma'' \models I_l(\bar{x})$. If $l = l_*$ there is nothing left to be proved, since there are no outgoing edges. Otherwise, let l' be the $(n+1)$th cut point visited, with the corresponding state satisfying $\sigma' [\![\bar{x}]\!] = T_{(l,l')}(\sigma'' [\![\bar{x}]\!])$, the reachability condition $R_{(l,l')}(\sigma'' [\![\bar{x}]\!])$ also holding. Since all the verification conditions have been established (in the successful application of **F**), in particular we have the one for $\alpha = (l, l')$, for all $\bar{x}$. In particular, it holds also for $\sigma'' [\![\bar{x}]\!]$. Thus, it follows that $\sigma' \models I_{l'}(\bar{x})$ also holds, which concludes the proof of the preservation lemma.

□

We now return to the proof of the soundness theorem and show that it immediately follows from the preservation lemma. Consider any computation starting from an initial state satisfying the precondition. If the computation is infinite, it certainly does not violate the partial correctness assertion. If it is finite, then by the definition of a terminal configuration at some stage it reaches the cut point $l_* \in \mathbf{C}$. By the preservation lemma, the state at that point, say σ^*, satisfies the associated inductive assertion $I_{l_*}(\bar{x})$, which by definition is the postcondition q. Once again, the partial correctness assertion is not violated.

□

We now turn to the issue of the semantic completeness of the method **F**.

Theorem (semantic completeness of method F):

If $\models \{p(\bar{x})\}\, P\, \{q(\bar{x})\}$, then $\vdash_{\mathbf{F}} \{p(\bar{x})\}\, P\, \{q(\bar{x})\}$

Proof: We have to show that if P is partially correct w.r.t. the specification $\phi = \langle p(\bar{x}), q(\bar{x}) \rangle$, then we can find an appropriate set $\mathbf{C}$ of cut points and associate with them inductive assertions, so that all verification conditions are indeed satisfied. We remind the reader that the semantic completeness is only concerned with the existence of the sets of states at the various cut points, disregarding at this stage ways of expressing them as formulas in a specification language. Also, there is no request to construct these predicates effectively (that is, algorithmically), only to establish their existence.

First, we choose an *arbitrary* collection of cut points $\mathbf{C}$ which includes l_0, l_* and cuts all cycles in P. Clearly, such collections always exist ($\mathbf{C} = L_P$ being one such candidate). We now associate with every $l \in \mathbf{C}$ what is known as the **minimal predicate** at l, denoted by $I_l^*(\bar{x})$, which holds in a state σ iff there exists a prefix $\pi \stackrel{df.}{=} C_0 = \langle \sigma_0, \lambda_0 \rangle \rightarrow \cdots \rightarrow C_k = \langle \sigma_k, \lambda_k \rangle$ of a computation of P, such that (1) $\sigma_0 \models p(\bar{x})$, (2) $\sigma_k = \sigma$, and (3) $\lambda_k = l$.

In other words, $I_l^*(\bar{x})$ is satisfied only by values that are determined by states reachable in l during a computation starting from an initial state satisfying the precondition.

We now have to show that the collection of predicates $\{I_l^*(\bar{x}) \mid l \in \mathbf{C}\}$ satisfies all the verification conditions.

Consider an arbitrary basic path $\alpha = (l, l')$. Suppose that for some state σ it is the case that

$$\sigma \models I_l(\bar{x}) \wedge R_{(l,l')}(\bar{x})$$

By definition, there exists some prefix π of a computation of P (starting in an initial state which satisfies p), which reaches l with state σ. Since $\sigma \models R_{(l,l')}(\bar{x})$ by assumption, there is a prolongation π' of π which reaches l', say with state σ'. By the definition of a minimal predicate (for l'), $\sigma' \models I_{l'}(\bar{x})$. By the path characteristics, we know that

$$\sigma'[\![\bar{x}]\!] = T_{(l,l')}(\sigma[\![\bar{x}]\!])$$

and hence $\sigma \models I_{l'}(T_{(l,l')}(\bar{x}))$, establishing the verification condition, and with it the semantic completeness theorem.

□

EXERCISE:

Show the satisfaction of the boundary conditions for I_{l_0}, I_{l_*}. (Here is where the assumption of partial correctness of the given program is actually used.)

□

Remarks:

(1) Note the difference between an arbitrary collection of inductive assertions and the special collection of minimal predicates defined in the completeness proof. An arbitrary assertion I_l is indeed satisfied by all states reaching l, but possibly also by unreachable states. On the other hand, I_l^* is satisfied only by reachable states. That is why it is called a minimal state predicate for l. The way the minimal predicates were defined, under the semantic assumption that the program is partially correct w.r.t. the specification, is typical of a completeness proof. Usually, minimal predicates are harder to find, and may contain more information than needed in the proofs. In actual proofs, one finds abstractions of the minimal predicates, that are weak enough to satisfy the required invariance, but strong enough to establish the ultimate claim.

(2) Clearly, we ignored the issue of expressibility of I_l^* in terms of a formula in some specification language, using state variables only. However, as a mathematical entity I_l^* is well defined.

(3) Another issue ignored in the discussion in this chapter is the way the proofs of the verification conditions themselves are obtained. Do we have a formalized proof system for proving them? Here, we were satisfied with semantic reasoning (in the computational structure), that is with the existence of an 'oracle' for true arithmetic statements.

In particular, note that no use was made of properties of I_0 in these proofs, which therefore carry to arbitrary domains of computation.

(4) In principle, applying the proof of the semantic completeness theorem to actual programs and specifications yields an actual proof of partial correctness for the given case. In practice, in particular in view of the issues ignored, this is not a way to construct proofs. Some more insight and heuristics are needed, to find assertions which are directly meaningful and expressible by the state variables. Several such heuristics appear in the literature, references presented at the end of the chapter. However, it is very important to know that a correctness proof (for a correct program), even if very unnatural, always exists.

We shall return to discussions of completeness and its many facets in the next chapter.

3.4 Well-founded sets: proving termination

In this section we present a proof method for proving termination of flow programs. Combined with the proof method of the previous section for partial correctness, and in view of the separation lemma, we have a way of proving total correctness.

The termination property is a special case of a family of properties known as **liveness** properties (which we shall consider in more detail subsequently). A common attribute of such properties is that they cannot be proved by induction on the computation, as all inductive assertions are satisfied also in infinite computations (as follows from the preservation lemma). A different approach is needed.

We again start by proving termination for an example (again the integer division program), and then generalizing the ideas as a method for the general case.

EXAMPLE:

We prove $\langle x_1 = X_1 \geqslant 0 \wedge x_2 = X_2 > 0 \rangle\, P_{idiv} \langle \mathit{true} \rangle$. Note the difference in the precondition on x_2 as compared with the corresponding partial correctness assertion.

Here too some intermediate assertions are needed. However, as no claim is made about the final states (except for their existence), less information has to be carried by the intermediate assertions.

The interesting intermediate assertion associated with label l_4 is $J_{l_4}(x_1, x_2, q, r) \overset{df.}{=} [x_2 = X_2 > 0 \wedge r \geqslant 0]$. In order to see this, we have again to show the properties (ESTABLISH) and (PRESERVE), which in this case are:

$$(x_1 = X_1 \geqslant 0 \wedge x_2 = X_2 > 0) \Rightarrow (x_2 = X_2 > 0 \wedge x_1 \geqslant 0),$$
$$(x_2 = X_2 > 0 \wedge r \geqslant 0 \wedge r \geqslant x_2) \Rightarrow (x_2 = X_2 > 0 \wedge r - x_2 \geqslant 0)$$

Both claims are easily verified.

We now observe the following crucial property of the simple path (l_4, l_4), that is the cycle in the graph of P_{idiv}: *during every traversal of it, the final value of r is always smaller than its initial value*. In other words, every traversal around the (only) cycle decreases r. This observation is an immediate conclusion of computing $T_{(l_4, l_4)}$.

By way of contradiction, suppose that there is an infinite computation π of P_{idiv}, starting in an initial state that satisfies the precondition. By the definition of a computation, π must pass infinitely often through l_4, traversing infinitely often the cycle. We thus get an infinite sequence of configurations $C_i = \langle \sigma_i, \lambda_i \rangle$, $i \geqslant 0$, satisfying

(1) for all $i \geqslant 0$, $\lambda_i = l_4$,

(2) for all $i \geqslant 0$, $\sigma_i \models J_{l_4}(\bar{x})$, by which $\sigma_i [\![r]\!] \geqslant 0$, and

(3) for all $i \geqslant 0$, $\sigma_i [\![r]\!] > \sigma_{i+1} [\![r]\!]$.

This is a contradiction, as there does not exist an infinite decreasing sequence of nonnegative integers.

Note that this proof would not apply if the precondition would allow $X_2 \geqslant 0$, as for $X_2 = 0$ no decrease in r would occur. That is the reason for having changed the specification used for partial correctness; the latter is not violated by a 0 value, causing an infinite computation.

Anticipating the general case, we slightly change the presentation of the proof. We introduce a **parametrized inductive assertion** with an additional parameter n (not occurring in the program), which is a natural number. We denote it by $J'_{l_4}(\bar{x}, n) \overset{df.}{=} [x_2 = X_2 > 0 \wedge r = n \geqslant 0]$. The new (PRESERVE) property is stated as $J'_{l_4}(\bar{x}, n) \wedge r \geqslant x_2 \Rightarrow J'_{l_4}(T_{(l_4, l_4)}(\bar{x}), n - x_2)$. Thus, the preservation is always with a smaller value of the (natural number) parameter.

In this example, the additional parameter n is somewhat redundant, as it is invariantly equal to r. In general, it need not be a value of a state variable, but only dependent on the state.

□

This principle, stating the impossibility of an infinite decreasing

To prove $\langle p(\bar{x})\rangle\, P\, \langle true \rangle$:

Well-founded set: Choose a well-founded, partially ordered set $(W, <)$.

Cut points: As for **F**.

Parametrized inductive assertions: With each $l \in \mathbf{C}$ associate a parametrized inductive assertion $I_l(\bar{x}, w)$, where $w \in W$.

Verification conditions:

$(INIT)$: $\forall \bar{x}: [p(\bar{x}) \Rightarrow \exists w: I_{l_0}(\bar{x}, w)]$

(DEC): For each basic path $\alpha = (l, l')$,

$$\forall \bar{x}: [I_l(\bar{x}, w) \wedge R_\alpha(\bar{x}) \Rightarrow \exists w' < w: I_{l'}(T_\alpha(\bar{x}), w')]$$

Figure 3.4 The method $\mathbf{F}^*$.

---

sequence of natural numbers, underlies the general approach to proving termination. However, for flexibility and convenience in actual proofs, a somewhat more general version of this principle is used.

Definition: A partially ordered set $(W, <)$ is **well founded** iff there does not exist an infinite sequence $w_i \in W$, $i \geqslant 0$, such that $w_0 > w_1 > w_2 > \ldots$.

□

Following are some simple examples of well-founded sets:

(1) The natural numbers under their usual ordering constitute a well-founded set.

(2) For an alphabet Σ, the set of all finite words over Σ, denoted usually by Σ^*, under the prefix ordering, is a well-founded set. Here the order is indeed partial.

(3) Generalizing (2), the set of trees, ordered by the subtree relation, is also well founded.

The set of positive rationals is not well founded under the usual ordering, as there are infinite decreasing sequences of rationals, for example the sequence $r_n \stackrel{df.}{=} 1/n$. Observe that the existence of minimal elements does not imply well-foundedness.

In Figure 3.4 we formulate the proof method $\mathbf{F}^*$ for proving termination (again, under the assumption of single entry and exit).

The method implies a decrease in the well-founded parameter, known also as the **variant**, along every basic path. This, in turn, implies that only a finite number of traversals of basic paths is possible, and therefore the finiteness of the computation. Note that the method does not require that I_{l_*} needs to be satisfied by minimal elements of W only. Sometimes it is easier to find natural proofs where the exact bound on the abstract distance from termination is not precisely known (see the *gcd* proof later in this section). This degree of freedom, of not having to terminate with a minimal parameter value, is quite significant for another variant of the rule (considered in an exercise), where the variant (which is a natural number) has to decrease exactly by one along every basic path. The current rule does imply, however, that for $l \neq l_*$ $I_l(\bar{x}, w)$ is never satisfied by a parameter value w which is a minimal element in W. This is because the consequent of the clause *DEC*, implying the existence of a strictly smaller w', cannot be established for a minimal w.

3.4.1 Soundness and semantic completeness of F*

In this section we establish the soundness and semantic completeness of the method **F*** for proving termination.

Theorem (soundness of method F*):

$$\text{If } \vdash_{\mathbf{F}^*} \langle p(\bar{x})\rangle\, P\, \langle true\rangle, \text{ then } \models \langle p(\bar{x})\rangle\, P\, \langle true\rangle.$$

Proof: Suppose the rule has been successfully applied to P and its specification, but still there exists an infinite computation π of P, starting in an initial state that satisfies the precondition. Thus, π visits cut points in C infinitely many times, by their choice. Therefore (making use of an appropriate generalization of the preservation lemma), there exists an infinite decreasing sequence of elements $w_i \in W$, $i \geqslant 0$, the ones obtained from the verification conditions. This contradicts the well-foundedness of W.

□

Obtaining a contradiction to well-foundedness is a typical structure of soundness proofs for rules for proving termination, and we shall encounter it again subsequently.

Theorem (semantic completeness of method F*):

$$\text{If } \models \langle p(\bar{x})\rangle P \langle true\rangle, \text{ then } \vdash_{\mathbf{F}^*} \langle p(\bar{x})\rangle P \langle true\rangle$$

Proof: Again, under the assumption of the termination of P (for initial states that satisfy the precondition), we have to show the ability to choose cut points and parametrized inductive assertions, so that all verification conditions (guaranteeing decrease of the variant) are satisfied.

As the well-founded set, we uniformly choose the natural numbers **N** under their usual ordering. The cut points are again chosen arbitrarily, such that every loop contains at least one cut point. As for the parametrized inductive assertions, for each $l \in \mathbf{C}$ we define $J_l^*(\bar{x}, n)$, as $I_l^*(\bar{x})$ (from the completeness proof of **F**), with the additional requirement that n equals the length of the rest of the computation (measured in basic paths), leading to *halt*. This length is well defined, since we are given that the program terminates. The proof of the verification condition is similar to the partial correctness case, with the additional observation that the rest of a longer partial computation becomes shorter, is 0 at the end of the computation, and is positive everywhere else.

□

Conclusion:

For every flow program P and specification $\phi = \langle p, q\rangle$,

(1) A proof $\vdash_{\mathbf{F}^*}\langle p\rangle P\ \langle true\rangle$ can always use $W \stackrel{df.}{=} \mathbf{N}$, with its standard ordering.

(2) The method **F*** can always be applied so that only 0 satisfies I_{l_*}.

As we shall see, this uniform use of natural numbers for proving termination will cease to be possible for nondeterministic programs under fairness assumptions (Chapter 5).

EXAMPLE (termination of gcd computation):

We end this section with another correctness proof of a flow program P_{gcd} for computing the greatest common divisor of two positive natural numbers X_1, X_2. The program is shown in Figure 3.5. We consider both partial correctness and termination, proved separately, each by its respective proof method. As the total correctness assertion, we show

$$\langle x_1 = X_1 > 0 \wedge x_2 = X_2 > 0\rangle P_{gcd}\langle y_2 = gcd(X_1, X_2)\rangle$$

We take here *gcd* as a known numeric function, so that we can use its properties in the proof.

We first apply **F** to prove partial correctness. The cut points are $\{l_0, l, l_*\}$, and an inductive assertion for l is

$$I_l(x_1, x_2, y_1, y_2) \stackrel{df.}{=} [x_1 = X_1 > 0 \wedge x_2 = X_2 > 0 \wedge \\ y_1 + y_2 > 0 \wedge gcd(y_1, y_2) = gcd(X_1, X_2)]$$

We check all the verification conditions.

($l_0 \to l$) We have to show that $p(\bar{x}) \Rightarrow (p(\bar{x}) \wedge gcd(X_1, X_2) = gcd(x_1, x_2) \wedge x_1 + x_2 > 0)$, which holds trivially.

($l \to l_1 \to l$) Here the important fact is the symmetry of *gcd*, a known fact.

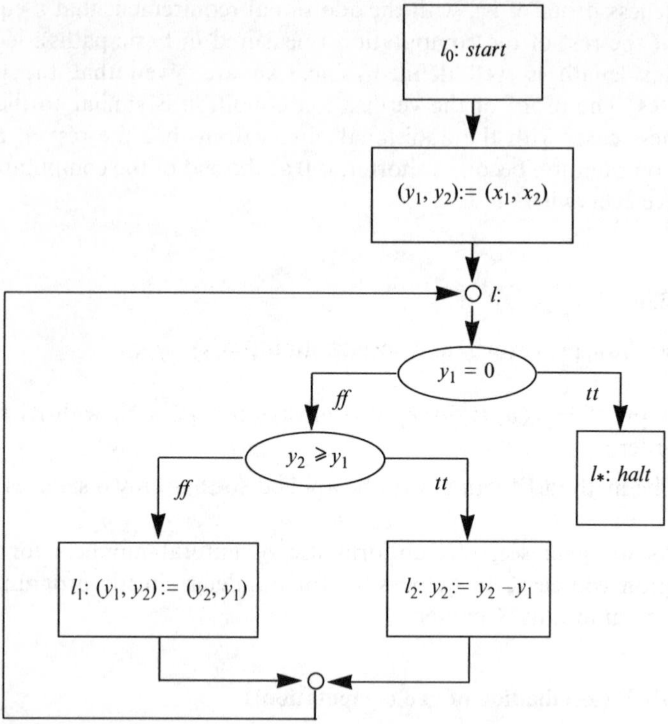

Figure 3.5 The flow program $\mathbf{P}_{gcd}$: greatest common divisor.

($l \rightarrow l_2 \rightarrow l$) The only nontrivial part we have to show is $I_l(x_1, x_2, y_1, y_2) \wedge y_1 \neq 0 \wedge y_2 \geqslant y_1 \Rightarrow gcd(y_1, y_2) = gcd(y_1, y_2 - y_1)$, also a known property of the *gcd* function.

($l \rightarrow l_*$) Again, a known fact about *gcd* is $n > 0 \Rightarrow gcd(n, 0) = n$.

This establishes partial correctness. We now use **F*** to show termination. As the well-founded set we choose $\mathbf{N} \times \mathbf{N}$, ordered lexicographically. In other words,

$$\langle n_1, n_2 \rangle <_l \langle n_1', n_2' \rangle \Leftrightarrow (n_1 < n_1') \vee (n_1 = n_1' \wedge n_2 < n_2')$$

The cut points are the same, and the parametrized inductive assertion at l is

$$I_l'(x_1, x_2, y_1, y_2, n_1, n_2) \overset{df.}{=} 0 \leqslant y_1 = n_1 \wedge 0 \leqslant y_2 = n_2$$

We use a simplification of the rule (see exercise), requiring a decrease of the variant only along cycles.

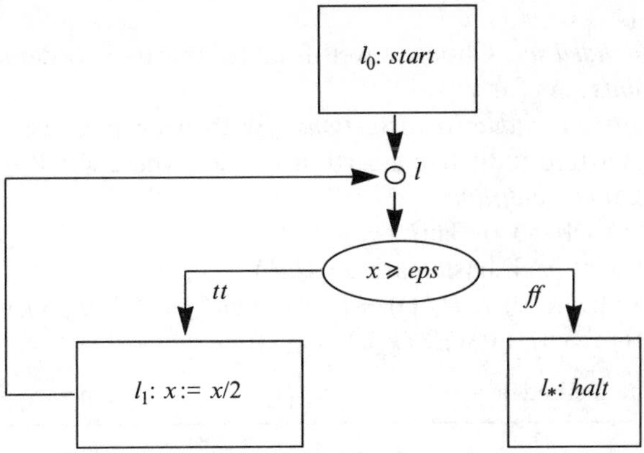

Figure 3.6 Termination over real numbers.

($l \rightarrow l_1 \rightarrow l$) Here we have to show that $y_1 \neq 0 \wedge y_2 < y_1 \Rightarrow \langle y_2, y_1 \rangle <_l \langle y_1, y_2 \rangle$, which follows from the definition of the lexicographical order.

($l \rightarrow l_2 \rightarrow l$) Here we have to show that $y_1 > 0 \wedge y_2 \geqslant y_1 \Rightarrow \langle y_1, y_2 - y_1 \rangle <_l \langle y_1, y_2 \rangle$, which holds, as y_1 remains fixed while y_2 decreases. Thereby, we have proved also termination.

An apparent alternative variant might be thought to be $y_1 + y_2$. However, it decreases along one cycle but remains fixed along the other. By the completeness proof, some trickier variant in **N** exists, but might be less natural to find.

Finally, note that when *halt* is reached, the parameter satisfying I_{l_*} is not a lexicographically minimal pair. It is harder to apply in this case the version of the rule requiring that only minimal parameters satisfy the inductive assertion associated with *halt*.

□

EXAMPLE (termination over real numbers):

Consider the program P_{log} in Figure 3.6, computing over real numbers. We want to use method **F*** to prove

$$\langle x = X \wedge eps > 0 \rangle P_{log} \langle true \rangle$$

that is termination for any initial value of x.

Clearly, the successive values of x form a monotonically decreasing sequence (of real numbers). However, because the real numbers (under their usual ordering) are not well founded, we cannot use the value of x directly as the variant parameter required by the method.

To prove $\langle p(\bar{x})\rangle P \langle q(\bar{x})\rangle$:

Well-founded set: Choose a well-founded, partially ordered set $(W, <)$

Cut points: As for **F**

Parametrized inductive assertions: With each $l \in \mathbf{C}$ associate a parametrized inductive assertion $I_l(\bar{x}, w)$, where $w \in W$.

Verification conditions:

$(INIT)$: $\forall \bar{x}:[p(\bar{x}) \Rightarrow \exists w: I_{l_0}(\bar{x}, w)]$

(DEC): For each basic path $\alpha = (l, l')$,

$\forall \bar{x}: [(I_l(\bar{x}, w) \wedge R_\alpha(\bar{x})) \Rightarrow (\exists w' \in W: w' < w \wedge I_{l'}(T_\alpha(\bar{x}), w'))]$

$(TERM)$: $\forall \bar{x}:[I_{l_*}(\bar{x}, w) I_{l_0}(\bar{x}, w) \Rightarrow q(\bar{x})]$

Figure 3.7 The method $\mathbf{F}^\dagger$.

The obvious choice of cut points is $\mathbf{C} = \{l_0, l, l_*\}$. As the parametrized invariant we take

$$I_l(x, eps, n) \overset{df.}{=} \left[x > eps \wedge n = \left\lfloor log_2\left(\frac{X}{eps}\right)\right\rfloor - log_2\left(\frac{X}{x}\right)\right] \vee [x < eps \wedge n = 0]$$

Note that the difference between the logarithms is nonnegative due to the condition $x > eps$. We now show that the verification conditions of rule $\mathbf{F}^*$ obtain.

(INIT) If $X > eps$ we take initially $n = log_2(X/eps)$. Note that $log_2(X/X) = 0$. Otherwise, we choose $n = 0$.

(DEC) There is one path to consider, namely (l, l_1, l). Suppose I_l holds with $n > 0$. The result follows from the equality

$$\log_2\left(\frac{X}{x/2}\right) = \log_2\left(\frac{X}{x}\right) + 1$$

□

We conclude this section by formulating proof method $\mathbf{F}^\dagger$, which is a combination of **F** and **F***, for proving total correctness directly (without the separation into partial correctness and termination). The main purpose for introducing this combined method is for a convenient comparison with other methods. The method is presented in Figure 3.7.

The main difference between this formulation of the inductive assertions method and the two previous ones is that here the parametrized assertions have to carry enough information to establish also the postcondition upon termination. The formulation of the soundness and semantic completeness theorems for this variant as well as their proofs are deferred to exercises.

3.5 Intermittent assertions: proving total correctness

In this section we present another proof method, known as the method of **intermittent assertions**, that aims directly towards total correctness, not making use of the separation lemma. One advantage of this method is that it naturally generalizes to a proof method of liveness properties of concurrent programs, especially the ones known as **reactive** programs. The natural correctness criterion for such programs does not imply termination. Rather, correct eventual response is required. It also naturally leads to consideration of **temporal logic** as the formalism for specification and proof. Thus, the discussion here is introductory, preparing the stage for further development, which is beyond the scope of this book. Some researchers in the field consider this method to be more natural, fitting better to the operational intuitions program designers have. We shall not attempt to settle this argument here.

The intermittent assertions method also relies on induction, but in contrast to the inductive assertions method, the induction is on the elements of the domain of computation. Before embarking on the details of the method, we formulate the induction principle used.

Structural induction:

Let $(W, <)$ be a well-founded, partially ordered set, and let $p(w)$ be a (monadic) predicate over W.

$$\text{If } \forall w \in W: \{[\forall v \in W: v < w \Rightarrow p(v)] \Rightarrow p(w)\}, \text{ then } \forall w \in W: p(w)$$

□

In other words, if, for each element w, the satisfaction of p by w can be deduced from the satisfaction of p by all smaller elements, then p is satisfied by every element w in W. Note that for the minimal elements of W, satisfaction of p has to be established unconditionally, as there are no smaller elements.

This is a well-known induction principle (having the 'course of values' induction on natural numbers as a special case), and we shall not prove here its validity. It is useful in many computational contexts, when one uses data structures such as lists or trees, which are well founded w.r.t. the substructure ordering.

We now return to the explanation of the intermittent assertions method. It also uses intermediate assertions as its main tool, but with a different interpretation. The previous methods rely on the preservation property, that is the intermediate assertion holds *whenever* the computation reaches the cut point with which it is associated. The new method, on the other hand, relies on the *existence* of a stage in a computation where a cut point is visited and the associated assertion is satisfied. Note that the correctness assertions do claim the existence of such a stage, and therefore are suitable to handle also termination.

Definition: For a flow program P, label l in L_P, and a state predicate $I(\bar{x})$: P satisfies the **intermittent assertion** $l:I(\bar{x})$ iff on every computation π of P there exists a configuration $C_i=\langle\sigma_i,\ l\rangle$ s.t. $\sigma_i \models I(\bar{x})$.

□

Our main correctness assertion is a relation between two intermittent assertions (not necessarily with different locations). It is denoted as

$$l_{i_1}: I_1(\bar{x}) \xrightarrow{\ \ 2\ \ } l_{i_2}: I_2(\bar{x})$$

where $l_{i_1}, l_{i_2} \in L_P$. Such an assertion is satisfied by a program iff for every computation, whenever at some stage control reaches l_{i_1} with a state satisfying I_1, then at some later time control (in the same computation) reaches l_{i_2} with a state satisfying I_2. Note that this is not an ordinary logical implication between I_1 and I_2. Neither is it a logical implication between $l_{i_1}: I_1$ and $l_{i_2}: I_2$, since both assertions are evaluated at different states (at different stages of the same computation). In addition, we require a temporal ordering among the two states (the respective values of the existentially quantified state). We will refer to this relation as **leads_to**, that is one intermittent assertion leads to another. Sometimes it is also called a **reachability** assertion. In this notation, the total correctness assertion is expressed as

$$l_0: p(\bar{x}) \xrightarrow{\ \ 2\ \ } l_*: q\,(\bar{x}).$$

Note that here the scope of specification variables is the whole reachability assertion. Thus, $l_0: x = X \xrightarrow{\ \ 2\ \ } l_*: x > X$ can be interpreted as 'the final value of x is greater than its initial value.' In both intermittent assertions X has the same denotation. Recall that the rule INST is applicable in this system too.

The proof method, denoted by **E** (for 'eventuality') uses the following axioms and rules for the '$\xrightarrow{\ \ 2\ \ }$' relation.

The first axiom is a variation on the verification condition for intermediate assertions, making use of the fact that the end point of a basic interval is always reachable from its origin, provided that the reachability condition is satisfied.

Basic-interval axiom:

If $\forall \bar{x}$: $[I_l(\bar{x}) \Rightarrow R_\alpha(\bar{x}) \wedge I_{l'}(T_\alpha(\bar{x}))]$ for $\alpha = (l, l')$ a basic interval, then l: $I_l(\bar{x}) \xrightarrow{\ \ 2\ \ } l': I_{l'}(\bar{x})$.

□

The second axiom can be interpreted as 'the present is included in the future': If a condition already holds, then it holds eventually.

Present axiom:

If $\forall\bar{x}:p(\bar{x}) \Rightarrow q(\bar{x})$, then $l\colon p(\bar{x}) \rightsquigarrow l\colon q(\bar{x})$, for every $l \in L_P$.

□

The third rule combines the effect of two consecutive intermittent assertions (sharing a cut point). It reflects the transitivity of the eventuality in time. Most often is the use of this axiom left implicit.

Transitivity of leads_to:

$$\frac{l_1\colon I_1(\bar{x}) \rightsquigarrow l_2\colon I_2(\bar{x}),\ l_2\colon I_2(\bar{x}) \rightsquigarrow l_3\colon I_3(\bar{x})}{l_1\colon I_1(\bar{x}) \rightsquigarrow l_3\colon I_3(\bar{x})}$$

□

Finally, for the case where the visits to control points are not consecutive, structural induction on data elements may be used.

Inductivity of leads_to:

If for all $w \in W$,
$\forall v < w\colon [l\colon I(\bar{x}, v) \rightsquigarrow l'\colon I'(\bar{x}, v)] \Rightarrow [l\colon I(\bar{x}, w) \rightsquigarrow l'\colon I'(\bar{x}, w)]$
then
$\forall w\colon [l\colon I(\bar{x}, w) \rightsquigarrow l'\colon I'(\bar{x}, w)]$

□

One of the appeals of this method is that for a control point in a loop, the reachability assertion need not directly connect consecutive visits to that point; rather, two mutually relevant visits are related to each other, possibly separated by many 'irrelevant' visits. This is useful in particular for flow programs that are an optimized transform of a recursive program.

We now present an example of a program that counts the number of leaves in a binary tree. The program P_{tcount} in this example makes use of the data structures of trees and stacks (of trees) which are common in such applications. We shall not enter into the description of formalisms for defining such structures and their operations as a domain of computation. See the section on suggestions for further reading for directives in that direction. Here we assume familiarity with them, as we did with integers. For (binary) trees, we use the notation $\underline{l}(t)$, $\underline{r}(t)$ for the left and right subtrees, respectively. The predicate *isleaf*(t) holds iff t is a leaf. For stacks, we use () for the empty stack, and *push*, *pop*, and *top* for the stack operations. Strictly speaking, we are proving that the program below is correct in a **class of interpretations**, those satisfying the axioms for trees and stacks used in the proof. We do not elaborate more on this distinction. See the suggestions for further reading for references to more thorough consideration of this issue.

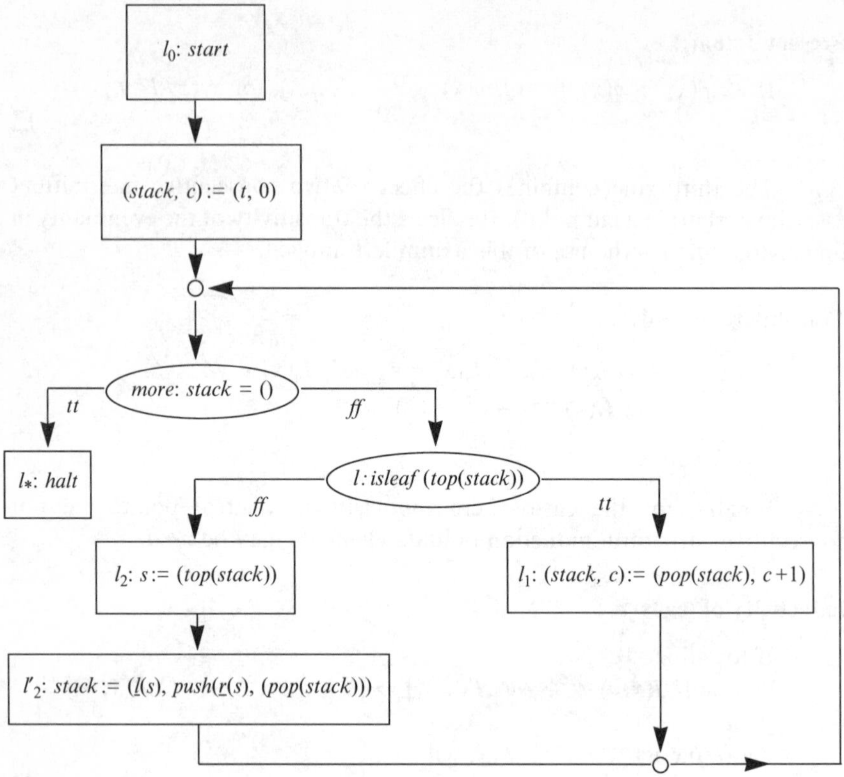

Figure 3.8 A program for counting the leaves of a binary tree.

EXAMPLE (counting the leaves of a binary tree):

The program P_{tcount} is shown in Figure 3.8. We use the following recursive definition of the function *count*(t), the number of leaves of a binary tree t.

$$count(t) \overset{df.}{=} \text{if } isleaf(t) \text{ then } 1 \text{ else } count(\underline{l}(t)) + count(\underline{r}(t))$$

We use self-describing mnemonic names for the variables. The total correctness assertion we want to establish is

$$l_0 : true \xrightarrow{\;\;2\;\;} l_* : c = count(t) \qquad \textbf{(3.1)}$$

We start with a reachability assertion characterizing the main loop in the program.

$$more: c = n \wedge stack = push(t', stack') \xrightarrow{\;\;2\;\;}$$
$$more: c = n + count(t') \wedge stack = stack' \qquad \textbf{(3.2)}$$

Here n, t' and *stack'* are specification variables.

Suppose that correctness assertion 3.2 has been proved. We now derive correctness assertion 3.1 using it. By applying the basic-interval axiom to (l_0, *more*) we get

$$l_0\colon true \rightsquigarrow more : c = 0 \wedge stack = push(t, ()) \tag{3.3}$$

where the r.h.s. intermittent assertion is an instance of the 1.h.s. of (3.2), where $n = 0, t' = t, stack' = ()$. Applying the same substitution to the r.h.s. of (3.2), we get

$$more\colon c = 0 \wedge stack = push(t, ()) \rightsquigarrow$$
$$more\colon c = 0 + count(t) \wedge stack = ()$$

By applying the basic-interval axiom once again to (*more*, l_*), we get

$$more\colon c = 0 + count(t) \wedge stack = () \qquad l_*\colon c = count(t) \tag{3.4}$$

An application of the transitivity of the *leads_to* rule to (3.3) and (3.4) completes the derivation.

We now return to establishing the reachability assertion (3.2). The proof is by structural induction on t'. Assume that (3.2) holds for every subtree t^* of t'. We distinguish between two cases:

(1) *t' is a leaf:* By the definition of the function *count*, $count(t') = 1$ for this case. By applying the basic-interval axiom to the path (*more*, l_1, *more*), we immediately obtain

$$more\colon c = n \wedge stack = push(t', stack') \rightsquigarrow$$
$$more\colon c = n + 1 \wedge stack = stack' \tag{3.5}$$

which establishes (3.2) for this case. It reflects removing the leaf from the top of the stack and counting it as a leaf.

(2) *t' is not a leaf:* Applying the basic-interval axiom to the path (*more*, l_2, *more*), we get

$$more\colon c = n \wedge stack = push(t', stack') \rightsquigarrow$$
$$more\colon c = n \wedge stack = push(\underline{l}(t'), push(\underline{r}(t'), stack')) \tag{3.6}$$

This reflects removing t' from the tree and pushing its two subtrees instead.

As the top element in the stack $\underline{l}(t')$ is a subtree of t', we may apply the induction hypothesis and get

$$more\colon c = n \wedge stack = push(t', stack') \rightsquigarrow$$
$$more\colon c = n + count(\underline{l}(t')) \wedge stack = push(\underline{r}(t'), stack') \tag{3.7}$$

Applying the induction hypothesis again, this time for $\underline{r}(t')$, we finally get

$$\begin{aligned}&more\colon c = n \wedge stack = push(t', stack') \xrightarrow{\quad} \\ &more\colon c = n + count(\underline{l}(t')) + count(\underline{r}(t')) \wedge stack = stack' \qquad \textbf{(3.8)}\end{aligned}$$

By the recursive definition of $count(t')$ for this case, we end up with

$$\begin{aligned}&more\colon c = n \wedge stack = push(t', stack') \xrightarrow{\quad} \\ &more\colon c = n + count(t') \wedge stack = stack'\end{aligned}$$

□

As in the previous method, finding the right intermittent assertions is a creative step and cannot be done mechanically. It relies on the understanding of how the program obtains the right result. Note in the example that a visit to *more* in which a tree is pushed into the stack is related to the visit where both of its subtrees have been removed from the stack with their leaves having been counted. This is an example of the association of 'relevant' events mentioned before.

In order to prove total correctness using intermediate assertions and well-founded sets, one would need an inductive assertion

$$I_{more}(t, c, stack) \overset{df.}{=} \left[count(t) = c + \sum_{t^* \in stack} count(t^*) \right]$$

which forces the consideration of the whole contents of the stack, in contrast to the current proof, that is 'interested' only in the top of the stack. The variant for the termination part could be $\langle count(t) - c,\ count(top(stack)) \rangle$, ordered lexicographically.

In order to establish the semantic completeness of this method, we use an indirect argument. We transform a proof by one method into a proof by another method. Such comparisons of proof methods are often studied, exhibiting more intricate relationships among methods than their mere completeness. The meaning of 'transforming' here is constructing the assertions needed by one method from the assertions used by the other method. We use for the reduction the stronger version of the intermediate assertions method.

Theorem (reducing $\mathbf{F}^\dagger$ to E):

Every proof of $\langle p(\bar{x}) \rangle\ P\ \langle q(\bar{x}) \rangle$ using method $\mathbf{F}^\dagger$ can be transformed into a proof of $l_0 \colon p(\bar{x}) \xrightarrow{\quad} l_* \colon q(\bar{x})$, (the corresponding total correctness assertion) using method **E.**

Proof: Suppose that the given proof of $\langle p(\bar{x}) \rangle\ P\ \langle q(\bar{x}) \rangle$ used the set of cut points $\mathbf{C} \subseteq L_P$, intermediate assertions $I_l(\bar{x}, w)$, $l \in \mathbf{C}$, with $w \in W$, where W is a well-founded set. We want to show that $\vdash_{\mathbf{E}} l_0 \colon p(\bar{x}) \xrightarrow{\quad} l_* \colon q(\bar{x})$. Let l_i,

$0 \leqslant i < |\mathbf{C}|$, be some fixed enumeration of $\mathbf{C}$, with $l_0 = start$, $l_{|\mathbf{C}|-1} = l_* = halt$. We derive the following collection of reachability assertions, one for each i, $0 \leqslant i < |\mathbf{C}|$:

$$[l_i : I_{l_i}(\bar{x}, w) \xrightarrow{\ 2\ } l_* : q(\bar{x})]$$

The theorem then follows from the case $i = 0$.

Suppose the collection of reachability assertions holds for all $w' < w$, and assume $l_j : I_{l_j}(\bar{x}, w)$ for some $0 \leqslant j < |\mathbf{C}|$. If $w = 0$ then $j = |\mathbf{C}| - 1$, the computation ends and $I_{|\mathbf{C}|-1} \Rightarrow q$ holds by the inductive assertions proof. The required conclusion follows by the present axiom. Otherwise, there is some basic path $\alpha = (l_j, l_k)$ along which the computation proceeds. By the basic-interval axiom, the use of which being justified by the verification condition of method $\mathbf{F}^\dagger$ for α, we obtain $I_{l_k}(\bar{x}, w')$ for some $w' < w$. By the induction hypothesis the required conclusion follows.

□

A consequence of this theorem is the semantic completeness of the intermittent assertions method (for intermittent assertions expressing total correctness).

A natural question arising is about the reduction in the opposite direction: can an intermittent assertions proof be converted into a proof using intermediate assertions and well-founded sets? As both methods are complete, some kind of a reduction transformation should exist. This issue has been considered recently (see references at the end of the chapter).

3.5.1 Verifying cyclic programs

We end this section with another application of the intermittent assertions proof method, this time to a different kind of program. As we mentioned before, the kind of specification we used for state-transforming programs is inappropriate for many other kinds of programs. A wide and interesting class of such programs is distinguished by the fact that they are not intended to terminate. Therefore, they cannot be regarded as state transformers. Rather, such programs interact, during their infinite life span, with their environment. The appropriate correctness criterion should therefore state some properties of their intended behavior, that is the way they interact with the environment. Examples of such programs are operating systems, database management systems, airline reservation systems, or banking systems. We use the generic names **cyclic** and **reactive** for such systems. As it turns out, intermittent assertions, connecting a stimulus to the program with the eventual response to it, are a natural tool for their specifications. In many cases, some real-time properties of systems fall into this class. We do not consider them here.

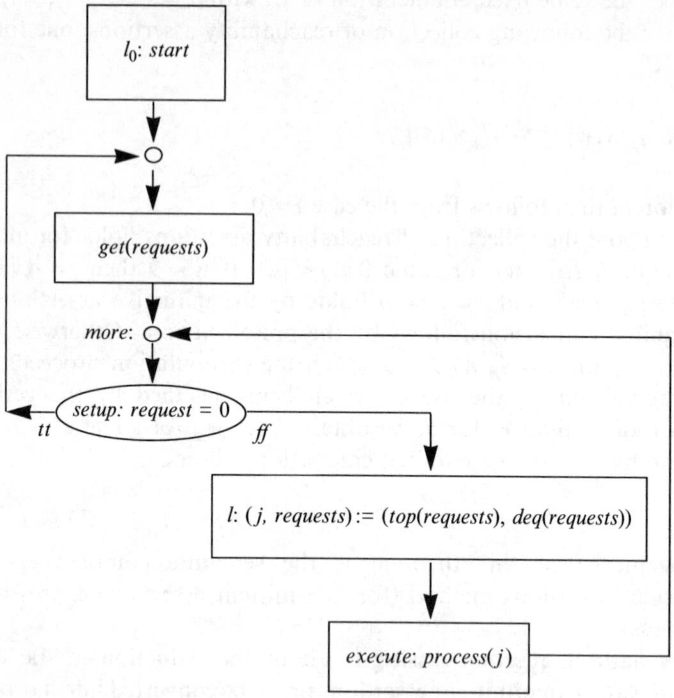

Figure 3.9 The program P_{OPS}.

As this class can be also studied with the tools applicable to concurrent programs, we shall not fully develop the subject here. Rather, we present the reader with one simple example, showing the flavor of the approach. The chapters on concurrent and distributed programs present some more discussions of such properties.

EXAMPLE:

Consider a program P_{OPS} (see Figure 3.9), whose task is to receive from the environment (on some input channel) lists of requests and process every such request. To this end, the program maintains a queue, holding the yet unprocessed requests. Again, we shall not develop a formal theory of queues. We use the notations ( ) for the empty queue, *top*(q) for the first element in the queue, and *deq*(q) for the rest of a queue, after the removal of its first element.

We also have to extend the programming language with some kind of an input statement. We will denote it by *get*(x), with the intuitive operational semantics of delay until some value v is available on the input channel, and the execution is then equivalent to the assignment $x := v$. The elements are referred to as **jobs,** not further specified. As this is only an example and not a full development of a theory, we avoid formalizing this operational semantics. The reader is invited to consider such a definition; in particular, the representation of availability of inputs needs to be explicit, as well as a delay. The program is presented in Figure 3.9. The section *process* represents a terminating program section, not modifying the contents of the *requests* variable. The program operates on each element of the queue until it becomes empty, at which time a new input is obtained, and the whole operation repeats. The property to be proved is

$$\forall job: [more: job \in requests \overset{2}{\longrightarrow} execute: j = job]$$

Remarks:

(1) This is not a full specification (or correctness criterion) of P_{OPS}. For example, one may require that *j* should not be processed unless it was a member of *requests*. We prove here only the one property mentioned.

(2) There is a certain deficiency in this kind of specification, since it refers to internal labels of the program, which need not be a part of an externally visible state. There are ways of presenting a more abstract version of this kind of specification, which serve better as an external representation, from which the internal specification can be derived.

We now turn to the proof of the above reachability assertion. We present in a more informal style, 'detaching' the intermittent assertions. Suppose that $more: job \in requests$ holds. In other words, there exist lists r_1, r_2, s.t. $requests = (r_1 \cdot job \cdot r_2)$ (with possibly r_1 or r_2 being empty). In particular, this implies $requests \neq ()$. Thus, by the basic-interval axiom, we get $setup: requests = (r_1 \cdot job \cdot r_2) \neq ()$. We proceed by structural induction on r_1:

$r_1 = ()$: After $job := top\ (requests)$ we immediately obtain by the basic-interval axiom that $execute: j = job$.

$r_1 \neq ()$: By considering the simple path around the loop, we get $setup: (deq(r_1) \cdot job \cdot r_2)$. As $deq(r_1) < r_1$, we use the induction hypothesis and get the required conclusion.

□

3.6 Conclusions

In this chapter, we have considered a class of programs whose correctness criteria are based on their view as state transformers. For the two kinds of correctness assertions introduced in Chapter 2, appropriate proof methods for establishing them were presented. For partial correctness, the inductive assertions methods associate state predicates with control locations, to hold in the respective intermediate states, and the verification conditions guarantee that local correctness (of loop-free subcomputations) propagates and implies the correctness of the whole program. The argument involves induction on the length of the computation. For termination, the well-founded set method associates with intermediate states an abstract measure of progress, the variant, whose values are decreasing as the computation proceeds. As those values are taken out of a well-founded set, having no infinite decreasing sequences, termination is implied. We have considered also a third method, intermittent assertions, that does not separate partial correctness from termination. It is based on reachability relations among states, implying the reachability of a 'good' final state from a 'good' initial one. Structural induction on data is used to overcome cycles. For each of the proof methods, we showed the two central properties of soundness and semantic completeness.

A common attribute of all the methods presented in this chapter is that they are **endogenous**: in order to verify a program, the whole program has to be globally considered. All the proof methods indeed break the argument into some finite number of simpler assertions about basic paths, but the latter are not syntactic subunits of the program. The computational induction on the progress of the computation is not represented as an induction on the textual structure of the program. In the next chapter, an alternative viewpoint is taken, known as **exogenous** or as **compositional**. According to this view, a property of a whole program is obtained by considering properties of syntactically determined subprograms. This approach is also commonly known as a **syntax-directed** proof method. In order to apply this approach, some assumptions on the programming language are needed, sometimes referred to as being 'structured': the flow of computation is related in a simple way to the syntactic structure of the program. This approach has the obvious advantage that only the specification of a subprogram, and not the subprogram itself, matters in the correctness proof. This is a **modular** approach: if a subprogram is replaced by another one, respecting the same specification, the higher-level proof is not affected. Another property of this approach is that proofs can be presented in a way more similar to the usual concept in deductive systems, with axioms and deduction rules.

Bibliographic notes and suggestions for further reading

Bibliographic notes First hints for a methodology of formal program verification appear as early as in [29] and [30]. An early example of verification using inductive assertions appears in [31]. A crucial contribution to proving partial correctness by intermediate assertions and termination by well-founded variants is due to Floyd [9], which gave momentum to the whole research area. Floyd attributes the method also to [32]. The idea of intermittent assertions proofs appears first in [33], interpreted as an application of modal logic. An application of structural induction to verification originates from there too, including the leaves-counting example. The method gained its name and its current formulation in [34], where the reduction theorem is presented. The 'leads_to' operator appears in [35]. Independently, at about the same time, the application of the method for cyclic (and concurrent) programs was presented in [36, 37]. A more syntax-directed exposition was independently presented in [38]. An early reference to soundness is [39]. The triggering of interest in soundness and completeness was due to [40].

Suggestions for further reading Both the inductive assertions method and the well-founded set method are presented (in a slightly modified notation) in [11], with many additional examples and exercises. In [41] another variant of the inductive assertions method is presented, called **subgoal induction**, in which intermediate states are related to the corresponding final states inductively, instead of relating them to initial states as in Floyd's method. In [42] one can find another variant of the intermittent assertions method. The influence of this method on the semantics of the programming language LUCID can be found for example in [43, 44]. A further comparative study of the various computational inductions can be found in [45]. A two-way reduction among the intermittent assertions and the intermediate assertions methods is presented in [46], though in a different setting. A thorough study of program verification over axiomatically defined collections of interpretations is presented in [28]. They also consider more general data domains in the setting of multisorted first-order logic and deal also with exceptions (error states). Several theories of data structures equipped with structural induction are presented in [47]. Formalization of Floyd's method in second-order predicate logic is described in [48]. A different presentation of termination proofs is presented in [49], and [50] contains many heuristics for systematic construction of intermediate assertions, given a program and its specification. A similar problem is dealt with in [51]. An early treatment of clean termination is in [52], and a more recent one, based on the notion of free logic, appears in [53].

EXERCISES

3.1 Is the following implication valid for *PLF*?

$$val(S_1, \sigma) = val(S_2, \sigma) \text{ implies } \pi(S_1, \sigma) = \pi(S_2, \sigma)$$

3.2 **Multiple entries/exits:** Formulate method **F** without the restriction to single entries and exits.

3.3 **Termination rule:** Formulate a rule for proving termination of *PLF* programs, in which the variant decreases by exactly 1 along each basic path, reaching 0 only upon termination. Show the semantic completeness of your rule.

3.4 **Trivial intermediate assertions:** Which requirement of rule **F**, when applied to an arbitrary *PLF* program and $p \not\equiv true$, $q \not\equiv true$, is violated by uniformly choosing $I_l \equiv true$ for every $l \in \mathbf{C}$ (other than l_0, l_*)?

3.5 **Cyclic decrease:** Formulate a termination rule requiring a decrease of the variant only upon each cycle (instead of each basic path). Is your rule semantically complete?

3.6 **Minimality:** Prove that every non-empty subset of a well-founded set has at least one minimal element (that is, an element with no strictly smaller ones in the subset).

3.7 **Well-foundedness of lexicographic order:** Prove that if $(W, <)$ is well founded, so is $W \times W$, ordered lexicographically.

3.8 Consider the program P_{root} in Figure 3.10, computing square roots of real numbers by the method of Newton–Raphson. Prove that $\langle 1 \leqslant x = a < 2 \rangle\ P_{root} \langle true \rangle$.

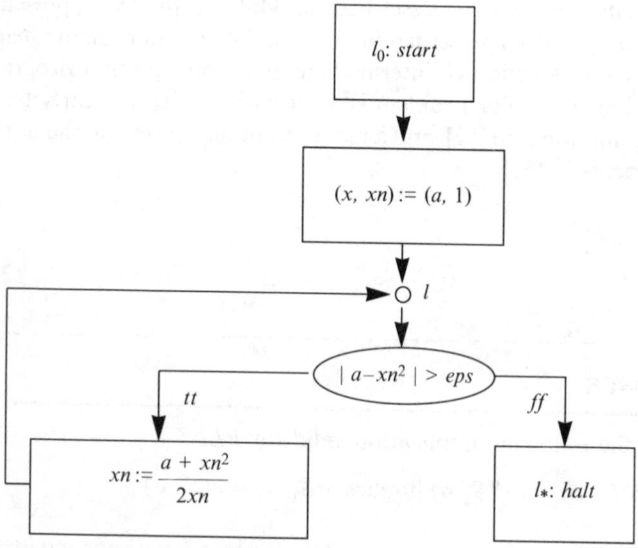

Figure 3.10 Square root computation.

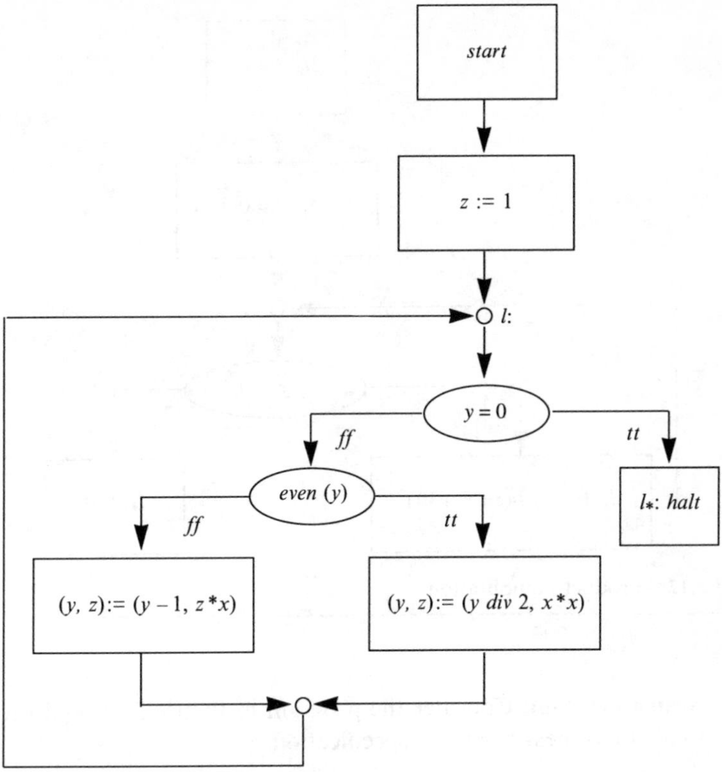

Figure 3.11 Exponentiation computation.

3.9 Consider the program P_{exp} in Figure 3.11, over natural numbers. Prove that $\langle x = X \wedge y = Y \geqslant 0 \rangle\ P_{exp}\ \langle z = X^{**}Y \rangle$.

(1) Use method **F** to prove partial correctness, and method **F*** for termination.

(2) Use method $\mathbf{F}^{\dagger}$ to prove total correctness (without separation).

(3) Use method **E** to prove total correctness.

3.10 Consider the program in Figure 3.12, and prove its partial correctness with respect to the specification

$$\langle x = X \wedge y = Y \geqslant 0 \rangle\ P_{prod}\ \langle z = X^{*}Y \rangle$$

Is it also totally correct with respect to the same specification?

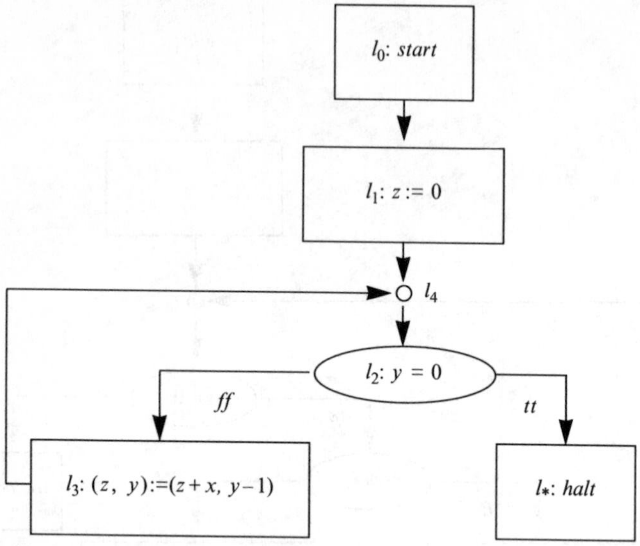

Figure 3.12 Product computation.

3.11 **Nested iteration:** Consider the program in Figure 3.13, and prove its total correctness w.r.t. the specification

$$\langle exp = EXP \geqslant 0 \wedge base = BASE,\ r = BASE^{EXP} \rangle$$

3.12 Prove the soundness and semantic completeness of $\mathbf{F}^{\dagger}$.

3.13 **Extended PLF:** Give a precise operational semantics, by means of an appropriate transition system, to an extension of *PLF* with a *get*(*x*) and a *put*(*x*) input and output statements. Does your semantics reflect *delay* of *get*(*x*) until the availability of input?

3.14 For $P \in PLF$, suppose that $\{I_l \mid l \in \mathbf{C}\}$ was used in showing $\vdash_{\mathbf{F}} \{p\}\ P\ \{q\}$, and let $\{I_l^* \mid l \in \mathbf{C}\}$ be the minimal predicates (as defined in the completeness proof of **F**). Show that

$$\forall \bar{x}: [I_l^*(\bar{x}) \Rightarrow I_l\ (\bar{x})]$$

3.15 **Full sets of cut points:** Show that if for some **C** $\{I_l \mid l \in \mathbf{C}\}$ satisfies the requirements of **F**, then there is a *completion* $\{I_l \mid l \in L_P\}$ which does so too.

3.16 Does $l_0 : true \xrightarrow{2} l_* : false$ express nontermination?

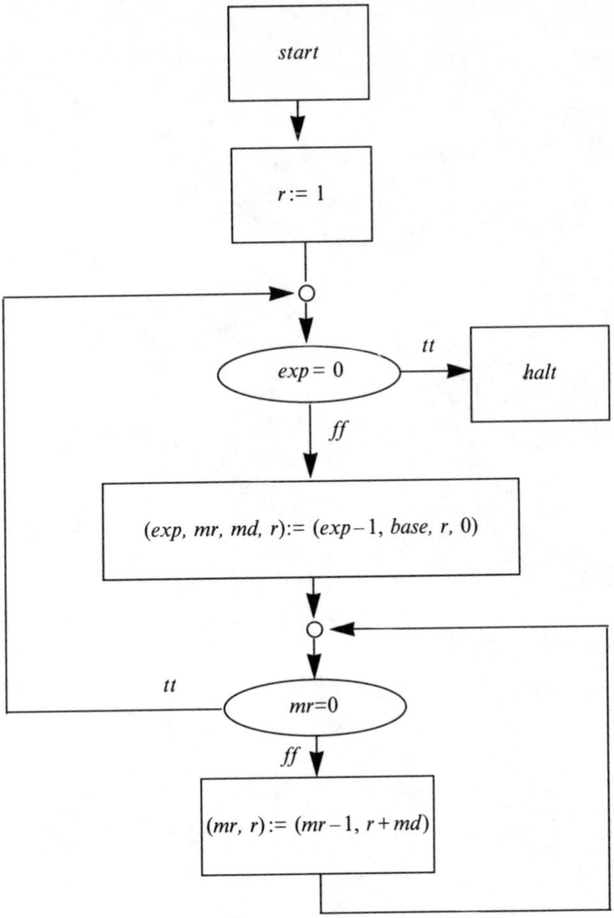

Figure 3.13 Nested iteration.

3.17 Multiple basic paths with same origin: Show that if $\alpha_1=(l, l')$ and $\alpha_2=(l, l'')$ are two different basic paths with the same origin, then $\models_I \forall \bar{x}:\neg(R_{\alpha_1}(\bar{x}) \wedge R_{\alpha_2}(\bar{x}))$.

What is the role of this fact in method **E**?

3.18 Fifo specification: Can the requirement of a Fifo service regime for requests (in P_{OPS}) be formulated as a reachability assertion?

Chapter 4
THE COMPOSITIONAL APPROACH

4.1 Introduction

In this chapter, we consider the compositional approach to program verification. We remain in the realm of deterministic programs (state transformers), but change the programming language in order to facilitate this approach. The specifications (correctness assertions) remain the same: partial correctness and termination. We consider a language *PLW*, whose programs are known also as **while-programs**, and sometimes also as 'ALGOL-like' programs, since their first significant appearance was in the language ALGOL 60. This language is a natural restriction of *PLF* (flow programs), where programs have the important property that the flow of control is strongly related to the syntactic structure of the program. Therefore, there is no need to consider the graph of a program, and its linear textual representation is sufficient for defining the progress of control during computation. The abstract syntax of a programming language always equips a program with a tree form, enabling the use of induction on this structure. We note that no loss of expressive power is imposed by this restriction. For every flow program, one can find an equivalent **while-program**. The equivalence relation here is equality of the values of the original variables of the flow program (in the final state), ignoring the value of any additional variables added for the sake of the translation.

For such a language, the proof methods can be compositional, that is adhering to the following principle (the restriction to binary compositions is expository and inconsequential):

Compositionality principle: If a program S is composed of syntactic components S_1, S_2, then the specification of S depends only on the specifications of S_1 and S_2 (without referring to the internal structure of S_1 and S_2).

In other words, every property of a program should be provable from corresponding properties of its (immediate) syntactic components, and should not depend on the syntactic units themselves. This property induces a modularity, which is very important at the program design level. For example, replacing some component by another one respecting the same specifications does not affect the validity of the correctness proof for the whole program. Instead of replacing subprograms, one can deal also with programs with 'syntactic holes', under some assumption (an assertion about the hole), to be implemented later.

Such proof systems are known also as **exogenous:** once a subprogram has been shown to satisfy a correctness assertion, the subprogram itself can be 'forgotten' for the rest of the proof. We do not have to keep in mind the whole program all the time, in contrast to the previous formulation of the inductive assertions method.

Another advantage of the compositional approach is that proofs using it can be conveniently presented in the usual deductive style. A proof consists of a sequence of formulas expressing correctness assertions, where each formula either is an axiom, or is derived from previous formulas by means of a derivation rule. There is a natural correspondence to the syntax of the language. **Axioms** represent some properties of atomic statements (without further specified syntactic subunits), while **derivation rules** (referred to also as **proof rules**) correspond to the various syntactic constructs of language compounds. As a result, the theory to be presented in this chapter stresses syntactic representability and the logic-based view of the program verification activity.

There is an approach to semantics of programming languages which regards such a deductive system as the (axiomatic) **definition** of the given language. A correct implementation should be a model of the axiomatic definition. For example, an axiomatic definition of (almost) full Pascal has been given (reference given at the end of the chapter). The role of soundness and completeness in this framework is reversed: it is a claim about an alternate semantic definition (for example, operational, as given here) and not about the proof system. In our presentation, we shall adhere to the previously stated approach, where the operational semantics is the definition, and the deductive system should be made to correspond to it, providing sound and possibly complete reasoning tools.

The discovery of the existence of compositional proof systems gave a strong momentum to the structured programming methodology. It became clear that there is a strong correlation between the ease of defining (and using) compositional proof rules and other 'metrics' of program quality: ease of implementation, readability, modifiability, modularity, and so on. Language design has also been affected, where languages and their constructs began to be designed with proof rules in mind. The language EUCLID is one example of such an approach.

4.2 Structured programs

In this section, we introduce the programming language *PLW*, to whose programs we refer as **while-programs,** or structured programs. Below is a description of the abstract syntax of the language, defined recursively. Here S is meta-variable, ranging over statements (used as a synonym to programs). The indexing of occurrences of S is not part of the syntax, only for a convenient reference to different components.

$$S{::}x{:=}e\,|\,skip\,|\,S_1;S_2\,|\,\textbf{if}\ B\ \textbf{then}\ S_1\ \textbf{else}\ S_2\ \textbf{fi}\,|\,\textbf{while}\ B\ \textbf{do}\ S_1\ \textbf{od}$$

As before, e and B are expressions (over the operators of the domain of computation) not further specified. The statements $x{:=}e$ (assignment) and *skip* are **atomic** (having no syntactic subunits). The other statements (referred to as **sequential composition**, **branching**, and **iteration**, respectively) are **compound**. For example, the immediate subunits of $S_1;S_2$ are S_1,S_2. As is usual in this context, the problem of parsing a given program is ignored, and in all definitions the subunits are taken to be given. As an example, consider a *PLW* program for integer division.

$$\begin{aligned} S_{idiv}{::}\,& r{:=}x;\ q{:=}0;\\ & \textbf{while}\ r \geqslant y\ \textbf{do}\ r{:=}r-y\ ;\ q{:=}q+1\ \textbf{od} \end{aligned}$$

Operational semantics

We now turn to a definition of the operational semantics of *PLW*. There is no need here for an explicit location counter λ. Instead, control is represented by the **syntactic continuation** component in a configuration. Here it is a program $S \in PLW$, representing the 'rest of the computation' still to be executed. Recall the empty syntactic continuation, denoted by E, satisfying $E;S = S;E = S$, for every $S \in PLW$. Note again that E is not a *PLW* program, and is used only in the definition of the semantics.

Definition:

(1) A **configuration** C is a pair $C = \langle S, \sigma\rangle$, where $S \in PLW$ is a syntactic continuation and σ is a state.

(2) A configuration $C = \langle S, \sigma \rangle$ is **terminal** iff $S = E$.

□

A terminal configuration occurs when nothing is left to be executed. Actually, since a subunit may have more than one occurrence in a program, a unique labeling is needed. However, to simplify notation we leave the exact determination of occurrences to the context. We now turn to defining the **transition** relation '$\rightarrow$' among *PLW* configurations. The definition is by induction on the structure of S.

Definition: Let '$\rightarrow$' be the least relation among configurations, satisfying the following:

(1) $\langle x := e, \sigma \rangle \rightarrow \langle E, \sigma[e \mid x] \rangle$.

(2) $\langle skip, \sigma \rangle \rightarrow \langle E, \sigma \rangle$.

(3) If $\langle S, \sigma \rangle \rightarrow \langle S', \sigma' \rangle$, then for every $T \in PLW$ $\langle S; T, \sigma \rangle \rightarrow \langle S'; T, \sigma' \rangle$.

(4) If $\sigma[\![B]\!] = tt$, then $\langle$**if** B **then** S_1 **else** S_2 **fi**, $\sigma \rangle \rightarrow \langle S_1, \sigma \rangle$.
If $\sigma[\![B]\!] = ff$, then $\langle$**if** B **then** S_1 **else** S_2 **fi**, $\sigma \rangle \rightarrow \langle S_2, \sigma \rangle$.

(5) If $\sigma[\![B]\!] = tt$, then $\langle$**while** B **do** S **od**, $\sigma \rangle \rightarrow \langle S$; **while** B **do** S **od**, $\sigma \rangle$.
If $\sigma[\![B]\!] = ff$, then $\langle$**while** B **do** S **od**, $\sigma \rangle \rightarrow \langle E, \sigma \rangle$.

□

It can be easily verified that a finite computation has to end in a terminal configuration (as every nonterminal configuration is not '$\rightarrow$'-maximal). Also, every infinite '$\rightarrow$'-sequence of configurations is maximal. The determinism of *PLW* is again exhibited by the fact that, by the definition of '$\rightarrow$', there is a unique computation from any given initial configuration. Note that here we have only an implicit characterization of the computations as sequences, as induced by the definition of the transition relation. A consequence of the above definition is presented as a lemma, characterizing the form of computations induced by the above semantics. It fits the expected intuitive meanings of the constructs involved.

Lemma (computations):

Let $C_0 = \langle S_0, \sigma_0 \rangle$.

(1) *Atomic statement:* If S_0 is atomic, then $\pi(C_0)$ has the form $C_0 \rightarrow C_1$, with C_1 terminal and σ_1 conforming to (1) or (2), respectively, in the definition of '$\rightarrow$'.

(2) *Sequential composition:* If $S_0 = S_1;S_2$, then $\pi(C_0)$ has one of the following forms:

(a) $C_0 \rightarrow C_1 \rightarrow \cdots$, where $C_i = \langle T_i; S_2, \sigma_i \rangle$, $i \geqslant 0$, and $\langle T_i, \sigma_i \rangle$, $i \geqslant 0$ is a (nonterminating) computation of S_1 on σ_0.

(b) $C_0 \xrightarrow{*} C_i = \langle S_2, \sigma_i \rangle \rightarrow C_{i+1} \rightarrow \cdots$, for some $i \geq 0$, and $C_j = \langle T_j, \sigma_j \rangle$, $j \geq i$ is a (nonterminating) computation of S_2.

(c) $C_0 \xrightarrow{*} \langle S_2, \sigma' \rangle \xrightarrow{*} \langle E, \sigma'' \rangle$, where $C_0 \xrightarrow{*} \langle E, \sigma' \rangle$ induces a computation of S_1 on σ_0 and $\langle S_2, \sigma' \rangle \xrightarrow{*} \langle E, \sigma'' \rangle$ is a computation of S_2 on σ'.

(3) *Branching:* If $S_0 =$ **if** B **then** S_1 **else** S_2 **fi**, then $\pi(C_0)$ has one of the following forms:

(a) $C_0 \rightarrow C_1 = \langle S_1, \sigma_1 \rangle \rightarrow \cdots \rightarrow C_i \rightarrow \cdots$, where $\sigma_0 \models B$ and C_i, $i \geq 1$, is a (nonterminating) computation of S_1 on σ_0.

(b) $C_0 \rightarrow C_1 = \langle S_1, \sigma_1 \rangle \xrightarrow{*} \langle E, \sigma' \rangle$,where$\sigma_0 \models BandC_1 \xrightarrow{*} \langle E, \sigma' \rangle$isa (terminating) computation of S_1 on σ_1.

(c) Similar to (a) with $\neg B$ replacing B and S_2 replacing S_1.

(d) Similar to (b) with $\neg B$ replacing B and S_2 replacing S_1.

(4) *Repetition:* If $S_0 =$ **while** B **do** S **od**, then $\pi(C_0)$ has one of the following forms:

(a) $C_0 \rightarrow \langle E, \sigma_0 \rangle$, with $\sigma_0 \models \neg B$.

(b) $C_0 \xrightarrow{*} C_i = \langle S_0, \sigma_1 \rangle \xrightarrow{*} \cdots \xrightarrow{*} C_k = \langle S_0, \sigma_k \rangle \rightarrow \langle C_{k+1}, \sigma_{k+1} \rangle \rightarrow \cdots$ for some $k \geq 0$, where for $0 \leq j < k$ $\sigma_j \models B$, $\langle S_0, \sigma_j \rangle \xrightarrow{*} \langle S_0, \sigma_{j+1} \rangle$ is a terminating computation of S and C_m, $m \geq k$, is a (nonterminating) computation of S.

(c) $C_0 \xrightarrow{*} C_i = \langle S_0, \sigma_1 \rangle \xrightarrow{*} \cdots \xrightarrow{*} C_k = \langle S_0, \sigma_k \rangle \xrightarrow{*} \cdots$ where for $0 \leq k$ $\sigma_k \models B$, and $\langle S_0, \sigma_k \rangle \xrightarrow{*} \langle S_0, \sigma_{k+1} \rangle$ is a computation of S.

(d) $C_0 \xrightarrow{*} \langle S_0, \sigma_1 \rangle \xrightarrow{*} \cdots \xrightarrow{*} \langle E, \sigma_k \rangle$, where for $0 \leq j < k$, $\sigma_j \models B$, $\sigma_k \models \neg B$, and $\langle S_0, \sigma_j \rangle \xrightarrow{*} \langle S_0, \sigma_{j+1} \rangle$ is a computation of S for $j < k$.

□

EXERCISE:

Prove that $\mathbf{M}[\![((S_1; S_2); S_3)]\!](\sigma) = \mathbf{M}[\![(S_1; (S_2; S_3))]\!](\sigma)$ for any state σ and *PLW* programs S_i, $1 \leq i \leq 3$. Based on this property, we can freely consider S_1; S_2; S_3. In the above claim, can we replace $\mathbf{M}$ by π?

□

4.3 A deductive system H for partial correctness

In this section we introduce a deductive system **H** for proving partial correctness assertions, embodying the compositional approach to verification of *PLW* programs. Such a system, like ordinary deductive systems in logic, has two components:

(1) *Axioms:* These are some basic partial correctness assertions relating to the atomic statements (which have no proper syntactic subunits). For *PLW*, the atomic statements are the assignment statement and *skip*.

(2) *Proof rules:* These are deduction rules that enable deducing a partial correctness assertion about a compound program from partial correctness assertions about the ('top level') syntactic subunits.

Having such a system, we can then define a **proof** in the familiar logical way: a finite sequence of partial correctness assertions (or state assertions), where each assertion either is an axiom or is derivable from previous (in the sequence) assertions by the application of a proof rule. Thus, (the program-dependent part of) proofs have their usual 'mechanical' flavor, based on form, in contrast to the semantics-dominated proof methods of the previous chapter.

A. The system H

Assignment axiom:

For every assignment statement $x := e \in PLW$ and every state assertion p,

$$\{p^x_e\} x := e \{p\} \tag{ASS}$$

is an axiom. Strictly speaking, this is an **axiom scheme,** a template of countably many axioms. We refer to all such schemes as axioms.

□

The meaning of this axiom is, that in order for an arbitrary postcondition to hold after the assignment, the value of the assigned term should satisfy the same condition before the assignment. The reader should compare this meaning with that of the computation of T_α in method **F.**

EXAMPLE:

$$\{y+1 \geqslant 0\} x := y+1 \; \{x \geqslant 0\}.$$

□

It is instructive to note that a natural candidate for an assignment axiom, namely, $\{true\}\; x := e\; \{x = e\}$, is not a sound axiom. In case e contains a free occurrence of x, the two occurrences of x refer to x's value in different states, and these values need not be equal. In particular, $\{true\}\; x := x+1\; \{x = x+1\}$ leads to a clear absurdity, where a contradicting postcondition is obtained.

Skip axiom:

For every state assertion p,

$$\{p\}\; skip\; \{p\} \tag{SKIP}$$

is an axiom.

□

This axiom clearly captures the intention of *skip* not modifying the state, leaving true every condition that was true before and no other one.

Now we present the derivation rules, one for each way of combining statements.

Sequential composition rule:

$$\frac{\{p\}\ S_1\ \{r\},\ \{r\}\ S_2\ \{q\}}{\{p\}\ S_1;S_2\ \{q\}} \qquad \text{(SEQ)}$$

Here we see again the idea of the intermediate assertion r, serving both as the postcondition of S_1 and as the precondition of S_2. In the conclusion, this assertion is 'forgotten' and not carried through the rest of the proof. By a simple inductive argument, we can derive a somewhat stronger version of this rule that enables the handling of arbitrary long straight-line sections, composed by sequential composition.

$$\frac{\{p\}\ S_1\{r_1\},\cdots,\{r_{n-1}\}\ S_n\ \{q\}}{\{p\}\ S_1;\cdots;S_n\ \{q\}} \qquad \text{(SEQ)}$$

□

EXAMPLE:

Let us try and prove the correctness of a straight-line section that interchanges the values of two variables, say x and y. Thus, we want to prove

$$\{x = X \wedge y = Y\}\ z{:=}x;\ x{:=}y;\ y{:=}z\ \{y = X \wedge x = Y\}$$

A proof is the following:

(1) $\{z = X \wedge x = Y\}\ y{:=}z\ \{y = X \wedge x = Y\}$ (ASS)

(2) $\{z = X \wedge y = Y\}\ x{:=}y\ \{z = X \wedge x = Y\}$ (ASS)

(3) $\{x = X \wedge y = Y\}\ z{:=}x\ \{z = X \wedge y = Y\}$ (ASS)

(4) $\{x = X \wedge y = Y\}\ z{:=}x;\ x{:=}y;\ y{:=}z\ \{y = X \wedge x = Y\}$ (1),(2),(3),(SEQ)

□

EXERCISE:

Can the semantically equivalent specification

$$\{x = X \wedge y = Y\}\cdots\{x = Y \wedge y = X\}$$

be derived solely by means of the assignment axiom and the sequential composition rule?

□

Conditional branching rule:

$$\frac{\{p \wedge B\}\, S_1 \{q\},\ \{p \wedge \neg B\}\, S_2\, \{q\}}{\{p\}\, \textbf{if}\ B\ \textbf{then}\ S_1\ \textbf{else} S_2\ \textbf{fi}\, \{q\}} \qquad \text{(COND)}$$

□

Here again one can recognize the traces of the verification conditions for flow programs, when the reachability conditions B and $\neg B$, respectively, are added to the precondition of the rule assumptions. Clearly, to establish the postcondition after a branching structure, it has to be established by each branch, under the precondition of the whole construct and the reachability condition.

Usually, in order to be able to apply this rule we need an additional ability of logically manipulating state assertions. In order to see this need, consider the following example. Suppose we want to prove

$$\{x \geqslant 0 \wedge y \geqslant 0\}\ \textbf{if}\ x > y\ \textbf{then}\ x := x - y\ \textbf{else}\ y := y - x\ \textbf{fi}\ \{x \geqslant 0 \wedge y \geqslant 0\}$$

Clearly, we have to use (twice) the assignment axiom for establishing the two premises of the (COND) rule. So we might start with

$$(1)\ \{x - y \geqslant 0 \wedge y \geqslant 0\}\ x := x - y\ \{x \geqslant 0 \wedge y \geqslant 0\} \qquad \text{(ASS)}$$

However, the precondition so obtained differs from the one required for (COND) in two respects. First, the conjunct $x \geqslant 0$ (in the p part) does not appear in it. Furthermore, the B part appears in an arithmetically equivalent form, namely $x - y \geqslant 0$ instead of $x \geqslant y$: it is also weaker than the condition in the **if** statement, which is $x > y$.

Similarly, we get for the other branch

$$(2)\ \{x \geqslant 0 \wedge y - x \geqslant 0\}\ y := y - x\ \{x \geqslant 0 \wedge y \geqslant 0\} \qquad \text{(ASS)}$$

It also differs in a similar way with regards to the required precondition.

Consequently, we need some formal means of logically manipulating state assertions within correctness proofs. The appropriate rule is introduced right after the program-dependent rules. In the meantime, we assume that such manipulations are permitted. Note that this ability was present in the previous, noncompositional proof methods also. However, it was 'hidden' in the more semantic presentation. Here we stress the deductive approach and need an explicit rule allowing these manipulations. Having such a formal means, we may end the example proof by

$$(3)\ \{x \geqslant 0 \wedge y \geqslant 0\}\ \textbf{if}\ x > y\ \textbf{then}\ x := x - y\ \textbf{else}\ y := y - x\ \textbf{fi}\ \{x \geqslant 0 \wedge y \geqslant 0\}$$

(1),(2),(COND)

EXAMPLE:

Consider a statement computing the absolute value of an integer x. We would like to prove

$\{true\}$ **if** $x>0$ **then** $y:=x$ **else** $y:=-x$ **fi** $\{y \geqslant 0\}$

(1) $\{x \geqslant 0\}\ y:=x\ \{y \geqslant 0\}$ (ASS)
(2) $\{x \leqslant 0\}\ y:=-x\ \{y \geqslant 0\}$ (ASS)
(3) $\{true\}$ **if** $x>0$ **then** $y:=x$ **else** $y:=-x$ **fi** $\{y \geqslant 0\}$ (1),(2),(COND)

Note again the logical manipulations, where $\neg x>0$ is taken as $x \leqslant 0$ and where the precondition is weakened.

□

Repetition rule:

$$\frac{\{p \wedge B\}\ S\ \{p\}}{\{p\}\ \textbf{while}\ B\ \textbf{do}\ S\ \textbf{od}\ \{p \wedge \neg B\}} \qquad \text{(REP)}$$

Here we can clearly see the difference between the compositional approach and the global approach. The body of the loop, S, is conceived as an **invariant preserver,** p being the **loop invariant.** Instead of considering basic paths (loop free), the whole body of the loop is used, calling for a subproof to establish the rule's premiss. Note again, that termination of the whole statement is not implied, and that adding $\neg B$ to the postcondition assumes termination.

□

We present more examples of using the rules, in particular (REP), in what follows.

To end the presentation of **H**, we present a rule of a somewhat different nature, dealing with the purely logical manipulations mentioned above. It states that one is always allowed to strengthen the precondition and to weaken the postcondition. This rule is independent of the particular programming language used, and depends only on the definition of partial correctness.

Consequence rule:

$$\frac{p \Rightarrow p_1, \{p_1\}\ S\ \{q_1\}, q_1 \Rightarrow q}{\{p\}\ S\ \{q\}} \qquad \text{(CONS)}$$

Note that here two of the rule's premisses are not partial correctness assertions, but claims about the domain, which need to be provable themselves. Several completeness notions are induced by attributing a different status to such parts in the proof. In general, there is a wish for a clear separation between program- and language-dependent parts in a proof, and pure mathematical facts about the domain of computation. Usually, the usage of the (CONS) rule is left implicit, not explicitly indicated in the proof. However, appeals to this rule, like proofs of the verification conditions in the previous chapter, are usually the tricky parts of correctness proofs. There one can see why the program 'really works'. While in the example presented usually the data-dependent reasoning is straightforward, it can become quite complicated, utilizing deep mathematical insight. As far as our methodology is concerned, again there is hope, since much of the commonly used software does not depend on such advanced mathematical reasoning.

□

In the remainder of this book, we retain the assumption that proofs may use 'for free' any true state assertion about the domain of computation. Denote by $Tr_{\mathbf{I}}$ the collection of all true first-order state assertions over **I**. We thus augment **H** with $Tr_{\mathbf{I}}$ as additional axioms. In general, $Tr_{\mathbf{I}}$ need not be recursively enumerable. This means that some axioms are not effectively recognizable as such, a deviation from usual logical practice. The advantage of retaining such an approach is a clear separation between program-dependent elements of a proof from data-dependent elements, allowing us to focus on the former.

Notation: We denote by $Tr_{\mathbf{I}} \vdash_{\mathbf{H}} \mathbf{c}$ the provability of the partial correctness assertion **c** in the above system.

□

EXAMPLE:

Following is a detailed example of a full proof of the partial correctness of the integer division program S_{idiv}. We want to prove, under the assumption of all true arithmetic statements, that:

$\{x \geqslant 0 \wedge y \geqslant 0\}$
S_{idiv}:: $q := 0;\ r := x;$
  while $r \geqslant y$ **do** $r := r - y;\ q := q + 1$ **od**
$\{x = q \cdot y + r \wedge 0 \leqslant r < y\}$

Below is a proof of this correctness assertion in **H**.

(1) $\{x = 0 \cdot y + x \wedge x \geqslant 0\}\ q := 0\ \{x = q \cdot y + x \wedge x \geqslant 0\}$ (ASS)
(2) $\{x = q \cdot y + x \wedge x \geqslant 0\}\ r := x\ \{x = q \cdot y + r \wedge r \geqslant 0\}$ (ASS)
(3) $\{x = 0 \cdot y + x \wedge x \geqslant 0\}\ q := 0;\ r := x\ \{x = q \cdot y + r \wedge r \geqslant 0\}$
(1),(2),(SEQ)
(4) $x \geqslant 0 \wedge y \geqslant 0 \Rightarrow x = 0 \cdot y + x \wedge x \geqslant 0$ (ARITHMETIC)
(5) $\{x \geqslant 0 \wedge y \geqslant 0\}\ q := 0;\ r := x\ \{x = q \cdot y + r \wedge r \geqslant 0\}$
(1),(4),(CONS)

Here the loop invariant has been established.

(6) $\{x = (q+1)\cdot y+r-y \wedge r-y \geqslant 0\}\ r:=r-y$
$\{x = (q+1)\cdot y+r \wedge r \geqslant 0\}$ (ASS)
(7) $\{x = (q+1)\cdot y+r \wedge r \geqslant 0\}\ q:=q+1\ \{x = q\cdot y+r \wedge r \geqslant 0\}$ (ASS)
(8) $\{x = (q+1)\cdot y+r-y \wedge r-y \geqslant 0\}\ r:=r-y;\ q:=q+1$
$\{x = q\cdot y+r \wedge r \geqslant 0\}$ (6),(7),(SEQ)
(9) $\{x = q\cdot y+r \wedge r \geqslant 0 \wedge r \geqslant y \Rightarrow x = (q+1)\cdot y+r-y \wedge r-y \geqslant 0$
(ARITHMETIC)
(10) $\{x = q\cdot y+r \wedge r \geqslant 0 \wedge r \geqslant y\}\ r:=r-y;\ q:=q+1$
$\{x = q\cdot y+r \wedge r \geqslant 0\}$ (8),(9),(CONS)

This shows preservation of the loop invariant by the loop body.

(11) $\{x = q\cdot y+r \wedge r \geqslant 0\}$ **while** $r \geqslant y$ **do** $r:=r-y;\ q:=q+1$ **od**
$\{x = q\cdot y+r \wedge 0 \leqslant r < y\}$ (10),(REP)
(12) $\{x = X \geqslant 0 \wedge y = Y \geqslant 0\}\ q:=0;\ r:=x;$
while $r \geqslant y$ **do** $r:=r-y;\ q:=q+1$ **od** $\{x = q\cdot y + r \wedge 0 \leqslant r < y\}$
(5),(11),(SEQ)

This example is typical of formalized proofs, which tend to be lengthy and composed of small steps. Its advantage is that it can be mechanically checked (except for the arithmetic parts).

□

EXERCISE:

(1) Modify the specification of the above division program so that q and r are, respectively, the quotient and remainder of the *initial* values of x and y; modify the proof accordingly.

(2) In addition to (1), add to the specification and proof the invariance of the values of x and y.

□

In many cases, this linearized presentation is found inconvenient, for example if intended as an accompanying documentation. In Section 4.4.1 we consider an alternative presentation of proofs, called **proof outlines,** sometimes found to be more convenient.

4.4 Soundness and relative completeness of H

In this section we show total soundness of the system **H** and consider several completeness notions for it, focusing on the one known as **relative completeness** (and sometimes also as 'completeness in the sense of Cook'). Here one makes actual use of the formal definition of the (operational) semantics.

Theorem (strong soundness of H):

For every interpretation **I** if $Tr_{\mathbf{I}} \vdash_{\mathbf{H}} \{p\}\ S\ \{q\}$, then $\models_{\mathbf{I}} \{p\}\ S\ \{q\}$

Proof: The structure of the proof is by induction on the length of the formal proof of the partial correctness assertion. We first show that the axioms are valid, and then that each inference rule preserves validity.

(ASS) Suppose that $\sigma \models_{\mathbf{I}} p^x_e$. By clause (1) in the computations lemma, the resulting state of executing $x := e$ in σ is the variant $\sigma' = \sigma[e|x]$. The result follows from the substitution theorem (Chapter 2).

(SKIP) By clause (2) of the computations lemma, the resulting state of *skip* equals the initial state, and hence both satisfy the same state assertions.

(SEQ) Suppose that $Tr_{\mathbf{I}} \vdash_{\mathbf{H}} \{p\}\ S_1\ \{r\}$ and $Tr_{\mathbf{I}} \vdash_{\mathbf{H}} \{r\}\ S_2\ \{q\}$ both hold. By the induction hypothesis, we obtain that $\models_{\mathbf{I}} \{p\}\ S_1 \{r\}$ and $\models_{\mathbf{I}} \{r\}\ S_2 \{q\}$ are satisfied. Let $\sigma \models_{\mathbf{I}} p$. We distinguish between three cases (in accordance with the computations lemma):

(1) The computation $\pi(\langle S_1, \sigma\rangle)$ is infinite. In this case, the computation $\pi(\langle S_1; S_2, \sigma\rangle)$ is also infinite, and hence $\models_{\mathbf{I}} \{p\}\ S_1; S_2\ \{q\}$ trivially holds.

(2) The computation $\pi(\langle S_1, \sigma\rangle)$ is finite and ends in $\langle E, \sigma_1\rangle$, and the computation $\pi(\langle S_2, \sigma_1\rangle)$ is infinite. Again we have that the computation $\pi(\langle S_1; S_2, \sigma\rangle)$ is infinite, and hence $\models_{\mathbf{I}} \{p\}\ S_1; S_2\ \{q\}$ trivially holds.

(3) The computation $\pi(\langle S_1; S_2, \sigma\rangle)$ is finite. In that case, by the computation lemma it has the form $\langle S_1; S_2, \sigma\rangle \xrightarrow{*} \langle S_2, \sigma_1\rangle \xrightarrow{*} \langle E, \sigma'\rangle$. From the induction assumption on S_1 we have that $\sigma_1 \models_{\mathbf{I}} r$. Furthermore, from the induction assumption on S_2, we have that $\sigma' \models_{\mathbf{I}} q$. Consequently, $\models_{\mathbf{I}} \{p\}\ S_1; S_2\ \{q\}$ holds.

(COND) This is similar to the previous case.

(REP) Suppose that $Tr_{\mathbf{I}} \vdash_{\mathbf{H}} \{p \wedge B\}\ S\ \{p\}$. By the induction hypothesis, $\models_{\mathbf{I}} \{p \wedge B\}\ S\ \{p\}$ is satisfied. Let $\sigma \models_{\mathbf{I}} p$. We again distinguish between cases according to the computations lemma. The only nontrivial case is when the computation $\pi(\langle \mathbf{while}\ B\ \mathbf{do}\ S\ \mathbf{od}, \sigma\rangle)$ terminates. In this case it has the form $C_0 \xrightarrow{*} \cdots \xrightarrow{*} C_i \xrightarrow{*} \cdots \xrightarrow{*} C_k$ for some $k \geqslant 0$, where $C_0 = \langle \mathbf{while}\ B\ \mathbf{do}\ S\ \mathbf{od}, \sigma\rangle$, $C_i = \langle \mathbf{while}\ B\ \mathbf{do}\ S\ \mathbf{od}, \sigma_i\rangle$ with $\sigma_i \models_{\mathbf{I}} B$, $0 \leqslant i < k$, and $C_k = \langle E, \sigma_k\rangle$ with $\sigma_k \models_{\mathbf{I}} \neg B$. By a simple inductive argument, repeatedly using the induction assumption about S, we get that $\sigma_i \models_{\mathbf{I}} p$ for $0 \leqslant i \leqslant k$. In particular, the case $i = k$ implies the required result.

(CONS) Finally, the validity of the consequence rule follows directly from the definition of states and partial correctness.

□

We now turn to the issue of completeness. The **semantic completeness** of **H** can be established by similar arguments as for the noncompositional case. However, in the current framework, which has a strict notion of proof, we are interested really in the existence of proofs as they are defined. This means that all reasoning must be carried out through axioms and proof rules, and all the assertions must be expressible in the specification language considered.

Our first observation is that **H** is not complete on its own in this absolute sense. For example, for e free of x, every partial correctness assertion of the form $\{true\}\ x := e\ \{x = e\}$ is valid but unprovable, unless we have a deductive system for proving $true \Rightarrow e = e$ and can then use rule (CONS).

So, let us consider augmentations of **H** with an axiomatic system for reasoning about the underlying interpretation over which we compute. In this case, Gödel's incompleteness theorem implies that for rich enough structures (such as the integers) the set of true assertions is not recursively enumerable. Therefore, the set of valid partial correctness assertions $\{true\}\ skip\ \{p\}$ is also not recursively enumerable, and **H** cannot be totally complete.

This situation seems to have little to do with the semantics of the programming language. Therefore, a natural tendency is to isolate the problems of proving facts about the domain from proving facts about programs. So, suppose again that we have an oracle for truth in the domain. This can be expressed as proving the partial correctness assertion **c** under the assumption of $Tr_{\mathbf{I}}$, the set of all true facts in the interpretation **I**.

Even in this sense **H** is not totally complete, as now problems of expressibility arise. There are formalisms in which the required intermediate assertions (mainly loop invariants) are not expressible by formulas.

Definition: For an interpretation **I**, predicate p, and program S, let
$post_{\mathbf{I}}(p, S) \stackrel{df.}{=} \{\sigma' \mid \exists \sigma : \sigma \models_{\mathbf{I}} p \wedge \mathbf{M}[\![S]\!](\sigma) = \sigma' \neq \bot\}$

This is the set of all the states resulting from the activation of S on initial states satisfying p.

$$pre_{\mathbf{I}}(S, q) \stackrel{df.}{=} \{\sigma' \mid \forall \sigma : \mathbf{M}[\![S]\!](\sigma') = \sigma \neq \bot \Rightarrow \sigma \models_{\mathbf{I}} \{q\}$$

This is the set of all the initial states generating, by the activation of S, final states satisfying q.

□

Definition: A specification language SL is **expressive** w.r.t. a programming language PL and interpretation **I** iff for every predicate $p \in SL$ and every program $S \in PL$, the predicate $post_{\mathbf{I}}(p, S)$ is expressible (by a formula) in SL.

□

We are led to the following relativized notion of completeness. An equivalent one can be formulated in terms of $pre_{\mathbf{I}}$.

> **Definition:** A deductive system **G** for proving partial correctness assertions is **relatively complete** iff for every specification language *SL*, programming language *PL*, and interpretation **I**, if *SL* is expressive w.r.t. *PL* and **I**, then $\models_{\mathbf{I}}\{p\}\ S\ \{q\}$ implies $Tr_{\mathbf{I}} \vdash_{\mathbf{G}} \{p\}\ S\ \{q\}$. □

Theorem (relative completeness of H):

> **H** is relatively complete.

Proof: Let *SL* be such that it is expressive w.r.t. **I** and *PLW*. The claim is shown by induction on the structure of the program *S*. Under the assumption of the semantic validity of the conclusion of a rule, it is shown that the premisses are valid, and, hence, provable by the induction assumption. We again consider all the possibilities for *S*.

Assignment: Suppose that $\models_{\mathbf{I}}\{p\}\ x:=e\ \{q\}$. Let $\sigma \models_{\mathbf{I}} p$. By the assumption of partial correctness and the computations lemma, we get $\sigma[e|x] \models_{\mathbf{I}} q$. By the substitution theorem, $\sigma \models_{\mathbf{I}} q^x_e$, and hence $\models_{\mathbf{I}} p \Rightarrow q^x_e$. Hence by the axiom of assignment and the rule of consequence we get $Tr_{\mathbf{I}} \vdash_{\mathbf{H}} \{p\}\ x:=e\ \{q\}$.

Skip: This is immediate.

Sequential composition: Suppose that $\models_{\mathbf{I}} \{p\}\ S_1 ; S_2\ \{q\}$. Define a state assertion r by $r \overset{df.}{=} post_{\mathbf{I}}(p,\ S_1)$. Here we make use of expressiveness, in that r is expressible in the specification language *SL*. From the definition of $post_{\mathbf{I}}$ and the computations lemma, both $\models_{\mathbf{I}}\{p\}\ S_1\ \{r\}$ and $\models_{\mathbf{I}}\{r\}\ S_2\ \{q\}$ hold. By the induction hypothesis, we get $Tr_{\mathbf{I}} \vdash_{\mathbf{H}} \{p\}\ S_1\ \{r\}$ and $Tr_{\mathbf{I}} \vdash_{\mathbf{H}} \{r\}\ S_2\ \{q\}$. By the rule (SEQ) the result follows.

Branching: This is similar.

Repetition: This is the most interesting case. Suppose that $\models_{\mathbf{I}} \{r\}$ **while** *B* **do** *S* **od** $\{q\}$. We need to find a loop invariant p, that satisfies the premiss of the (REP) rule, and in addition, $\models_{\mathbf{I}} r \Rightarrow p$ and $\models_{\mathbf{I}} p \wedge \neg B \Rightarrow q$ hold. Semantically, we again would like to use as p the minimal predicate, satisfied exactly by the states reachable by any number of iterations of *S*, starting from an initial state satisfying the precondition r. Here we would like to use the following iterative definition of a sequence of state predicates p_i, $i \geqslant 0$.

$$p_0 \overset{df.}{=} r,\ p_{i+1} \overset{df.}{=} post_{\mathbf{I}}\ (p_i \wedge B,\ S)$$

All these predicates are expressible by the expressiveness assumption. Clearly the infinite disjunction $\bigvee_{i \geqslant 0} p_i$ expresses our required invariant, as an easy inductive argument shows that r_i characterizes the states reachable from r by up to i iterations of S. How can this infinite disjunction be finitely expressed by a formula?

Let $\bar{y} = (y_1, \cdots, y_n)$ be the list of all variables free in S, r, q, and let $\bar{z}$ be a list (of the same length) of new variables. Denote by S^* the following program:

$$S^* :: \textbf{while } B \wedge \bigvee_{i=1,n} y_i \neq z_i \textbf{ do } S \textbf{ od}$$

and let $p^* \overset{df.}{=} post_\text{I}(r, S^*)$. We claim that $p \overset{df.}{=} \exists \bar{z}{:}p^*$ is a finite representation of the loop invariant. It is expressible by the expressiveness assumption. Note that the state transformation of S^* is the same as that of the given program (w.r.t. $\bar{y}$) since it has the same loop body. Furthermore, the **while** condition is strengthened in a way controlable by the choice of $\bar{z}$, independent of the program. By means of this strengthening of the **while** condition we are able to capture states arising after some finite number of iterations of the loop body, not necessarily until $\neg B$ holds.

To see that $\models_\text{I} r \Rightarrow p$, we choose for $\bar{z}$ the initial values of $\bar{y}$. In that case, S^* is exited after zero iterations and by the definition of $post_\text{I}$ we have that p^* is satisfied for this choice of $\bar{z}$.

To see that $\models_\text{I} p \wedge \neg B \Rightarrow q$, we note that if $p^* \wedge \neg B$ holds for some choice of $\bar{z}$, then $\bar{y}$ has the final values in the computation of the original loop. Therefore, $q\ (\bar{y})$ holds by the assumption of partial correctness of the loop.

Finally, to see that p is preserved by the body of the loop S, let $\sigma \models_\text{I} p^* \wedge B$. By the definition of p^*, $\sigma[\![\bar{y}]\!]$ is the result of executing the body of the loop some finite number of times on an initial state satisfying r. Thus, we can choose $\bar{z}$ as $\mathbf{M}\,[\![S]\!](\sigma)[\![\bar{y}]\!]$, the values of $\bar{y}$ after yet another traversal and we get that $\models_\text{I} \{p \wedge B\}\ S\ \{p\}$. By the induction hypothesis, we get that $Tr_\text{I} \vdash_\text{H} \{p \wedge B\}\ S\ \{p\}$, and the required consequence is derived by means of (REP) and the rule of consequence.

□

Expressiveness We saw above that the relative completeness property depends on the structure to be such that the assertion language be expressive w.r.t. it and the programming language (though it can be shown that this is not a necessary condition for completeness). How strong is this assumption of expressibility?

The typical structure for which specifications based on first-order logic are expressive, for many typical programming languages, is the standard model of **Peano arithmetic**. Such models are the natural numbers 'as we know them', with the usual interpretation of zero, addition, multiplication, and ordering. This is a very rich structure, with the ability to code finite sequences of numbers by a single number. Several coding schemes are known, and their description can be found in many standard textbooks on logic and recursion theory. They were used by Gödel in his famous proof of the incompleteness theorem. His original coding scheme was based on the unique decomposition of integers into forms such as $2^{n_1} \times 3^{n_2} \cdots \times pr_k^{n_k}$, where pr_k is the kth prime number. The actual details of coding schemes are immaterial here, but they need the power of full arithmetic for their representation.

The way this coding scheme is used to express strongest postconditions is very similar to the arithmetic completeness proof, shown in the next section for total correctness assertion. Essentially, one 'unwinds' the effect of a repetition, claiming the existence of some (existentially quantified) number n of intermediate states with the appropriate properties. This sequence is coded and represented as a single element of the domain.

A typical example of an inexpressive structure is a standard model for what is known as **Preburger arithmetic**, which has only addition and no multiplication. As is known from logic, the only (unary) predicates expressible by first-order formulas in this weak arithmetic are those known as **eventually periodic** sets. For such a set, there is a bound, say m, and a period, say k, such that for every member n in the set, if $n > m$, then $n + k$ is also in the set. Thus, operations such as multiplication or squaring cannot be expressed, since they are not eventually periodic. On the other hand, they are easy to program, using **while** loops. Hence, expressiveness fails in this situation.

Special form proofs

While we have shown that the system **H** is relatively complete, one is often interested in the existence of proof having special forms. The existence of such proofs of a predetermined form is not guaranteed by the relative completeness theorem. It may be the case that additional rules have to be introduced in order to obtain the proofs of the required form. We present two examples of special proof forms, which are methodologically important for the practicality of the proof system.

A. Incremental proofs Suppose one is interested in proving a correctness assertion where the postcondition q happens to be a conjunction of two (or more) state assertions $q_1 \wedge q_2$. In applying our current system, one has to find an intermediate assertion strong enough to carry information needed for the establishment of both conjuncts simultaneously, even in cases where the two conjuncts are totally unrelated. Thus, it is useful to add an extra proof rule, that allows for an incremental proof, achieving a separation of concerns: prove each conjunct separately. This is formulated by the following proof rule:

$$\frac{\{p\}\,S\,\{q_1\},\ \{p\}\,S\,\{q_2\}}{\{p\}\,S\,\{q_1 \wedge q_2\}} \qquad \text{(AND)}$$

The extension to any finite number of conjuncts is clear. The soundness of this rule is also clear, since in order to violate a conjunction, at least one conjunct has to be violated.

B. Proof by cases It is often the case that a precondition can be split into two (or more) cases, each needing a different proof. Again, in applying the current system, the intermediate assertions have to keep track of both cases simultaneously. Methodologically, it is beneficial to allow a separate proof for each case and then deducing correctness in all cases. This is expressed by the following proof rule:

$$\frac{\{p_1\}\,S\,\{q\},\ \{p_2\}\,S\,\{q\}}{\{p_1 \vee p_2\}\,S\,\{q\}} \qquad \text{(OR)}$$

Again, the extension to any finite number of disjuncts as well as the soundness of the rule are both clear.

A particularly useful special case of the (OR) rule handles a temporary strengthening of the precondition by means of two complementary conditions.

$$\frac{\{p \wedge r\}\,S\,\{q\},\ \{p \wedge \neg r\}\,S\,\{q\}}{\{p\}\,S\,\{q\}}$$

This variant is derived from (OR) and (CONS) by noting that by De Morgan's law we have that $(p \wedge r) \vee (p \wedge \neg r)$ is equivalent to p.

A useful theorem, often applicable in concert with the conjunction rule, is the following theorem of invariance (known also as the **frame axiom**).

Theorem (invariance):

For $S \in PLW$, if $y \notin change\,(S)$, then $Tr_1 \vdash_H \{p(y)\}\ S\ \{p(y)\}$.

Proof: By induction on the structure of S.

(1) S is *skip*: Immediate.

(2) S is $x := e$: Since by assumption y is not x, the claim is obtained directly by the assignment axiom, causing no substitutions to be made.

(3) S is $S_1; S_2$: By the induction hypothesis we have $Tr_1 \vdash_H \{p(y)\}\ S_1\ \{p(y)\}$ and $Tr_1 \vdash_H \{p(y)\}\ S_2\ \{p(y)\}$. The result is obtained by an application of the sequential composition rule.

(4) S is **if** B **then** S_1 **else** S_2 **fi**: The argument is similar to case (3).

(5) S is **while** B **do** S_1 **od**: By the induction assumption, we have that $Tr_I \vdash_H \{p(y)\}\, S_1\, \{p(y)\}$. By (CONS), we get $Tr_I \vdash_H \{p(y) \wedge B\}\, S_1\, \{p(y)\}$. By (REP) we get $Tr_I \vdash_H \{p(y)\}$ **while** B **do** S_1 **od** $\{p(y) \wedge \neg B\}$. Finally, by (CONS) we obtain the required result $Tr_I \vdash_H \{p(y)\}$ **while** B **do** S_1 **od** $\{p(y)\}$.

□

A similar theorem is obtainable for more general languages than *PLW*, and its importance increases in the context of recursive procedures (Chapter 6).

4.4.1 Proof outlines

In this subsection we consider an alternative way of presenting partial correctness proofs, which has advantages in certain circumstances. We start again by an example. The proof of the partial correctness for the integer division program S_{idiv} (of Section 4.3) can be presented in the following form of an **annotated program.**

$\{x \geqslant 0 \wedge y \geqslant 0\}$
$S :: q := 0; r := x\ \{x = q \cdot y + r \wedge r \geqslant 0\}$
  while $r \geqslant y$ **do** $\{x = q \cdot y + r \wedge r \geqslant 0\} r := r - y;\ q := q + 1$ **od**
$\{x = q \cdot y + r \wedge 0 \leqslant r < y\}$

What we did is to insert the (key) assertions occurring in the proof as preconditions and postconditions of substatements. This is similar to using the inductive assertions as program annotations and serves as a useful documentation means. Clearly, an arbitrary annotation cannot serve its purpose. We would like to capture the idea that the collection of annotating assertions represents a proof in **H.** This leads to the following definition.

Definition: A proof outline for $\{p\}\, S\, \{q\}$ consists of an annotation of S with assertions before and after each substatement S' of S, referred to as $pre(S')$ and $post(S')$, respectively, satisfying:

(1) $p \Rightarrow pre(S)$, $post(S) \Rightarrow q$.

(2) For $S' :: skip$, $pre(S') \Rightarrow post(S')$.

(3) For $S' :: x := e$, $pre(S') \Rightarrow post(S')^x_e$.

(4) For $S' :: S_1; S_2$, $pre(S') \Rightarrow pre(S_1)$, $post(S_1) \Rightarrow pre(S_2)$, $post(S_2) \Rightarrow post(S')$.

(5) For $S' ::$ **if** B **then** S_1 **else** S_2 **fi**, $pre(S') \wedge B \Rightarrow pre(S_1)$, $pre(S') \wedge \neg B \Rightarrow pre(S_2)$, $post(S_1) \Rightarrow post(S')$, $post(S_2) \Rightarrow post(S')$.

(6) For $S' :: \textbf{while}\ B\ \textbf{do}\ S_1\ \textbf{od}$, $pre(S') \wedge B \Rightarrow pre(S_1)$, $pre(S') \wedge \neg B \Rightarrow post(S')$, $post(S_1) \Rightarrow pre(S')$.

□

Lemma (compositional preservation):

For every proof outline for $\{p\} S \{q\}$, in any execution of S from an initial state satisfying p, and for every subprogram S' of S, if S' is executed in a state σ and results in a state σ', then $\sigma \models pre(S')$ and $\sigma' \models post(S')$.

□

EXERCISE:

Prove the compositional preservation lemma by induction on the computation and the structure of S.

□

This lemma is the natural analog of the preservation lemma in Chapter 3. It is actually a generalization of the soundness of **H.** Thus, in proving the soundness and completeness of **H,** one could reason about proof outlines instead of proofs.

The definition above is given under the assumption that the annotation is **full,** in that sequential composition is applied in its binary form. In practice, a variant of the concept, for *n*-ary sequential compositions, is used.

From the definition of a proof outline, one can easily prove the following lemma.

Lemma (proof outline):

$Tr_{\mathrm{I}} \vdash_{\mathbf{H}} \{p\}\ S\ \{q\}$ iff there exists a proof outline for $\{p\}\ S\ \{q\}$.

□

The real importance of the concept of proof outlines will become clear when proofs of concurrent and distributed programs are considered (Chapters 7 and 8). There the proof outlines have a more significant role in the theory.

4.5 A deductive system H* for total correctness

In this section we extend the compositional approach and introduce a deductive system **H*** for proving total correctness assertions $\langle p \rangle\ S\ \langle q \rangle$ for *PLW* programs. From the definition of '$\rightarrow$' (and more directly from the computations lemma), it is clear that the only source for nontermination is the repetition statement **while** *B* **do** *S* **od**, so the only needed change is in the corresponding derivation rule. For all other rules, we just modify $\{\cdots\}$ to $\langle\cdots\rangle$

throughout all correctness assertions. We again want to use the idea of a decreasing well-founded variant, incorporated into the deductive framework. So, we again introduce the idea of **parametrization** (this time canonically with natural numbers), and use a parametrized loop invariant $pi(\bar{x}, n)$, where n is a fresh variable, not appearing free in S, ranging over natural numbers. Note that when occurring free, n is treated as a specification variable regarding quantification.

Repetition rule:

$$\frac{pi(\bar{x}, n+1) \Rightarrow B, \langle pi(\bar{x}, n+1)\rangle\ S\ \langle pi(\bar{x}, n)\rangle, pi(\bar{x}, 0) \Rightarrow \neg B}{\langle \exists n: pi(\bar{x}, n)\rangle\ \mathbf{while}\ B\ \mathbf{do}\ S\ \mathbf{od}\ \langle pi(\bar{x}, 0)\rangle} \qquad \text{(REP*)}$$

There are two differences between the conditions on the variant induced by this rule as compared with the ones induced by **F***.

(1) The decrease in n is exactly 1 in each iteration of S.

(2) Upon termination, only the minimal variant value 0 is reached.

Other formulations of the (REP*) rule are possible (see exercises), not imposing these restrictions (similar to the non-compositional case). They may make actual proofs easier, but complicate the structure of the soundness and completeness proofs. The proofs themselves look very similar to these in **H**, embodying the familiar usage of well-foundedness.

As an example of a proof using **H***, we show (with some shortcuts) that $Tr_{\mathbf{I}_0} \vdash_{\mathbf{H}^*} \langle \exists z \geqslant 0 : x = X = 2^z \wedge y = 0\rangle S_{\log} \langle X = 2^y\rangle$, for

$$S_{\log} :: \mathbf{while}\ even\ (x)\ \mathbf{do}\ x := x/2;\ y := y+1\ \mathbf{od}$$

As the parametrized invariant we choose

$$pi(x, y, n) \stackrel{df.}{=} \exists z \geqslant 0 : X = 2^z = x \cdot 2^y \wedge n = \log_2(x)$$

Following is the proof.

(1) $\exists z \geqslant 0 : x = X = 2^z \wedge y = 0 \Rightarrow pi(X, 0, \log_2(X))$ (ARITHMETIC)

(2) $\langle even\ (x) \wedge pi(x, y, n+1)\rangle x := x/2; y := y+1\ \langle pi(x, y, n)\rangle$ (ASS), (SEQ), (CONS)

This is based on the following arithmetic propositions: $even\ (x) \wedge X = x \cdot 2^y \Rightarrow X = (x/2) \times 2^{y+1}$, $even\ (x) \Rightarrow \log_2(x/2) = \log_2 x - 1$, and $x \geqslant 1 \Rightarrow \log_2(x) \geqslant 0$.

(3) $pi(x, y, n+1) \Rightarrow even(x)$ (ARITHMETIC)

(4) $pi(x, y, 0) \Rightarrow \neg even(x)$ (ARITHMETIC)

(5) $\langle \exists n : pi(x, y, n,)\rangle S_{\log} \langle pi(x, y, 0)\rangle$ (2),(3),(4),(REP*)

(6) $pi(x, y, 0) \Rightarrow x = 1$ (ARITHMETIC)

Then by a final application of (CONS) we get the required pre- and postconditions.

□

4.6 Arithmetical soundness and completeness of H*

In this section we consider the appropriate notions of soundness and completeness for a system such as **H***. The difference between this system and **H** is in the explicit reference to a variable ranging over natural numbers, which do not have to be in the given domain of computation. The property we would like to have is **total soundness**, namely, for every interpretation **I**, if $Tr_{\mathbf{I}} \vdash_{\mathbf{H}^*} \langle p \rangle S \langle q \rangle$, then also $\models_{\mathbf{I}} \langle p \rangle S \langle q \rangle$. Unfortunately, this strong property does not hold. For example, consider the program S:: **while** $x > 0$ **do** $x := x - 1$ **od**. In the standard model for the natural numbers $\mathbf{I}_0$ this is an always-terminating program, and we certainly can show $Tr_{\mathbf{I}_0} \vdash_{\mathbf{H}^*} \langle true \rangle S \langle true \rangle$. Consider now any nonstandard model **I** of the natural numbers. We can use exactly the same proof to obtain $Tr_{\mathbf{I}} \vdash_{\mathbf{H}^*} \langle true \rangle S \langle true \rangle$, but certainly the semantic counterpart $\models_{\mathbf{I}} \langle true \rangle S \langle true \rangle$ does not hold. In case the initial value of x is a nonstandard element, the computation need not terminate.

One way out is to remain in the domain of computations of natural numbers. This would conflict with many intended applications of our whole methodology, and with the logical flavor of the approach. It turns out that there is a more general approach: to consider interpretations which are extended with means of referring to natural numbers and their operations, in addition to the given domain and operations.

Definition:

(1) For a specification language SL, denote by SL^+ the **arithmetical extension** of SL, consisting of the minimal extension including L_{PE} (the language of Peano arithmetic), in which finite sequences of natural numbers can be encoded, and a unary predicate N (characterizing 'natural numbers').

(2) An interpretation $\mathbf{I}^+$ is **arithmetical** if its domain includes the standard natural numbers as a (sub)model of L_{PE}, with the arithmetic operations having their standard meanings.

□

Note that it does not matter how arithmetic operations are interpreted over elements not satisfying $N(x)$. We shall use the notation $A(n)$ as an abbreviation for $N(n) \Rightarrow A(n)$. For quantifiers, we have $\forall n{:}A(n)$ abbreviating $\forall n{:}N(n) \Rightarrow A(n)$ and $\exists n{:}A(n)$ abbreviating $\exists n{:}N(n) \wedge A(n)$.

We now want to relativize our concepts to arithmetic interpretations only.

Definition: A proof system **G** (for total correctness assertions) is

(1) **arithmetically sound** iff for every arithmetical interpretation $\mathbf{I}^+$, if $Tr_{\mathbf{I}^+} \vdash_{\mathbf{G}} \langle p \rangle S \langle q \rangle$, then also $\models_{\mathbf{I}^+} \langle p \rangle S \langle q \rangle$ and

(2) **arithmetically complete** iff for every arithmetical interpretation $\mathbf{I}^+$, if $\models_{\mathbf{I}^+} \langle p \rangle S \langle q \rangle$, then $Tr_{\mathbf{I}^+} \vdash_{\mathbf{G}} \langle p \rangle S \langle q \rangle$.

□

Theorem (arithmetical soundness of H*):

H* is arithmetically sound.

Proof: This is similar to the case of **H** and is omitted.

□

Note that the problem with the program S above disappears now, since we can formulate our intention by means of the following total correctness assertion: $Tr_{\mathbf{I}^+} \vdash_{\mathbf{H}^*} \langle N(x) \rangle\ S \langle true \rangle$ which indeed holds. The nonstandard elements that cause nontermination do not satisfy the precondition $N(x)$.

Theorem (arithmetical completeness of H*):

H* is arithmetically complete.

Proof: We consider the only interesting case, namely when S is a **while** program. Suppose that $\models_{\mathbf{I}^+} \langle p \rangle$ **while** B **do** S **od** $\langle true \rangle$ holds. What we need to show is how to construct a parametrized invariant $pi(\bar{x}, n)$ (abbreviated to $pi(n)$), to enable the application of the rule (REP*). The idea is similar to the one involved in using the expressiveness property for **H**. Here we make similar use of the assumption about the ability of coding finite sequences in an arithmetic structure. We are interested in the relation

$$R(\sigma, k) \stackrel{df.}{=} \models_{\mathbf{I}^+} N(k) \wedge \exists\sigma_0, \ldots, \exists\sigma_k : [\sigma = \sigma_0 \wedge \sigma_k \models_{\mathbf{I}^+} \neg B \wedge \bigwedge_{0 \leqslant i < k} (\sigma_{i+1} = \mathbf{M}[\![S]\!](\sigma_i) \wedge \sigma_i \models_{\mathbf{I}^+} B)]$$

This relation relates (initial) states to the maximal possible number of iterations of the loop when started in them. It can be shown (using standard tools from recursion theory, omitted here) that, by using the coding property, a formula $pi(n)$ expressing this relation in SL^+ can be constructed. Clearly, $pi(n)$ satisfies the three required premisses. First, $\models_{\mathbf{I}^+} pi(n+1) \Rightarrow B$ follows from the conjunct corresponding to $i = 0$ in the definition of R. Similarly, $\models_{\mathbf{I}^+} p(0) \Rightarrow \neg B$ follows by taking $k = 0$ in the definition of R (the third part holding vacuously). Finally, to see that $\models_{I^+} \langle pi(n+1)\rangle\; S\; \langle pi(n)\rangle$, note that the precondition implies the existence of a sequence of states $\sigma_0, \ldots, \sigma_{n+1}$. For the postcondition, the required sequence can be chosen as $\sigma'_i \stackrel{df.}{=} \sigma_{i+1}, 0 \leqslant i \leqslant n$. By the induction assumption on S we get $Tr_{I^+} \vdash_{H^*} \langle pi(n+1)\rangle\; S\; \langle pi(n)\rangle$, enabling the application of (REP*) to obtain the required result.

□

4.7 Array variables

4.7.1 Introduction

In this section we consider **array variables** (known also as **subscripted variables**), which are the most elementary data structure present in most programming languages. In spite of its apparent simplicity, such a data structure introduces a high complication both to the definition of its operational semantics, and even more so into its corresponding proof system. The reason for the extra complication is that introducing array variables collides with our most basic device, namely using the familiar syntactic substitution to capture the effect of an assignment. This use strongly manifests itself in the assignment axiom.

In handling those extra complications we shall focus on the essentials only, ignoring such important issues as array bounds and their violation by indices, multidimensionality of arrays, array-valued expressions, and later also passing arrays as parameters.

In order to see clearly the nature of the problem we are facing, consider the following apparent instance of the assignment axiom, interpreting arrays informally at this stage, based on common experience from programming languages.

$$\{true\}\; a[i] := 1\; \{a[i] = 1\} \qquad (?)$$

As it turns out, this is not a valid partial correctness assertion, as is evident by considering an initial state in which $a[1] = a[2] = 2$ holds, and choosing $i = a[2]$. Under these assumptions, the assignment $a[a[2]] := 1$ is actually $a[2] := 1$, leaving $a[1]$ unchanged, that is $a[1] = 2$. Thus, the following should hold.

$$\{a[1] = 2 \wedge a[2] = 2\}\; a[a[2]] := 1\; \{a[a[2]] = 2\} \qquad (*)$$

However, applying the consequence rule to (?) with $i = a[2]$, one obtains

$$\{a[1] = 2 \wedge a[2] = 2\}\; a[a[2]] := 1\; \{a[a[2]] = 1\} \qquad (**)$$

contradicting (*).

The immediate consequence is that, under the naive application of previous ideas to the new situation arising as a result of the presence of arrays, the assignment statement is unsound.

Fortunately, the soundness of the other proof rules that relate to the control structures is not affected by the introduction of arrays. Thus, our main concern is to reinstantiate the soundness of the assignment axiom.

To simplify the presentation even further, we shall assume a language without nested array references, excluding expressions such as $a[a[2]]$. This simplification by itself does not get rid of the unsoundness problem, since we still can obtain

$$\{0+1=a[y]\}\, a[x]:=0\, \{a[x]+1=a[y]\} \qquad (??)$$

as an apparent valid instance of the assignment axiom. However, taking an initial state in which $a[1]=x=y=1$ holds, thereby satisfying the pre-condition, the assignment to $a[x]$ actually modifies $a[y]$ too, thereby violating the postcondition. This is known as the problem of the **aliasing** of array elements.

4.7.2 Operational semantics and array substitutions

The syntactic extension of *PLW* considered here assumes a set of syntactically recognized **array variables.** An array variable a can be indexed by any arithmetical expression e, in the form $a[e]$, provided e itself does not refer to (indexed) array variables. Indexed array variables can appear in every context in which simple variables may appear. In particular, they can appear as targets of an assignment statement, for example, $a[e]:=e'$. We leave to context the determination of which variables are array variables, ignoring issues such as the ill-formedness of assignments, for example $a:=a[1]$.

A. Operational semantics

Our first task is to extend the notion of a state so that a state can assign values to indexed array variables too. We therefore stipulate that a state has, in addition to its original component of mapping simple variables to their domain, another (disjoint) component which maps pairs of the form $\langle a, i\rangle$ to the (same) domain. Here a is an array variable and i is an integer value (constant). Under this stipulation, we now may put $\sigma[\![a[e]]\!] \stackrel{df.}{=} \sigma[\![\langle a, \sigma[\![e]\!]\rangle]\!]$, where the inner application of the state is the ordinary one, because of our assumption that e is array free.

This definition of a state induces a natural extension of the interpretation of state assertions in a state. For example,

$$\sigma \models a[x+y]>0 \text{ if and only if } \sigma[\![\langle a, \sigma[\![x]\!]+\sigma[\![y]\!]\rangle]\!]>0$$

Note, however, that no quantification over array variables is allowed in the assertion language. It does admit quantification over variables serving as indices, for example $\forall 1 \leqslant x \leqslant n \colon a[x] = 0$.

Next, we naturally extend the notion of a state variant, to allow for states differing from a given state only in the value of some $\langle a, i\rangle$ component.

Definition: For an (extended) state σ, expression e (possibly involving array components), and array component $b[e']$, the **a-variant** of σ (w.r.t. e and $b[e']$), denoted by $\sigma[e\,|\,b[e']]$, is defined by

$$\sigma[e\,|\,b[e']][\![\langle c, i\rangle]\!] \stackrel{df.}{=} \begin{cases} \sigma[\![e]\!] & \text{if } c \text{ is } b \text{ and } \sigma[\![e']\!] = i \\ \sigma[\![\langle c, i\rangle]\!] & \text{otherwise} \end{cases}$$

□

Thus, this is an (extended) state agreeing with σ on any simple variable, any array variable other than b, and any component of b except the one indexed by $\sigma[\![e']\!]$, and assigning the value of e in σ to that component of b. This notation is naturally extended to multiple array variables for simultaneous extended state modifications.

We now add to the definition of the transition relation the clauses that cover the array assignments, keeping the previous approach of generating a variant (only this time it is an a-variant).

$$\langle a[e] := e', \sigma\rangle \rightarrow \langle E, \sigma[e'\,|\,a[e]]\rangle$$

For example, we get that

$$\mathbf{M}[\![a[x] := a[x] + 1]\!](\sigma[1\,|\,x, 10\,|\,a[1]]) = \sigma[1\,|\,x, 11\,|\,a[1]])$$

for any state σ. Note that the under the obvious modification of its first clause, the computations lemma remains true.

B. Array substitution

We now turn to a revision of the notion of syntactic substitution for array components. We of course aim at a definition that will render the assignment axiom sound. For that matter, the evaluation of a state assertion after such substitution should produce the appropriate variant of the original state.

Before presenting the definition, we would like to draw the reader's attention to the fact that by our previous provisions, array references are always free, and hence amenable to substitution. Even in an assertion such as $\forall x \colon a[x] = 0$, $a[x]$ occurs free in spite of x occurring bound.

As a means for achieving our goal we define a **formal conditional** to be evaluated at evaluation time (in a given state), and not at substitution time. Its form is $cond\,(b, e_1, e_2)$, where b is some equality among expressions, and both e_1 and e_2 are expressions. We put

$$\sigma[\![cond(e = e', e_1, e_2)]\!] \stackrel{df.}{=} \begin{cases} e_1 & \text{if } \sigma[\![e]\!] = \sigma[\![e']\!] \\ e_2 & \text{otherwise} \end{cases}$$

Thus, evaluating a term containing a formal conditional in some state produces another term (not a value).

We now turn to the definition of array substitution. The only case that needs a careful consideration is replacing one array component by another one.

Definition:

$$(a[e])^{a[e']}_{e''} \stackrel{df.}{=} cond(e = e', e'', a[e])$$

□

Thus, by this definition, the test for equality between the indices of the replaced array element and any occurrence of another element of that array is recorded in the resulting expression by means of a formal conditional. Note that this definition depends on the provision of the absence of nested array references. The extension of array substitution to the general case appears as an exercise at the end of the chapter.

EXERCISE:

Why is the following definition of the array substitution inadequate?

$$(a[e])^{a[e']}_{e''} \stackrel{df.}{=} \begin{cases} e'' & e = e' \\ a[e] & \text{otherwise} \end{cases}$$

□

EXAMPLE:

Consider again the 'offending' assertion $a[x] + 1 = a[y]$ (from (??)). By applying our new definition of array substitution we get

$$(a[x] + 1 = a[y])^{a[x]}_0 = [cond(x = x, 0, a[x]) + 1 = cond(x = y, 0, a[y])]$$

which will not yield (??) in any state in which $x = y$ holds, since both formal conditionals will be resolved to 0 in any such state, yielding an identically false precondition, as expected.

□

There is one fine point that has to be made clear, namely the manipulation of formal conditionals within the scope of a (first-order) quantifier. Recall that such quantification does not bind the array variable, and its components remain free for substitution. The point becomes clear by considering the following example.

EXAMPLE:

Let p be $\forall x{:}\, a[x] = 0$. What is $p_1^{a[7]}$? By applying the definition, we get $\forall x{:}\, cond(x = 7, 1, a[7]) = 0$. This assertion reduces to *false* (in any state, as expected), because for $x = 7$ the value of the formal conditional is 1, not equal to 0.

□

After all this preparation, we now get the array substitution lemma, the natural generalization of the substitution lemma, which renders the assignment axiom sound.

Lemma (array substitution):

$\sigma[e \mid a[e']] \models p$ *iff* $\sigma \models p_e^{a[e']}$

Proof: This follows directly from the definitions.

□

We now consider a complete program, showing how to incorporate the new machinery into the system **H**, in concert with all other rules.

EXAMPLE (linear search):

Let S be the following simplified version of the linear search program. Note that it does not have array assignments, only array references.

$S{::}\ k{:=}0;\ y{:=}n;$ **while** $k < n$ **do**
if $a[k] = x$ **then** $[y{:=}k;\ k{:=}k+1]$ **else** $k{:=}k+1$ **fi od**

For this program we want to prove within the augmented **H** the partial correctness assertion

$\{x = X \wedge n = N \geqslant 0 \wedge \forall 0 \leqslant i < n{:}\, a[i] = A[i]\}$
S
$\{x = X \wedge n = N \wedge \forall 0 \leqslant i < n{:}\, a[i] = A[i] \wedge$
$\exists 0 \leqslant i < n{:}\, A[i] = x \Rightarrow 0 \leqslant y < n \wedge A[y] = x \wedge$
$\neg\exists 0 \leqslant i < n{:}\, A[i] = x \Rightarrow y = n\}$

To shorten the notation, we abbreviate $\exists l \leqslant i < u{:}\, A[i] = x$ to *member* (x, l, u) and $0 \leqslant i < n{:}\, a[i] = A[i]$ to $a = A$. We let p and q denote the pre- and post- condition, respectively.

The loop invariant $I(a, x, n, y, k)$ is

$$x = X \wedge n = N \geqslant 0 \wedge a = A \wedge 0 \leqslant y \leqslant n \wedge 0 \leqslant k \leqslant n \wedge$$
$$member\ (x, 0, k) \Rightarrow A[y] = x \wedge \neg member\ (x, 0, k) \Rightarrow y = n$$

(1) $\{true\}\ k := 0\ \{I(a, x, n, y, k)\}$ (ASS),(SEQ),(CONS)

The last three conjuncts of I are established by the first three assignments; in the second conjunct the antecedent becomes false and in the third conjunct the consequent becomes true. The other conjuncts are trivial.

(2) $\{I(a, x, n, k, k+1) \wedge k < n\}\ y := k; k := k+1\ \{I(a, x, n, y, k)\}$
(ASS),(SEQ),(CONS)

(3) $\{I(a, x, n, y, k+1) \wedge k < n\}\ k := k+1\ \{I(a, x, n, y, k)\}$
(ASS),(CONS)

(4) $I(a, x, n, y, k) \wedge k < n \wedge a[k] = x \Rightarrow I(a, x, n, k, k+1)$
(ARITHMETIC)

(5) $I(a, x, n, y, k) \wedge k < n \wedge a[k] \neq x \Rightarrow I(a, x, n, y, k)$
(ARITHMETIC)

(6) $\{I(a, x, n, y, k) \wedge k < n\}$
if $a[k] = x$ **then** $[y := k;\ k := k+1]$ **else** $k := k+1$ **fi**
$\{I(a, x, n, y, k)\}$ (2),(3),(4),(5),(COND),(CONS)

(7) $I(a, x, n, y, k) \wedge k \geqslant n \Rightarrow q$ (ARITHMETIC)

(8) $\{p\}\ S\ \{q\}$ (1),(6),(7),(REP),(SEQ)

Note that since no array assignment is present in this example, no use is made of formal conditionals. As for the termination of this program, a total correctness proof would use as its variant for the parametrized invariant $w = n - k$, which is nonnegative as implied by I, and obviously decreases in each interation by $k := k+1$.

□

EXAMPLE:

For a second example, one which does contain array assignments, we use a simple program that assigns 0 to $a[i]$, $1 \leqslant i \leqslant n$. Let

S:: $k := 0$; **while** $k < n$ **do** $a[k] := 0; k := k+1$ **od**

We want to derive in **H** with array assignments the partial correctness assertion

$$\{n = N\}\ S\ \{n = N \wedge \forall 0 \leqslant i < n : a[i] = 0\}$$

The proof is rather simple, too.

(1) $\{n=N\}\ k:=0\ \{n=N \wedge 0 \leqslant k \leqslant n \wedge \forall 0 \leqslant i<k\colon a[i]=0\}$ (ASS),(CONS)

(2) $\{k<n \wedge n=N \wedge 0 \leqslant k \leqslant n \wedge \forall 0 \leqslant i<k+1\colon a[i]=0\}$
$a[k]:=0;\ k:=k+1$ (ASS)(SEQ),(CONS)
$\{n=N \wedge 0 \leqslant k \leqslant n \wedge \forall 0 \leqslant i<k\colon a[i]=0$

Note that the occurrence of a formal conditional here, implied by (ASS), is eliminated via (CONS). This is explained below in more detail.

(3) $k \geqslant n \wedge n=N \wedge 0 \leqslant k \leqslant n \wedge \forall 0 \leqslant i<k+1\colon a[i]=0 \Rightarrow$
$n=N \wedge \forall 0 \leqslant i<n\colon a[i]=0$ (ARITHMETIC)

(4) $\{n=N \wedge 0 \leqslant k \leqslant n \wedge \forall 0 \leqslant i<n\colon a[i]=0\}$
while $k<n$ **do** $a[k]:=0;\ k:=k+1$ **od** (2),(3),(REP)(CONS)
$\{n=N \wedge \forall 0 \leqslant i<n\colon a[i]=0\}$

(5) $\{n=N\}\ S\ \{n=N \wedge \forall 0 \leqslant i<n\colon a[i]=0\}$ (1),(4),(SEQ)

Note that the actual array substitution that takes place in (2) is

$$(\forall 0 \leqslant i<k+1\colon a[i]=0)_0^{a[k]}$$

which produces $\forall 0 \leqslant i<k+1\colon cond(i=k, 0, a[i])=0$, which after a little reflection is seen to be the right precondition. For $0 \leqslant i<k$ the formal conditional reduces to $a[i]=0$, while for $i=k$ it reduces to $0=0$.

□

In the suggestions for further reading, at the end of the chapter, the reader may find references to the literature containing more complicated examples of correctness proofs of programs with arrays.

The approach presented so far can be referred to as the **component assignments** approach, as it preserves the direct assignment to array elements. Another approach to handling arrays has also been suggested, according to which an expression $a[e]:=e'$ is interpreted as $a:=f(a, e, e')$. This approach may be termed the **full assignment** approach, according to which a component assignment is represented as an assignment to the whole array of an array-valued expression. In this case, a state should map an array variable to a (whole) array value, and the syntactic assignment becomes $p^a_{f(a,e,e')}$. It is basically a matter of taste to choose between the two approaches. Here the first was preferred because it resembles more closely the actual programming notation commonly used.

4.8 Conclusions

In this chapter we focused on a compositional proof system for partial and for total correctness assertions for structured programs. We showed how to present the same ideas discussed in the previous chapter, namely computational induction and decreasing well-founded variants, in a deductive framework. As a major methodological outcome (for the construction of correct programs), we have an abstract view of iterations: preserving an invariant on the one hand, while decreasing a well-founded variant (thereby ensuring progress towards termination) on the other hand.

We then studied several notions of soundness and completeness arising in the considered context. In particular, we showed that the deductive system considered for partial correctness is **relatively complete** (that is, allows deductions using as assumptions all true predicates in the underlying structure, provided that the required loop invariants can be expressed in the assertion language). Similarly, we considered the **arithmetic completeness** of the deductive system for total correctness assertions (that is, provability in an extended language, enabling explicit reference to natural numbers).

The existence of sound and complete (in some form) compositional proof systems for correctness assertions is obviously a very desirable situation. Unfortunately, this situation cannot always be guaranteed, especially in the presence of several quite complicated programming constructs. In particular, in the context of concurrency, the correctness assertions themselves have to have a more complicated structure than either partial or total correctness assertions, in order to facilitate compositional complete proof systems.

As we mentioned before, the desirability of the existence of such systems becomes a major drive in the design of modern programming languages.

We concluded the chapter with a discussion of array assignments. This is a more delicate issue, which, if not treated cautiously, may easily interfere with the soundness of the system. We shall return to examples using arrays in the chapters on concurrency and distributedness. As we do not consider very intricate usage of arrays, we shall reason about their assignments in a semisemantical mode, avoiding the notational inconvenience introduced by the fully formal approach. Such reasoning is confined to small steps in a program, and it does not rely on the lower-level details of the operational semantics, the latter possibly inviting confusion.

Bibliographic notes and suggestions for further reading

Bibliographic notes The first compositional proof system, on which we based **H**, appears in [10] (except for the rule (COND), which is from [39]), and has influenced since the whole research discipline of program verification and axiomatic semantics. The term 'compositional', though, emerged much later. An extensive review of compositional proof methods for deterministic programs is [54], from which the example proof was taken. The notion of relative completeness originates from [40], for a more complicated language including procedures and scope rules. A completeness proof w.r.t. a denotational semantics for a system like **H** appears in [17]. The appendix there contains a proof of expressiveness of first-order Peano arithmetic, due to J.I. Zucker. The (AND) and (OR) rules appear (in the context of total correctness proofs) in [55], and are discussed also in [56], where a proof of the invariance theorem also appears. The notion of arithmetic completeness is due to Harel, for example in [57], though presented in the context of dynamic logic, which has partial correctness and total correctness assertions as a special case. An early compositional proof system for total correctness (in a different notation) is [55]. The system **H*** follows Apt's presentation [54], inspired by Harel's corresponding rules in dynamic logic. Precursors to proof outlines, called **annotated programs**, were considered in [15] and [58]. The unsoundness of the assignment axiom for arrays as exhibited in assertion (?) is from [17] (attributed there to Peter Van Emde Boas). The other example, that of assertion (??), appears in [59]. The whole presentation of the array rules follows [17] and [59]. The unsoundness of the assignment axioms for arrays is mentioned also in [60], which treats also **pointer** variables and their assignments, and some other 'storage features'. An early rule for array assignment, based on the full assignment approach, appears in [61]. Another treatment based on the latter approach appears in [14], extended also to records and combinations of both. There, however, no independent semantics is given, and the whole issue of soundness is not raised. Another early treatment of the semantics of array assignments and their associated substitutions, in the context of dynamic logic, is in [62], presented also in [63]. The total assignments to array variables had already been described in [64], a paper with many precursory ideas about the semantics of programming languages.

Suggestions for further reading An interesting survey of compositional proof methods, mainly for total correctness, as interpreted uniformly by translation into dynamic logic, appears in [65]. An early syntax-directed proof system for programs with (a restricted use of) *goto*s appears in [66], using proofs from assumptions. Other proof systems for languages with explicit *goto* statements can be found in [67],[38],[17, Chapter 10 (by A. de Bruin)] and [58]. For axiomatic definitions of the semantics of specific programming languages by means of compositional proof systems, see [61] for Pascal and [68] for EUCLID. An interesting interdisciplinary discussion of compositionality in logic, mathematics, linguistics, and computer science is [69]. A convincing example of a construction of a nontrivial program together with its correctness proof can be found in [53]. An extension of **H**, in which one can deduce partial correctness assertions for one program from partial correctness assertions on other programs (the latter not being syntactic components of the former), is presented in [166]. Another extension of partial correctness, accompanied by the corresponding extensions of **H**, can be found in [71]. Many examples of partial correctness proofs (in **H**) of *PLW* programs using arrays can be found in [25]. While mentioning the absence of rules to handle array assignments, which is done in an *ad hoc* manner (confined to swapping only), the issue of unsoundness of the presented assignment axiom is not mentioned there, as no independent semantics is given. The problem of expressing *PLF* programs by means of equivalent *PLW* programs is described, amongst many other places, in [72]. It became part of the 'goto-less' programming controversy, sometimes unjustly referred to as 'structured programming'. It is surveyed also in [73], a general survey on issues of program schemes and their associated decision problems. A discussion showing that expressiveness is not a necessary condition for relative completeness appears in [171].

EXERCISES

4.1 Describe *comp* $(\langle S_{idiv}, \sigma\rangle)$, where $\sigma \models x = 7 \wedge y = 3$.

4.2 **Forward assignment axiom [9]:** For an arbitrary precondition p, find a postcondition q such that the alternative assignment axiom $\{p\}\, x := e\, \{q\}$ (together with the rest of **H**) is a sound and relatively complete proof system.

4.3 **One directional conditional statement:** Define **if** B **then** S **fi** $\overset{df.}{=}$ **if** B **then** S **else** *skip* **fi**. Derive a sound and relatively complete partial correctness rule for this construct.

4.4 **Alternative iteration rule:** Formulate an alternative partial correctness rule for the **while** statement, having as consequence

$\{p\}$ **while** B **do** S **od** $\{q\}$.

Derive your new rules from the ones in **H**.

4.5 **Trivial correctness assertions:** In the previous chapter, you were asked to show that $\models_I \{true\}\, P\, \{true\}$, for any P. Show that $Tr_I \vdash_H \{true\}\, P\, \{true\}$, for every $P \in PLW$.

4.6 **Uniqueness of proof outlines:** Prove that every partial correctness assertion has a unique proof outline (up to logical equivalence of state assertions) or present a partial correctness assertion with two different proof outlines.

4.7 Soundness of H w.r.t. another semantics: Consider the following alternative semantic definition of *PLW*. The semantics defines for each program $P \in PLW$ and state σ the sequence of states *comp* (P, σ). The sign '·' denotes sequence concatenation. Sequences of length one are identified with their elements.

(1) $comp\,[\![skip]\!](\sigma) = \sigma$

(2) $comp\,[\![x := e]\!](\sigma) = \sigma[\sigma[\![e]\!] \mid x]$

(3) $comp\,[\![\textbf{if}\ B\ \textbf{then}\ S_1\ \textbf{else}\ S_2\ \textbf{fi}]\!](\sigma) = \begin{cases} \sigma\cdot comp\,[\![S_1]\!](\sigma) & \text{if}\ \sigma \models B \\ \sigma\cdot comp\,[\![S_2]\!](\sigma) & \text{if}\ \sigma \models \neg B \end{cases}$

(4) $comp\,[\![\textbf{while}\ B\ \textbf{do}\ S_1\ \textbf{od}]\!]$

$$(\sigma) = \begin{cases} \sigma & \text{if}\ \sigma \models \neg B \\ comp\,[\![S_1]\!](\sigma)\cdot comp\,[\![\textbf{while}\ B\ \textbf{do}\ S_1\ \textbf{od}]\!](\sigma') & \text{if}\ \sigma \models B \end{cases}$$

(5) $comp\,[\![S_1 ; S_2]\!](\sigma) = comp\,[\![S_1]\!](\sigma)\cdot comp\,[\![S_2]\!](\sigma')$ where

$$\sigma' \overset{df.}{=} last\,(comp\,[\![S_1]\!](\sigma))$$

Redefine the notions of 'computation' and 'satisfaction of a partial correctness assertion' to fit this semantics. Prove the soundness of **H** w.r.t. this semantics (without proving the equivalence of both semantic definitions). In what sense are conditions (1)–(5) a definition of 'comp'?

4.8 Relation to predicate transformers: Prove that for any interpretation **I**,

$$\models_{\mathbf{I}} \{p\}S\{q\} \Leftrightarrow \{\sigma \mid \sigma \models_{\mathbf{I}} p\} \subseteq pre_{\mathbf{I}}(S, q)$$
$$\Leftrightarrow post_{\mathbf{I}}(p, S) \subseteq \{\sigma' \mid \sigma' \models_{\mathbf{I}} q\}$$

4.9 Inexpressiveness: Suppose that the only operations allowed in r.h.s. of assignment statements are '+1' and '−1'. Show that the first-order language with these two operations only and a constant '0' is not expressive with respect to **while** programs and the integers (where the operations are interpreted as adding and subtracting, respectively, and '0' is interpreted as zero).

You may consult a logic book, for example [74].

4.10 Alternative variant decrease: Formulate an equivalent termination rule for the repetition statement, which

(1) allows an arbitrary decrease after each iteration, and
(2) does not require reaching 0 (exactly) upon termination.

4.11 Shift rule [75]:

(1) Derive the following rule in **H**:

$$\frac{\{p \wedge q\}\, S\,\{r\}}{\{p\}\, S\,\{q \Rightarrow r\}}$$

provided $var(q) \cap var(S) = \varnothing$.

(2) Replace the syntactic restriction on q and S by a more general semantic restriction.

(3) Use the **shift** rule to prove $\{p\}\, S\,\{r\}$, where $p \equiv (x = X < y = Y)$, $q \equiv [even\ (X+Y) \Rightarrow x = y = (X+Y)\ /2) \wedge (odd\ (X+Y) \Rightarrow x = (X+Y+1)/2 \wedge y = (X+Y-1)/2)]$, and S:: **while** $x < y$ **do** $x := x+1; y := y-1$ **od**.

4.12 Define the corresponding notion of proof outline for **H***.

4.13 **Reducing H to F:** Provide a representation of *PLW* programs as *PLF* programs. Deduce from your representation that for every proof outline for $\{p\}\, S\ \{q\}$ in **H,** there is an application of **F** with such cut points that allow $pre(S')$ to serve as $I_l(\bar{x})$ for l corresponding (in your representation) to S', for every substatement S' of S.

4.14 **Alternative atomic statements rules [28]:** Suppose that in **H** the assignment axiom is replaced by the rule

$$\frac{p \Rightarrow q^{x}_{e}}{\{p\}\, x := e\,\{q\}}$$

and the *skip* axiom is replaced by

$$\frac{p \Rightarrow q}{\{p\}\, skip\,\{q\}}$$

How would this change affect the relative completeness of **H**?

4.15 **Identically false precondition:** For an arbitrary $S \in PLW$ and post-condition q, show that $Tr_{\mathrm{I}} \vdash_{\mathbf{H}} \{false\}\, S\,\{q\}$ without an appeal to the relative completeness proof.

4.16 **AND–OR rules [56]:** Show that all the applications of the *AND–OR* rules can be effectively eliminated from proofs in **H**.

4.17 Under the assumption that $\models_{\mathrm{I}} \{p_1 \wedge p_2\}\, S\,\{q_1 \wedge q_2\}$, is it true that either $\models_{\mathrm{I}} \{p_1\}\, S\,\{q_1\}$ or $\models_{\mathrm{I}} \{p_2\}\, S\,\{q_2\}$?

4.18 General array substitution [17]: Define the semantics of array assignments and array substitutions without the provision for the absence of nested array references. Show the soundness of the assignment axiom under your extensions.

4.19 Truth preservation [53]: Define the truth of a partial correctness assertion in a given state by $\sigma \models \{p\}\, S\{q\}$ iff one of the following conditions holds.

(1) $\sigma \not\models p$

(2) $\mathbf{M}[\![S]\!](\sigma) = \bot$

(3) $\mathbf{M}[\![S]\!](\sigma) \models q$

Which of the rules of **H** is preserving truth in a state? Relate your answer to the strong soundness of **H** (that is, its validity preservation).

4.20 (1) Extend **H** with an assignment axiom for parallel assignments.

(2) Prove that $tr_{\mathbf{I}_0} \vdash_{\mathbf{H}} \{p\}\, S\{q\}$ using your extension, where:

$p = (x = X \wedge y = Y \geqslant 0)$
$q = (z = X^Y)$
$S{::}\ z := 1;$
  while $y \neq 0$ **do**
    if $even\ (y)$ **then** $(y, x) := (y\ div\ 2,\ x * x)$
        else $(y, z) := (y - 1,\ z * x)$
    fi
    od

(3) Prove $Tr_{\mathbf{I}_0} \vdash_{\mathbf{H}^*} \langle x = X \wedge y = Y \geqslant 0\rangle\, S\, \langle true\rangle$

Chapter 5
VERIFYING NONDETERMINISTIC PROGRAMS

5.1 Introduction

In this chapter, we extend the compositional approach to verification of nondeterministic programs. A similar, but endogenous, extension for nondeterministic flow programs is also possible. Nondeterministic programs are characterized by the fact that, for a given initial state, the program may exhibit more than one computation, and, therefore, more than one outcome (final state). In particular, it is possible that for a given initial state some of the possible computations terminate, while others do not terminate. There are two natural representations of nondeterminism in programming languages: the first one, to which we refer as **control driven** (on which we focus here as a main one) is by nondeterministic branching. The second one, to which we refer as **data driven,** is by a nondeterministic choice of a value to be assigned to a variable. In principle, these two representations are equivalent, in that each of them is powerful enough to simulate the other under a natural simulation relation. It is common to restrict the control-driven nondeterminism to a finite number of control continuations (even to a bounded number). The data-driven nondeterminism, however, is usually concerned also with a choice out of a countable domain. We return later to this issue in more detail.

In this context, it is still natural to view programs as state transformers. However, the execution does not define any longer a function but a **relation** between initial and their corresponding final states. A pair of states σ and σ'

stands in the relation associated with a nondeterministic program iff σ' is a possible final state when the program is executed on the initial state σ. Thus, the specification method we considered so far, by means of preconditions and postconditions, is still applicable, with a modified interpretation of the satisfiability of the correctness assertions. These correctness assertions are again partial correctness (coming in two variants, as explained below) and total correctness. Another kind of correctness assertion for nondeterministic programs appears in the exercises.

The interpretation of nondeterminism we are going to use throughout this chapter is based on what is known as **don't care** nondeterminism, according to which nondeterminism is resolved, when encountered, in an arbitrary way (unless **fairness** is involved, as discussed later). Thus, for a program to be correct, every computation must succeed. In particular, to be considered a terminating program, every computation (from an admissible initial state) of that program must terminate. A more concrete motivation for this approach is **abstraction,** for example of implementation details, leaving for a correct implementation a range of choices according to 'internal' criteria. Thus, a correct implementation is not 'forced' to reproduce every computation or final outcome allowed by the semantics. The 'real' computation might even be deterministic. This issue manifests itself in the meaning of specifications, that is in the definition of satisfaction of correctness assertions, at which we soon arrive.

Another important point about the interpretation of nondeterminism held here is the complete absence of any probabilistic assumptions. No probability distribution among possible nondeterministic choices is present. On the contrary, we may use nondeterminism (and in particular its fair version, to be introduced below) as abstracting away some probabilistic properties of correct implementations.

This approach to nondeterminism should be contrasted to the one prevailing in the theory of computation, where correctness is defined **existentially**: a program succeeds if at least one of its computations succeeds. This kind of nondeterminism, known also as **don't know** nondeterminism, abstracts away from an exhaustive search over all possible computations (usually implemented using backtracking as is done, for example, in Prolog). The 'don't care' nondeterminism is of course much more efficient to implement. The main theoretical advantage of the 'don't know' nondeterminism is in complexity theory and in discussion of **expressive power** (for example, the equivalence of the deterministic and nondeterministic variants of a given model of computation).

Our main interest in extending the theory of program verification to nondeterministic programs is to understand fully the power of our methodology. Also, as concurrency can often be modeled by nondeterminism, the extension here leads to further extensions for verification of concurrent programs, which are of practical importance too.

For the expression of nondeterministic programs, we first consider a programming language *Guarded Commands* (*GC*), which is a natural extension of *PLW* and admits, as we show, a relatively complete compositional proof system both for partial and for total correctness. We start by considering 'pure' nondeterminism, which is indeed resolved arbitrarily, without any further restrictions. Then, we pass to the consideration of one of the more interesting developments in this theory, namely **fairness.** This is a global restriction on the way (infinite) sequences of nondeterministic resolutions can occur. It affects drastically the termination of nondeterministic programs. Some kinds of fairness assumptions are present in many modern programming languages, in particular in the context of concurrency. However, its effect can be better explained and handled in the context of nondeterminism. We shall see that one way of dealing with fair nondeterminism is by reducing it to data-selection nondeterminism, using a construct which is known as **random assignments**. A major novelty of the fairness assumption is the insufficiency of the natural numbers as the universal domain for well-founded variants in termination proofs; rather, recursive ordinals are required.

5.2 Guarded commands

In this section, we introduce the structured programming language *Guarded Commands* (*GC*) for nondeterministic programs, where nondeterminism originates from multiple possibilities of a continuation of a computation. This is a very simple language for the expression of nondeterministic, state transforming programs, naturally generalizing *PLW*. It was originally introduced (by E.W. Dijkstra) for the description of systematic development of programs together with their correctness proofs. Here we remain within the framework of a posteriori verification and its theory.

The abstract syntax of *GC* is given below, where *S* and *G* are meta-variables.

$$S{::}\ x := e \mid skip \mid S_1 ; S_2 \mid [G] \mid {*}[G]$$
$$G{::}\ B \rightarrow S \mid B \rightarrow S \,[]\, G.$$

The first three elements, namely assignment, *skip*, and sequential composition, are similar to their counterparts in the deterministic *PLW*. The structure $[G]$ is called **nondeterministic selection** and the structure $*[G]$ is called **nondeterministic repetition**. The structure *G* itself is called a **guarded command**. The Boolean expression (over states) *B* is called a **guard**. A generic nondeterministic selection is denoted by $[B_1 \rightarrow S_1 [] \cdots [] B_n \rightarrow S_n]$, for some $n \geqslant 1$, also abbreviated as $[\underset{i \in \Delta}{[]} B_i \rightarrow S_i]$, where $\Delta \overset{df.}{=} \{1, \ldots, n\}$ is the set of **directions.** Similarly, for repetitions we use the abbreviation $*[\underset{i \in \Delta}{[]} B_i \rightarrow S_i]$.

Note that nondeterministic selections and repetitions can be nested arbitrarily within each other.

The informal description of the intended semantics is as follows. For a nondeterministic selection statement, the set of all guards true in the current state is evaluated. If this set is empty, then the computation **fails**. Otherwise, an arbitrary direction $i \in \Delta$, such that B_i is true in the current state, is selected, S_i is executed, and the statement terminates. For a nondeterministic repetition, again the set of all guards true in the current state is evaluated. If this set is empty, then the computation **terminates**. Otherwise, an arbitrary direction $i \in \Delta$, such that B_i is true in the current state, is selected, S_i is executed, and the whole procedure is repeated, either forever, or until the occurrence of a state in which all the guards are false. Failure of a computation is represented by a special failure state. The failure state propagates itself, causing the failure of the whole program.

EXAMPLE:

The following statement $S_{\max}$ assigns to m the maximum of the values of x and y:

$$S_{\max} :: [x \geqslant y \rightarrow m := x \, [] \, y \geqslant x \rightarrow m := y].$$

It has two possible computations in the case $x = y$ (still, both yield the same outcome).

□

EXAMPLE:

The following program S_{b_choice} selects an arbitrary natural number in the range $[0 \ldots N]$, $N \geqslant 0$, and assigns it to x.

$$S_{b\_choice} :: x := 0; y := 0; *[y < N \rightarrow y := y + 1; [\mathit{true} \rightarrow x := y \, [] \, \mathit{true} \rightarrow \mathit{skip}]].$$

□

EXERCISE:

Write a nondeterministic program that sorts four variables x_i, $1 \leqslant i \leqslant 4$, by means of value exchanges only. The nondeterminism should reflect the order of independent interchanges.

□

Operational semantics

We now turn to the formal definition of an operational semantics of GC. Once again, we use a transition relation among configurations, which are similar to those for *PLW*, but with syntactic continuations being *GC* programs. We again systematically omit the references to **I**, the underlying interpretation over which the computation takes place. However, we do introduce a new state, denoted by **f**, capturing the situation of a failing computation. Again, by convention, this state is not proper and does not satisfy any state assertion formulated in terms of program variables. Also, all variants of **f** are equal to **f** by convention.

Definition: Let '→' be the least relation among *GC* configurations, satisfying the following.

(1) $\langle x := e, \sigma\rangle \rightarrow \langle E, \sigma[\mathrm{e}|x]\rangle$.

(2) $\langle skip, \sigma\rangle \rightarrow \langle E, \sigma\rangle$.

(3) if $\langle S, \sigma\rangle \rightarrow \langle S', \sigma'\rangle$, then for every $T \in GC$, $\langle S; T, \sigma\rangle \rightarrow \langle S'; T, \sigma'\rangle$.

(4) For $i \in \Delta$, if $\sigma[\![B_i]\!] = tt$, then $\langle [\underset{i\in\Delta}{\square}\ B_i \rightarrow S_i], \sigma\rangle \rightarrow \langle S_i, \sigma\rangle$. If $\underset{i\in\Delta}{\wedge}\ \sigma[\![B_i]\!] = ff$, then $\langle [\underset{i\in\Delta}{\square}\ B_i \rightarrow S_i], \sigma\rangle \rightarrow \langle E, \mathbf{f}\rangle$.

(5) For $i \in \Delta$, if $\sigma[\![B_i]\!] = tt$, then $\langle *[\underset{i\in\Delta}{\square}\ B_i \rightarrow S_i], \sigma\rangle \rightarrow \langle S_i; *[\underset{i\in\Delta}{\square}\ B_i \rightarrow S_i], \sigma\rangle$. If $\underset{i\in\Delta}{\wedge}\ \sigma[\![B_i]\!] = ff$, then $\langle *[\underset{i\in\Delta}{\square}\ B_i \rightarrow S_i], \sigma\rangle \rightarrow \langle E, \sigma\rangle$.

□

Recall that a computation is a maximal '→' sequence. However, now there are several possible computations from a given initial configuration. Note that in the semantics nondeterminism is represented by the meta-level ability to apply more than one '→'-rule to a given configuration, resolved arbitrarily. We say that a direction $i \in \Delta$ is **enabled** in a configuration $C = \langle S; S', \sigma\rangle$, iff $S = *[\underset{i\in\Delta}{\square}\ B_i \rightarrow S_i]$ or $S = [\underset{i\in\Delta}{\square}\ B_i \rightarrow S_i]$, and in both cases $\sigma \models B_i$. When the syntactic continuation is clear from the context, we say that direction i is enabled in σ. We denote by $\Pi(S, \sigma)$ the collection of all computations of S on an initial state σ. We then put $\mathbf{M}_{\mathbf{GC}}[\![S]\!](\sigma) \overset{df.}{=} \{val(\pi) | \pi \in \Pi(S, \sigma)\}$. Note that it is possible now to have $\mathbf{f} \in \mathbf{M}_{\mathbf{GC}}[\![S]\!](\sigma)$. Also, $\bot \in \mathbf{M}_{\mathbf{GC}}[\![S]\!](\sigma)$ iff there exists a diverging computation of **S** on σ. A failing computation is finite, neither properly terminating nor diverging. In this chapter, we abbreviate $\mathbf{M}_{\mathbf{GC}}$ to **M**.

Once again we have as a characterization of computations the following properties, directly following from the definition of '→'.

Lemma (nondeterministic computations):

Let $C_0 = \langle S_0, \sigma_0\rangle$.

(1) Atomic statements and sequential composition: these are as before.

(2) *Selection:* If $S_0 = [\underset{i\in\Delta}{\square} B_i \to S_i]$, then $\pi(C_0)$ has one of the following forms:

(a) $C_0 \to \langle E, \mathbf{f}' \rangle$, where $\sigma \models \neg \bigvee_{i\in\Delta} B_i$.

(b) $C_0 \to C_1 = \langle S_i, \sigma \rangle \to \cdots$, where $i \in \Delta$ and $\sigma_0 \models B_i$, and $\langle S_i, \sigma \rangle \to \cdots$ is in $\Pi(C_1)$.

(3) *Repetition:* If $S_0 = {}^*[\underset{i\in\Delta}{\square} B_i \to S_i]$, then $\pi(C_0)$ has one of the following forms:

(a) $C_0 \to \langle E, \sigma_0 \rangle$, with $\sigma_0 \models \bigwedge_{i\in\Delta} \neg B_i$.

(b) $C_0 \overset{*}{\to} \langle S_0, \sigma_1 \rangle \overset{*}{\to} \cdots \overset{*}{\to} \langle S_0, \sigma_k \rangle \to \langle T_{k+1}, \sigma_{k+1} \rangle \to \cdots$ for some $k \geqslant 0$, where for every j, $0 \leqslant j < k$ there exists a direction l_j such that $\sigma_j \models B_{l_j}$, $\langle S_0, \sigma_j \rangle \overset{*}{\to} \langle S_0, \sigma_{j+1} \rangle$ is a finite computation of S_{l_j} and there exists a direction $l \in \Delta$ such that $\langle S_0, \sigma_k \rangle \to \langle T_{k+1}, \sigma_{k+1} \rangle \to \cdots$ is either a nonterminating or a failing computation of S_l.

(c) $C_0 \overset{*}{\to} \langle S_0, \sigma_1 \rangle \overset{*}{\to} \cdots \overset{*}{\to} \langle S_0, \sigma_k \rangle \overset{*}{\to} \cdots$ where for every k, $0 \leqslant k$, there is a direction $l_k \in \Delta$, such that $\sigma_k \models B_{l_k}$ and $\langle S_0, \sigma_k \rangle \overset{*}{\to} \langle S_0, \sigma_{k+1} \rangle$ is a finite computation of S_{l_k}.

(d) $C_0 \overset{*}{\to} \langle S_0, \sigma_1 \rangle \overset{*}{\to} \cdots \overset{*}{\to} \langle E, \sigma_k \rangle$, where for every j, $0 \leqslant j < k$ there exists a direction $l_j \in \Delta$, such that $\sigma_j \models B_{l_j}$, $\sigma_k \models \bigwedge_{i\in\Delta} \neg B_i$ and $\langle S_{l_j}, \sigma_j \rangle \overset{*}{\to} \langle S_0, \sigma_{j+1} \rangle$ is a finite computation of S_{l_j}.

□

EXERCISES:

(1) Extend *GC* to include empty guarded commands (that is, with zero directions), by letting an empty selection fail and an empty repetition immediately exit.

(2) Define a deterministic sublanguage of *GC* 'equivalent' to *PLW*; define exactly the notion of equivalence used.

□

We now have to revise slightly the definition of the satisfaction of the correctness assertions for nondeterministic programs. There are two natural variants, one ignoring failures and the other one considering them. We proceed with the variant that considers failures and leave the other variant to an exercise.

Definition: For $S \in GC$, specification $\langle p, q \rangle$ and interpretation $\mathbf{I}$

(1) $\models_{\mathbf{I}} \{p\}\, S\, \{q\} \Leftrightarrow \forall \sigma, \sigma' : [\sigma \models_{\mathbf{I}} p \wedge \sigma' \in \mathbf{M}[\![S]\!](\sigma) \wedge \sigma' \neq \bot \Rightarrow \sigma' = \mathbf{f} \wedge \sigma' \models_{\mathbf{I}} q]$, and

(2) $\models_I \langle p \rangle S \langle q \rangle \Leftrightarrow \forall \sigma, \sigma' : [\sigma \models_I p \wedge \sigma' \in \mathbf{M}[\![S]\!](\sigma) \Rightarrow \sigma' \neq \bot \wedge \sigma' \neq \mathbf{f} \wedge \sigma' \models_I q]$.

□

This definition reflects the intentional specification of all computations having the required behavior. It is important, at this point, to understand the exact meaning of the correctness assertions as specifications for nondeterministic programs. Consider the program S_{b_choice} mentioned above. A possible specification could be: find a program S such that $\{true\}\ S\ \{0 \leqslant x \leqslant N\}$ holds, (or even $\langle true \rangle\ S\ \langle 0 \leqslant x \leqslant N \rangle$ holds). While S_{b_choice} is a correct solution (as can be verified by the rules presented in the next section), so is the trivial program $x := 0$. The point is, that neither the partial nor the total correctness assertion implies the 'converse' requirement, that every state satisfying the postcondition is a possible outcome of the program. The reason for not imposing the latter requirement is that it is not detectable by merely activating the program as a black box (even infinitely often). No sequence of activations of the box can determine its content. The infinite sequence of 0s as the (only) outcome can occur with S_{b_choice} as well (recall that no probabilities on outcomes are assumed). In the suggestions for further reading we mention further references to discussions of this issue.

EXERCISE:

Give a formal specification to the interchange-sorting program you wrote in a previous exercise.

□

Remark:

The separation lemma (separating total correctness to partial correctness and termination) holds also in the case of nondeterministic programs.

It is possible to arrange all the configurations occurring in the computations of $\Pi(S, \sigma)$ as a **tree,** denoted by $T_{S,\sigma}$. Each path in this tree represents a computation of S on σ. The branching structure reflects the nondeterministic choices present in a given computation. For a repetitive S, the definition of $T_{S,\sigma}$ is recursive, and may yield an infinite tree in case S is nonterminating. It is very important to note that all such trees are **finitely branching**, where the degree is always bounded by the maximal number of directions in any selection or repetition substatement S' of S. The tree $T_{S_{b\_choice}}$ (which is independent of the initial states) is shown for $N = 2$ in Figure 5.1. To simplify the presentation, only the state component of each configuration is depicted in a node.

We end this section with an important observation about the semantics

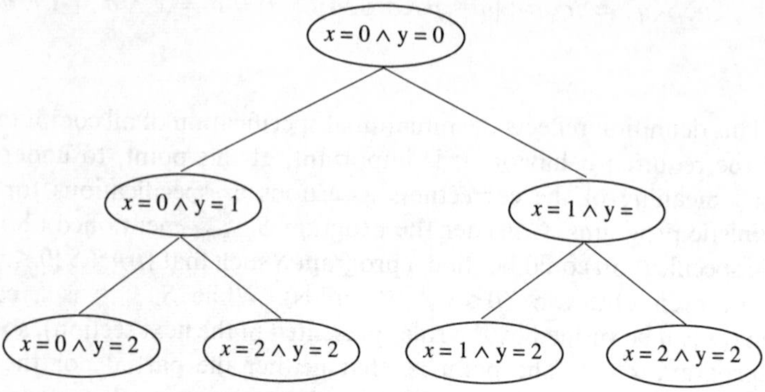

Figure 5.1 The tree $\mathbf{T}_{S_{b\_choice}}$.

of *GC*, namely its **bounded nondeterminism**, which is lost once a fair semantics is imposed in the sequel. This property has a crucial influence on the kind of well-founded sets needed for termination proofs.

Theorem (bounded nondeterminism):

> For every program $S \in GC$ and initial state σ, either $\mathbf{M}[\![S]\!](\sigma)$ is finite, or $\bot \in \mathbf{M}[\![S]\!](\sigma)$.

Proof: Consider the tree $T_{S,\sigma}$ which, as mentioned before, is infinite if and only if $\mathbf{M}[\![S]\!](\sigma)$ is infinite. If it is infinite, then, since it is finitely branching, it has an infinite path by König's lemma. This path is an infinite computation of S on σ. Hence, $\bot \in \mathbf{M}[\![S]\!](\sigma)$.

□

As a consequence, it is impossible to present a terminating *GC* program that chooses an arbitrary natural number such that every natural number is a possible outcome for it. As we see later in this chapter, such a program can be presented under fairness assumptions.

5.3 A deductive system D for partial correctness

In this section we introduce a compositional deductive system **D** for proving partial correctness assertions for nondeterministic *GC* programs. We retain from the system **H** the axioms for assignments and *skip*, the rule for sequential composition, as well as the language-independent consequence rule. We eliminate the rules for conditional branching and repetition from system **H**, replacing them by rules for their nondeterministic counterparts.

Nondeterministic selection rule:

$$\frac{p \Rightarrow \bigvee_{i\in\Delta} B_i,\ \{p \wedge B_i\}\, S_i\, \{q\},\ i\in\Delta}{\{p\}\,[\, \underset{i\in\Delta}{[]}\ B_i \rightarrow S_i]\,\{q\}} \qquad \text{(SEL)}$$

The first premiss of the rule ensures that no failure occurs. The second premiss reflects the requirement that all directions should lead to a correct outcome, all satisfying the required postcondition. For each direction, the enabledness condition for that direction is added to the precondition. Thus, we obtain the natural generalization of the (COND) rule of the **H** system.

□

Nondeterministic repetition rule:

$$\frac{\{p \wedge B_i\}\, S_i\, \{p\},\ i\in\Delta}{\{p\}\ {*}[\, \underset{i\in\Delta}{[]}\ B_i \rightarrow S_i]\,\{p \wedge \bigwedge_{i\in\Delta} \neg B_i\}} \qquad \text{(ND} - \text{REP)}$$

This characterization of a nondeterministic repetition is again the natural generalization of its deterministic counterpart. A loop invariant is introduced, preserved by every possible direction within the body of the loop. Upon termination all guards are false.

□

EXERCISE:

What is the meaning of this rule in case all guards are identically false?

□

Following is an example of a proof in **D.**

EXAMPLE:

We show that $Tr_{\mathbf{I}_0} \vdash_{\mathbf{D}} \{x \geqslant 1\}\, S_{div}\, \{y|x\}$, for S_{div} as shown in Figure 5.2. Here $x|y$ is the divisibility predicate, holding when (the natural number) y is divisible by (the natural number) x.

(1) $\{x \geqslant 1\}\, z := 1\, \{1 \leqslant z \leqslant x\}$ (ASS),(CONS)
(2) $\{1 \leqslant z \leqslant x\}\, y := 1\, \{1 \leqslant z \leqslant x \wedge y|x\}$ (ASS),(CONS)
(3) $\{x \geqslant 1\}\, z := 1; y := 1\, \{1 \leqslant z \leqslant x \wedge y|x\}$ (1),(2),(SEQ)
(4) $\{1 \leqslant z \leqslant x \wedge z|x \wedge y|x\}\ y := z\, \{1 \leqslant z \leqslant x \wedge y|x\}$ (ASS),(CONS)
(5) $\{1 \leqslant z \leqslant x \wedge z|x \wedge y|x\}\ \mathit{skip}\ \{1 \leqslant z \leqslant x \wedge y|x\}$ (SKIP),(CONS)

$$S_{div} :: z := 1;\ y := 1;$$
$$*[z < x \rightarrow z := z+1;\ [z|x \rightarrow [true \rightarrow y := z \,[]\, true \rightarrow skip] \,[]\, \neg z|x \rightarrow skip]].$$

Figure 5.2 A nondeterministic program for an arbitrary divisor.

(6) $1 \leqslant z \leqslant x \wedge z|x \wedge y|x \Rightarrow true$ (LOGIC)

(7) $\{1 \leqslant z \leqslant x \wedge z|x \wedge y|x\}$
$[true \rightarrow y := z \,[]\, true \rightarrow skip]$ (4),(5),(6),(SEL),(CONS)
$\{1 \leqslant z \leqslant x \wedge y|x\}$

(8) $\{1 \leqslant z \leqslant x \wedge \neg z|x \wedge y|x\}\, skip\, \{1 \leqslant z \leqslant x \wedge y|x\}$ (SKIP),(CONS)

(9) $1 \leqslant z \leqslant x \wedge y|x \Rightarrow z|x \vee \neg z|x$ (LOGIC)

(10) $\{1 \leqslant z \leqslant x \wedge y|x\}$ (7),(8),(9),(SEL),(CONS)
$[z|x \rightarrow [true \rightarrow y := z \,[]\, true \rightarrow skip]$
$[]$
$\neg z|x \rightarrow skip]$
$\{1 \leqslant z \leqslant x \wedge y|x\}$

(11) $\{1 \leqslant z \leqslant x \wedge z < x \wedge y|x\}\ z := z+1 \{1 \leqslant z \leqslant x \wedge y|x\}$
(ASS),(CONS)

(12) $\{1 \leqslant z \leqslant x \wedge z < x \wedge y|x\}$ (10),(11),(SEQ)
$z := z+1;[z|x \rightarrow [true \rightarrow y := z \,[]\, true \rightarrow skip]$
$[]$
$\neg z|x \rightarrow skip]$
$\{1 \leqslant z \leqslant x \wedge y|x\}$

(13) $\{1 \leqslant z \leqslant x \wedge y|x\}$
$*[z < x \rightarrow z := z+1;[z|x \rightarrow [true \rightarrow y := z \,[]\, true \rightarrow skip]$
$[]$ (12),(ND–REP),(CONS)
$\neg z \rightarrow x \rightarrow skip]]$
$\{y|x\}$

(14) $\{x \geqslant 1\} S_{div} \{y|x\}$ (3),(13),(SEQ),(CONS)

□

EXERCISES:

(1) In the above proof, where exactly has $x|x$ been used?

(2) Is the program S_{div} correct under the same postcondition and the precondition $x \geqslant 0$? If so, prove the correctness under your modified specification.

(3) Replace S_{div} by another divisor program, which halts as soon as some (nondeterministically chosen) divisor y of x is obtained (without necessarily always testing the whole interval $[1 \ldots x]$). Verify your solution.

□

5.3.1 Soundness and relative completeness of D

In this subsection we show the total soundness of the system **D** and its relative completeness. The presentation is a natural generalization of the deterministic case.

Theorem (total soundness of D):

For every interpretation **I**

if $Tr_{\mathbf{I}} \vdash_{\mathbf{D}} \{p\}\ S\ \{q\}$, then $\models_{\mathbf{I}} \{p\}\ S\ \{q\}$

Proof: The structure of the proof is by induction on the length of the formal proof of the partial correctness assertion. The only difference from the soundness proof for the nondeterministic case is that the inductive argument in the cases of (SEL) and (ND-REP) is based on the nondeterministic computations lemma.

□

We now turn to the issue of relative completeness.

Theorem (relative completeness of D):

D is relative complete.

Proof: Let SL be such that it is expressive w.r.t. **I** and GC. We again consider all the possibilities for S. The only different case is for the nondeterministic repetition. This time, the sequence of predicates p_i, $i \geqslant 0$, is defined so as to take care of the fact that at each traversal, several directions may be possible. We get

$$p_0 \overset{df.}{=} r,\ p_{i+1} \overset{df.}{=} \bigvee_{j \in \Delta} post_{\mathbf{I}}(p_i \wedge B_j, S_j)$$

Again, an easy inductive argument shows that p_i characterizes the states reachable from r by up to i iterations of the body (in all possible ways). The encoding program becomes (with m the length of $\bar{z}$):

$$S^* :: *[\underset{j \in \Delta}{\square}\ B_j \wedge \bigvee_{k=1,\,m} y_k \neq z_k \rightarrow S_j]$$

Once again, $p^* \overset{df.}{=} post_{\mathbf{I}}\ (r, S^*)$, with $p \overset{df.}{=} \exists \bar{z} : p^*$ being the finite representation of the loop invariant. It is expressible by the expressiveness assumption. The rest of the argument is similar to the deterministic case.

□

5.4 A deductive system D* for total correctness

In this section we extend the compositional approach and introduce a deductive system **D*** for proving total correctness assertions $\langle p\rangle\ S\ \langle q\rangle$ for nondeterministic *GC* programs. Again, the presentation follows closely the deterministic case. From the definition of '$\rightarrow$' it is again clear that the only source for nontermination is the nondeterministic repetition statement $*[\underset{i\in\Delta}{[]}\ B_i \rightarrow S_i]$, so again the only change needed is in the corresponding derivation rule. For all other rules, we just modify $\{\cdots\}$ to $\langle\cdots\rangle$ throughout all correctness assertions. We again want to use the idea of a decreasing well-founded variant, and we again use a parametrized loop invariant (still canonically with natural numbers). Anticipating the forthcoming discussion, we choose a slightly different format of presenting the rule, with mnemonic names for its various clauses.

Let m be a fresh variable, not appearing free in S, ranging over natural numbers.

Nondeterministic-repetition rule:

$$INIT: p \Rightarrow \exists m : pi(m)$$

$$CONT: pi(m+1) \Rightarrow \bigvee_{i\in\Delta} B_i$$

$$DEC: \langle pi(m) \wedge m > 0 \wedge B_i\rangle\ S_i\ \langle \exists k : k < m \wedge pi(k)\rangle, i\in\Delta$$

$$TERM: \frac{pi(0) \Rightarrow \bigwedge_{i\in\Delta} \neg B_i}{\langle p\rangle\ *[\underset{i\in\Delta}{[]}\ B_i \rightarrow S_i]\ \langle pi(0)\rangle} \qquad \text{(ND–REP*)}$$

Note that in clause *DEC k*, the smaller value with which the invariant $pi(m)$ is re-established after the execution of S_i, may depend on the chosen direction i. The idea behind the rule is the expected one, a decrement of the well-founded variant along every enabled direction . However, there need not exist a uniform decrement for all enabled directions. In particular, it is not necessary to have uniformly $k = m-1$.

□

EXAMPLE:

As an example proof in **D***, consider proving termination of the following version of the bounded-choice program $S_{b\_choice'}$ (in Figure 5.3). We want to establish $\langle N>0\rangle S_{b\_choice'}\langle true\rangle$.

$$S_{b\_choice'} :: *[goon \wedge x<N \rightarrow x:=x+1\ []\ goon \rightarrow goon:=ff].$$

Figure 5.3 $S_{b\_choice'}$.

As the parametrized invariant we choose

$$pi(x, goon, n) \overset{df.}{=} N>0 \wedge \textit{if } goon \wedge x<N \textit{ then } n = N-x+1$$
$$\textit{else if } goon \wedge x \geqslant N \textit{ then } n = 1$$
$$\textit{else } n = 0.$$

(1) $N>0 \Rightarrow \exists n{:}[N>0 \wedge [\textit{ if } goon \wedge x<N \textit{ then } n = N-x+1$
$\textit{else if } goon \wedge x \geqslant N \textit{ then } n = 1$
$\textit{else } n = 0]].$

(ARITHMETIC)

Here, if $goon = f\!f$ we may take $n = 0$. If $goon = tt \wedge x \geqslant N$ we take $n = 1$; otherwise, we take $n = N-x+1$, with the initial value of x.

(2) $N>0 \wedge [\textit{if } goon \wedge x<N \textit{ then } n = N-x+1$
$\textit{else if } goon \wedge x \geqslant N \textit{ then } n = 1$
$\textit{else } n = 0] \wedge n>0 \Rightarrow goon = tt.$

(ARITHMETIC)

(3) $\langle N>0 \wedge [\textit{if } goon \wedge x<N \textit{ then } n = N-x+1$
$\textit{else if } goon \wedge x \geqslant N \textit{ then } n = 1$
$\textit{else } n = 0] \wedge n>0\rangle$

$x := x+1$
$\langle N>0 \wedge \exists m{:}\ [m<n \wedge [\textit{if } goon \wedge x<N \textit{ then } m = N-x+1$
$\textit{else if } goon \wedge x \geqslant N \textit{ then } m=1$
$\textit{else } m=0]]\rangle.$

(2),(ASS),(CONS)

Here we can take $m = n-1$.

(4) $\langle N>0 \wedge [\textit{if } goon \wedge x<N \textit{ then } n = N-x+1$
$\textit{else if } goon \wedge x \geqslant N \textit{ then } n=1$
$\textit{else } n = 0] \wedge n>0\rangle$

$goon := f\!f$
$\langle N>0 \wedge \exists m{:}\ [[m<n \wedge \textit{if } goon \wedge x<N \textit{ then } m = N-x+1$
$\textit{else if } x \geqslant N \textit{ then } m = 1$
$\textit{else } m = 0]]\rangle.$

(ASS),(CONS)

Here we always take $m = 0$.

(5) $N>0 \wedge [\textit{if } goon \wedge x<N \textit{ then } n = N-x+1$
$\textit{else if } goon \wedge x \geqslant N \textit{ then } n = 1$
$\textit{else } n = 0] \wedge n = 0 \Rightarrow goon = f\!f.$

(ARITHMETIC)

(6) $\langle N>0\rangle S_{b\_choice'}\langle true\rangle$ (1),(2),(3),(4),(5),(ND-REP*)(CONS)

Note that in (3) and (4) the decrement of the well-founded variant is different, depending on the direction taken.

□

5.4.1 Arithmetical soundness and completeness of D*

In this subsection we consider arithmetical soundness and completeness for the system **D***. The problem is again the explicit reference to a variable ranging over natural numbers, which need not be in the given domain of computation. The solution is a natural generalization of the one for the deterministic case.

Theorem (arithmetical soundness of D*):

D* is arithmetically sound.

Proof: This is similar to the case of **H*** and omitted.

□

Theorem (arithmetical completeness of D*):

D* is arithmetically complete.

Proof: The proof generalizes the construction of the proof of arithmetical completeness in the deterministic case to the nondeterministic case, making a very essential use of the bounded nondeterminism theorem. Suppose that $\models_{I^+}\langle p\rangle *[\underset{i\in\Delta}{\square}\ B_i \rightarrow S_i]\ \langle true\rangle$ holds. What we need to show is how to construct a parametrized invariant $pi(\bar{x},\ m)$ (abbreviated $pi(m)$), to enable the application of the rule (ND-REP*). This time, we are interested in the relation

$$R(\sigma, k) \overset{df.}{=} \models_{I^+}\mathsf{N}(k) \wedge \exists k' \leqslant k \exists \sigma_0, \ldots, \exists \sigma_{k'}:$$
$$[\sigma = \sigma_0 \wedge \sigma_{k'} \models_{I^+} \bigwedge_{j\in\Delta} \neg B_j \wedge \bigwedge_{0\leqslant i<k'} (\bigvee_{j\in\Delta} (\sigma_{i+1} = \mathbf{M}[\![S_j]\!](\sigma_i) \wedge \sigma_i \models_{I^+} B_j))]$$

This relation relates (initial) states to the maximal possible number of iterations of the loop (in all possible directions) when started in them. The existence of such k follows from the bounded nondeterminism theorem, and is the length of the longest path in $T_{S,\sigma}$. It can be shown again that by using the coding property a formula $pi(m)$ expressing this relation in SL^+ can be constructed and that it satisfies the required premisses. The argument is similar to the deterministic case.

□

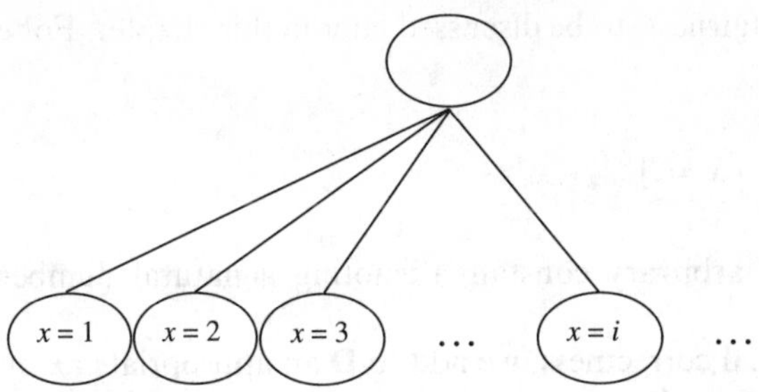

Figure 5.4 $T_{x:=?,\sigma}$.

5.5 Random assignments

In this section we consider the other form of nondeterminism mentioned in the introduction of this chapter, namely that of **data selection.** This type of nondeterminism is also of the 'don't care' kind, similarly to the control-driven nondeterminism present in *GC*. We add the following clause to the definition of the syntax of *GC* to obtain that of GC_R:

$$S :: \cdots \mid x := ?$$

The semantics of the **random assignment** statement $x := ?$ is defined by adding a corresponding additional clause to the definition of '$\rightarrow$' in the semantics of *GC* (Section 5.2). This clause is

$$\langle x := ?, \sigma \rangle \rightarrow \langle E, \sigma[n \mid x] \rangle, \; n \in \mathbf{N}$$

In other words, when executed in a configuration with state σ, the random assignment produces (in finite time) any variant of σ out of the set $\{\sigma[n \mid x] \mid n \in \mathbf{N}\}$ (that is, it assigns to x an arbitrary natural number). A better name for this construct would be **nondeterministic assignment**, since it is devoid of any probabilistic connotation, usually attributed to randomness.

Clearly, by the introduction of this primitive into the programming language, GC_R does not satisfy the bounded nondeterminism theorem of Section 5.2. In contrast to the rest of the language, which is uninterpreted, random assignments in this context are interpreted, using natural numbers. This is a very strong primitive. In terms of computation trees, it produces a countably branching tree $T_{x:=?,\sigma}$ (see Figure 5.4), indicating a connection with fairness, having a similar property. Taking such a primitive always to terminate transcends the effective semantics of *GC*.

Note that here also nothing is assumed about the outcomes of a repeated selection by means of a repeated execution of a random assignment. In particular, the usual partial correctness and total correctness specifications do not imply that any particular natural number will eventually be selected in an infinite repetition of random assignments. Such an assumption has the same power as fairness, to be discussed later in this chapter. For example, the program

$$*[x \neq n_0 \rightarrow x := ?]$$

where n_0 is an arbitrary constant (denoting a natural number), need not terminate.

For partial correctness, we add to **D** an appropriate axiom to capture the semantics of random assignments:

$$\{\forall x : p\}\ x := ?\ \{p\} \qquad \text{(RAND)}$$

This axiom reflects the semantic fact that an arbitrary value is assigned to x. Thus, in order for $p(x)$ to hold after the assignment, it should be the case that every value of x satisfies p prior to the assignment.

EXERCISE:

Under what condition about p is the following axiom an equivalent alternative to (RAND)?

$$\{p\}\ x := ?\ \{p\} \qquad \text{(RAND')}$$

□

We need to modify the proof rule (ND-REP*) for proving the termination of iterative statements in GC_R, since it is no longer always applicable with natural numbers. The (countable) ordinals are needed, because of the presence of random assignments, which share with fairness the effect of preventing *a priori* bounds on the computation length. We preserve the same name for the extended rule. Actual examples may use arbitrary (countable) well-founded sets. The new form of the rule is now given.

Nondeterministic repetition rule:

$$INIT: p \Rightarrow \exists \alpha : pi(\alpha)$$

$$CONT: pi(\alpha) \wedge \alpha > 0 \Rightarrow \bigvee_{i \in \Delta} B_i$$

$$DEC: \langle pi(\alpha) \wedge \alpha > 0 \wedge B_i \rangle\ S_i\ \langle \exists \beta : \beta < \alpha \wedge pi(\beta) \rangle, i \in \Delta \qquad \text{(ND-REP*)}$$

$$TERM: \frac{pi(0) \Rightarrow \bigwedge_{i \in \Delta} \neg B_i}{\langle p \rangle\ *[\underset{i \in \Delta}{[]}\ B_i \rightarrow S_i]\ \langle pi(0) \rangle}$$

□

EXAMPLE:

Following is an example termination proof using the extended version of the (ND-REP*) rule with a countable ordinal. We show $Tr_{I_0} \vdash_{D^*} \langle y \geqslant 0 \rangle\ S\ \langle y = 0 \rangle$, where

$$
\begin{aligned}
S{::}\ {*}[&x = 0 \wedge y > 0 \rightarrow y := ?; x := 1\\
&\square\\
&x \neq 0 \wedge y > 0 \rightarrow y := y - 1\\
&]
\end{aligned}
$$

As the parametrized invariant we choose

$$pi(\alpha) \overset{df.}{\equiv} (x = 0 \Rightarrow \alpha = \omega) \wedge (x \neq 0 \Rightarrow \alpha = y \geqslant 0)$$

(Recall that ω denotes the first infinite ordinal.) We now show satisfaction of all clauses of (ND-REP*).

INIT: We have to show $y \geqslant 0 \Rightarrow \exists \alpha \colon pi(\alpha)$. We take $\alpha = \omega$ in case the initial value of x is 0, and we take α equal to the initial value of y otherwise.

CONT: Immediate.

DEC: We consider each direction separately. For the first direction, we have to show

$$\langle pi(\alpha) \wedge \alpha > 0 \wedge x = 0 \rangle\ y := ?; x := 1\ \langle \exists \beta \colon \beta < \alpha \wedge pi(\beta) \rangle$$

The precondition implies $\alpha = \omega$. We thus may choose $\beta = y$ to satisfy the postcondition. Note that actually a use of (RAND) with $\forall y \exists \beta \colon \beta < \alpha \wedge pi(\beta)^x_1$ and the consequence rule are involved in this step of the proof. For the second direction the reasoning is even simpler, since $y - 1 < y$.

TERM: Immediate.

□

EXERCISE:

In the above example, can we replace the precondition by *true* and preserve the postcondition?

□

It is not hard to realize that restricting (ND-REP*) to natural-number valued parameters is not powerful enough for this example. Suppose that such $pi(k)$ could be found, satisfying all the required clauses. In this case, if $\sigma_0 \models pi(k)$, then clearly the number of iterations of the body of S when started in the initial state σ_0 is at most k. However, no such bound exists for $\sigma_0 \models x = 0$, a contradiction.

Soundness of the modified rule (for a language containing variables ranging over ordinals) is proved similarly to the previous proof for *GC*. The (semantic) completeness proof is somewhat more complicated and is presented below.

Theorem:

The augmented version of (ND-REP*) is semantically complete.

Proof: Suppose that $\models \langle p \rangle\ S\ \langle true \rangle$ holds, for S a typical GC_R nondeterministic repetition. Let $\sigma_0 \models p$ and consider the (possibly countably branching) tree T_{S,σ_0}. By the assumption, this tree is well-founded, that is it has no infinite paths. We apply to this tree a standard ranking by ordinals. First, all leaves are ranked 0. Each other node is ranked with the least upper bound of the successors of the ranks of all its immediate descendant nodes. Let α be the rank of the root. We now may define the parametrized invariant based on this ranking. We define $pi(\sigma, \beta)$ to hold iff there exists a node labeled σ which is ranked by β.

□

EXERCISE:

The above construction depends on the initial state σ_0. Extend it to depend only on the precondition p.

□

EXERCISE:

Show that the parametrized invariant as constructed above satisfies all the clauses of the extended (ND-REP*) rule.

□

5.6 Proving fair termination

5.6.1 Introduction to fair termination

In this section we consider a fair semantics for *GC* and extend the use of a decreasing well-founded variant to prove fair termination of *GC* programs. Intuitively, fairness w.r.t. the directions of a nondeterministic repetition means that, in a sequence of repeated nondeterministic choices, no direction that could be selected sufficiently often is indefinitely postponed. We shall

S_{ub_choice}:: $x := 0$; $b :=$ *true*
$*[1: b \rightarrow x := x+1$
$[]$
$2: b \rightarrow b :=$ *false*
].

Figure 5.5 Example – random (natural) number generator.

make this more precise and define exactly the fair semantics. The definition has the form of a global restriction imposed on the collection (or tree) of all the infinite computation sequences generated by the standard *GC* semantics presented before. There is no effective way of producing a direct operational semantics in the *sos* format that would generate all and only fair computations. We consider here one type of fairness only. Other types are considered in exercises and references are given in the suggestions for further reading.

In order to simplify the presentation we confine our attention to what we hereafter refer to as **flat** nondeterministic selection statements. A typical flat nondeterministic selection statement has the form $*[\underset{i \in \Delta}{[]} B_i \rightarrow S_i]$, where S_i has no nested repetition statements in it; it may have nested nondeterministic selections, though. Until the end of this chapter, all references to typical repetitions are assumed to be flat ones. We shall mainly be interested in **fair termination** (*FT*) of nondeterministic programs, that is termination under fairness assumptions.

Before embarking on the details of proofs, following is an example of a fairly terminating program and an example of a non-fairly terminating program.

EXAMPLE:

Consider the program S_{ub_choice} for a random generator of natural numbers (in Figure 5.5). This is a nonterminating program. It has only one infinite computation sequence, namely $(1)^\omega$, increasing x forever. The tree $T_{S_{ub\_choice,\sigma}}$ (for an arbitrary σ) is shown in Figure 5.6. Obviously, this computation is not fair, since direction 2 is always enabled but never taken. Any attempt to execute direction 2 sets b to *ff* and the program terminates. Hence this program is *FT*.

□

EXAMPLE:

The program P in Figure 5.7 is not *FT* for any state σ s.t. $\sigma[\![x]\!] > 0$. For example, the infinite sequence $(1, 2)^\omega$ is a possible infinite fair computation of P for such a state.

□

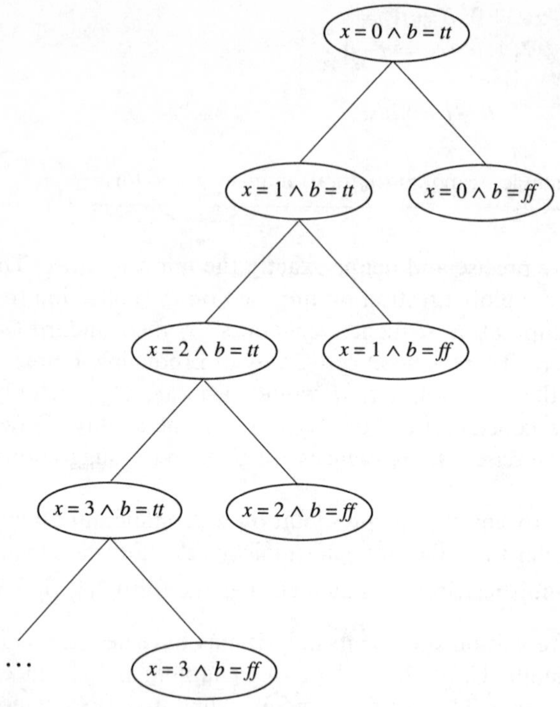

Figure 5.6 The tree $T_{S_{ub\_choice,\sigma}}$.

```
P:: *[1:x>0 → x:=x+1
     []
     2:x>0 → x:=x−1
     ].
```

Figure 5.7 A non-fairly terminating program.

Recall that the basic proof principle behind the rule (ND−REP*) requires a decrease of a well-founded variant along every enabled direction. We replace this strict-decreasing requirement with the following intuitive alternative: at each intermediate stage of execution (of a typical non-deterministic repetition), choose a (non-empty) subset of all the directions (called **helpful directions**) such that

(1) whenever a helpful direction is taken, the well-founded variant decreases, and

(2) fairness forces helpful directions to be chosen eventually.

Thus, along an infinite fair computation helpful directions must be repeatedly chosen, which would imply an infinite decreasing sequence of ranks, contradicting well-foundedness. What we are doing can be interpreted as follows: we are relativizing the notion of termination by making certain infinite sequences of the standard semantics as 'not counting' and showing that all others, that do count, are finite. Had we a semantics which generates only fair computations, then such a program would be properly terminating.

There are two natural ways of choosing the helpful directions at intermediate stages.

(1) Basing the selection upon the rank, measuring some abstract 'distance' from termination. Each rank has its own set of helpful directions.

(2) Basing the selection upon state predicates, each such predicate determining directions which are helpful when it holds on a given state.

We present both methods and leave the mutual reduction among them as an exercise.

In Section 5.6.3 another solution to the same problem, based on a different intuition, is presented. There, the idea is to augment the program with a section that can be considered as a **scheduler** that ensures fairness, built using the previously considered random assignment primitive. Then, a proof rule is obtained by reducing the fair termination of the original program to ordinary termination of the augmented (transformed) program.

In order to define the fair semantics of GC, we proceed in two stages: first, the '$\rightarrow$' transitions are used, as defined before; then, a global condition is imposed, excluding all computations not satisfying it as unfair. We freely identify computations with paths in $T_{S,\sigma}$.

Definition: For a typical nondeterministic repetition

$$S{::}\ *[\mathop{[]}_{i\in\Delta} B_i \rightarrow S_i] \in GC$$

and an infinite computation $\pi \in T_{S,\sigma}$ (for any initial state σ), π is **strongly fair,** iff every direction infinitely often enabled along π is executed infinitely often along π. A **finite** path is always fair.

□

Consequently, a path π is **unfair** iff there is a direction $i_0 \in \Delta$ that is infinitely often enabled along π but taken only finitely many times. Such a π contains a suffix along which direction i_0 is infinitely often enabled but never taken. We say that π is i_0**-unfair.** Note that this definition has a strong syntactic flavor in that fairness is confined to direction selections at a given syntactic location of the program. In the discussion, we often describe a path by a word over the finite alphabet Δ, being an infinite word for an infinite computation. Since no other form of fairness is considered here, we abbreviate strong fairness to fairness.

To prove $\ll p \gg S:: *[\ \underset{i\in\Delta}{[]}\ B_i \rightarrow S_i] \ll q \gg$:

Choose a well-founded, partially ordered set $(W, <)$, a **parametrized invariant** $pi(w)$, $w \in W$ and, for each $w \in W$, $w > 0$, a partition of Δ into $\Delta^d_w \cup \Delta^s_w$ with $\Delta^d_w \neq \emptyset$, all satisfying the following:

(1) (INIT) $p \Rightarrow \exists w: pi(w)$.

(2) (CONT) $(pi(w) \wedge w>0) \Rightarrow \bigvee_{i\in\Delta} B_i$.

(3) (TERM) $pi(0) \Rightarrow \bigwedge_{i\in\Delta} \neg B_i \wedge q$.

(4) (DEC) $\ll pi(w) \wedge w>0 \wedge B_j \gg S_j \ll \exists v: v<w \wedge pi(v) \gg$, for all $j \in \Delta^d_w$.

(5) (NOINC) $\ll pi(w) \wedge w>0 \wedge B_i \gg S_i \ll \exists v: v \leqslant w \wedge pi(v) \gg$, for all $i \in \Delta^s_w$.

(6) (IOE) $\ll pi(w) \wedge w>0 \gg \bar{S}_w:: *[\ \underset{j\in\Delta^s_w}{[]}\ (B_j \wedge \neg \bigvee_{k\in\Delta^d_w} B_k) \rightarrow S_j] \ll true \gg$.

Figure 5.8 Rule **FT** (fair termination).

We now can define the fair semantics meaning function $\mathbf{M}^{\mathrm{f}}$. The only difference is in the condition for the inclusion of $\perp$. We define $\perp \in \mathbf{M}^{\mathrm{f}}[\![S]\!](\sigma)$ iff S has an infinite fair computation on σ.

Our aim is to suggest methods for proving that a given flat nondeterministic repetition S does not have infinite fair paths.

Definition: A typical nondeterministic repetition $S \in GC$ is *FT* iff for every state σ, $\perp \notin \mathbf{M}^{\mathrm{f}}[\![S]\!](\sigma)$. In other words, S terminates fairly iff all fair paths of $T_{S,\sigma}$ are finite.

□

Note that the tree $T_{S,\sigma}$ can be infinite, having infinite unfair paths. The relativization to states satisfying a precondition is as usual.

We use the notation $\ll p \gg\ S \ll true \gg$ to denote the fair termination of S under a precondition p, and $\ll p \gg\ S \ll q \gg$ to denote the fair total correctness of S w.r.t. $\langle p, q \rangle$.

As before, we have the following lemma, separating the concerns of partial correctness (properties of the final state) from termination. The former does not depend on the fairness assumption.

Lemma (fairness separation):

For every typical nondeterministic repetition $S \in GC$, specification $\langle p, q \rangle$, and interpretation $\mathbf{I}$,

$$\models_{\mathbf{I}} \ll p \gg S \ll q \gg \text{ iff } \models_{\mathbf{I}} \{p\}\, S\, \{q\} \text{ and } \models_{\mathbf{I}} \ll p \gg S \ll true \gg$$

□

EXERCISE:

Prove the lemma.

□

For later use we need the following definition.

Definition: A computation path $\pi \in T_{S,\sigma}$ is ***i*-avoiding** if it contains no occurrences of direction $i \in \Delta$.

□

5.6.2 The helpful directions method

A. Ordinal directed helpful directions

In this subsection we present one variant of the helpful directions proof method for proving fair termination of *GC* programs. Linking the discussion to the example in the previous subsection, we first present the intuition behind the method as applied to that example, and then generalize it to a rule.

EXAMPLE:

Consider again the example program S_{ub_choice} (Figure 5.5) for a random generator of natural numbers. At every intermediate stage of the computation, we can divide the directions into two kinds. When direction 1 is executed, clearly no progress is made towards termination, as it can be repeated indefinitely. On the other hand, any attempt to execute direction 2 sets *b* to *ff* and the program terminates. In this sense, direction 2 is 'helpful'. Note that direction 2 remains enabled throughout the computation.

□

This is the intuition behind the suggested proof rule for the general case: at any stage, let us choose the directions along which a certain well-founded variant decreases; let the other directions be nonincreasing w.r.t. that variant. If a helpful direction is infinitely often enabled, then, by the fairness assumption, eventually a decreasing direction has to be executed. Thus, all fair computation sequences are guaranteed to be finite. We generalize this reasoning to the following rule, **FT** (see Figure 5.8). In this subsection we are again concerned with a semantic proof principle. References to a discussion of syntactic expressibility are presented at the end of the chapter.

In the formulation, we leave out all state arguments, which are implicit. In this rule, Δ_w^d stands for **decreasing** at 'distance' w, while Δ_w^s stands for **steady** (or, non-decreasing at 'distance' w).

Explanation:

(1)–(3) These clauses ensure that the parametrized invariant is established initially and that the program terminates only when reaching a minimal element of $(W, <)$, denoted generically by 0.

(4) This clause ensures that along every direction in Δ_w^d, if it is taken, there is a decrease of the well-founded variant. Note that at least one decreasing direction is required.

(5) This clause guarantees that along every direction in Δ_w^s, if it is taken, there is no increase of the well-founded variant. Thus, an infinite computation, proceeding along Δ_w^s directions only, and not decreasing, is possible. Such a sequence, however, should be unfair. To this end we have the next clause.

(6) The role of this clause is to establish an eventual enabledness of some decreasing direction in Δ_w^d, as long as $pi(w)$ holds (for $w>0$). This ensures infinitely often enabledness of such a direction, or a decrease in $pi(w)$. It imposes a recursive application of the rule to an auxiliary program $\bar{S}_w$ (called also the **derived program**). By convention, $\bar{S}_w = skip$ if $\Delta_w^s = \emptyset$. Its termination can be proved using $W = \{0\}$, a trivial boundary case. The derived program $\bar{S}_w$ fairly terminates (where fairness is with respect to its own directions) because of one of two reasons:

(a) $\bigwedge_{j \in \Delta_w^s} \neg B_j$ is true, hence no Δ_w^s-move is possible and (possibly) only Δ_w^d-moves are left.

(b) For some $k \in \Delta_w^d$, B_k is true, that is a Δ_w^d -move is enabled. Hence, this clause guarantees that along infinite Δ_w^s -computations, Δ_w^d -moves are infinitely often enabled, that is, such computations are unfair.

Note that the derived program has fewer directions than the original one. This is why the proof itself terminates, not entering an infinite sequence of recursive applications of the rule.

Actually, the use of the derived program is a 'coding trick' by means of which the eventual occurrence (of a condition) in one program is reduced to termination of another program. We appeal to it in order to remain strictly within the framework of termination. Furthermore, its use depends on some 'closure properties' of the underlying programming language (*GC* in our case), allowing the expression of the derived program.

Remarks:

(1) If we take $\Delta_w^s = \emptyset$ (and hence $\Delta_w^d = \Delta$) for all $w \in W$, $w>0$, the rule reduces to the nondeterministic termination rule (ND-REP*).

```
E:: b:=true;x:=0;
    *[  1:b→x:=x+1
        ▯
        2:b ∧ even(x)→b:=false
        ].
```

Figure 5.9 Program E – intermittent enabledness of the helpful direction.

(2) In proving clauses (4)–(6) of the rule, application of the rest of the partial correctness rules in **D** is allowed.

(3) In clauses (4) and (5) we could as well appeal to the partial correctness counterparts of the stated assertions, as a result of the flatness assumption.

We now present a proof for $Tr_{I_0} \vdash_{FT} \ll true \gg U \ll b \gg$, where U is the repetition in the body of S_{ub_choice}. Choose as the well-founded set $W = \{0,1\}$ with $0 < 1$, $\Delta_1^S = \{1\}$, $\Delta_1^d = \{2\}$, and as the parametrized invariant

$$pi(x, b, w) \overset{df.}{=} (w = 1 \Rightarrow b) \wedge (w = 0 \Rightarrow \neg b)$$

We now check that all clauses of the proof rule are satisfied.

(INIT): Since $b = true$ holds initially for U, take $w = 1$ to establish pi.

(CONT),(TERM): Immediate.

(DEC): When direction 2 is executed, b changes from *true* to *false* and hence w drops from 1 to 0.

(NOINC): b remains *true* under direction 1: $x := x + 1$, and $pi(w)$ is independent of x, so pi stays true with $w = 1$.

(IOE): Trivial. The derived program has one direction only, with a guard $b \wedge \neg b$, vacuously terminating.

EXAMPLE:

The previous example does not take advantage of the function of a derived program. We consider a slightly more complicated program E (see Figure 5.9), where the helpful direction is only intermittently enabled. We prove $Tr_{I_0} \vdash_{FT} \ll b \gg E' \ll true \gg$, where E' is the repetition in E's body. Choose W, pi, Δ_1^s, Δ_1^d, as for the previous random natural number generator example. As for clause (IOE), the derived program is

$$\bar{E}_1 :: *[b \wedge \neg(b \wedge even(x)) \rightarrow x := x + 1]$$

$$
\begin{aligned}
S_{fair\_rand}:: *[&1: x=0 \rightarrow y:=y+1 \\
&\square \\
&2: x=0 \rightarrow x:=1 \\
&\square \\
&3: x>0 \wedge y>0 \rightarrow y:=y-1 \\
&].
\end{aligned}
$$

Figure 5.10 Simulating random assignment via fairness.

which is deterministic and terminates after one iteration at most. We omit details of the subproof, which reduces to use of (REP*).

□

EXAMPLE:

Consider a *GC* program (in Figure 5.10) that under the assumption of fairness simulates the GC_R program in the example in Section 5.5 (p. 117). For this program, we may use the natural numbers as the well-founded set for the establishment of $\vdash_{\mathbf{FT}} \ll x=0 \gg S_{fair\_rand} \ll true \gg$. First, we choose $W=\{0, 1, 2\}$ (ordered as usual), with the parametrized invariant as follows.

$$
\begin{aligned}
pi(x, y, w) \stackrel{df.}{=} &(w=2 \Rightarrow x=0 \wedge y \geqslant 0) \\
&(w=1 \Rightarrow x>0 \wedge y>0) \\
&(w=0 \Rightarrow x>0 \wedge y=0).
\end{aligned}
$$

As the helpful directions we take $\Delta_2^d = \Delta_1^d \stackrel{df.}{=} \{2\}$. Clause (IOE) for $w=2$ is immediate, yielding one identically false guard. To show (IOE) for $w=1$, we take $W=\mathbf{N}$ (the natural numbers), this time with the simple parametrized invariant $y=n$. The situation may be contrasted with the corresponding random-assignment program, where ω was needed. The helpful-directions method introduces a kind of separation of concerns, where the first two alternatives, simulating $y:=?$, are seen as a 'layer', and a simple well-founded set is used to show that the lower layer is reached by fairness. Then, that layer is treated separately as a deterministic program, using **N**. In particular, note that Δ_1^d contains a helpful direction which is never enabled. This is because the 'lower level' terminates independently of fairness, and the nonincreasing direction is actually decreasing.

□

For more examples of fair termination proofs (including ones requiring higher ordinals), the reader is referred to the references provided by the suggestions for further reading.

B. Soundness and semantic completeness of the FT rule

In this subsection we prove soundness and semantic completeness of the **FT** proof rule. Throughout the section, all the satisfaction relations are over some interpretation **I**, not explicitly indicated.

Theorem (total soundness of rule FT):

For a typical nondeterministic repetition $S \in GC$ (recall that typical here implies also *flat*):

if $Tr_{\mathbf{I}} \vdash_{\mathbf{FT}} \ll p \gg S \ll q \gg$, then $\models_{\mathbf{I}} \ll p \gg S \ll q \gg$

Proof: Assume that $Tr_{\mathbf{I}} \vdash_{\mathbf{FT}} \ll p \gg S \ll q \gg$, that is we have a well-founded, partially ordered set $(W, <)$, a partition of Δ into Δ^s_w, $\Delta^d_w \neq \varnothing$ for each $w > 0$, and a parametrized invariant $pi(w)$ satisfying clauses (1)–(6) of the **FT** rule.

Assume, by way of contradiction, that for some state σ_0, T_{S,σ_0} contains an infinite fair path with σ_i, $i \geqslant 0$ being the state after the ith traversal of the body of S. Consider the corresponding sequence of directions d_i taken, $i \geqslant 0$. By an inductive argument (similar to the unfair case), we get a sequence of W-elements w_i, $i \geqslant 0$, such that $pi(\sigma_i, w_i), i \geqslant 0$. The sequence of directions cannot contain an infinite subsequence $d_{i_j}, j \geqslant 0$, of $\Delta^d_{w_i}$-moves, since by clause (DEC) this would imply the existence of an infinite decreasing sequence of elements in W, contradicting W's well-foundedness. Thus, from some k onwards, $pi(\sigma_k, w)$ holds for the same $w \in W$, and all moves d_j for $j > k$ are Δ^s_w-moves (by clause (NOINC)). Finally, by clause (IOE), Δ^d_w- moves are infinitely often enabled, contradicting the assumption that $\sigma_i, i \geqslant 0$, is fair.

□

Theorem (semantic completeness of rule FT):

For a typical nondeterministic repetition $S \in GC$,

if $\models_{\mathbf{I}} \ll p \gg S \ll q \gg$, then $Tr_{\mathbf{I}} \vdash_{\mathbf{FT}} \ll p \gg S \ll q \gg$

Proof: Assume that $\ll p \gg S \ll q \gg$ holds. Then we have to find a well-founded, partially ordered set $(W, <)$, partitions Δ^s_w, Δ^d_w of Δ with $\Delta^d_w \neq \varnothing$ for each $w > 0$ and a parametrized invariant $pi(w)$ (given by a collection of pairs (w, σ)) such that clauses (1)–(6) of rule **FT** hold. We have to derive everything needed from the computation trees. We are given that the computation tree T_{S,σ_0}, for every state σ_0 satisfying p, either is finite or contains at least one infinite, hence unfair, computation sequence.

The basic idea is to construct another (possibly countably branching) tree T^*_{S,σ_0}, some of whose nodes are obtained by collapsing certain infinite families of nodes in T_{S,σ_0}, all elements of unfair sequences, such that T^*_{S,σ_0} is well founded, that is contains finite paths only. Then we use the same idea as the one in the random assignment case, ranking T^*_{S,σ_0} by means of (countable) ordinals to obtain the parametrized invariant. A direction originating in state σ and remaining in the same infinite family belongs to Δ^s_w, for the corresponding rank w. A move that leaves such a family belongs to Δ^d_w. Special care must be taken that these partitions do not depend on the initial state labeling σ_0, the root of the computation tree. Rather, all the initial states satisfying the precondition should induce the same partitions, as the rule requires. We now present the details of the construction. To simplify notations, we identify a node in the tree with its label (a state).

Definition: Let $\sigma \in T_{S,\sigma_0}$ and $d \in \Delta$. Define σ's d-cone $CONE_d(\sigma)$ as follows:
$CONE_d(\sigma) = \{\sigma\} \cup$ the set of all occurrences of states in T_{S,σ_0} residing on infinite d-avoiding computation paths starting in σ.
Direction d is called the cone's **directive**, and the node labeled σ is called the cone's **root.**

□

Note that a cone is never empty, always containing its root.

Definition: $C = CONE_d(\sigma)$ is **trivial** iff $C = \{\sigma\}$.

□

A computation path is said to **leave** a d-cone $CONE_d(\sigma)$ at node $\eta \in CONE_d(\sigma)$, if the next state-occurrence of the path, following η, is outside $CONE_d(\sigma)$.

Lemma (cone exit):

Let $\sigma \in T_{S,\sigma_0}$, and let $\eta \in CONE_d(\sigma)$ for some $d \in \Delta$. Then, a computation sequence leaves $CONE_d(\sigma)$ at η if and only if it either is finite or contains a d-move.

Proof: Suppose that an infinite path π starts at η, leaves the cone and contains no d-move. Since $\eta \in CONE_d(\sigma)$, there is some finite path π' joining σ to η, along which no d-move was taken. Hence the concatenation $\pi'\pi$ is contained in $CONE_d(\sigma)$, contradicting the assumption that π leaves $CONE_d(\sigma)$ at node η.

The other direction is trivial.

□

Next we define inductively a hierarchy **A** of families of states A_i, covering T_{S,σ_0}. Here i denotes the level at which the family A_i is defined. Actually, at each such level there may be countably many such A_i. To simplify the notation we avoid the extra index distinguishing them, leaving the distinction to the context. Such a family A_i is to be contracted to a (single) node in the well-founded tree T^*_{S,σ_0}. Some A_i are nontrivial cones, while others, having no direction-avoiding infinite paths leaving them, are trivial.

Base step: We distinguish between two cases:

(1) If the initial state σ_0 is the origin of some infinite d-avoiding path, for some $d \in \Delta$, let d_0 be such a direction.

(2) Otherwise, let d_0 be any direction enabled in σ_0.

In both cases, let $A_0 = CONE_{d_0}(\sigma_0)$ be a cone at level 0, with root σ_0 and directive d_0. Note that in the second case, A_0 is a trivial cone.

Induction step: Let A_i be at level i, with root σ_i. We distinguish between the following cases.

(1) $A_i = CONE_{d_i}(\sigma_i)$ and π is some infinite path leaving A_i. By the cone exit lemma π is not d_i-avoiding. Let σ_{i+1} be a state resulting from the first d_i-move after π leaves A_i.

(2) $A_i = CONE_{d_i}(\sigma_i)$ and π is some finite path leaving the cone. Let σ_{i+1} be the first state after π leaves the cone.

(3) $A_i = \{\sigma_i\}$ where σ_i is not a leaf. Take as σ_{i+1} any child of σ_i in T_{S,σ_0}.

(4) If $A_i = \{\sigma_i\}$ and σ_i is a leaf, A_i has no descendants.

After determining σ_{i+1}, we now construct A_{i+1}. Consider the collection D of all d for which there is an infinite d-avoiding path originating at σ_{i+1} along which d is infinitely often enabled. If $D \neq \emptyset$, let d_{i+1} be the direction chosen least recently, possibly not at all, as a cone directive along $\sigma_0 \to \sigma_1 \to \cdots \to \sigma_{i+1}$, and define $A_{i+1} = CONE_{d_{i+1}}(\sigma_{i+1})$ to be a descendant of A_i at level $i+1$, with root σ_{i+1} and directive d_{i+1}. In case of a tie, the direction with the smallest index is chosen. By 'least recently' it is meant, that if d has been chosen as a cone directive at σ_k, $0 \leqslant k \leqslant i+1$, then every other $d' \in D$ (and not d) has been chosen as a directive along $\sigma_{k+1}, \ldots, \sigma_{i+1}$. Thus, when iterating, we vary the cone directive maximally, which means that if some direction d may serve as a cone directive again and again along some path, eventually it will be selected as such. If $D = \emptyset$, we again choose d_{i+1} as any enabled direction, generating A_{i+1} as a trivial cone.

Remark:

If some A_i is a nontrivial cone it always has descendants, that is it is never a leaf in the contracted tree. This is important in establishing clause (2) of the rule. This does not hold when applying the cone construction to arbitrary programs (not necessarily fairly terminating).

Lemma (cone chain):

In the hierarchy **A** there does not exist an infinite sequence of descendant cones $CONE_{d_i}(\sigma_i)$ s.t. $\sigma_i, i \geqslant 0$, resident on an infinite path of T_{S,σ_0}.

Proof: The main idea is to show that an infinite unfair path cannot 'cross' (enter and exit) infinitely many different cones (in the above constructed cover). Rather, it has an infinite tail that remains within some cone. The proof utilizes the maximal variability as described in the inductive construction of **A**.

Suppose that such an infinite, thus unfair, sequence of states $\sigma_i, i \geqslant 0$, exists. Thus, there is some $\bar{d} \in \Delta$ such that the path σ_i is $\bar{d}$-unfair. Take the least such $\bar{d}$. Then there is an i_0 such that the infinite tail originating at σ_{i_0} is $\bar{d}$-avoiding. Hence, there is also a $j_0 \geqslant i_0$, such that either $\bar{d}$ did not occur at all on the initial subpath $\sigma_0 \rightarrow \cdots \rightarrow \sigma_{j_0}$ or it occurred less recently than any other move. Hence $\bar{d} = d_{j_0}$ in the inductive construction of $CONE_{d_{j0}}(\sigma_{j_0})$ (by the directive choice criterion of maximal variability), and the path $\sigma_i, i \geqslant 0$, would have an infinite tail contained in $CONE_{d_{j0}}(\sigma_{j_0})$, contrary to assumption.

□

Now we define T^*_{S,σ_0} as suggested above. Its nodes are all the families A_i in the hierarchy **A**, and its edges are either original edges entering cones, or original edges leaving cones, and, otherwise, edges outside cones. By the cone chain lemma, the tree T^*_{S,σ_0} is well founded, that is it contains finite paths only (though, possibly, infinitely many of them). Note again that by the previous remark a leaf is never a nontrivial cone.

In order to get rid of the undesired σ_0-dependence of $W, \Delta^s_w, \Delta^d_w$ and pi, we do one more construction: combine all the trees T^*_{S,σ_0} s.t. $\sigma_0 \models p$ into the infinitary well-founded tree T^*_S, by identifying their roots.

Now the situation is similar to the random assignment case. The tree T^*_S is ranked by ordinals as before. Call this rank the **basic rank.**

However, the basic ranking allows the case that two different nodes, being cones with different directives, have received the same rank. This would destroy the uniqueness of the choice of the decreasing directions as depending on the rank only, required by the proof rule. Thus, uniqueness has to be restored. This is achieved by a **rank shift**: suppose that at some level of the basic ranking, say λ, there are equiranked cones with different directives, say of order type α. Then rerank these consecutively by $\lambda+1, \ldots, \lambda+\alpha$, and proceed to the next level $\lambda+\alpha+1$.

Let ρ denote the resulting ranking function of T^*_S. As W we choose the ordinals ranking T^*_S, an initial segment of the countable ordinals, with their usual ordering. Using it, we define the parametrized invariant pi and partitions (Δ^s_w, Δ^d_w) (see Figure 5.11).

$$pi(\sigma, w) \overset{df.}{\equiv} \exists \eta, d\colon \sigma \in CONE_d(\eta) \wedge \rho(CONE_d(\eta)) = w$$

and, for $w > 0$,

$$\Delta_w^d = \{d \mid \exists \eta : \rho(CONE_d(\eta)) = w\}$$
$$\Delta_w^s = \Delta - \Delta_w^d.$$

Figure 5.11 Parametrized invariant and partitions.

Thus, states are ranked according to the cones in which their occurrences reside, and $pi(w, \sigma)$ may be satisfied by σ with more than one w. Note that the rank shift of T_S^* assures that Δ_w^s is well defined, while the fact that **A** is a cover guarantees that pi is well defined.

Next, we show that clauses (1)–(6) of the rule **FT** hold.

Clauses (INIT), (CONT), (TERM): Immediate.

Clause (DEC): Assume $pi(w) \wedge w > 0 \wedge B_i$ holds in σ, for $i \in \Delta_w^d$. By the definition of $pi, \sigma \in T^*_{S,\sigma_0}$ for some σ_0 such that $\sigma_0 \models p$ holds. We distinguish between two cases:

(a) There is a nontrivial cone with directive i containing σ and ranked w, say $CONE_i(\eta)$. By the cone exit lemma, the i-move leaves the cone at some $\delta \in CONE_i(\eta)$, and hence reaches a state with a lower rank, since the ranking was bottom up in T_S^*.

(b) The state occurrence σ is a trivial cone, and is ranked w. Indeed, any enabled move, and in particular the i move, leads to a descendant node with a smaller rank.

Clause (NOINC): Assume $pi(w) \wedge w > 0 \wedge B_i$ holds in σ, for $i \in \Delta_w^s$. Again $\sigma \in T^*_{S,\sigma_0}$ and $\sigma_0 \models p$ holds for some state σ_0. Then $\sigma \in CONE_d(\eta)$ for some η and d with $d \neq i$. If move i remains in the cone, by construction the rank remains the same. Otherwise, it leaves the cone, and hence the rank decreases.

Clause (IOE): To see that the derived program fairly terminates, note that every infinite fair computation of the derived program is suffix of a fair computation of the original program, which does not exist, since the program is given to be fairly terminating.

Now apply an inductive argument on the number of directions in the derived program. Thus, we establish the applicability of **FT**, and hence its semantic completeness.

□

Applying the construction above to the tree $T_{S_{ub\_choice,\sigma_0}}$ of the body of the random natural number generator example (with $\sigma_0 \models x = 0 \wedge b = true$),

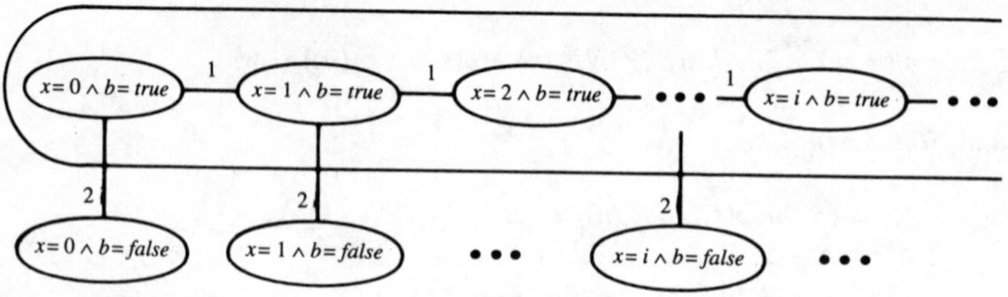

Figure 5.12 $CONE_2(\sigma_0)$.

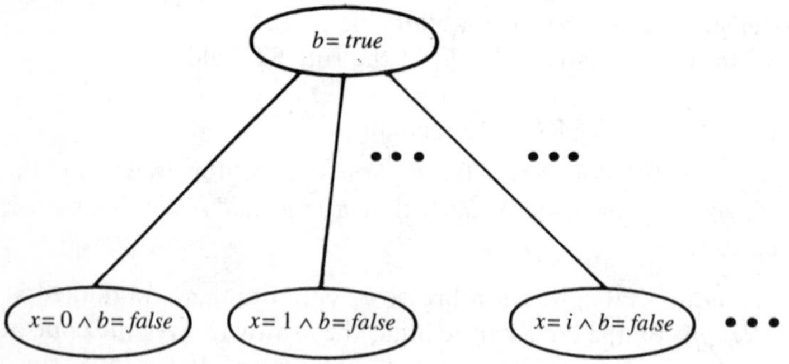

Figure 5.13 $T_{S^*_{ub\_choice,\sigma_0}}$.

yields the following cone and exits (see Figure 5.12), which yields the collapsed tree $T_{S^*_{ub\_choice,\sigma_0}}$ shown in Figure 5.13.

C. State directed helpful direction

In this subsection we present another variant of the helpful directions method, where the choice of which direction is helpful depends on state predicates, rather than on abstract distance from termination. The rule **FT′** is shown in Figure 5.14.

Explanation:

The predicate Q_i, $i \in \Delta$, is intended to characterize states for which direction i is helpful. The condition $Q = \bigvee_{i \in \Delta} Q_i$ should be invariant during the whole computation, implying that at any stage there exists a helpful direction.

(M1) Boundary conditions.

(M2) The rank never increases after taking an enabled direction.

(M3) When i is the helpful direction, but some other enabled direction has

To prove $\ll p \gg S \ll q \gg$:

Find a well-founded, partially-ordered set $(W, <)$, a **parametrized invariant** $pi(w)$, **direction predicates** Q_i, $i \in \Delta$, where $Q \overset{df.}{=} \bigvee_{i \in \Delta} Q_i$, such that

(M1) $p \Rightarrow Q \wedge \exists w: pi(w), (Q \wedge pi(w) \wedge w > 0) \Rightarrow \bigvee_{i \in \Delta} B_i, (Q \wedge pi(0) \Rightarrow (\neg \bigvee_{i \in \Delta} B_i) \wedge q$

(M2) $\ll Q \wedge pi(w) \wedge w > 0 \wedge B_i \gg S_i \ll Q \wedge \exists v: v \leqslant w \wedge pi(v) \gg$, $i \in \Delta$

(M3) $\ll Q_i \wedge pi(w) \wedge w > 0 \wedge B_j \gg S_j \ll pi(w) \Rightarrow Q_i \gg$, $i \in \Delta, j \neq i$.

(M4) $\ll Q_i \wedge pi(w) \wedge w > 0 \wedge B_i \gg S_i \ll \exists v: v < w \wedge pi(v) \gg$, $i \in \Delta$.

(M5) $\ll Q_i \gg \bar{S}_i \ll true \gg$, where for every $i \in \Delta$

$$\bar{S}_i :: *[\underset{j \in \Delta}{\square} B_j \wedge \neg B_i \rightarrow S_j]$$

Figure 5.14 Rule **FT′**.

---

been taken, preserving the rank, then i is still a helpful direction for the resulting state.

(M4) When an enabled helpful direction is taken, the rank decreases.

(M5) Again the familiar requirement of termination of the derived program, inducing a recursive application of the rule. Note that the derived program is independent of w.

EXAMPLE (greatest common divisor):

We now present an application of the rule **FT′** to a program *GCD* (see Figure 5.15), which abstracts a concurrent computation of the greatest common divisor (gcd) of two positive natural numbers. The concurrency can be construed by the first two guards being executed by one processor, while the two last are to be executed by another processor. Explicit concurrency is considered in Chapters 7 and 8. Clearly, this program is not terminating without a fairness assumption; we want to prove $\ll y_1 > 0 \wedge y_2 > 0 \gg GCD \ll true \gg$ using rule **FT′**.

As the well-founded set we choose again $W = \mathbf{N}$, the natural numbers, with their usual ordering. As the parametrized invariant, we take

$$pi(y_1, y_2, n) \overset{df.}{=} ((y_1 \neq y_2 \Rightarrow n = y_1 + y_2) \wedge (y_1 = y_2 \Rightarrow n = 0))$$

As the direction predicates we take

$$Q_1(y_1, y_2) \overset{df.}{=} y_1 \geqslant y_2 > 0$$

$$
\begin{aligned}
GCD:: *[&1: y_1 > y_2 \rightarrow y_1 := y_1 - y_2 \\
&\square \\
&2: y_2 > y_1 \rightarrow skip \\
&\square \\
&3: y_1 > y_2 \rightarrow skip \\
&\square \\
&4: y_2 > y_1 \rightarrow y_2 := y_2 - y_1 \\
].&
\end{aligned}
$$

Figure 5.15 Program *GCD*.

$Q_2(y_1, y_2) \overset{df.}{=} false$ (that is, this direction is helpful for no state)

$Q_3(y_1, y_2) \overset{df.}{=} false$

$Q_4(y_1, y_2) \overset{df.}{=} y_2 > y_1 > 0$

Thus, $Q \equiv y_1 > 0 \wedge y_2 > 0$ is clearly invariant; also, $Q \wedge pi(0)$ implies $y_1 = y_2$ implying termination (M1). The value of $y_1 + y_2$ never increases, since the *ys* are either decremented or left unchanged (M2). In case $y_1 + y_2$ did not decrease, it is due to having taken directions $\{2, 3\}$ – executing a *skip* – and, hence, preserving the direction predicate (M3). Clause (M4) also holds, since decreasing y_i, $i = 1, 2$, decreases also $y_1 + y_2$ (possibly reducing n to 0, in case $y_1 = y_2$ after decreasing any of the *ys*). Finally, the recursive application is immediate. Thus, we established the strongly fair termination of *GCD*.

□

5.6.3 The explicit scheduler method

In this section we present one variant of an alternative method for proving fair termination of *GC* programs. The main idea of this approach is to reduce the fair termination problem of *GC* programs to ordinary (nondeterministic) termination of GC_R programs (the augmentation of *GC* with random assignments).

The reduction method uses random assignment (of natural numbers) to represent explicitly the fair scheduler within the program. Once this transformation is carried out, the resulting nondeterministic program can be proved to terminate by using a variant decreasing along every direction whenever the original program is fairly terminating. Finally, the effect of the transformation is simulated within a proof rule, which now serves for proving properties of the original, untransformed, program.

$$
\begin{aligned}
&S{::}\ {*}[1{:}\,B_1 \rightarrow S_1 \,[]\, 2{:}\,B_2 \rightarrow S_2].\\
&\mathbf{T}_f^2(S){::}\ z_1 := ?;\ z_2 := ?;\\
&\qquad {*}[1{:}\,B_1 \wedge z_1 \leqslant z_2 \rightarrow S_1;\ z_1 := ?;\ [B_2 \rightarrow z_2 := z_2 - 1 \,[]\, \neg B_2 \rightarrow skip]\\
&\qquad []\\
&\qquad 2{:}\,B_2 \wedge z_2 < z_1 \rightarrow S_2;\ z_2 := ?;\ [B_1 \rightarrow z_1 := z_1 - 1 \,[]\, \neg B_1 \rightarrow skip]]
\end{aligned}
$$

Figure 5.16 Explicit scheduler transformation for two directions.

A. The explicit scheduler transformation

We start by presenting a transformation $\mathbf{T}_f^2: GC \rightarrow GC_R$, which for a repetition statement $S \in GC$ produces a program $\mathbf{T}_f^2(S) \in GC_R$. To overcome notational difficulties, we first discuss programs with two directions only. A fair scheduler is explicitly represented in $\mathbf{T}_f^2: GC \rightarrow GC_R$ by means of random assignments, as shown in Figure 5.16.

The transformation introduces two new variables (not occurring in S), z_1 and z_2, which range over integers. The assignments to these variables and the extra inequalities added to the guards represent the fair scheduling policy in the following way, informally expressed.

During a computation of $\mathbf{T}_f^2(S)$ the values of the variables z_1 and z_2 represent the respective **priorities** assigned to the directions 1 and 2. Consequently, z_1 and z_2 are called **priority variables**. We say that S_1 has a higher priority than S_2 if $z_1 \leqslant z_2$ holds (and vice versa for $z_2 < z_1$). The guards $B_1 \wedge z_1 \leqslant z_2$ and $B_2 \wedge z_2 < z_1$ guarantee that the direction with the higher priority is scheduled for execution. Note that if both priority variables are equal, S_1 gets executed. After every execution of a direction, say i, the priority of the other direction, which was not chosen, say j, gets increased (by decrementing z_j by 1) if that other direction was enabled, whereas the priority of direction i is reset to some arbitrary nonnegative value. Gradually increasing the priority of direction j excludes the possibility of postponing j's right for execution forever, if indeed direction j keeps on being enabled while ignored. This guarantees fairness. At the very beginning of a computation of $\mathbf{T}_f^2(S)$ both priority variables are initialized to arbitrary nonnegative values. The value $z_j + 1$ describes also the maximum number of computation steps (iterations of the body of S) which may happen before direction j is eventually scheduled for execution, provided it keeps being enabled whenever ignored.

$\mathbf{T}_f^2(S)$ allows all and only fair computations of program S.

Definition: For computation sequences

$$\pi = \sigma_0 \rightarrow_{i_0} \cdots \sigma_j \rightarrow_{i_j} \cdots \text{ and } \pi' = \sigma_0' \rightarrow_{i_0} \cdots \sigma_j' \rightarrow_{i_j} \cdots$$

(1) π' is an **extension** of π to the variables $z_1, \ldots, z_n$ if the states σ_j' differ from σ_j at most in the variables $z_1, \ldots, z_n$.

(2) π is a **restriction** of π' to the variables $x_1, \ldots, x_m$ if every state σ_j is obtained from σ'_j by resetting every variable $z \notin \{x_1, \ldots, x_m\}$ to its value in σ'_0, that is by defining

$$\sigma_j[z] = \begin{cases} \sigma'_0[z] & \text{if } z \notin \{x_1, \ldots, x_m\} \\ \sigma'_j[z] & \text{otherwise} \end{cases}$$

□

Lemma (faithfulness of $\mathbf{T}^2_f$):

(1) If π is a fair computation sequence of S then there exists an extension π' of π to be the (new) variables z_1 and z_2 so that π' is a computation sequence of $\mathbf{T}^2_f(S)$.

(2) Conversely, if π' is a computation sequence of $\mathbf{T}^2_f(S)$ then its restriction π to the variables of S is a fair computation sequence of S.

This lemma states that $\mathbf{T}^2_f$ is a **faithful transformation** in the sense that for every program S, $\mathbf{T}^2_f(S)$ simulates exactly all and only fair computation sequences of S.

Proof:

(1) Consider a fair computation sequence $\pi = \sigma_0 \to_{i_0} \cdots \sigma_j \to_{i_j} \cdots$ of S with $i_j \in \{1, 2\}$. We extend π to a sequence

$$\pi' = \sigma'_0 \to_{i_0} \cdots \sigma'_j \to_{i_j} \cdots$$

by providing values to the variables z_1 and z_2. For $l \in \{1, 2\}$ we define

$$\sigma'_j[z_l] = \begin{cases} |\{m \mid j < m \leqslant k_0 \wedge \sigma_m \models B_l\}| & \text{if } \exists k \geqslant j : i_k = l \\ 1 + |\{m \mid j \leqslant m \wedge \sigma_m \models B_l\}| & \text{otherwise} \end{cases}$$

where $k_0 = min\{k \mid k \geqslant j \wedge i_k = l\}$. To see that $\sigma'_j[z_l] \in \mathbf{N}$ holds for all j and l, we have to show that in both cases the cardinality of a finite subset of $\mathbf{N}$ is taken. The first case represents the case where direction l is taken at some stage k, $k \geqslant j$. Thus, the set $\{k \mid k \geqslant j \wedge i_k = l\}$ is not empty and k_0 is well defined, bounding the set whose cardinality is taken. The second case, namely $\forall k \geqslant j$: $i_k \neq l$, means that from σ_j onwards, the lth direction is never taken again. Since π is fair, this can only be the case if direction l is only finitely often enabled. In this case, there exists a bound on the values of m in the definition.

Note that in every state σ'_j exactly one variable z_l has the value 0, namely z_{i_j}. Furthermore, the value of the other priority variable is at least 1. So the scheduler built into the program $\mathbf{T}^2_f(S)$ will indeed choose the direction i_j in the state σ'_j. Also it is easy to check that the values of

$T^n_f(S)$:: for *all* $i \in \Delta$ *do* $z_i := ?$;
  *[$\underset{i\in\Delta}{[]}$ i: $B_i \wedge turn = i \rightarrow S_i$; $z_i := ?$;
  for *all* $j \in \Delta - \{i\}$ *do* $[B_j \rightarrow z_j := z_j - 1 \,[]\, \neg B_j \rightarrow skip]$
  ].

Figure 5.17 Transformation $T^n_f(S)$.

the variables z_1, z_2 in the states σ'_j are defined consistently with the corresponding assignments in $\mathbf{T}^2_f(S)$.Thus π' is indeed a computation sequence of $\mathbf{T}^2_f(S)$.

(2) Let π' be a computation sequence of $\mathbf{T}^2_f(S)$ and let π be its restriction to the variables of S. It is obvious that π is a valid computation sequence of S. However, we have to prove that this computation sequence is fair.

Suppose this is not the case. Then π is infinite, that is $B_1 \vee B_2$ is always true, but one direction of S, say i, is from a certain moment on never taken, even though it is infinitely often enabled. By the definition of $\mathbf{T}^2_f(S)$ the value of the variable z_i becomes arbitrarily small and from some moment on smaller than -1. However, this is impossible because in every state σ'_j of π' the following invariant

$$IN_2 \equiv (z_1 \geqslant -1 \wedge z_2 \geqslant -1) \wedge (z_1 = -1 \rightarrow z_2 \geqslant 0) \wedge (z_2 = -1 \rightarrow z_1 \geqslant 0)$$

holds. This is shown by induction on j in the computation sequence. Initially, both z_1 and z_2 are initialized with random assignments and are nonnegative, establishing IN_2. Assume $\sigma_j \models IN_2, j \geqslant 0$. W.1.o.g assume further that $\sigma_j \models z_1 \leqslant z_2$, implying that the transition to σ_{j+1} is along direction 1. First, upon termination of this direction z_1 is reset with a random assignment, so $\sigma_{j+1} \models z_1 \geqslant 0$. From $\sigma_j \models IN_2$ we get that $\sigma_j \models z_2 \geqslant -1$. If $z_2 = -1$ is the case, then by $z_1 \leqslant z_2$ we get $\sigma_j \models z_1 \leqslant -1$, contradicting IN_2. Hence, $\sigma_j \models z_2 \geqslant 0$. Then, $\sigma_{j+1} \models z_2 \geqslant -1$, but we already have $\sigma_{j+1} \models z_1 \geqslant 0$, re-establishing IN_2.

□

Next this transformation is extended to a typical nondeterministic repetition $S \in GC$ with any number of directions. The transformation $\mathbf{T}^n_f(S)$ (see Figure 5.17) is a systematic extension of the one for the two directions case. The $z_1, \ldots, z_n$ are new variables not occurring in S which range over the integers. The expression $turn = i$ is an abbreviation defined by

$$turn = i \overset{df.}{\equiv} (i = \min\{j \mid z_j = \min\{z_1, \ldots, z_n\}\})$$

To prove $\ll p \gg S :: *[\underset{i\in\Delta}{[]} B_i \rightarrow S_i] \ll q \gg$:

Choose a well-founded, partially ordered set $(W, <)$, a parametrized invariant $pi(w, z_1, \ldots, z_n)$, satisfying:

(1) (INIT) $p \rightarrow \forall z_1, \ldots, z_n \geqslant 0 \exists w : pi(w, z_1, \ldots, z_n)$

(2) (CONT) $pi^{in}(w, z_1, \ldots, z_n) \wedge w > 0 \Rightarrow \bigvee_{i\in\Delta} B_i$

(3) (TERM) $pi^{in}(0, z_1, \ldots, z_n) \Rightarrow (\neg \bigvee_{i\in\Delta} B_i) \wedge q$

(4) (DEC) $\ll pi^{in}(w, z_1, \ldots, z_n) \wedge B_i \wedge turn = i \gg$

S_i

$\ll \forall z_i \exists v : v < w \wedge pi^{in}(v, \tilde{z}_1, \ldots, \tilde{z}_n) \gg$, $i \in \Delta$, where

$$\tilde{z} = \begin{cases} z_k & k = i \vee k \neq i \wedge \neg B_k \\ z_k - 1 & k \neq i \wedge B_k \end{cases}$$

and $pi^{in} \equiv pi \wedge IN_n$

Figure 5.18 Rule **ESFT**.

which holds if i is the smallest index such that z_i has the minimal value among $z_1, \ldots, z_n$. The variables $z_1, \ldots, z_n$ are once again priority variables used to realize a schedule in $\mathbf{T}^n_f(S)$ which allows only fair computations. At every stage in the computation of $\mathbf{T}^n_f(S)$ the enabled direction with the smallest index and the maximal priority, say i, is executed. After this execution the priorities of all other directions j, $j \neq i$, get incremented (that is, z_j decremented) by 1 whereas the priority of i gets reset to an arbitrary nonnegative value. The coding of *for all ... do* in *GC* is left as an exercise.

The transformation $\mathbf{T}^n_f(S)$ also satisfies the faithfulness lemma. In proving direction (2), recall that in the transformed program in the two-directional case the variables z_1 and z_2 were always $\geqslant -1$. For $\mathbf{T}^n_f(S)$, analogously $z_1, \ldots, z_n \leqslant -n + 1$ is always true. This follows from the more general invariant

$$IN_n \equiv \bigwedge_{i=1,n} |\{k \mid z_k \leqslant -i\}| \leqslant n - i$$

EXERCISE:

Complete the proof of invariance.

□

B. The explicit scheduler proof rule

In this subsection we present a proof rule **ESFT** (explicit scheduler fair termination) for proving fair termination based on the transformation in the previous subsection (see Figure 5.18). The rule simulates the transformation in its clauses, 'absorbing' it.

Soundness and semantic completeness of the rule **ESFT** follow from the faithfulness of T_f^n and the corresponding results for the proof rule (ND-REP*) for GC_R.

EXAMPLE:

We start with the simplest fairly terminating program.

$$\vdash_{\mathbf{ESFT}} \ll true \gg *[1: b \rightarrow skip \,[]\, 2: b \rightarrow b := false] \ll true \gg$$

We need a parametrized invariant $pi(w, z_1, z_2)$. Recall that w is intended to count the numbers of loop traversals; thus, in this example, using the natural numbers as the well-founded set suffices. To determine w consider the possible cases. First, if b is initially *false* the program terminates immediately so that $w = 0$ holds. Otherwise $w > 0$ holds. Suppose the second direction $S_2 :: b := false$ is taken first. Then $w = 1$ holds, as this direction forces termination. If the first direction $S_1 :: skip$ is taken first, the exact number w of loop traversals is not directly predictable, and it depends by fairness on the number of times S_2 may be neglected. The maximal number of times S_2 may be neglected is given by $z_2 + 1$. The '$+1$' is necessary here because S_1 may be executed once even if $z_2 = 0$ holds (as follows from the invariant IN_2). We end up with the following parametrized invariant:

$$\begin{aligned} pi(w, z_1, z_2) \equiv\ & (\neg b \Leftrightarrow w = 0) \\ & \wedge (b \wedge turn = 1 \Rightarrow w = 2 + z_2) \\ & \wedge (b \wedge turn = 2 \Rightarrow w = 1) \end{aligned}$$

As it turns out $pi(w, z_1, z_2)$ satisfies indeed the premisses of the proof rule **ESFT**. Note how the variable z_2 reflects the assumption of fairness. With z_2 it is possible to find a variant w which decreases with every loop execution, but without z_2 this is impossible. This clearly indicates the absorbing of the scheduler into the proof rule.

□

EXERCISE:

Complete the details of the application of **ESFT**.

□

EXAMPLE (symmetric termination):

The previous example was particularly simple because there was a fixed direction which was responsible for termination. Here is a more symmetric program.

$$A :: *[\mathop{[]}_{i \in \Delta} i : \neg(\bigwedge_{i \in \Delta} b_i) \rightarrow b_i := true]$$

Here the value of the Boolean variable b_i being *true* can be interpreted as reporting that some ith subprogram S_i has already been executed. The program A terminates as soon as every direction has been executed at least once. The claim to be proved is

$$\vdash_{\mathbf{ESFT}} \ll true \gg A \ll true \gg$$

To prove this claim, an estimation of the maximal number of executions of the body of A is needed. So assume that currently the ith direction S_i is being executed, that is that $turn = i$ holds. Then w depends on how many times the other directions j, $j \neq i$, may still be neglected. However, this can be measured in terms of the priority variables z_j, $j \neq i$. Taking the invariant IN_n for these variables into account a first estimation of w in case of $turn = i$ is

$$w = n + \max_{j \in \Delta} \{z_j \mid j \neq i\}$$

This equality clearly holds at the beginning of a computation but is not kept invariant in the course of such a computation. As soon as the jth direction has been executed the corresponding priority variable z_j is reset arbitrarily whereas the maximum number of times the loop is left to be executed decreases by at least 1. However, this deficiency can be fixed easily by using the variables b_j which indicate whether direction j has already been executed. For $turn = i$ let

$$q_i \overset{df.}{\equiv} (w = n + max\ \{if\ b_j\ then\ -n+1\ else\ z_j \mid j \in \Delta, j \neq i\})$$

where $-n+1$ is the smallest value z_j can assume.

Finally, define

$$pi(w, z_1, \ldots, z_n) \overset{df.}{\equiv} [(\bigwedge_{i \in \Delta} b_i \Leftrightarrow w = 0) \wedge \bigwedge_{i \in \Delta} (\neg b_i \wedge turn = i \Rightarrow q_i)]$$

It turns out that $pi(w, z_1, \ldots, z_n)$ indeed satisfies the premises of proof rule **ESFT**.

□

EXERCISE:

Verify the above claim.

□

5.7 Conclusions

In this chapter, we first extended the compositional approach to proofs of both partial correctness and total correctness to nondeterministic programs in the language of guarded commands. The two main underlying principles, those of using invariants for partial correctness and well-founded variants for termination, carry through naturally. The novel feature is the presence of multiple directions, and each direction has to lead to correct results. In particular, each direction should cause a decrease in the variant to establish termination. The soundness and completeness results also have their natural generalization.

A crucial feature of this kind of nondeterminism is its being bounded, in the sense that every initial state either generates a finite number of computations or else generates also a nonterminating computation. We then studied another kind of nondeterminism by the random assignment construct, which enables a choice of an arbitrary natural number in a finite time. The novel proof-theoretic issue raised here is the use of infinite ordinals as values of the variant in termination proofs. This is due to the unbounded nondeterminism, a distinctive feature of random assignments. We showed that the suitable extension of the repetition rule is semantically complete. Regarding the issue of syntactic completeness, consult the section on suggestions for further reading.

Finally, the issue of fairness was introduced, where a natural restriction is imposed on infinite sequences of nondeterministic choices. This restriction guarantees that under a proper assumption about its enabledness, each direction will eventually be selected. Fairness shares with random assignments the presence of unbounded nondeterminism. In the proof methods for fair termination presented, infinite ordinals are needed. Directions are partitioned into helpful, the ones causing a decrease in the variant value, and steady, the ones which do not cause an increase in that value. A rather complicated construction establishes the semantic completeness of this approach. Again, a reference to a study of syntactic completeness in a stronger logic is given in the suggestions for further reading.

Then, a second method, a transformational one, for establishing fair termination was introduced. It uses random assignments to incorporate a fair scheduler into the transformed program, reducing thereby the fair termination of the original program to ordinary termination of the transformed one.

The conclusion of this chapter is that the compositional verification methods introduced for deterministic programs are powerful enough to extend naturally to nondeterminism, which also does not need a different specification method. The situation is going to change once concurrency is introduced. As for fair termination, a change in the condition under which the variant has to decrease is the main difference.

Bibliographic notes and suggestions for further reading

Bibliographic notes The first treatment of the correctness of nondeterministic programs appears in [39], where a language containing an *or* construct is studied. A similar construct is studied also in [17]. The language *GC* was introduced by Dijkstra [23], [76]. The rules of the deductive system **D** are an adaptation of Harel's rules for dynamic logic [57]. A survey of correctness proofs that inspired the current presentation is [77]. The arithmetic soundness and completeness proofs also originate in [57]. The significance of bounded nondeterminism was first pointed out in [23]. A comprehensive study of random assignments appears in [78], which is also the source of the example proof in Section 5.5 (in a somewhat different formulation). The need for infinite ordinals for termination proofs of unbounded nondeterminism was pointed out by [79]. A comprehensive survey of the study of fairness is [80]. The helpful direction methods originate in [81], [82] (ordinal directed) and [83] (state directed). The explicit scheduler method originates in [84].

Suggestions for further reading The denotational semantics of nondeterminism and the construction of power domains can be read in [85] and [86]. [17] also studies the denotational semantics of nondeterministic programs and their correctness. Some further variants of random assignments and their relationship to fairness are discussed in [80, Chapter 3]. There one can also find a comprehensive study of more fairness notions, both in the context of *GC* and in other formalisms. It also contains more examples of proof of fair termination, including use of higher ordinals. The syntactic completeness proof for the proof rule for termination of programs with random assignments, using a variant of Park's μ-calculus [87], appears in [78]. The syntactic completeness of fair termination proof rules is studied in [88] in a similar formalism (surveyed also in [80, Chapter 6].) More on fairness can be read also in [89], [90]. A treatment of 'all-levels' fairness appears in [91]. A general application of the construction in the proof of the semantic completeness of the helpful directions method appears in [92]. A very general treatment of generalization of fairness appears in [93]. Required nondeterminism is considered in [94] and [95] (the latter in a temporal logic context). A recent interpretation of nondeterminism in the classical theory of computation (Turing machines), influenced by developments in programming languages, and in particular by fairness, appears in [96].

EXERCISES

5.1 **Failure ignoring:** Formulate a correctness assertion that allows for a program to fail (that is, to end with **f**) but disallows nontermination. Show how to modify the system **D** to accommodate this correctness assertion.

5.2 Invariance theorem: Extend the invariance theorem to *GC*.

5.3 Proof outlines:

(1) Formulate an exact definition of proof outlines for *GC* and **D** (extending that of *PLW* and **H**).

(2) Prove that the two characterizing lemmata for proof outlines are satisfied by your definition.

5.4 Existential termination [97]: Formulate a proof rule for the following correctness assertion: from any initial state satisfying the precondition p, there exists a terminating computation of S.

(1) Prove soundness and semantic completeness of your rule w.r.t. the standard semantics of *GC* as presented in the text. (Compare also with the diamond operator of dynamic logic [57].

(2) Do the same for the property *there exists a nonterminating computation* of S

5.5 Distinguishability [97]: Consider the following three *GC* programs.

S_0:: *skip*
S_1:: *[*true* → *skip*]
S_2:: [*true* → *skip* [] *true* → S] (Here, S is an arbitrary *GC* program.)

Which of the programs are pairwise distinguishable by means of partial correctness, total correctness, or existential termination assertions (Exercise 5.4)?

5.6 Or programs [17]: Consider another nondeterministic extension of *PLW*. Instead of guarded commands, the command S_1 **or** S_2 is introduced, with the following clause defining its semantics as an arbitrary branch:

$$\langle S_1 \textbf{ or } S_2, \sigma\rangle \rightarrow \langle S_i, \sigma\rangle,\ i = 1, 2$$

Also, add Boolean tests $p?$ as atomic statements (composed sequentially, like assignments).

(1) Attribute a precise semantics to tests and show how to simulate *GC* in this language.

(2) Develop sound and semantically complete proof rules for total correctness in this language. (Compare also with the programming language used in dynamic logic [57].)

(3) Provide correctness assertions for this language fitting the 'demonic nondeterminism' (as discussed in Section 5.1).

5.7 **Angelic nondeterminism:** Consider the following proof rules.

$$\frac{\langle p\rangle\, S_1\, \langle q\rangle}{\langle p\rangle\, S_1 \textbf{ or } S_2\, \langle q\rangle}, \quad \frac{\langle p\rangle\, S_2\, \langle q\rangle}{\langle p\rangle\, S_1 \textbf{ or } S_2\, \langle q\rangle}$$

Provide an operational semantics for *or*-programs rendering them sound.

5.8 **Idempotence of GC:** Let P:: $*[g \rightarrow S]$ and P':: $*[g \rightarrow S \,[]\, *g \rightarrow S]$. Show that

$$\vdash_{\mathbf{D}}\{p\}\ P\ \{q\} \text{ iff } \vdash_{\mathbf{D}}\{p\}\ P'\ \{q\}$$

by actually converting each proof to its counterpart (that is, without directly relying on completeness).

5.9 **Interreducibility of the helpful directions methods:** Prove that every fair termination proof $\ll p \gg\ S\ \ll q \gg$ (for S:: $*[\underset{i\in\Delta}{[]}\ B_i \rightarrow S_i]$) using the ordinal directed helpful directions method (rule **FT**) can be converted to a proof of the same using the state directed helpful directions method (rule **FT′**) and vice versa.

5.10 **Reducibility of the helpful directions methods to the explicit scheduler method:** Prove that every fair termination proof $\ll p \gg\ S\ \ll q \gg$ (for S:: $*[\underset{i\in\Delta}{[]}\ B_i \rightarrow S_i]$) using the ordinal directed helpful directions method (rule **FT**) can be converted to a proof of the same using the explicit scheduler method (rule **ESFT**).

5.11 **[98]:** Prove termination of the following program (over integers), using (ND–REP*):

$$\begin{aligned}
&*[x>0 \rightarrow (x, y) := (x-1, ?)\\
&\ \ []\\
&\ \ y>0 \rightarrow y := y-1]
\end{aligned}$$

5.12 Provide an alternative version of rule (ND-REP*) in which termination is not necessarily reached with a minimal value of the variant. Which clauses of (ND-REP*) have to be modified?

5.13 Use rule FT to prove the following fair termination assertion:

$\ll true \gg \ S \ \ll true \gg$

where

$$
\begin{aligned}
S{::}\ *[&1: xup \rightarrow x := x+1\\
&\quad\Box\\
&2: yup \rightarrow y := y+1\\
&\quad\Box\\
&3: xup \rightarrow xup := false\\
&\quad\Box\\
&4: yup \rightarrow yup := false\\
&\quad\Box\\
&5: x > 0 \rightarrow x := x-1\\
&\quad\Box\\
&6: y > 0 \rightarrow y := y-1\\
&]
\end{aligned}
$$

Chapter 6
VERIFYING PROGRAMS WITH PROCEDURES

6.1 Introduction

In this chapter, we extend the **compositional** approach to verification of programs with **procedures**. The procedure construct is one of the main *abstraction* constructs in programming languages and an important unit of modularity as such. By means of an **invocation** of a procedure (known as a procedure **call** in the programming jargon), with an appropriate **parametrization**, multiple use is made of a uniquely defined, and uniquely specified, program section. The latter can be viewed as an abstract action, enriching the repertoire of basic actions provided by the underlying programming language.

We would like that the proof method for programs with procedures reflects as closely as possible the way that such programs are designed, developed, and used. Thus, we would like to see a single proof that the body of a procedure satisfies some specification, which then can be adapted to derive the appropriate conclusion about the various invocations of the procedure. Such proofs are known as **canonical** proofs.

Special attention has to be paid to the apparent circularity associated with **recursion**, whereby within the body of some procedure the same procedure is re-invoked. To overcome this apparent circularity, we shall need to augment the proof system with a meta-rule, which has a **provability** claim as one of its assumptions, in addition to correctness assertions. An extra complication due to recursion is another source of nontermination: an infinite sequence of recursive calls. Thus, proving total correctness requires also showing the absence of such sequences by means of an appropriate rule.

Because of the usefulness of procedures and their invocations in programming practice, programming languages were led to the inclusion of very complicated combinations of procedures with other constructs, very liberal parametrizations (including procedures as parameters), scope roles, nested definitions, and much more. As a result, the verification issues for such programs are more delicate than for the simpler constructs considered so far. They even lead to non-existence of relatively complete proof rules, and to various inconsistent attempts. In a sense, in dealing with procedures and parameters the logical aspects dominate the methodological aspects more than for other constructs. Sometimes it is felt that procedures reside on the line separating 'verifying the algorithm' from 'verifying a program'. However, even if such a separation can be maintained, methodologically the latter is as important as the former.

A comprehensive treatment is beyond the scope of the current level of presentation. We shall consider some of the more typical simple uses of procedures and parameters, both giving the flavor of the problem and its solutions and giving sufficient background for stepping forward towards concurrent and distributed programs.

We shall advance in several stages in an attempt to achieve a separation of concerns, treating separately the aspect of reasoning about the transfer of control implied by procedure invocations, then including recursion, then considering the implication of simple parametrization modes, and, finally, considering declarations of local variables.

Since the kind of specification we are considering here remains the same as before, and is irrelevant to the question whether a procedure body is deterministic or not, our treatment is free of this distinction too.

6.2 Parameterless, nonrecursive procedures

We start by introducing the simplest procedural extension of a base language *PL* (being either *PLW* or *GC* in our case), denoted by *PROC*(*PL*). Since the variation of the base language *PL* is restricted here, we abbreviate the extension to just *PROC*, leaving the determination of the base language to the context.

A program consists of a **procedure declaration**, associating some body with a procedure name, followed by some statement possibly containing activation statements to declared procedures. The syntax is given by

$P{::}\ D;S$

$D{::}\ \textbf{procedure}\ \langle pname_1\rangle : S_1, \ldots, \textbf{procedure}\ \langle pname_n\rangle : S_n, n \geqslant 1$

$S{::}\ \textbf{call}\ \langle pname\rangle \,|\,$ as for base language....

P::**procedure** *add_1*: $x:=x+1$;
  while $y>0$ **do call** *add_1*; $y:=y-1$ **od**.

Figure 6.1 A simple procedure example.

We assume here that the $\langle pname_i \rangle$, $1 \leqslant i \leqslant n$, the **procedure names**, are pairwise distinct identifiers, generically denoted by $proc_i$ for some arbitrary enumeration. Furthermore, we require that programs are well formed in that for every **call** $\langle pname \rangle$, the procedure $\langle pname \rangle$ is indeed declared in the program. Note that nested definitions of procedures are precluded by this definition. The statement S_i in the declaration of $proc_i$ is called its body. We further stipulate in this section that the calling graph generated by connecting $proc_i$ to $proc_j$ iff S_i contains a statement **call** $proc_j$ is acyclic, that is recursion is excluded here, its treatment being deferred to Section 6.3. Note that procedures here are not parametrized, and that they operate on the same state variables as their activating environment.

As a simple example, consider the program in Figure 6.1. This procedure adds the value of x to y, by repeatedly invoking the *add_1* procedure which adds 1 to x, subtracting 1 from y each time.

The intended semantics of the *PROC* language is that whenever a procedure *proc* is activated by means of a **call** *proc* statement, execution proceeds with the body of the procedure *proc*. If and when the execution of this body terminates, execution resumes with the statement immediately following the activating **call** *proc* (if there is such).

In order to formalize the semantics, we add to the collection of rules defining the transition relation of the base language another rule, handling the procedure activation. Strictly speaking, we have to add another component to a configuration, whose role is to record all the procedure definitions in a program, as a means of association of a procedure body with a procedure name. Since this component is not changed during transitions, we omit it in order to keep the notation simple, leaving the determination of this association implicit.

Thus, the following clause is added to the definition of '$\rightarrow$'.

$$\langle \textbf{call}\ proc, \sigma_0 \rangle \rightarrow \langle S, \sigma_0 \rangle$$

provided that the declaration **procedure** *proc*: S is part of the program under consideration.

This kind of replacement rule is known also as **macro expansion** of the procedure. Note that under the assumption that the base language contains the sequential composition transition rule, we get that

$$S_1; \textbf{call}\ proc; S_2 \equiv S_1; S; S_2$$

where S is the body of procedure *proc*.

As an immediate consequence of the extended definition of transitions for *PROC*, we get the following extension of the corresponding computation lemma for the base language.

Lemma (computations extension):

If $C_0 = \langle \mathbf{call}\ \text{proc}, \sigma_0 \rangle$, then $\pi(C_0) = \pi(\langle S, \sigma_0 \rangle)$, where S is the body of procedure *proc* (recall that the declarations are implicitly in the configuration).

□

We now capture the meaning of a procedure call by an appropriate proof rule. The underlying idea is rather simple, because of all the restrictions we have imposed: in order to derive a correctness assertion about an invocation statement, derive the same correctness assertion about the body of the invoked procedure. Thus, we get the following rule of invocation.

Rule of invocation:

$$\frac{\{p\}\, S\, \{q\}}{\{p\}\ \mathbf{call}\ proc\, \{q\}} \qquad \text{(INVOC)}$$

provided that *proc* has body S.

□

EXAMPLE:

As an example of using this rule, we return to the example program P in Figure 6.1, and establish $\{x = X \wedge y = Y \geqslant 0\}\ P\ \{x = X + Y\}$. As a preparatory step, we prove the general partial correctness assertion $\{x = Z\}\ x := x+1\ \{x = Z+1\}$ about the body of the *add_1* procedure. Actually, we have to preserve across the call also the assertion $y \geqslant 1$. We return later to the issue of passing assertions about variables not affected by a procedure across its body. As the loop invariant, we take $x = X + Y - y \wedge y \geqslant 0$.

(1) $\{x+1 = Z+1 \wedge y \geqslant 1\}\ x := x+1\ \{x = Z+1 \wedge y \geqslant 1\}$ (ASS)
(2) $x = Z \wedge y \geqslant 1 \Rightarrow x+1 = Z+1 \wedge y \geqslant 1$ (ARITHMETIC)
(3) $\{x = Z \wedge y \geqslant 1\}\ x := x+1\ \{x = Z+1 \wedge y \geqslant 1\}$ (1), (2), (CONS)
(4) $\{x = X + Y - y \wedge y \geqslant 1\}\ \mathbf{call}\ add\_1\ \{x = X + Y - y + 1 \wedge y \geqslant 1\}$
(3), (INVOC), (INST)

under the instantiation of Z to $X + Y - y$. Note its adherence to the restriction on *INST* (Exercise 2.10), which is due to the fact that $y \notin var$ (*add_1*).

(5) $\{x = X + Y - y + 1 \wedge y \geqslant 1\}\ y := y - 1\ \{x = X + Y - y \wedge y \geqslant 0\}$
(ASS), (CONS)

(6) $\{x = X+Y-y \wedge y \geqslant 1\}$
call *add_1*; $y := y-1$
$\{x = X+Y-y \wedge y \geqslant 0\}$ (4), (5), (SEQ)

(7) $x = X+Y-y \wedge y \geqslant 0 \wedge y > 0 \Rightarrow x = X+Y-y \wedge y \geqslant 1$
(ARITHMETIC)

(8) $\{x = X+Y-y \wedge y \geqslant 0\}$
call *add_1*; $y := y-1$
$\{x = X+Y-y \wedge y \geqslant 0\}$ (6),(7),(CONS)

(9) $\{x = X+Y-y \wedge y \geqslant 0\}$
while $y > 0$ **do call** *add_1*; $y := y-1$ **od** (8), (REP)
$\{x = X+Y-y \wedge y \geqslant 0 \wedge y \leqslant 0\}$

After another use of (SEQ) and some simplification by (CONS), we get

$\{x = X \wedge y = Y \geqslant 0\}\ P\ \{x = X+Y\}$

□

The argument for soundness and relative completeness of the extended **H** system is straightforward, relying directly on the extended computations lemma. First, soundness can be shown as follows. If $Tr_{\mathbf{I}} \vdash \{p\}$ **call** *proc* $\{q\}$ in this system, then $Tr_{\mathbf{I}} \vdash \{q\}\ S\ \{q\}$ for S the body of *proc*. By the soundness of **H** for the base language (see Exercise 6.9), and by induction on procedure calls within S (possibly to other procedures) we have $\models_{\mathbf{I}} \{p\}\ S\ \{q\}$, and by the extended computations lemma $\models_{\mathbf{I}} \{p\}$ **call** *proc* $\{q\}$. Completeness is shown as follows. Assume $\models_{\mathbf{I}} \{p\}$ **call** *proc* $\{q\}$. By the extended computations lemma, we also have $\models_{\mathbf{I}} \{p\}\ S\ \{q\}$. By the relative completeness of **H** (assuming an expressive interpretation), we get $Tr_{\mathbf{I}} \vdash_{\mathbf{H}} \{p\}\ S\ \{q\}$ for S, and by an application of the invocation rule we finally get $Tr_{\mathbf{I}} \vdash_{\mathbf{H} \cup \{INVOC\}} \{p\}$ **call** *proc* $\{q\}$.

Note that at this point, since procedures are nonrecursive, no further provision is needed for proving termination. All that is needed is to pass to the total correctness proof system for the base language (**H*** or **D*** in our case), and prove termination of procedure bodies and of the initial S.

EXAMPLE:

Consider again the program P in Figure 6.1. We show that

$\vdash_{\mathbf{H}^* \cup \{INVOC\}} \langle y \geqslant 0 \rangle\ P\ \langle true \rangle$

Since the body of *add_1* contains no iteration, its termination proof is trivial. As for the initial S, we choose as the parametrized invariant $pi(n) \overset{df.}{=} (y = n \geqslant 0)$ and apply (REP*).

□

EXERCISE:

Complete the proof of this termination assertion.

□

In the next section, after the introduction of recursion, another source of nontermination is introduced, namely an infinite sequence of recursive invocations. We defer the details of termination proofs of recursive procedures to a later section.

Obviously, parameterless, nonrecursive procedures are not too interesting. Therefore, in the next sections we relax the restrictions imposed here.

6.3 Parameterless, recursive procedures

In this section we admit **recursion**, that is we allow for cycles in the calling graph presented in the previous section, but retain the exclusion of parametrization and scope rules. To keep the notation simple, the presentation is in terms of simple recursion, where the body of some procedure *proc* may itself contain a (re)invocation statement of the same procedure *proc*. The extension to **mutual recursion** of several procedures, for example where $proc_1, proc_2$, (assumed different) invoke each other, is left for the exercises. We first consider partial correctness proofs, and then turn to termination.

Note that no change is needed in the definition of the operational semantics. For example, for the declaration **procedure** *pr*: **if** $x \leqslant 0$ **then** *skip* **else** $[x := x-1;$ **call** *pr*$]$ **fi**, we get the following computation for an initial state $\sigma[2|x]$.

$$
\begin{aligned}
\langle \mathbf{call}\, pr, \sigma[2|x]\rangle \rightarrow\ & \langle \mathbf{if}\ x \leqslant 0\ \mathbf{then}\ skip\ \mathbf{else}\ [x := x-1;\ \mathbf{call}\ pr]\ \mathbf{fi}, \sigma[2|x]\rangle \rightarrow \\
& \langle x := x-1;\ \mathbf{call}\ pr, \sigma[2|x]\rangle \rightarrow \\
& \langle \mathbf{call}\ pr, \sigma[1|x]\rangle \rightarrow \\
& \langle \mathbf{if}\ x \leqslant 0\ \mathbf{then}\ skip\ \mathbf{else}\ [x := x-1;\ \mathbf{call}\ pr]\ \mathbf{fi}, \sigma[1|x]\rangle \rightarrow \\
& \langle x := x-1;\ \mathbf{call}\ pr, \sigma[1|x]\rangle \rightarrow \\
& \langle \mathbf{call}\ pr, \sigma[0|x]\rangle \rightarrow \\
& \langle \mathbf{if}\ x \leqslant 0\ \mathbf{then}\ skip\ \mathbf{else}\ [x := x-1;\ \mathbf{call}\ pr]\ \mathbf{fi}, \sigma[0|x]\rangle \rightarrow \\
& \langle skip, \sigma[0|x]\rangle \rightarrow \\
& \langle E, \sigma[0|x]\rangle.
\end{aligned}
$$

Why is recursion posing a problem for proofs? There seems to be an apparent circularity in the reasoning involved.

First, trying to interpret the computations extension lemma for recursive procedures induces a circular characterization of $\pi(\langle \mathbf{call}\ proc, \sigma_0\rangle)$. This circularity can be understood as a fixed point equation, to be solved over an appropriately ordered domain of computations. Similarly, any attempt to derive a partial correctness assertion about an invocation, by means of the invocation rule, requires a previous subderivation of the same correctness assertion about the body of the recursive procedure invoked. However, since the procedure is recursive, its body itself contains (recursive) invocations of the procedure, so in order to prove the correctness assertion about the body, yet another correctness assertion (possibly w.r.t. the same specification) has to be derived about the 'inner' invocation, which seemingly leads to an infinite regression.

The way out is to mimic the induction involved in the execution of recursive procedures, by producing a meta-rule, one of the premisses of which is not merely a correctness assertion; rather it is a premiss about the existence of a proof from assumption: under the assumption of a partial correctness assertion about the 'inner' invocation statement, the same specification is provable about the body of the invoked procedure, discharging the assumption. This leads to the formulation of the following meta-rule of recursion.

Rule of recursion:

$$\frac{\{p\}\ \mathbf{call}\ proc\,\{q\} \vdash_{\mathrm{H}} \{p\}\, S\,\{q\}}{\{p\}\ \mathbf{call}\ proc\,\{q\}} \qquad \text{(REC)}$$

provided that S is the declared body of procedure *proc*.

□

Note that the presence of a meta-rule slightly changes the induced notion of a proof as a sequence of partial correctness formulas (or formulas from Tr_{I}), by allowing assumptions too. Every application of the recursion rule discharges the assumption about the invocation. To keep the notation simple, we shall record assumptions by indenting the proof section using them, indenting back upon discharging the assumption.

Following is an example of a proof using the recursion rule. Let

P:: **procedure** *power_2*:
if $x = 0$ **then** $y := 1$ **else** $[x := x-1;$ **call** *power_2*; $x := x+1; y := y*2]$ **fi**;
call *power_2*

We want to show that $\{x \geqslant 0\}\ P\ \{y = 2^x\}$.

(1) $\{x \geqslant 0\}$ **call** *power_2* $\{y = 2^x\}$ (ASSUMPTION)
(2) $\quad \{y*2 = 2^x\}\, y := y*2\, \{y = 2^x\}$ (ASS)
(3) $\quad \{y*2 = 2^{x+1}\}\, x := x+1\, \{y*2 = 2^x\}$ (ASS)
(4) $\quad \{y*2 = 2^{x+1}\}\, x := x+1;\, y := y*2\, \{y = 2^x\}$ (2), (3), (SEQ)
(5) $\quad y = 2^x \Rightarrow y*2 = 2^{x+1}$ (ARITHMETIC)
(6) $\quad \{x \geqslant 0\}$ **call** *power_2* $\{y*2 = 2^{x+1}\}$ (1), (5), (CONS)
(7) $\quad \{x \geqslant 0\}$ **call** *power_2*; $x := x+1;\, y := y*2\, \{y = 2^x\}$
(4), (6), (SEQ)

(8) $x \geqslant 0 \wedge x \neq 0 \Rightarrow x-1 \geqslant 0$ (ARITHMETIC)
(9) $\{x-1 \geqslant 0\}\, x := x-1\, \{x \geqslant 0\}$ (ASS)
(10) $\{x-1 \geqslant 0 \wedge x \neq 0\}\, x := x-1\, \{x \geqslant 0\}$ (8), (9), (CONS)
(11) $\{x \geqslant 0 \wedge x \neq 0\}$
$x := x-1$; **call** *power_2*; $x := x+1$; $y := y * 2$
$\{y = 2^x\}$ (7), (10), (SEQ)
(12) $x \geqslant 0 \wedge x = 0 \Rightarrow 2^x = 1$ (ARITHMETIC)
(13) $\{2^x = 1\}\, y := 1\, \{y = 2^x\}$ (ASS)
(14) $\{x \geqslant 0 \wedge x = 0\}\, y := 1\, \{y = 2^x\}$ (12), (13), (CONS)
(15) $\{x \geqslant 0\}$ **if** $x = 0$ **then** $y := 1$
else [$x := x-1$; **call** *power_2*;
$x := x+1$; $y := y * 2$] **fi**
$\{y = 2^x\}$ (11), (14), (COND)
(16) $\{x \geqslant 0\}$ **call** *power_2* $\{y = 2^x\}$ (1)–(15), (REC)

EXERCISE:

(1) In the above program, replace $y := y * 2$ by $y := y * x$, and prove the postcondition $y = fac(x)$ (with the same precondition), where *fac* is the factorial function.

(2) Explain the absence of an appeal to the invocation rule in the above proof.

□

It is very important here to note the role of logical variables within the rule of recursion. Recall our stipulation, that these are implicitly universally quantified, the scope of quantification being the whole correctness assertion. Suppose that $p \equiv q \overset{df.}{\equiv} x = X$. Then the actual meaning of

$$\{p\}\ \textbf{call}\ proc\ \{q\} \vdash \{p\}\ S\{q\}\ \text{is}\ \forall X{:}\{p\}\ \textbf{call}\ proc\ \{q\} \vdash \forall X{:}\ \{p\}\ S\{q\}.$$

Thus, there is no connection between the occurrence of X in the assumption and that in the consequence. In the above example, the derivability assertion would paraphrase to the following: from the assumption that x preserves its value across a procedure call, it is provable that x preserves its value across the body S. Different recursive invocations within the body S can use the assumption with different instantiations of X, by the instantiation rule, each referring to the respective value of x just before the corresponding activation.

To see the implication of the above observation, we show the provability of $\{x = X\}$ **call** *power_2* $\{x = X\}$.

(1) $\{x = Z\}$ **call** *power_2* $\{x = Z\}$ (ASSUMPTION)
(2) $\{x = X\}\, y := y * 2\, \{x = X\}$ (ASS)
(3) $\{x = X-1\}\, x := x+1\, \{x = X\}$ (ASS), (CONS)
(4) $\{x = X-1\}$ **call** *power_2* $\{x = X-1\}$ (1), (INST)

The instantiation is of Z to $X-1$.

(5) $\{x-1 = X-1\}\, x := x-1\, \{x = X-1\}$ (ASS)

(6) $x = X \Rightarrow x-1 = X-1$ (ARITHMETIC)

(7) $\{x = X\}\, x := x-1\, \{x = X-1\}$ (ASS)

(8) $\{x = X\}$ x $:= x-1$; **call** *power_2*; $x := x+1$; $y := y*2\, \{x = X\}$ (3), (4), (7), (SEQ)

(9) $\{x = X \wedge x \neq 0\}$
$x := x-1$; **call** *power_2*; $x := x+1$; $y := y*2$
$\{x = X\}$ (8), (CONS)

(10) $\{x = X\}\, y := 1\, \{x = X\}$ (ASS)

(11) $\{x = X \wedge x = 0\}\, y := 1\, \{x = X\}$ (10), (CONS)

(12) $\{x = X \wedge x = 0\}$ **if** $x = 0$ **then** $y := 1$
else [$x := x-1$; **call** *power_2*;
$x := x+1$; $y := y*2$] **fi**
$\{x = X\}$ (9), (11), (COND)

(13) $\{x = X\}$ **call** *power_2* $\{x = X\}$ (1)–(12), (REC)

We now turn† to the establishment of the soundness and relative completeness of $\mathbf{H} \cup \{REC\}$, the extended system for proving partial correctness assertions of *PROC* programs with recursive procedures. We immediately face a problem: what could be the meaning of soundness of a meta-rule such as (REC)? As long as we considered 'standard' proof rules, for which the premisses and the conclusion all were correctness assertions, the meaning of soundness of separate rules was clearly defined: preservation of validity of the correctness assertions. However, the premiss of (REC) is not itself a correctness assertion. Rather, it is a provability claim, which has no semantic interpretation in our framework, and hence no truth value either. So, what exactly should be preserved by such a rule?

In order to obtain the right answer, we have to recall why we attributed soundness to separate rules to start with. Clearly, what we are really interested in is the soundness of the proof system as a whole, that is, that every formally derivable correctness assertion is indeed semantically valid. The attribution of soundness to separate rules was merely a means (and a successful one) of establishing the overall soundness by induction on the number of rule applications.

Thus, we should stick to the soundness of the whole extended system, and use the fact that the meta-rule still induces proofs from assumptions in the usual sense. We may interpret the provability claim in the premiss as a claim about 'shorter' executions, and establish the validity of correctness assertions obtained for 'longer' executions (where the 'length' is expressed as the number of recursive invocations).

Note, however, that we are not attributing validity to 'intermediate'

† The treatment here is different from the usual one, as for example in [54].

stages in a proof, depending on an assumption. Only conclusions after the discharging of the assumption of (REC) should be established as valid, for (REC) to be accounted for as sound.

As a first preparatory step, we define a sequence $S^{(i)}$, $i \geqslant 0$ of **recursion-free** programs that capture what might be called the (consecutive) **unfoldings** of the given recursive procedure *proc* with body S. Let Ω denote the nowhere terminating program Ω :: **while** *true* **do** *skip* **od**. The definition is by induction on i.

$$S^{(0)} \stackrel{df.}{=} \Omega$$

$$S^{(i+1)} \stackrel{df.}{=} S[S^{(i)}/\mathbf{call}\ proc]$$

where $S[S'/\mathbf{call}\ proc]$ is obtained from $S \in PROC$ by replacing every occurrence of **call** *proc* with S'.

EXAMPLE:

Consider again the procedure *power_2*, and let S be its body. We get

$S^{(0)} = \Omega$
$S^{(1)} = \mathbf{if}\ x = 0\ \mathbf{then}\ y := 1\ \mathbf{else}\ [x := x-1; \Omega; x := x+1; y := y * 2]\ \mathbf{fi}$
$S^{(2)} = \mathbf{if}\ x = 0\ \mathbf{then}\ y := 1\ \mathbf{else}\ [x := x-1;$
$[\mathbf{if}\ x = 0\ \mathbf{then}\ y := 1\ \mathbf{else}\ [x := x-1; \Omega; x := x+1; y := y * 2]\ \mathbf{fi}];$
$x := x+1; y := y * 2]\ \mathbf{fi}$
etc.

We now relate this sequence with the recursive procedure *proc*.

□

Definition:

(1) For a computation $\pi = C_i = \langle S_i, \sigma_i \rangle$, $i \geqslant 0$, its **state projection** is the sequence of states σ_i, $i \geqslant 0$.

(2) Two computations (of possibly different programs) **correspond** if their state projections are equal up to finite repetition of identical states.

□

Lemma (transition):

(1) *Downward transition:* For $S_1 \neq \mathbf{proc}; S'$ (for any S'), $\langle S_1, \sigma_1 \rangle \rightarrow \langle S_2, \sigma_2 \rangle$ in *proc* iff $\langle S_1[S^{(n)}/proc], \sigma_1 \rangle \rightarrow \langle S_2[S^{(n)}/proc], \sigma_2 \rangle$, for any $n \geqslant 0$, in $S^{(n+1)}$.

(2) *Upward transition*: For $S_1 \neq S^{(n)}; S'$ (for any S' and $n \geqslant 0$), $\langle S_1, \sigma_1 \rangle \rightarrow \langle S_2, \sigma_2 \rangle$ in $S^{(n+1)}$ iff $\langle S_1[\mathbf{call}\ proc/S^{(n)}], \sigma_1 \rangle \rightarrow \langle S_2[\mathbf{call}\ proc/S^{(n)}], \sigma_2 \rangle$, in *proc*.

Proof: The proof is by induction on the structure of S_1, following the cases in the computations lemma.

□

This lemma is easily extended to finite subcomputations by induction on their lengths, as expressed in the following corollary.

Corollary:

(1) *Downward subcomputation:* Every finite subcomputation $\langle S_1, \sigma_1\rangle \xrightarrow{*} \langle S_2, \sigma_2\rangle$ with no invocation of *proc*, has a corresponding finite subcomputation $\langle S_1[S^{(n)}/\mathbf{call}\ proc], \sigma_1\rangle \xrightarrow{*} \langle S_2[S^{(n)}/\mathbf{call}\ proc], \sigma_2\rangle$ of $S^{(n+1)}$.

(2) *Upward subcomputation:* Every finite subcomputation $\langle S_1, \sigma_1\rangle \xrightarrow{*} \langle S_2, \sigma_2\rangle$ of $S^{(n+1)}$, with no intermediate configuration of the form $\langle S^{(n)};\ S,\ \sigma\rangle$, has a corresponding finite subcomputation $\langle S_1[\mathbf{call}\ proc/S^{(n)}], \sigma_1\rangle \xrightarrow{*} \langle S_2[\mathbf{call}\ proc/S^{(n)}], \sigma_2\rangle$ of *proc*.

□

Lemma (unfolding):

(1) If π is a finite computation of $\langle \mathbf{call}\ proc, \sigma_0\rangle$, then there exists some $n \geqslant 0$ s.t. π corresponds to a finite computation of $\langle S^{(n)}, \sigma_0\rangle$.

(2) Conversely, for any $n > 0$, if π is a finite computation of $\langle S^{(n)}, \sigma_0\rangle$, then π corresponds to a finite computation of $\langle \mathbf{call}\ proc, \sigma_0\rangle$.

Proof:

(1) Let π be a finite computation of $\langle \mathbf{call}\ proc, \sigma_0\rangle$. Hence, it contains only finitely many recursive invocations of *proc*. We proceed by induction on r, the number of recursive invocations of *proc* in π.

Basis: $r = 1$. Let $\pi = \langle \mathbf{call}\ proc, \sigma_0\rangle \rightarrow \langle S, \sigma_0\rangle \rightarrow \langle S_1[S^{(n)}/proc]\ \sigma_1\rangle \rightarrow \cdots \rightarrow \langle S_k[S^{(n)}/proc]\ \sigma_k\rangle$ be a computation of **call** *proc* with only one recursive invocation (in its first transition). By the downward transition corollary, $\pi' = \langle S[S^{(n)}/proc], \sigma_0\rangle \rightarrow \langle S_1[S^{(n)}/proc], \sigma_1\rangle \rightarrow \cdots \rightarrow \langle S_k[S^{(n)}/proc], \sigma_k\rangle$ is a computation of $S^{(n+1)}$ corresponding to π.

Induction step: Suppose the claim holds for $r \leqslant m$ and let π have $m+1$ recursive calls. By the operational semantics, π has the form

$$\langle \mathbf{call}\ proc, \sigma_0\rangle \rightarrow \langle S, \sigma_0\rangle \xrightarrow{*} \langle \mathbf{call}\ proc;\ S', \sigma_1\rangle \xrightarrow{*} \langle S', \sigma_1'\rangle \xrightarrow{*} \langle E, \sigma^*\rangle$$

for some S', where $\pi^* = \langle \mathbf{call}\ proc, \sigma_1\rangle \xrightarrow{*} \langle E, \sigma_1'\rangle$ is a computation with m recursive invocations only. By the induction hypothesis, there is some $n > 1$

s.t. π^* corresponds to a finite computation $\pi^{*\prime}$ of $\langle S^{(n)}, \sigma_1 \rangle$, having the form $\langle S^{(n)}, \sigma_1 \rangle \xrightarrow{*} \langle E, \sigma_1' \rangle$. Since $\langle S, \sigma_0 \rangle \xrightarrow{*} \langle \textbf{call}\, proc; S', \sigma_1 \rangle$ is a subcomputation of *proc*, we get by the downward transition corollary that

$$\langle S[S^{(n)}/proc], \sigma_0 \rangle \xrightarrow{*} \langle S^{(n)}; S'[S^{(n)}/proc], \sigma_1 \rangle$$

is a subcomputation of $S^{(n+1)}$. Similarly,

$$\langle S'[S^{(n)}/proc], \sigma_1' \rangle \xrightarrow{*} \langle E, \sigma^* \rangle$$

is a subcomputation of $S^{(n+1)}$. Consequently,

$$\langle S^{(n+1)}, \sigma_0 \rangle \xrightarrow{*} \langle S^{(n)}; S'[S^{(n)}/proc], \sigma_1 \rangle \xrightarrow{*} \langle S'[S^{(n)}/proc], \sigma_1' \rangle \xrightarrow{*} \langle E, \sigma^* \rangle$$

is the corresponding computation of $\langle S^{(n+1)}, \sigma_0 \rangle$.

(2) Let π be a finite computation of $\langle S^{(n)}, \sigma_0 \rangle$, $n \geqslant 1$. The argument proceeds by induction on n.

Basis: $n = 1$. Since $\pi = \langle S^{(1)}, \sigma_0 \rangle$ is finite, by the operational semantics it did not reach $\Omega = S^{(0)}$. Hence, by the upward subcomputation corollary, there is a finite corresponding computation of $\langle S, \sigma_0 \rangle$ (not invoking *proc* recursively), and therefore also a corresponding computation of $\langle \textbf{call}\ proc, \sigma_0 \rangle$.

Induction step: Suppose the claim holds for $S^{(k)}$, $1 \leqslant k \leqslant m$, and let π be a finite computation of $S^{(m+1)}$. From the definition of $S^{(m+1)}$ it follows that π can be presented in the form $\alpha_1 \pi_1 \cdots \alpha_l \pi_l \alpha_{l+1}$ for some $l \geqslant 0$, where for $1 \leqslant j \leqslant l$ the computations π_j are finite computations of $S^{(m)}$. By the induction hypothesis, each π_j has a corresponding computation π_j' in *proc*. Since no α_i contains computations of $S^{(m)}$, by the upward subcomputation corollary there are corresponding subcomputations α_i' of *proc*. The computation

$$\pi' = \alpha_1' \pi_1' \cdots \alpha_l' \pi_l' \alpha_{l+1}'$$

is a computation of *proc* corresponding to π.

□

Proposition:

If $Tr_1, \{p\}\, \textbf{call}\, proc\, \{q\} \vdash_{\mathbf{H}} \{p\}\, S\, \{q\}$, then $Tr_1, \{p\}\, S^{(n)}\, \{q\} \vdash_{\mathbf{H}} \{p\}\, S^{(n+1)}\, \{q\}$ for every $n \geqslant 0$.

Proof: Consider any application of a rule in **H** using $\{p\}\, \textbf{call}\, proc\, \{q\}$ as one of its premisses. In its conclusion, there is some occurrence of **call** *proc* in the program part. By the definition of $S^{(n+1)}$, the corresponding program section is obtained by replacing that occurrence with $S^{(n)}$. Thus, the same rule can be applied in the proof of $\{p\}\, S^{(n+1)}\, \{q\}$ by using the assumption $\{p\}\, S^{(n)}\, \{q\}$.

For example, consider a proof fragment of Tr_{I},

$$\{p\}\,\mathbf{call}\,proc\,\{q\} \vdash_{\mathbf{H}} \{p\}\,S\,\{q\}$$

where the recursive invocation of *proc* is sequentially composed, say with an assignment statement $x := e$.

(i)	$\{p\}\,\mathbf{call}\,proc\,\{q\}$	(ASSUMPTION)
(j)	$\{(p')^x_e\}\,x := e\,\{p'\}$	(ASS)
(k)	$p' \Rightarrow p$	(LOGIC)
(h)	$\{(p')^x_e\}\,x := e\,\{p\}$	(j), (k), (CONS)
(g)	$\{(p')^x_e\}\,x := e;\,\mathbf{call}\,proc\,\{q\}$	(i), (h), (SEQ)

If we replace line (i) by

$$(i)\quad \{p\}\,S^{(n)}\,\{q\}$$

which is assumed, we can derive

$$(g)\quad \{(p')^x_e\}\,x := e;\,S^{(n)}\,\{q\} \qquad (i),\ (h),\ \text{(SEQ)}$$

as before.

□

By an inductive argument, using the fact that $\vdash_{\mathbf{H}} \{p\}\,\Omega\,\{q\}$ as a basis, and the proposition as the induction step, we obtain:

Conclusion:

If

$$Tr_{\mathrm{I}}, \{p\}\,\mathbf{call}\,proc\,\{q\} \vdash_{\mathbf{H}} \{p\}\,S\,\{q\}$$

then, for every $n \geqslant 0$,

$$Tr_{\mathrm{I}} \vdash_{\mathbf{H}} \{p\}\,S^{(n)}\,\{q\}$$

□

Finally, by the soundness of **H**, we have:

Conclusion:

If

$$Tr_{\mathrm{I}}, \{p\}\,\mathbf{call}\,proc\,\{q\} \vdash_{\mathbf{H}} \{p\}\,S\,\{q\}$$

then, $\models_{\mathbf{I}} \{p\}\, S^{(n)}\, \{q\}$.

□

Theorem (strong soundness of H $\cup$ {*REC*}):

For $P \in PROC$, if $Tr_{\mathbf{I}} \vdash_{\mathbf{H} \cup \{REC\}} \{p\}\, P\, \{q\}$ then $\models_{\mathbf{I}} \{p\}\, P\, \{q\}$.

Proof: The only interesting case is when $\{p\}$ **call** *proc* $\{q\}$ is deduced by means of (REC). Assume the premiss of the rule holds, and suppose that it is not the case that $\models_{\mathbf{I}} \{p\}$ **call** *proc* $\{q\}$. Clearly, every computation of **call** *proc* which generates infinitely many recursive invocations of the procedure *proc* is nonterminating, and hence cannot violate the partial correctness by definition. Thus, we may assume that there exists a terminating computation of **call** *proc*, starting in a configuration with an initial state σ_0 such that $\sigma_0 \models_{\mathbf{I}} p$, and ends in a terminal configuration with a state σ^*, such that $\sigma^* \models_{\mathbf{I}} q$ does not hold. By the unfolding lemma, this computation is also a computation of $S^{(n)}$, for some $n \geqslant 0$, violating the partial correctness of the latter w.r.t. the same specification, as obtained from the second conclusion above (under the assumption that (REC) was successfully applied).

□

We now turn to show the relative completeness of **H** $\cup$ {*REC*}.

Theorem:

H $\cup$ {*REC*} is relatively complete.

Proof: Let *SL* be expressive for **I** and *PROC*, and assume that $\models_{\mathbf{I}} \{p\}$ **call** *proc* $\{q\}$ holds. We have to show that $Tr_{\mathbf{I}} \vdash_{\mathbf{H} \cup \{REC\}} \{p\}$ **call** *proc* $\{q\}$. Let $\bar{x}$ be the list of all program variables free in *S*, the body of the procedure *proc*. As a preliminary step, we first consider a proof of $\{p\}\, S\, \{q\}$ from a recursive assumption of a special form, known also as the **most general** partial correctness assertion, namely $\{\bar{x} = \bar{X}\}$ **call** *proc* $\{r\}$, where *r* expresses

$$post_{\mathbf{I}}(\bar{x} = \bar{X}, \mathbf{call}\ proc)$$

Here the expressiveness assumption is used. The list $\bar{X}$ is a list of fresh specification variables, not occurring in *p* or in *q*. The role of this predicate is similar to that of its counterpart in the completeness proof of **H**. It characterizes all states originating after an arbitrary number of recursive calls.

We now proceed by induction on the structure of *S*, where the only interesting case is for *S* equal to **call** *proc*. Thus, we want to show that $Tr_{\mathbf{I}}, \{\bar{x} = \bar{X}\}$ **call** *proc* $\{r\} \vdash_{\mathbf{H} \cup \{REC\}} \{p\}$ **call** *proc* $\{q\}$.

First, $\{p^{\bar{x}}_{\bar{X}}\}$ **call** *proc* $\{p^{\bar{x}}_{\bar{X}}\}$ is obtained by the invariance theorem for *PROC* (see exercise), since $p^{\bar{x}}_{\bar{X}}$ does not refer to any program variables by its construction. By the conjunction rule, we get $\{\bar{x} = \bar{X} \wedge p^{\bar{x}}_{\bar{X}}\}$ **call** *proc* $\{r \wedge p^{\bar{x}}_{\bar{X}}\}$. An easy application of the definition of r shows that $\models_{\mathbf{I}} (r \wedge p^{\bar{x}}_{\bar{X}} \Rightarrow q)$. For, assume that $\sigma \models_{\mathbf{I}} r \wedge p^{\bar{x}}_{\bar{X}}$. By the definition of r, there exists a state σ_0 s.t. $\mathbf{M}[\![$**call** *proc*$]\!](\sigma_0) = \sigma$, and $\sigma_0[\![\bar{x}]\!] = \bar{X}$. So, $\sigma_0 \models_{\mathbf{I}} \bar{x} = \bar{X} \wedge p^{\bar{x}}_{\bar{X}}$ (the latter conjunct being independent of σ). Since $\models_{\mathbf{I}} (\bar{x} = \bar{X} \wedge p^{\bar{x}}_{\bar{X}} \Rightarrow p)$, we have that $\sigma_0 \models_{\mathbf{I}} p$. By the initial partial correctness assumption $\models_{\mathbf{I}} \{p\}$ **call** *proc* $\{q\}$, *we thus get* $\sigma \models_{\mathbf{I}} q$, as required. So, by the consequence rule, we have

$$\{\bar{x} = \bar{X} \wedge p^{\bar{x}}_{\bar{X}}\}\ \textbf{call}\ proc\ \{q\}.$$

Finally, by instantiating $\bar{X}$ to $\bar{x}$ we get $\{p\}$ **call** *proc* $\{q\}$. This instantiation is valid, though referring to program variables, since by assumption X does not occur in q.

To complete the completeness proof, we have to show the provability of the most general partial correctness assertion. By the definition of r we have that $\models_{\mathbf{I}} \{\bar{x} = \bar{X}\}$ **call** *proc* $\{r\}$. Since by definition $\mathbf{M}[\![$**call** *proc*$]\!] = \mathbf{M}[\![S]\!]$, we also have $\models_{\mathbf{I}} \{\bar{x} = \bar{X}\}\ S\ \{r\}$. By the preliminary step above,

$$Tr_{\mathbf{I}}, \{\bar{x} = \bar{X}\}\ \textbf{call}\ proc\ \{r\} \vdash_{\mathbf{H} \cup \{REC\}} \{p\}\ S\ \{q\}$$

So, by *REC* we get the required consequence $Tr_{\mathbf{I}} \vdash_{\mathbf{H} \cup \{REC\}} \{p\}$ **call** *proc* $\{q\}$.

□

To understand how this proof works, consider the following recursive procedure over the integers.

procedure d: **if** $x = 0$ **then** *skip*
else $x := x - 1$; **call** d; $x := x + 2$ **fi**

An easy calculation shows that $post_{\mathbf{N}}(x = X, \textbf{call}\ d) = (x = 2X)$. Suppose we want to prove $\{x > Y > 1\}$ **call** d $\{x > 2Y\}$. By the above construction, the recursive assumption generated, after taking into account the effects of the body S, is $\{x = X - 1 \wedge X > Y\}$ **call** d $\{x = 2X - 2 \wedge X > Y\}$. Indeed, the postcondition implies $x > 2Y - 2$, and after the increment of x the postcondition $x > 2Y$ is obtained for S, as required.

6.3.1 Proving termination of recursive procedures

As already mentioned before, the introduction of recursion is another source of nontermination: an infinite sequence of recursive invocations. The simplest example manifesting this phenomenon is the following program:

P:: **procedure** *diverge*: **call** *diverge*;
call *diverge*

which never terminates. As a somewhat less obvious example, consider

$$P:: \textbf{procedure } d\_2: \textbf{if } x=0 \textbf{ then } skip \textbf{ else } x:=x-2; \textbf{ call } d\_2; x:=x+2 \textbf{ fi}.$$

This procedure does not terminate in initial states in which the value of x is odd. Contrast this with the procedure d above, which terminates for $x \geqslant 0$, satisfying the same partial correctness assertion.

We already know that termination proofs appeal to an inductive argument, using a well-founded, partially ordered set. In order to arrive at the right compositional proof rule for proving termination of recursive procedures, we start by inspecting an informal proof of $\langle x \geqslant 0 \rangle$ **call** d $\langle true \rangle$. Suppose $x = X$ initially. If $X = 0$, then the body of d terminates immediately, without generating any further recursive invocations of d. Otherwise, $X > 0$. After the decrement of x, we have $x = X - 1 \geqslant 0$. By the induction assumption, the next **call** d terminates, and hence the whole body terminates, terminating the initial invocation.

The essence of the argument is that in the sequence of states just before the consecutive recursive invocations **call** d, the values of x constitute a decreasing sequence of natural numbers, thus being finite.

How can this argument be generalized to arbitrary recursive procedures? In contrast to the similar situation for PLW programs, where we could associate a parametrized invariant with the iterative statement and show its reestablishment with a decrease in the variant, the corresponding parametrized invariant for recursive invocation has to rely again on the methodology of proof from assumptions.

We thus arrive at the following formulation of a recursion meta-rule for total correctness, for a deterministic base language. The extension to a nondeterministic base language has to bypass the uniform decrement of 1 in the parameter, and its exact formulation appears as an exercise.

Recursion rule:

$$\frac{\forall n: [\langle pi(n) \rangle \textbf{ call } proc \langle q \rangle \vdash \langle pi(n+1) \rangle\, S\, \langle q \rangle],\ \neg pi(0)}{\langle \exists n: pi(n) \rangle \textbf{ call } proc \langle q \rangle} \qquad \text{(REC*)}$$

provided that the declaration **procedure** $proc$: S is present in the program and $n \notin var(S, q)$.

□

Note the difference in the scope of the universal quantifier on n, which is the whole provability assertion. This is essential for soundness of the rule.

In order to show that $\vdash_{\mathbf{H^*} \cup \{REC^*\}} \langle x \geqslant 0 \rangle$ **call** d $\langle true \rangle$, we may choose the parametrized invariant

$$pi(x, n) \overset{df.}{=} x \geqslant 0 \wedge x + 1 = n$$

EXERCISES:

(1) Complete the above proof.

(2) Show why the similar 'proof', with the same parametrized invariant, fails for the procedure *d_2*.

(3) Show that $\vdash_{\mathbf{H}^* \cup \{REC^*\}} \langle x \geqslant 0 \wedge even(x) \rangle$ **call** $d\_2 \langle true \rangle$.

□

We shall return to the termination proofs after the introduction of parameter passing. The informal interpretation of the role of the variant n is a measure of the number of active invocations until termination. Here an invocation is active if the instance of the body has not yet terminated. Under that interpretation, the provability assumption means that, under the assumption that the 'inner' invocation generates n recursive invocations, there is a proof that the body needs no more than $n+1$ such invocations.

Theorem (arithmetic soundness and completeness of (REC*)):

For $\mathbf{I}^+$ an arithmetical interpretation, $P \in PROC(PL)$, **D** a proof system for total correctness for *PL*,

$$Tr_{\mathbf{I}^+} \vdash_{\mathbf{D} \cup \{REC^*\}} \langle p \rangle\ P\ \langle q \rangle \Leftrightarrow \models_{\mathbf{I}^+} \langle p \rangle\ P\ \langle q \rangle.$$

The soundness proof is as usual, generating an infinite decreasing sequence of natural numbers under the assumption of nontermination, a contradiction. For semantic completeness, $pi(n)$ is defined as the set of states from which the program terminates by n active recursive invocations, and under the assumption of arithmetical interpretation, such predicates can be expressed. We omit the details.

□

We could avoid the special convention of the scope of the universal quantification over n being the whole provability assumption by appealing to a somewhat different intuition. Suppose we can find a parametrized invariant such that, under the assumption that the 'inner' invocations do not increase it, it is decreased by the body. Then, a similar soundness argument would apply.

This might be formulated as the following alternative recursion rule.

Alternative recursion rule:

$$\frac{\neg pi(0), \langle pi(n) \rangle \mathbf{call}\, proc \langle \exists m : m \leqslant n \wedge pi(m) \rangle \vdash \langle pi(n) \wedge n > 0 \rangle S \langle \exists m : m < n \wedge pi(m) \rangle}{\langle \exists n : pi(n) \rangle \mathbf{call}\, proc \langle true \rangle.}$$

(REC′)

□

Note that here n is a usual specification variable, separately quantified implicitly in the antecedent and in the consequent of the provability assumption.

However, for the procedure d as above, we cannot use the same parametrized invariant as with the previous rule. The reason is that the body of d 'restores' x after the exit of the recursive invocation. The solution is to augment the program with **auxiliary variables** which have no effect on the computation, but 'remember' state information for the proof. For example, we could add to d another variable, say y, which records the values of x just before recursive invocations, and which is not modified after the exit of the invocation, carrying the 'old' state to the end of the body. We get the following modification d' of d.

procedure d' : **if** $x = 0$ **then** *skip*
else $x := x - 1$; $y := y - 1$; **call** d' ; $x := x + 2$ **fi**.

Now we can use the invariant $pi(y,\ n) \stackrel{df.}{=} y \geqslant 0 \wedge y + 1 = n$ to satisfy the modified rule.

EXERCISE:

Show that replacing $m \leqslant n$ by $m < n$ in the postcondition of the assumption of the provability claim in (REC′) is incorrect. Under what condition does $m = n$ arise in the proof of d'?

□

6.4 Parameter passing

In this section we augment the *PROC* language with a parameter passing construct and local variable declaration facilities, without which there is not much use for procedures. Again, as a first stage, we consider nonrecursive procedures. The basic reasoning principle is some substitution of the actual parameters in correctness assertions that have been proved for the procedure in terms of its formal parameters. This reasoning should reflect the parameter binding occurring during execution. Different modes of parameter passing induce different kinds of substitutions.

However, some care must be taken to avoid certain 'blind substitution', which leads to invalid reasoning. Consider the following simple procedure, using a self-explanatory notation for parametrization.

procedure $inc\_1(x, y)$: $x := y + 1$.

Clearly, a valid postcondition for inc_1's body is $x = y + 1$. Suppose we take this to be the postcondition of the procedure call, and agree that in order to deduce a property of an invocation **call** *inc*_1(a, b), we simply substitute a for x and b for y, to obtain $a = b+1$ as the conclusion. However, after **call** *inc*_1(c, c) we get the contradictory postcondition $c = c+1$. The source of the problem here is known as **aliasing,** whereby apparently different names coincide when bound in certain ways, as in the example. In the body of the procedure, x and y are considered to be different variables, apparently having independent values. However, the procedure call in the example identifies both with c. There are ways of complicating the rules and dealing correctly with aliasing. Here we shall prohibit such calls (see the suggestions for further reading for references to such treatments).

However, aliasing is not the only source of pitfalls. Consider the following procedure declaration.

procedure *inc* (x): $x := x+1$.

We certainly should be able to prove $\{x = y\}$ **call** *inc* (x) $\{x = y+1\}$. By blind substitution, we would obtain $\{y = y\}$ **call** *inc*(y) $\{y = y+1\}$, another obviously false conclusion, this time arising from a parameter appearing in the specification.

Thus, the conclusion is that a finer analysis of the way conclusions about parametrized activations are drawn is needed.

We now introduce an extension of *PROC* with parametrized activations. We restrict the discussion to two modes of parametrization, known as **value** parameters and **result** parameters (others appear as exercises). The former supply values to the procedure, and are not allowed to be modified within its body, while the latter are used to transfer values from the procedure to its invoking environment. Furthermore, to avoid here the more delicate issues of **scope rules** (for example dynamic compared with static scopes), we stipulate that procedures do not refer at all to global variables (that is, variables which are neither parameters nor locally declared). We first consider 'pure' procedures, which use only parameters; then we consider the declaration of local variables also.

A procedure declaration and invocation now have the following form.

P:: D;S.
D:: **procedure** *<pname>*(**val** ⟨var_list_1⟩; **var**⟨var_list_2⟩): S
S:: **call** *<pname>*$(\bar{e};\bar{x})$ | as for base language ...

where var_list_i, $i = 1,2$ are lists of variables, called, respectively, the **value** and the **result formal parameters**, and $\bar{e}, \bar{x}$ are, respectively, lists of expressions and of variables, called the **value** and the **result actual parameters**. The following constraints are assumed.

(1) The lists var_list_i, $i = 1,2$ are disjoint and each contains pairwise distinct elements.

(2) The lengths of $\bar{e}$ and $\bar{x}$ are equal to the lengths of var_list_1 and of var_list_2, respectively.

(3) The list $\bar{x}$ has pairwise distinct elements, and no expression in $\bar{e}$ refers to a variable in $\bar{x}$.

(4) In the body S of the procedure, $var\_list_1 \cap change\ (S) = \varnothing$.

Here *change* (*S*) is defined as the collection of variables which either are assigned to directly, or appear as result actual parameters in some invocation statement in *S*. Also, $var(pname) \stackrel{df.}{=} var(S) \cup \bigcup_{i=1,2} var\_list_i$.

In addition, we initially assume that the call graph is acyclic, that is the absence of recursion. Note that the offending invocations considered above are not allowed in the extended *PROC*.

The intended meaning of a procedure invocation is first binding the formal **value** parameters to the corresponding actual values, then executing the body, and finally returning the result values in the result parameters. However, since the names of the parameters may conflict with names of state variables outside the body, we also need to create a new instance of the parameters, before binding them. This is particularly important for recursion, where several instances of the parameters coexist, only one of which is 'active'.

A major difference imposed on the semantic definition is the need of a 'reservoir' of **fresh** variables, to be used in order to express nonpersisting state components such as parameters, and later also local variables. Intuitively, such entities are 'created' upon invocation of a procedure, and 'cease to exist' upon completion of such an invocation. Our current framework, in which states assign values to all the potential variables, is inconvenient to accommodate treatment of such allocations, which in real implementations are most often handled by stacks, or other complicated memory structures.

Thus, for the rest of this section, we shall adopt a different definition of states, namely finite mappings from variables to values. We denote by $dom(\sigma)$ the **domain**† of σ, that is the collection of variables mapped by σ. To take advantage of this finiteness for our need, we introduce two state reformation operations, that expand and restrict the support of a state. This immediately poses another problem: When a 'new' variable, say x, is added, as a result of a declaration, to a state σ, what is the value of $\sigma[\![x]\!]$? We stipulate a special value, **u**, interpreted as an undefined, or unassigned, value, and take it to be the value of a fresh state variable prior to the first (in time) assignment to this variable by the program.

(1) *include* (x, σ), with $x \notin dom(\sigma)$, is the expansion of σ by x, mapping x to **u**.

(2) *exclude* (x, σ) is the state obtained by removing x from the support of σ, leaving x unmapped by σ.

† This is sometimes called also the **support**.

Both operations are naturally extended for $\bar{x}$ instead of x.

Another small obstacle is that the definition by transition rules has to unwind the recursion, and introduce an explicit deallocation statement, 'planted' in the right place, to represent the LIFO deallocation assumed. Thus, we augment the language with a **release** (<*var_list*>) statement (not appearing in the verified programs).

The operational semantics is defined by replacing the rule for an invocation transition by the following alternate rule. Let $\bar{y}'$ be a list of fresh variables, not in $dom(\sigma_0)$, of the same length as $\bar{y}$.

$$\langle \mathbf{call}\ proc\ (\bar{e};\bar{x}),\ \sigma_0\rangle \rightarrow \langle \bar{y}' := \bar{e};\ S\,[\bar{y}' \mid \bar{y}];\ \bar{x} := \bar{z};\ \mathbf{release}\,(\bar{y}'),\ include\,(\bar{y}',\sigma_0)\rangle$$

provided that P contains the declaration **procedure** *proc* $(\bar{y};\bar{z})$: S. The renamed body $S[\bar{y}' \mid \bar{y}]$ is obtained from S by renaming all the free occurrences of $\bar{y}$ into $\bar{y}'$, as usual.

This rule captures the operational idea that executing a procedure activation consists of first expanding the state, then assigning the actual value parameters to their formal 'fresh' counterparts, then executing the body, which possibly updates the result formal parameters, and upon termination of the body execution ends with assigning the final values of the result formal parameters to their actual counterparts and releasing the fresh variables. This last effect is achieved by the releasing transition

$$\langle release\ (\bar{y}'), \sigma\rangle \rightarrow \langle E,\ exclude\ (\bar{y}', \sigma)\rangle$$

EXERCISE:

Explain why we had to introduce an extra deallocation statement, but need not do the same for the allocation.

□

The change in the definition of a state enforces a corresponding modification of the satisfaction of a state assertion by a state. We now have to account for the interpretation of variables in the assertion, which are not in the support of the state. The convention adopted is to interpret all such variables as implicitly universally quantified. It turns out that using this convention allows for preserving all other definitions, in particular the ones of satisfaction of a correctness assertion by a program.

We now turn to the formulation of a proof rule for deriving partial correctness properties of a parametrized invocation. One immediate candidate that suggests itself from the definition of the semantics is

$$\frac{\{p\}\ \bar{y}' := \bar{e};\ S\,[\bar{y}' \mid \bar{y}];\ \bar{x} := \bar{z}\ \{q\}}{\{p\}\ \mathbf{call}\ proc\ (\bar{e};\bar{x})\ \{q\}}$$

(with a number of syntactic restrictions). However, such a rule is not canonical, requiring a separate proof of the 'modified body' for each invocation. Rather, we are looking for a way to derive some general property of the body, and adapt it to each invocation, in terms of the actual parameters of that invocation.

First, we reinstate the invocation rule in a slightly modified form.

$$\frac{\{p'\}\ S\ \{q'\}}{\{p'\}\ \mathbf{call}\ \mathit{proc}\ (\bar{y};\bar{z})\ \{q'\}}$$

provided that P contains the declaration **procedure** *proc* $(\bar{y};\bar{z})$: S, and $\mathit{free}\ (p') \subseteq \bar{y} \cup \bar{z}$, $\mathit{free}\ (q') \subseteq \bar{z}$.

The meaning of this rule is that a partial correctness assertion about a 'dummy' invocation, which takes all the actual parameters as the corresponding formal ones, can be inferred from the corresponding assertion about the body. Note that the postcondition restricts only the result parameters. Reference in the postcondition to initial values of value parameters is again achieved by using free specification variables.

Once we have a means to deduce partial correctness assertions about this dummy invocation, we now may adapt it, taking into account the specific actual parameters of the invocation. Consider an invocation **call** *proc* $(\bar{e};\ \bar{x})$, and suppose that the required partial correctness assertion about it is of the form $\{p\}$ **call** *proc* $(\bar{e};\ \bar{x})$ $\{q\}$. In view of the assignment of actual value parameters to their corresponding formal parameters, which precedes the body S of procedure *proc*, clearly $p \Rightarrow (p')^{\bar{y}}_{\bar{e}}$ should hold, so that the body is executed from a state satisfying its assumed precondition. Similarly, in view of the post-assignment of the result parameters following S, q' has to imply the appropriate variant of q. Suppose that the effect of S with the value parameters $\bar{e}$ is the assignment of $\bar{a}$ to $\bar{z}$, the formal result parameters. This turns out to be also the assignment to the actual result parameters $\bar{x}$, and hence has to satisfy the postcondition q of the invocation. Thus we end up with the additional requirement in the precondition $\forall \bar{a}{:}[(q')^{\bar{z}}_{\bar{a}} \Rightarrow q^{\bar{x}}_{\bar{a}}]$. Accumulating all these requirements leads to the rule of adaptation† below.

Rule of adaptation:

$$\frac{\{p'\}\ \mathbf{call}\ \mathit{proc}\ (\bar{y};\ \bar{z})\ \{q'\}}{\{(p')^{\bar{y}}_{\bar{e}} \wedge \forall \bar{a}{:}\ [(q')^{\bar{z}}_{\bar{a}} \Rightarrow q^{\bar{x}}_{\bar{a}}]\}\ \mathbf{call}\ \mathit{proc}\ (\bar{e};\ \bar{x})\ \{q\}} \qquad \text{(ADAPT)}$$

Recall the assumed universal quantification on all specification variables.

□

† In the literature, this rule appears with more restrictions, for example non-aliasing, which were imposed here as restriction on the programming language considered.

P:: **procedure** *inc_1*$(y;z)$: $z:=y+1$;
call *inc_1*$(u;v)$.

Figure 6.2 Example procedure.

EXAMPLE:

Let us return to the procedure *inc_1*, with its formal parameters passed by value and by result, respectively (see Figure 6.2). Suppose we want to establish $\{u=0\}\ P\ \{v^2=v\}$.

(1) $\{y=Y\}\ z:=y+1\ \{z=Y=1\}$ (ASS)
(2) $\{y=Y\}$ **call** *add_1*$(z;y)$ $\{z=Y+1\}$ (1),(INVOC)
(3) $\{y=0\}$ **call** *add_1*$(z;y)$ $\{z=1\}$ (2), (INST)
(4) $\forall a:[a=1 \Rightarrow a^2=a]$ (ARITHMETIC)

Thus, this conjunct can be removed from the precondition.

(5) $\{u=0\}$ **call** *add_1*$(u;v)$ $\{v^2=v\}$ (3),(4),(ADAPT),(CONS)

□

This rule is strong enough to handle many of the frequently encountered procedure specifications. However, occasionally the precondition is too strong. Following is an example where this rule does not suffice.

EXAMPLE:

Suppose we want to specify a procedure *r_to_i* $(y;z)$, which returns in z an integer 'approximation' to the real y. In case y is an integer to start with, z should return the initial value of y itself. Rounding, truncating, taking ceiling or floor are all correct bodies, satisfying such a specification. We assume a predicate $int(x)$, characterizing the reals which are integers. The formal statement is $\{int(X) \wedge X \leqslant y \leqslant X+1\}$ $S\ \{z=X \vee z=X+1\}$.

□

EXERCISE:

(Tricky) Check that if $x=Y$ initially, then $z=Y$ upon termination is implied.

□

Consider now an invocation **call** *r_to_i*$(u;v)$, where the required postcondition is $v = 0$. The only way to apply (ADAPT) is with the *false* precondition, while $\models\{u = 0.0\}$ **call** $r\_to\_i(u; v)$ $\{v = 0\}$ certainly holds (in the standard reals and integers).

In the suggestions for further reading, a reference to a rule stronger than (ADAPT) is provided.

We end our discussion of procedures by considering two more issues. First, we augment the language with another construct, local variables declarations, allowing variables whose value is accessible only in the body of the procedure in which they are declared. Thus, any modification of the values of such variables is 'unsensed' outside the invoked procedure. The syntax of such a declaration is given by **new** <*var_list*>, and it can only appear at the header of a procedure declaration. Thus, the new form of a procedure declaration is now **procedure** $\langle pname\rangle$ $(\langle var\_list_1\rangle; \langle var\_list_2\rangle)$; **new**$\langle var\_list_3\rangle : S$.

To define the meaning of such declarations, we add to the operational semantics a transition defining a variable declaration as the expansion of the state with a fresh list of local variables, accompanied by the corresponding renaming the occurrences of the local variables in the body.

Let $\bar{y}'$ be a list of fresh variables, not in $dom(\sigma_0)$, of the same length as $\bar{y}$.

$$\langle \mathbf{new}\ \bar{y}: S, \sigma_0\rangle \rightarrow \langle S[\bar{y}' \mid \bar{y}];\ \mathbf{release}\ (\bar{y}),\ include\ (\bar{y}', \sigma_0)\rangle$$

Thus, any state information about $\bar{y}$ is not used within S, the **scope** of the declaration. The treatment is similar to that of value parameters, only without the initialization by binding.

Variable declaration rule:

$$\frac{\{p \wedge x = \mathbf{u}\}\ S[x \mid w]\ \{q\}}{\{p\}\ \mathbf{call}\ proc\ (y; z)\ \{q\}} \qquad \text{(VDEC)}$$

provided that P contains the declaration **procedure** $proc\ (\bar{y}; \bar{z})$; **new** $w: S$, and $x \notin free\ (p, S, q)$.

□

EXERCISE:

Give an example where the precondition $x = \mathbf{u}$ is indeed needed.

□

Finally, we have to re-incorporate recursion to the context of parametrized procedures with local variables. The recursion rule is slightly modified, to accommodate the parametrization.

Rule of parametrized recursion:

$$\frac{Tr_1, \{p\}\ \mathbf{call}\ proc\,(\bar{y};\bar{z})\,\{q\} \vdash \{p\}\,S\,\{q\}}{\{p\}\ \mathbf{call}\ proc\,(\bar{y};\bar{z})\,\{q\}} \qquad \text{(PREC)}$$

with similar restrictions as before.

□

We now put this machinery to work on examples.

EXAMPLE:

Consider the parametrized procedure for computing factorials in Figure 6.3. We want to show that $Tr_{1_0} \vdash \{a = A \geqslant 0\}$ **call** *fact* $(a; b)\ \{b = A!\}$. Following is a proof.

(1) $\{y = Y \geqslant 0$ **call** *fact* $y; z)\ \{z = Y!\}$ (ASSUMPTION)
(2) $\{z \times y = Y!\}\ z := z * y\ \{z = Y!\}$ (ASS),(CONS)
(3) $y = Y > 0 \Rightarrow [y - 1 = Y - 1 \geqslant 0 \wedge \forall c : [c = (Y-1)! \Rightarrow Y \times c = Y!]]$ (ARITHMETIC)
(4) $\{y = Y > 0\}$ **call** *fact* $(y-1; z)\ \{y \times z = Y!\}$ (1),(3),(ADAPT),(CONS)
(5) $\{y = Y > 0\}$ **call** *fact* $(y-1; z);\ z := z * y \{z = Y!\}$ (2),(4),(SEQ)
(6) $\{y = Y = 0\}\ z := 1\ \{z = Y!\}$ (ASS),(CONS)
(7) $\{y = Y \geqslant 0\}$ **if** $y = 0$
then $z := 1$
else call *fact* $(y-1; z);\ z := y * z$ **fi** $\{z = Y!\}$
(5),(6),(COND)
(8) $\{y = Y \geqslant 0\}$ **call** *fact* $(y; z)\ \{z = Y!\}$ (1)–(7), (PREC)
(9) $\forall c : [c = Y! \Rightarrow c = Y!]$ (ARITHMETIC)
(10) $\{a = A \geqslant 0\}$ **call** *fact* $(a; b)\ \{b = A!\}$ (8),(9),(ADAPT),(CONS)

□

EXERCISE:

Show how to derive the postcondition $b = a!$.

□

EXAMPLE (Pnueli):

Below we consider another example, a variant of Fibonacci's sequence, incorporating also local variables and more than one recursive call within the procedure's body.

Let α_1, α_2 be the two (different) roots of the quadratic equation

procedure *fact*$(y; z)$: **if** $y = 0$ **then** $z := 1$
else call *fact*$(y-1; z)$; $z := y * z$ **fi**.

Figure 6.3 Parametrized factorial procedure.

$u^2 - u - 1 = 0$. Actually, these are $(1 \pm \sqrt{5})/2$, and they satisfy the following property.

$$\alpha_1 + \alpha_2 = 1 \qquad \text{(F)}$$

Consider the program defined in Figure 6.4. We want to prove that $\{a = A \geqslant 0\}\ P\ \{b = \alpha_1^A + \alpha_2^A\}$. We present a proof below.

(1) $\{v = V \geqslant 0\}$ **call** *fib*$(v; x)$ $\{x = \alpha_1^V + \alpha_2^V\}$ (ASSUMPTION)
(2) $0 \leqslant V < 2 \Rightarrow 2 - V = \alpha_1^V + \alpha_2^V$ (ARITHMETIC)

(Case $V = 0$ is immediate. For $V = 1$, use property (F) above.)

(3) $\{0 \leqslant v = V < 2\}\ x := 2 - v\ \{x = \alpha_1^V + \alpha_2^V\}$ (ASS),(2),(CONS)
(4) $v = V \geqslant 2 \Rightarrow v - 1 = V - 1 \geqslant 0\ \wedge$ (ARITHMETIC)
$\forall c: [c = \alpha_1^{V-1} + \alpha_2^{V-1} \Rightarrow c = \alpha_1^{V-1} + \alpha_2^{V-1}]$
(5) $\{v = V \geqslant 2\}$ **call** *fib* $(v-1; y_1)$ $\{y_1 = \alpha_1^{V-1} + \alpha_1^{V-1}\}$
(1),(3),(4),(ADAPT),(INVOC),(CONS)
(6) $v = V \geqslant 2 \Rightarrow v - 2 = V - 2 \geqslant 0\ \wedge$
$\forall c: [c = \alpha_1^{V-2} + \alpha_2^{V-2} \Rightarrow c = \alpha_2^{V-2} + \alpha_2^{V-2}]$
(ARITHMETIC)
(7) $\{v = V \geqslant 2 \wedge y_1 = \alpha_1^{V-1} + \alpha_2^{V-1}\}$
call *fib* $(v-2; y_2)$ (1),(6),(ADAPT),(INVOC),(CONS)
$\{y_1 = \alpha_1^{V-1} + \alpha_2^{V-1} \wedge y_2 = \alpha_1^{V-2} + \alpha_2^{V-2}\}$
(8) $V \geqslant 2 \wedge y_1 = \alpha_1^{V-1} + \alpha_2^{V-1} \wedge y_2 = \alpha_1^{V-2} + \alpha_2^{V-2}\ \wedge$
$\alpha_1^2 - \alpha_1 - 1 = 0 \wedge \alpha_2^2 - \alpha_2 - 1 = 0$
$\Rightarrow y_1 + y_2 = \alpha_1^V + \alpha_2^V$ (ARITHMETIC)

(Recall the equation which α_i, $i = 1, 2$ solve).

(9) $\{v = V \geqslant 2\} x := y_1 + y_2 \{x = \alpha_1^V + \alpha_2^V\}$ (ASS),(8),(CONS)
(10) $\{v = V \geqslant 2\}$
call *fib* $(v-1; y_1)$; **call** *fib* $(v-2; y_2)$; $x := y_1 + y_2$
$\{x = \alpha_1^V + \alpha_2^V\}$ (5),(7),(9),(SEQ), (CONS)
(11) $\{v = V \geqslant 0\}$ (3),(10),(COND),(VDEC)
new y_1, y_2; **if** $v < 2$ **then** $x := 2 - v$
else [call *fib* $(v-1; y_1)$; **call** *fib* $(v-2; y_2)$; $x := y_1 + y_2]$ **fi**;
$\{x = \alpha_1^V + \alpha_2^V\}$

(A dummy renaming was applied here.)

P:: **procedure** *fib* $(v; x)$:
new y_1, y_2;
if $v < 2$ **then** $x := 2 - v$
else [**call** *fib* $(v-1; y_1)$; **call** *fib* $(v-2; y_2)$; $x := y_1 + y_2$];
call *fib* $(a; b)$.

Figure 6.4. A variant of Fibonacci's sequence.

(12) $\{v = V \geqslant 0\}$ **call** *fib* $(v; x)$ $\{x = \alpha_1^V + \alpha_2^V\}$ (1)–(11),(PREC)

Skipping the final adaptation details, as before,

$\{a = A \geqslant 0\}$ P $\{b = \alpha_1^A + \alpha_2^A\}$ (12),(ADAPT)

□

EXERCISE:

Prove the arithmetic claims in lines (2), (4), (6) and (8).

□

6.5 Conclusions

In this chapter, we have extended the compositional approach to programs with procedures, parameter passing, recursion, and local variables. We have not comprehensively covered the whole spectrum of problems raised by such programs. For example, we did not relate to other parameter passing modes such as call by name, nor did we consider more elaborate scope rules or passing procedures as parameters.

As we have seen, there are two main issues that have to be taken care of. The first one relates to various forms of name clashes and aliasing, that prohibit the modeling of semantic binding of parameters by means of simple syntactic substitutions. In most cases, we just restricted the programming language in such ways as to avoid the 'offending' name clashes. However, such restriction may conflict with the expressive power needed for natural programming, and there are more advanced treatments that can handle properly such constructs, having more elaborate proof rules. References are given at the end of the chapter. The second issue was the presence of recursion, that forced us to appeal to a more elaborate notion of a proof, by means of a meta-rule, relying on proof from assumptions, with the extra complication induced on soundness and completeness proofs.

Some combinations of constructs related to procedures become so complicated, that it can be shown that there do not exist sound and relatively complete proof rules for partial correctness for languages exhibiting these combinations. Such impossibilities transcend the deficiencies of inexpressive interpretations. One such list consists of the following items:

(1) procedure names as parameters,
(2) recursion,
(3) static scope,
(4) global variables, and
(5) internal procedures.

The suggestions for further reading provide references for such incompleteness results.

Another indication of the intricacy of rules dealing with the language constructs considered in this chapter is that several wrong rules have been proposed, the errors in which were caught much later. However, any serious methodological attempt at verification of actual software will have to deal with such mechanisms to be of any practical use. Thus, awareness of complications and limitations is of crucial importance when programs with procedures are concerned.

Bibliographic notes and suggestions for further reading

Bibliographic notes The treatment of procedures originates from [70], where the rules of invocation and recursion are presented. The case of parameterless, nonrecursive procedures is treated in [54]. The soundness proof of the system augmented with the recursion rule is different from the ones in the literature, for example [17], [54], the former extending the calculus of correctness assertions with implication among such assertions, the latter resorting to a Gentzen-like sequents version of the proof system. Some problems with this kind of indirect soundness proof (for total correctness) were recently pointed out in [99]. The completeness proof for the recursion rule is a modification of Gorelick's proof [100] (as presented in [54]), the latter not being specific about the scope of free specification variables in the recursion meta-rule presented here. Another proposal for syntactically distinguishing variables which refer to 'old values' appears in [16]. The meta-rule for total correctness was proposed in [101], with a similar rule stated for dynamic logic in [57]. The alternative termination rule, though known, does not seem to have been explicitly discussed in the literature. My attention to it was drawn by Shmuel Katz. The original introduction of the rule of adaptation is in [70]. A more extensive development appears in [14] for passing parameters by reference. Here we used a variant fitting to the assumed value result passing mode. The example where the adaptation rule fails is from [102]. A thorough analysis of various variants of the rule of adaptation, in the context of parameterless procedures, is presented in [103], together with their impact on relative completeness. It also contains a discussion of the nonsoundness of the Euclid rule [68]; this observation appears also in [104], [105] and later in [14]. No focused discussion of completeness in the parametrized case is explicitly present in the literature. The treatment of parameters and local variables via renaming and state reformation appears in [106] and is surveyed in [54]. The proof of the recursive factorial procedure is a variation on the one in [70].

Suggestions for further reading An explanation of the procedure proof rules in terms of weakest precondition predicate transformers can be found in [107]. A proof of the equivalence between the rule derived in [107] and the one in [14] (the variant of which was used here) appears in [108]. A derivation of a stronger rule (with a weaker precondition), in the framework of predicate transformer semantics, is presented in [102]. There the weakest precondition for adaptation is actually derived. A consideration of nested procedure definitions appears in [109], and in [110], where a richer assertion language is used. Relaxing the restrictions on non-aliasing is discussed in [107] and [104]. It is considered also in [111], where interaction with scope rules is handled too, by incorporating a 'syntactic environment' into the proof system, whereby variables are bound to locations and a state binds locations to values. A certain visualization of the various forms of proof rules for procedures and their effect on relative completeness is presented in [112]. More results about other parameter passing modes (and appropriate further references) can be found in [54]. The incompleteness results hinted at in the conclusions appear in [106], and are further elaborated in [113]. An example of a sound and absolutely complete proof system for partial correctness for a language with bounded iteration appears in [114].

EXERCISES

6.1 **Macro expansion:** For parameterless, nonrecursive procedures, define the syntactic transformation $P[proc \Leftarrow S]$ as the result of replacing every invocation statement **call** *proc* by S, where S is the body of *proc* from the declarations of P.

(1) Show that this transformation can be repeatedly applied finitely often only, ending with a program P^* with no procedure calls.

(2) Prove that $\mathbf{M}_{\mathbf{PROC(PLW)}}[\![P]\!] = \mathbf{M}_{\mathbf{PLW}}[\![P^*]\!]$.

6.2 **Mutual recursion:** Generalize the recursion rule to mutual recursion (assume two procedures only, to simplify notation), and give an example of an application of your generalized rule.

6.3 **Invariance theorem:** Extend the invariance theorem to *PROC*(*LP*), under the assumption that it holds for *LP* .

6.4 **Recursion rule for nondeterministic base language:** Formulate the analogous rule to (REC*) for the base language *GC*.

6.5 **Unfolding:** For a declaration **procedure** *proc*: *S*, define $\hat{S}^{(0)} =$ **call** *proc*, $\hat{S}^{(i+1)} = \hat{S}^{(i)}$ [*S*/**call** *proc*]. Prove that for every $i \geqslant 0$ and σ,

$$\pi(\langle S^{(i)}, \sigma\rangle) = \pi(\langle \hat{S}^{(i)}[\Omega/\textbf{call } proc], \sigma\rangle)$$

6.6 **Uninterpreted programs [115]:** Consider the recursive procedure

P:: **procedure** *f_fact* (*u*; *v*): **if** $u = 0$ **then** $v := 1$
else call *f_fact* $(u-1; v)$; $v := v * u$ **fi**
call *f_fact* (*x*; *y*).

(1) Show that $Tr_{1_0} \vdash \langle x = X\rangle\ P\ \langle y = x!\rangle$ using the rules for parametrized invocations.

(2) Explain why it is impossible to derive

$$Tr_1 \vdash \langle f(0) = 1 \wedge \forall z{:}[f(z+1) = (z+1) * f(z)]\rangle\, P \langle y = f(x)\rangle.$$

6.7 **Value–result parameters:** Extend the language *PROC* with procedures that have, in addition to formal value parameters and formal result parameters, also formal value–result parameters.

(1) Add a transition rule for procedure invocations, that upon invocation treats a value–result parameter as a value parameter, while upon exit the value–result parameter is treated as a result parameter.

(2) Provide an extension of the given rules to handle also value–result parameters.

(3) Consider the procedure declaration

procedure *swap* (*w*; *v*): $(w, v) := (v, w)$,

where *w*, *v* are value–result parameters. Use your extended rules to prove

$$\{x = X \wedge y = Y\}\ \textbf{call}\ swap\ (x, y)\ \{x = Y \wedge y = X\}.$$

procedure p; **if** $n \leqslant 0$ **then** *skip*
else $n := n - 1$; **call** p; $s := s + 1$; **call** p; $n := n + 1$ **fi**

Figure 6.5. Non-linear recursion.

6.8 **Nonlinear recursion [116]:** Consider the recursive procedure p in Figure 6.5. Prove, using the appropriate rules, that

$\{n = N \wedge s = 0\}$ **call** p $\{n = N \wedge s = 2^N - 1\}$

6.9 **Soundness preservation:** Show that adding the rules for procedures to **H** does not affect its soundness and relative completeness (for proving properties of procedure bodies).

AN INTERLUDE ON CONCURRENCY

In the two coming chapters, we extend our approach to verifying programs in languages with **concurrency** (or **parallelism**). Such programs consist of a collection of **processes,** components of the **concurrent composition** operator, which **communicate** with each other and (occasionally) **synchronize** with each other. We concentrate on two kinds of interprocess communications: by means of **shared variables** and by means of **message passing.** The name **distributed programs** is reserved for the latter variant. The presence of concurrency and interprocess communication of some kind is a distinctive feature of many modern programming languages, such as Ada, Modula-2 and occam. The design of correct concurrent programs turns out to be a much harder task than in the sequential case. Hence, the extension of the theory of program verification to concurrency has a great methodological and practical importance, at the same time considerably complicating the theory.

In this book, we stick to assertional proofs and mainly study the previously considered correctness criteria of partial and total correctness.

We also consider very briefly more general correctness criteria, which are best described in a framework providing a more general means for expressing them, for example temporal logic. These more general correctness properties are even more meaningful and significant for a kind of programs known as **reactive programs** (or systems). Such programs are perpetual, not intended ever to terminate. Their correctness is manifested in the way such programs interact with an external environment, and specifying them means imposing requirements on such interactions. The by now established names of these families of properties are **liveness** and **safety.** The former deals with various 'good' things happening eventually, of which termination is an instance. The latter deals with 'bad' properties invariantly not happening, of which partial correctness is an instance. There are several more precise characterizations of these families in the literature, all needing means of expression beyond first-order logic.

In our context, the main characteristic of this distinction is the approach towards proving properties in the corresponding families. A safety property, similarly to its specific instance of partial correctness, is proved by computational induction, using inductive assertions or invariants. In contrast, liveness properties, similarly to their instance of termination, are proved by an appeal to a well-founded, decreasing variant.

Here we restrict our attention to two novel correctness criteria: **freedom of deadlock** and **nonstarvation.** Basically, every language for concurrent programming has some language primitive the meaning of which implies **blocking** (hopefully temporarily) the process executing it. A **deadlock** occurs† when all the processes which have not terminated are indefinitely blocked, usually because of some circular interdependency. Clearly, this is an undesired situation, preventing a successful completion of the program. Thus, part of the proof burden for establishing correctness is to show that this situation cannot occur in the verified program. Also, most languages exhibit constructs the meaning of which implies a certain **competition** over the use of certain **resources.** These may take the power of the ability to access the memory, or the ability to advance and execute an instruction. Most often, these are abstractions of 'invisible queues'. A starvation occurs if, during an infinite computation, a competing component is indefinitely 'ignored' and not granted access to the required resources. The 'good' thing, of course, occurs when the resource is granted, and it is another proof burden to show that this event will necessarily occur.

A notable property of the semantics of concurrency which we consider here is its representation by means of **interleaving** of **atomic** actions of the various processes. The grain of atomicity, forming the unit of interleaving, must be carefully chosen. Thus, except for synchronization, no simultaneity of actions in concurrent components is assumed. In general, all possible interleavings are considered. Hence, no assumption is made about relative speed of processes' executions (in case the real execution involves multi-processing). This assumption is known also as **asynchronous computation**. Thus, the meaning of a concurrent program involves nondeterminism, the result of a computation depending on the 'actual' interleaving that took place. An alternative approach, known as **partial-order semantics**, does not interleave independent actions; rather it considers them as partially ordered (by some causality ordering), in particular allowing an interpretation of their simultaneous execution. We leave simultaneity to explicit synchronization and do not pursue this approach further here.

While the general issue of the adequacy of this approach may be scrutinized, it is adequate for the study of correctness proofs for the kinds of correctness properties under consideration. An important factor in the adequacy of the interleaving approach to concurrency is again the issue of fairness. One novel phenomenon regarding fairness in this context is the presence of **joint-actions**, namely actions performed synchronously by several processes simultaneously. The enabledness notion for such actions involves

† Sometimes referred to as **global deadlock.** A more general deadlock involves arbitrary subsets of active processes unable to advance. We deal here only with the former notion.

the joint-readying of the action by all its participants, raising some problems in the interpretation of fairness in this context.

Concurrency constitutes a challenge for the compositional approaches. One extreme approach to the verification of concurrent programs is the **global** approach, which tends almost to ignore the process structure of the program and to conduct global reasoning. This is a natural extension of the inductive assertions method to the current context. We shall not elaborate this approach here, and leave it as further reading. However, as it turns out there do not exist fully compositional proof methods for proving partial correctness of concurrent programs. The initial state–final state relationship conveyed by partial correctness is not strong enough to allow for compositionality, since reference to intermediate states (of a process) is needed for such proofs. The **visibility** of intermediate states is one of the main distinctions between concurrency and other module composition operators.

To realize this fact, consider (informally) the two processes P_1 and P_2 below, under the assumption that the grain of interleaving is complete assignment statements.

$$P_1 :: x := 0;\ y := 0$$
$$P_2 :: x := 0;\ x := x+1;\ y := 0;\ x := x-1.$$

Clearly, these two programs satisfy the same partial-correctness assertions, as they transform the state variables x and y in the same way. However, $P_1 \parallel Q$ behaves differently from $P_2 \parallel Q$ for some processes Q, where '$\parallel$' is the **parallel composition** operator. For example, suppose that $x<0$ holds initially and consider $Q :: z := x$. In the first case $z \leqslant 0$ holds as a postcondition of the concurrent composition, while in the second case $z = 1$ is also a possibility, in case the assignment $z := x$ is so interleaved as to succeed $x := x+1$ but to precede $x := x-1$.

EXERCISE:

What are the possible outcomes (values of x) of

$$[x := 1;\ x := x+1 \parallel x := 2]?$$

□

As a good approximation to compositionality, the notion of a **two-leveled** (or two-staged) proof is proposed. According to this approach, a proof consists of two stages:

(1) A **local** stage, where a correctness assertion is proved about each process separately (usually compositionally).

(2) A **global** stage, where a global correctness property of the whole program is deduced from the collection of the local correctness properties, provided that the collection of local proofs satisfy a consistency criterion. The exact consistency criterion needed depends on the details of the interprocess communication used.

The catch of the method, rendering it as noncompositional, is the latter provision, which refers to the proofs of the local correctness assertions, and not to the assertions themselves, as would be the case in a compositional approach. Thus, the second stage actually applies a meta-rule. Here proof outlines have a more significant role and are indispensable, in contrast to their minor role in verifying sequential programs.

Another new issue raised by concurrency and two-leveled proofs is the issue of **auxiliary variables**. Previously, all partial correctness proofs involved only the actual variables appearing in the program (that is, the proper state), as well as (universally quantified) specification variables that 'freeze' the initial state. As it turns out, having complete rules requires the addition of extra variables, and assignments to these variables that play a role only during the proof and not in the execution. Usually, such variables represent abstractions of the history of the computation which is not carried by the local state. Special proof-theoretic provisions are needed to handle these variables. These variables play also an important role in coordinating the independent 'knowledge' of processes in a distributed program within a two-staged proof.

An antipodal approach both to the global proof method and to the two-level proof method, based on the view of concurrency as nondeterministic interleaving, is a **reductionist** approach. According to this approach, the concurrent program is transformed to some other nondeterministic program, which explicitly represents nondeterministic selection of atomic actions by explicitly referring to a location counter. The correctness criteria of the original program are also transformed to some properties of the non-deterministic program and the previously described method is applied to the transformed program. This way, all the structural information conveyed by the process structure of the program, the interprocess communication and synchronization, is totally lost.

We do not pursue here this approach any further. A good verification method should fit as much as possible to the ways programs are conceived, designed, and presented. Only such methods have a chance of serving as guidelines to program design and correct construction and not only for a posteriori verification. While we deal here with foundational, formal issues, their informal use is always an additional methodological goal in the background.

Bibliographic notes and suggestions for further reading

Bibliographic notes The global approach to the verification of concurrent programs (in a flow-programs version) can be found in [117]. The reductionist approach can be found in [118], [119] and [120]. The informally stated distinction between liveness and safety properties originates in [35].

Suggestions for further reading A comprehensive treatment of the specification and verification of reactive systems will appear in [121]. An expository description of a specification method for concurrent programs, transcending the correctness criteria studied here, can be found in [122]. An alternative, non-imperative, treatment of *CSP* is presented in [123]. Other non-imperative formalisms for studying concurrency are *CCS* [124], [125] and *ACT* [126]. In those studies, the approach is algebraic, and the verification problem manifests itself in comparing two programs (in the same formalism) for equivalence (or, more generally, for partial order). A good source for many discussions of issues related to partial order semantics and to temporal logics (with many further references) is [127]. Yet another model for concurrency, not based on a language approach (rather, closer to classical automata theory) is that of Petri nets [128], [129]. Surveys of verification techniques for concurrent and distributed programs may be found in [130] and in [131].

Chapter 7
VERIFYING CONCURRENT PROGRAMS

7.1 Introduction

In this chapter we consider the verification of concurrent programs in which processes interact with each other using **shared variables**. The distinguishing property of this model for concurrent computation is that there is no direct connection between the assignments that any particular process performs and the values the same process obtains when it accesses the variables. The actual value depends on assignments to the shared variables performed by other processes. The preservation property of proof outlines (of a single process) is not guaranteed to hold for arbitrary proof outlines. The main goal is to identify those proof outlines for which it does hold.

On the other hand, assignment to shared variables is the way by which one process passes information to other processes. The means of guaranteeing the consistency of this way of passing information is by using **synchronization** primitives, that guarantee that certain kinds of 'bad interleavings' do not occur. The synchronization means to be considered here are of two kinds:

(1) *Low-level synchronization:* There is a built-in synchronization assumption of **mutual exclusion** between the basic operations on a shared variable. This mechanism guarantees that no undefined outcome can be produced by access to a variable at the same time that its value is being changed. This is expressed by choosing the assignment statements

with a single reference to a shared variable (critical reference†) as the basic atomic action of a process (known also as the **grain of interleaving**).

EXERCISE:

Try to relate the 'single critical reference' restriction to implementation considerations.

□

(2) *Higher-level synchronization:* On many occasions the mutual exclusion on the level of access to variables is not powerful enough. We consider here another means of guaranteeing the **atomicity** of larger program sections, having many accesses to shared variables. Atomicity means here that such a section, sometimes referred to as a **critical section**, is executed in an **uninterruptible** way. Thus, within such a section, the executing process has an exclusive access to the shared variables, with no other process being able to modify them during this access. Atomicity here is combined with **conditional delay**: the execution of such a section can be delayed until the shared variables are found to be in a consistent state, consistency expressed by means of a Boolean expression over the state. Finding the required state consistent and executing the critical section are combined, so that no other process can 'ruin' the state between the time it was detected to be consistent and the time of entry to the critical section. We say more about the relationship between synchronization and deadlock in a later section.

While synchronization is needed to obtain correct concurrent activity, it has the obvious property of reducing concurrency by delaying some activities. Good concurrent programming is the art of the balanced combination of all these factors. Thus, such programs may be quite tricky and complex, and the reasons for their correctness can be quite subtle.

In the next section we introduce a mini programming language, *SVL* (shared-variables language), and its formal operational semantics. We then pass to proving partial and total correctness and also to proving deadlock freedom. Since concurrency adds an extra complication, we return here to a presentation of correctness proofs in such a way that no explicit reference is made either to assignment axioms or to application of the consequence rule. This amounts to 'semantic reasoning' about short program sections. We also omit reference to $\mathbf{Tr}_\mathrm{I}$ in the meta-theory.

† This restriction is known also as 'Reynolds' law'.

7.2 The shared-variables language *SVL*

A **program** P consists of an intialized **concurrent composition** of **processes** P_i, $1 \leqslant i \leqslant n$, for some $n \geqslant 1$, denoted by $P :: P_0; [P_1 \| \cdots \| P_n]$, also abbreviated as $P :: P_0; [\, \|_{i=1,n}\, P_i]$†. Here P_0 is an initialization part defined by a *PLW* statement (Chapter 4). Each process P_i is defined by means of a statement S_i, where the statements include all the statements in *PLW* and the additional conditional delay statement **await** $B \rightarrow S$ **end**, where S is any *PLW* statement. Thus, no nesting of **await** statements is allowed. In examples we also use mnemonic names for processes. Note that a program is not defined as a statement here, so **nested concurrency** is also excluded. Note that n, the number of processes, should be **constant** (that is, independent of the program's state). This excludes **dynamic process creation** which has a much more complicated verification theory.

The informal semantics of the **await** statement is the following. The process executing it gains exclusive access to all the variables needed to test B, the **delaying condition**. If B is found *true*, control of the executing process directly continues to execute S atomically. If B is found *false*, access to the shared variables is released and the executing process is delayed until some later stage, when the whole scenario repeats itself. The concurrent composition is interpreted, as already mentioned, as the interleaving of atomic statements of the component processes. It **terminates** once every process has terminated.

As an example program in *SVL*, consider the following parallel computation of the factorial function $N!$. There are two processes; the first computes $1 * \ldots * k$ while the second computes $N * (N-1) * \ldots * (k+1)$, for an arbitrary $1 \leqslant k \leqslant N$.

EXAMPLE:

$P_{cfac} :: c1 := true;\ c2 := true;\ i := 1;\ j := N;\ n := N;$
$[P_1 :: \textbf{while}\ c1\ \textbf{do await}\ true \rightarrow \textbf{if}\ i+1 < j\ \textbf{then}\ i := i+1;\ n := n * i$
$\qquad\qquad\qquad\qquad\qquad\qquad\qquad \textbf{else}\ c1 := false\ \textbf{fi end od}$

$\|$

$P_2 :: \textbf{while}\ c2\ \textbf{do await}\ true \rightarrow \textbf{if}\ j-1 > i\ \textbf{then}\ j := j-1;\ n := n * j$
$\qquad\qquad\qquad\qquad\qquad\qquad\qquad \textbf{else}\ c2 := false\ \textbf{fi end od}]$

Note that the whole bodies of both loops are atomic here. The effect of the **awaits** synchronization is pure mutual exclusion. We return later to this program to prove its correctness.

□

† Traditionally, a syntax using the keywords **cobegin, coend,** or **parbegin, parend** is also used.

P_{buf} :: P_0 :: $in := 0$; $out := 0$; $i := 1$; $j := 1$;
[*producer* :: **while** $i \leqslant n$ **do**
$x := A[i]$;
await $in - out < b \rightarrow skip$ **end**;
buffer [*in* **mod** *b*] := *x*;
$in := in + 1$;
$i := i + 1$ **od**
||
[*consumer* :: **while** $j \leqslant n$ **do**
await $in - out > 0 \rightarrow skip$ **end**;
y := *buffer* [*out* **mod** *b*];
$out := out + 1$;
$B[j] := y$;
$j := j + 1$ **od**].

Figure 7.1 The bounded buffer program.

EXERCISE:

Why is the following program a wrong concurrent factorial computation?

$i := 1$; $j := N$; $n := N$;
[**while** $i + 1 < j$ **do await** $true \rightarrow i := i + 1$; $n := n * i$ **end od**
||
while $j - 1 > i$ **do await** $true \rightarrow j := j - 1$; $n := n * j$ **end od**]

□

EXERCISE:

Modify the solution so that both processes do at least one multiplication. Can this requirement be part of a specification expressed by means of a partial correctness assertion?

□

EXAMPLE:

The following example embodies one of the classic synchronization problems, known as the **bounded buffer**. It involves two processes, referred to generically as the **producer** and the **consumer**. The former process generates a sequence of values of some type which are used in some way by the latter process. In order to allow for varying rates of production and consumption of values, the two processes cooperate by means of a bounded buffer of (a fixed) size $b > 0$. The *producer* process can deposit a newly generated value only if the buffer is not **full** (that is, it contains less than *b* values). The consumer can retrieve a value only if the buffer is not **empty** (that is, it contains more than 0 values). To be concrete, we assume that the joint task of the pair of processes is to copy an array $A[1..n]$ local to the producer into $B[1..n]$ local to the consumer. The variables *in* and *out* keep track of the number of values added to the buffer and removed from the buffer, respectively. Thus, the buffer contains $in - out$ values. The program is presented in Figure 7.1.

A correctness proof of this program is presented in the next section.

□

Note that the notion of a state does not change when adding shared variables. Processes operate on the same state, known also as a **global state**.

We now present a formal definition of the operational semantics, again in the form of transition rules among configurations. We distinguish between two kinds of configurations. A **sequential configuration** has the same form as before. A **concurrent configuration** has the form $C = \langle [P_1 \| \cdots \| P_n], \sigma \rangle$.

First, we have all the '$\rightarrow$' transitions from PLW as transitions among sequential configurations. Consequently, assignments (with a single critical reference) and evaluation of Boolean conditions (in selection and repetition statements) are atomic. In addition, we have one more transition among sequential configurations, intended to capture the atomicity of the **await** statement:

$$\text{if } \sigma \models B \text{ and } \langle S, \sigma \rangle \stackrel{*}{\rightarrow} \langle E, \sigma' \rangle, \text{ then } \langle \textbf{await } B \rightarrow S \textbf{ end}, \sigma \rangle \rightarrow \langle E, \sigma' \rangle$$

The observant reader might have noticed that this clause does not precisely capture the usual informal semantics as explained above. It calls for an unbounded lookahead to 'predict' the termination of S (on σ) in order to grant exclusive access to the critical section. This is known to be undecidable in general. In particular, such an access will not be granted in case S happens not to terminate on σ.

In order to define a more 'realistic' and effective semantics, precluding the above-mentioned phenomenon, more invisible state components must be added to concurrent configurations, thereby complicating the treatment. We do present such a more elaborate semantic definition for the language considered in Section 7.5, where it fits more naturally. Another approach admits the construct **await** $B \rightarrow S$ **end** only for loop-free S, thereby avoiding the problem. Note, however, that our deviation using a 'predictive' definition of access to critical sections has no effect on partial correctness, which is concerned with terminating computations only.

Now we introduce the rule defining transitions among concurrent configurations, representing the arbitrary interleavings of local atomic actions:

if $\langle S_i, \sigma\rangle \rightarrow \langle S'_i, \sigma'\rangle$ then $\langle [S_1 \parallel \cdots S_i \parallel \cdots S_n], \sigma\rangle \overset{\langle i,\sigma\rangle}{\rightarrow} \langle [S_1 \parallel \cdots \parallel S'_i \parallel \cdots \parallel S_n], \sigma'\rangle$

for any $1 \leqslant i \leqslant n$. *The i* above the arrow records the identity of the process which does the move in a transition. This relation is inductively extended to $\langle [\underset{i=1,n}{\parallel} S_i], \sigma\rangle \overset{h}{\rightarrow} \langle [\underset{i=1,n}{\parallel} S'_i], \sigma'\rangle$, for $h = \langle i_1, \sigma_1\rangle \cdots \langle i_k, \sigma_k\rangle$, for some $k \geqslant 0$. We refer to h as the **history** of the computation **leading** to the above configuration.

A **concurrent computation** is again a maximal $\overset{h}{\rightarrow}$-sequence of concurrent configurations. The information coded in h is needed later, for the completeness proof of the proposed proof method for partial correctness. Note that by this definition a concurrent program exhibits nondeterminism, reflecting the different ordering of the interleaved atomic actions of the different processes. See Exercise 7.8 for the boundedness of the nondeterminism.

From the maximality requirement it only follows that *some* transition is performed as long as some transition is possible (enabled). In particular, it does not follow that each process will perform such a transition if possible. The latter requirement amounts to imposing fairness at the process level and is not considered here. Our weak progress assumption in the semantics is known as the **fundamental liveness** property. We return to this issue later in the chapter, when proofs of liveness properties are considered.

From the definition of '$\rightarrow$' it is clear that indeed the body of an **await** statement is executed atomically. Thus, states in which such a body is partially executed are 'invisible'. In order to reflect this fact in the proof theory, we introduce the notion of a normal substatement.

Definition: A substatement S of a concurrent program P is **normal** iff it is not a proper substatement of any **await** statement.

□

The most important property of a computation of a concurrent program, which is central to the completeness proof of the proposed proof system, is expressed by the lemma below.

Definition: For $P{::}\ P_0; [\underset{i=1,n}{\parallel} P_i]$, let $S_{i_1}, \ldots, S_{i_l}$ be a collection of $l \geqslant 1$ normal substatements of $P_{i_1}, \ldots, P_{i_l}$, respectively. This collection is $[\langle i_1, \ldots, i_l\rangle, \sigma]$-**reachable** via h iff there exists a prefix of a computation $\langle P, \sigma_0\rangle \overset{h}{\rightarrow} \langle [\underset{i=1,n}{\parallel} S_i], \sigma\rangle$, for some initial state σ_0, and arbitrary S_k for $k \in (\{1, \ldots, n\} - \{i_1, \ldots, i_l\})$.

□

The intuitive meaning of this reachability property is the existence of a prefix of a computation leading to a configuration, where it simultaneously is the case that each process P_{i_l} is about to execute S_{i_l} as its next statement. The following lemma states that separate reachability of normal substatements with the same state can be combined with joint reachability (still with the same state).

Lemma (merging):

If each of S_{i_j}, $1 \leqslant j \leqslant l$, is $[\langle i_j \rangle, \sigma]$-reachable via h, then the collection of $S_{i_1}, \ldots, S_{i_l}$ is $[\langle i_1, \ldots, i_l \rangle, \sigma]$-reachable via h.

□

This lemma is rather simple in our context, since bodies of processes are deterministic, and the given history does not leave a large degree of freedom for the control locations. It does hold, however, under more general conditions. The references are given at the end of the chapter.

By adapting the semantic notions introduced in the introduction to concurrent configurations, we obtain the following.

Definition:

(1) A concurrent computation **terminates** iff it is finite and its last configuration is of the form $\langle [E \| \cdots \| E], \sigma \rangle$, for some σ.

(2) A concurrent computation is **deadlocked** iff it is finite and it does not terminate.

(3) A concurrent computation **diverges** (is nonterminating) iff it is infinite.

□

The definition of *val* (π), for a concurrent computation π, carries over, with the additional provision of interpreting **f** as the value of a deadlocked computation. This yields the standard definition of $\mathbf{M}_{\mathrm{SVL}}$, again abbreviated as **M**. We will also need the following definition of **enabledness**.

Definition: A process P_i, $1 \leqslant i \leqslant n$, is **enabled** in a configuration $C = \langle [S_1 \| \cdots \| S_n], \sigma \rangle$ iff $S_i \neq E$, and if S_i is of the form **await** $B \rightarrow S$ **end**; S' (with S' possibly being E), then $\sigma \models B$.

□

We also relativize two notions in order to make distinctions about variables and the way they are shared. Thus, we need to capture local modifiability and local access to variables, where local means 'by a certain process'.

Definition: For a concurrent program $P :: P_0;\ [P_1 \| \cdots \| P_n]$, let *free* ($P_i$) be the set of all variables appearing in P_i and *change* (P_i) the set of all variables **modifiable** by P_i.

□

EXERCISE:

Give a precise inductive definition of *free* and *change* (use induction on the structure of S).

□

7.3 A deductive system O for partial correctness

As already stated, the proof system is a two-leveled one. We first present the rules for constructing **local proofs**, actually proof outlines, for each process separately. In some sense, such a local proof reflects what the process would do if it were executed in isolation, without other processes interfering with its actions.

Since the only new statement in a process body is the **await** statement, we adopt the **H** system, augmented with the following **await** rule.

Await rule:

$$\frac{\{p \wedge B\}\, S\, \{q\}}{\{p\}\ \mathbf{await}\ B \rightarrow S\ \mathbf{end}\ \{q\}} \qquad \text{(AWAIT)}$$

□

We take $\mathbf{H}^{\mathbf{a}}$ to be **H** augmented with the (AWAIT) rule.

Not surprisingly, the (AWAIT) rule is very similar to the rule for a conditional statement. Indeed, as far as partial correctness is concerned, the delaying effect of the **await** statement has no impact. The real essence of the (AWAIT) rule is the capturing of the atomicity of its execution. Whatever holds for S (under the condition B) in isolation holds for **await** $B \rightarrow S$ **end** too.

In order to define the corresponding notion of a proof outline, we have to account for the fact that the body of an **await** statement is executed atomically. As we mentioned already, proof outlines will be confronted for a consistency test at the second stage of a partial correctness proof. However, intermediate states within the body of an **await** statement are not visible due to this atomicity, and should not be so confronted. To obtain the definition of a proof outline for an *SVL* process, we adopt the definition of a proof outline for a *PLW* program, with the following two modifications:

(1) The state assertions *pre* (S') and *post* (S') are attributed only to **normal** subprograms S'.

(2) The following condition is added:

for S' :: **await** $B \rightarrow S$ **end**, $\{pre(S') \wedge B\}\, S\, \{post(S')\}$.

Alternatively, we could in (2) require the existence of a *PLW* proof outline for

$\{pre(S') \wedge B\}\, S\, \{post(S')\}$. The latter, however, would not be a part of the main outline, since it would refer to nonnormal substatements.

An immediate adaptation of the proof of the relative completeness of **H** yields the following corollary.

Proposition:

$\mathbf{H}^{\mathbf{a}}$ is relatively complete.

□

While the proof outline lemma (Section 4.4.1) holds also for the *SVL* local proof outlines (for $\mathbf{H}^{\mathbf{a}}$), the structured preservation lemma (Section 4.4.1) certainly does not hold. Suppose *post* (S') (in process P_i) has been just established by P_i executing S'. If some P_j, $j \neq i$, modifies a shared variable on which *post* (S') depends, the latter may cease to hold, although P_i is still at the same local control location, 'unaware' of the change.

Thus, the following naive concurrent composition rule is not valid (but compare with the exercise on disjoint concurrency):

$$\frac{\{p_i\}\, S_i\, \{q_i\},\ 1 \leqslant i \leqslant n}{\{\bigwedge_{i=1,n} p_i\}\, [\ \|_{i=1,n}\ S_i]\, \{\bigwedge_{i=1,n} q_i\}}$$

Hence, our aim is to strengthen the assumption of the concurrent-composition rule, so that the same consequence as above does follow. Our guideline is the compositional preservation lemma. If we manage to restrict our consideration only to proof outlines for which it does hold, then the concurrent-composition rule will be valid.

The central notion leading towards this goal is the notion of **noninterference** among local proofs (actually, among proof outlines).

Definition: A collection of local $\mathbf{H}^{\mathbf{a}}$ proof outlines $\{p_i\}\, S_i\, \{q_i\}$, $i = 1, n$, is **interference free** iff for every normal substatement S' of S_i and every normal substatement S'' of S_j, $j \neq i$, where S'' is either an assignment or an **await** statement, the following two conditions are satisfied:

(1) $\vdash_{\mathbf{H}^{\mathbf{a}}} \{pre(S') \wedge pre(S'')\}\, S''\, \{pre(S')\}$

(2) $\vdash_{\mathbf{H}^{\mathbf{a}}} \{post(S') \wedge pre(S'')\}\, S''\, \{post(S')\}$

□

Clearly, the meaning of interference freedom is that the structured preservation property holds for each proof outline, since executing any other atomic statement in some other process respects the assertions in the given

$[\{p_1 : x = 0 \vee x = 2\}$ $\{p_2 : x = 0 \vee x = 1\}$
S_1:: **await** $true \rightarrow x := x+1$ **end** $\parallel$ S_2:: **await** $true \rightarrow x := x+2$ **end**
$\{q_1 : x = 1 \vee x = 3\}$ $\{q_2 : x = 2 \vee x = 3\}]$

Figure 7.2 Interference-free proof outlines.

outline. Note that it need not be the case (and it rarely is) that the values of the shared variables are preserved. Only the intermediate assertions are preserved. Note also that *every* pair of atomic statements (in different processes) must be confronted. Thus, the number of interference-freedom tests grows as the product of the process lengths.

Definition: A **proof outline** for $\{p\} P \{q\}$, where $P :: [\underset{i=1,n}{\parallel} P_i]$, is an interference-free collection of local proof outlines $\{p_i\} P_i \{q_i\}$, $1 \leqslant i \leqslant n$, with the additional property that $p \Rightarrow \bigwedge_{i=1,n} p_i$, $\bigwedge_{i=1,n} q_i \Rightarrow q$. □

The main property of the proof outline of a concurrent program is expressed by the following lemma, extending the (sequential) compositional preservation lemma. Let a proof outline for $\{p\} P \{q\}$ be given.

Lemma (concurrent preservation):

Consider any computation of P starting in an initial configuration $C_0 = \langle P, \sigma_0 \rangle$, s.t. $\sigma_0 \models \bigwedge_{i=1,n} p_i$. In any intermediate configuration $C_k = \langle [\underset{i=1,n}{\parallel} S_i^{(k)}], \sigma_k \rangle$, $k \geqslant 0$, we have, for every $1 \leqslant i \leqslant n$: if $S_i^{(k)} \neq E$ then $\sigma_k \models pre(S_i^{(k)})$, where $pre(S_i^{(k)})$ is the precondition of $S_i^{(k)}$ in the ith local proof outline. In addition, $\sigma_0 \models post(P_i)$ in case $S_i^{(k)} = E$.

Proof: The proof is by induction on k. Initially, $\sigma_0 \models \bigwedge_{i=1,n} p_i$ holds by assumption. Assume that for some configuration $C_k = \langle [\underset{i=1,n}{\parallel} S_i^{(k)}], \sigma_k \rangle$ it is the case that $\sigma_k \models \bigwedge_{i=1,n} pre(S_i^{(k)})$. Let $C_k \overset{j}{\rightarrow} C_{k+1} = \langle [\underset{i=1,n}{\parallel} S_i^{(k+1)}], \sigma_k \rangle$. From the definition of '$\rightarrow$', for all $l \neq j$, $S_l^{(k)} = S_l^{(k+1)}$, so $pre(S_l^{(k+1)}) = pre(S_l^{(k)})$. From the soundness of $\mathbf{H}^a$ we know that if $S_j^{(k+1)} \neq E$, then $\sigma_{k+1} \models pre(S_j^{(k+1)})$. Also, by noninterference, $pre(S_l^{(k)})$, $l \neq j$, remains true at σ_{k+1}. Hence, $\sigma_{k+1} \models \bigwedge_{i=1,n} pre(S_i^{(k+1)})$, as required. For $S_i^{(k)} = E$ a similar argument obtains. □

EXAMPLE:

Consider the proof outlines in Figure 7.2, where substatements are labeled for reference. The sequential correctness of these two proof outlines is obvious. In order to show that they are interference free, we have to verify (in $\mathbf{H^a}$) the following four assertions.

(1) $\{pre(S_1) \wedge pre(S_2)\}\, S_2\, \{pre(S_1)\}$.

Substituting the assertions and program, we get

$$\{(x = 0 \vee x = 2) \wedge (x = 0 \vee x = 1)\}$$
$$\{x = 0\}\ \mathbf{await}\ \mathit{true} \rightarrow \{x = 0\}\, x := x+2\, \{x = 2\}\ \mathbf{end}\ \{x = 2\}$$
$$\{x = 0 \vee x = 2\}$$

which is a sequentially valid proof outline in $\mathbf{H^a}$.

(2) $\{post(S_1) \wedge pre(S_2)\}\, S_2\, \{post(S_1)\}$.

We get

$$\{(x = 1 \vee x = 3) \wedge (x = 0 \vee x = 1)\}$$
$$\{x = 1\}\ \mathbf{await}\ \mathit{true} \rightarrow \{x = 1\}\, x := x+2\, \{x = 3\}\ \mathbf{end}\ \{x = 3\}$$
$$\{x = 1 \vee x = 3)$$

which is also easily seen to be sequentially valid in $\mathbf{H^a}$.

(3) $\{pre(S_2) \wedge pre(S_1)\}\, S_1\, \{pre(S_2)\}$.
(4) $\{post(S_2) \wedge pre(S_1)\}\, S_1\, \{post(S_2)\}$.

□

EXERCISE:

Complete the details of the above noninterference proof.

Note that a sequentially correct proof outline, say for S_1, which has stronger intermediate assertions, for example

$$\{x = 0\}\ \mathbf{await}\ \mathit{true} \rightarrow \{x = 0\}\ x := x+1\ \{x = 1\}\ \mathbf{end}$$

would not be interference free with any outline for S_2.

□

As can be learned from the example, what we have to do in order to obtain interference freedom amongst local proofs is to weaken the intermediate assertions in every process in such a way that any atomic modification of the shared variables by another process will preserve these assertions. Thus, there is no magic here. One has to consider the global behavior. However, the system provides us with a systematic and structured method for conducting this reasoning in a naturally partitioned way. Finding the required assertions is a creative step, even more so than in the sequential case. Note that weakening too much would not do either, as the required local postcondition, needed for the concurrent composition rule presented below, would not be established.

We now present the concurrent composition rule (SCONC). Note that actually this is again a meta-rule, having a property of proof outlines in its premiss.

Concurrent composition rule:

$$\frac{\text{proof outlines } \{p_i\}\, S_i\, \{q_i\},\ 1 \leqslant i \leqslant n \text{ are } \textit{interference free}}{\{\bigwedge_{i=1,n} p_i\}\ [\ \|_{i=1,n}\ S_i]\ \{\bigwedge_{i=1,n} q_i\}} \qquad \text{(SCONC)}$$

□

We denote the system obtained by adding (SCONC) to $\mathbf{H}^{\mathbf{a}}$ (and yet another augmentation described below) as **O**. Note once again the important difference between this rule and previously considered rules. The premiss is formulated in terms of proof outlines, not of specifications (that is, correctness assertions). We return to this issue in the concluding section.

EXAMPLE:

Returning to the previous example, after having established the interference freedom of the local proofs, we now conclude by (SCONC) that $\{x = 0\}\,[S_1 \,\|\, S_2]\,\{x = 3\}$.

□

EXAMPLE:

Returning to the concurrent factorial example in Section 7.2, we now show $\vdash_{\mathbf{O}} \{\mathit{true}\}\, P_{\mathit{cfact}}\, \{n = N!\}$. For the concurrent composition we have to show

$$\vdash_{\mathbf{O}} \{c1 = \mathit{true} \wedge c2 = \mathit{true} \wedge i = 1 \wedge j = N \wedge n = N\}\,[P_1 \,\|\, P_2]\,\{n = N!\}$$

The loop invariant for P_1 is

$$I \overset{df.}{\equiv} i \leqslant j \wedge (\neg c1 \Rightarrow i + 1 = j) \wedge n * (i + 1) * \cdots * (j - 1) = N!$$

Clearly, the assignments in P_2's **await** do not interfere with I_1. Similarly, the loop invariant for P_2 is I_2, the same as I_1 but with $c2$ instead of $c1$. P_1's **await** does not interfere with it either. Finally, it is easy to see that by applying (SCONC) and the consequence rule, we obtain $\neg c1 \wedge \neg c2 \wedge I_1 \wedge I_2$ which implies $n = N!$.

□

EXAMPLE:

This example shows an important point about the interference-freedom tests: sometimes they hold *vacuously*! This happens when there is no computation in which control of the two processes is in front of S' and S'', respectively. Still, by definition such two atomic actions have to be confronted. What happens is that $pre(S') \wedge pre(S'')$ reduces to false (that is, are contradictory), and partial correctness holds vacuously.

To see this, consider the following proof outline:

$$\begin{array}{lll} & \{true\}\ x := 0;\ \{x \geqslant 0\} & \\ [P_1 :: \{x \geqslant 0\} & P_2 :: \{x \geqslant 0\} & \\ \quad x := 1 \quad \| & \quad \textbf{if } x \geqslant 0 \textbf{ then } \{x \geqslant 0\}\ \textbf{await } true \rightarrow x := x+1 \textbf{ end} & \\ \quad \{x \geqslant 0\} & \quad\quad \textbf{else } \{x < 0\}\ \textbf{await } true \rightarrow x := -1 \textbf{ end fi}] & \end{array}$$

Suppose P_1 is in front of $x := 1$ with the precondition $x \geqslant 0$. Clearly, the execution of **await** $true \rightarrow x := -1$ **end** would violate $x \geqslant 0$. However, the pre-condition of this atomic action is $x < 0$. Thus, the test to hold is

$$\{x \geqslant 0 \wedge x < 0\}\ \textbf{await } true \rightarrow x := -1 \textbf{ end } \{x \geqslant 0\}$$

which, indeed, holds vacuously.

□

Remark:

This phenomenon plays an even more crucial role in verifying distributed programs, as will be seen in Chapter 9.

Auxiliary variables

To motivate this issue we start with an example, a simple variant of a previous example. Consider the program

$$P :: x := 0;\ [\textbf{await } true \rightarrow x := x+1 \textbf{ end} \parallel \textbf{await } true \rightarrow x := x+1 \textbf{ end}]$$

Clearly, $\models_{\mathrm{I}_0} \{x = 0\}\ P\ \{x = 2\}$. Trying to imitate the previous example, we attempt the outline in Figure 7.3.

$[\{p_1\colon x=0 \vee x=1\}$ $\quad\quad$ $\{p_2\colon x=0 \vee x=1\}$
S_1: **await** *true* $\rightarrow x:=x+1$ **end** $\|$ S_2: **await** *true* $\rightarrow x:=x+1$ **end**
$\{q_1\colon x=1 \vee x=2\}$ $\quad\quad$ $\{q_2\colon x=1 \vee x=2\}]$

Figure 7.3 Attempted proof outlines.

However, applying (SCONC) we get $(x=1 \vee x=2) \wedge (x=1 \vee x=2)$, which is equivalent to $x=1 \vee x=2$, weaker than the sought postcondition $x=2$.

EXERCISE:

Are these proof outlines interference free?

□

Whence this difference between the seemingly almost identical examples?

In both cases, the proof reflects the behavior of two interleavings: S_1 followed by S_2 or vice versa. However, in the first example, the intermediate state σ_1 is different for the two interleavings: $\sigma_1 \models x=1$ in one case, while $\sigma_1 \models x=2$ in the other. On the other hand, in the second example the same intermediate state occurs in both interleavings, namely, $\sigma_1 \models x=1$. In other words, the state does not record enough information from the (history of the) computation to enable the distinction between the two interleavings, a distinction required in order to obtain correct and interference-free local proofs.

A way out of this situation is to augment the state with additional variables and assignments that will record (an abstraction of) the required information about the history. We do it in such a way as not to influence the very history we want to record.

We add two fresh variables, y to P_1 and z to P_2, both initialized to 0. When P_1 does its move, it sets y to 1, while P_2 does the same with z. Let the modified processes be P_1' and P_2', respectively. With the help of these additional variables we again can distinguish between two different intermediate states for the two possible interleavings. We get

$$\sigma_1 \models x=1 \wedge y=1 \wedge z=0 \text{ for } S_1' \text{ followed by } S_2'$$

and

$$\sigma_1 \models x=1 \wedge y=0 \wedge z=1 \text{ for } S_2' \text{ followed by } S_1'$$

This distinction can be captured in the local proof outline in Figure 7.4.

$$\{x = y = z = 0\}$$

$$\begin{array}{lll}
[\{p_1\colon (x=0 \wedge y=0 \wedge z=0) \vee & & \{p_2\colon (x=0 \wedge y=0 \wedge z=0) \vee \\
\quad (x=1 \wedge y=0 \wedge z=1)\} & & \quad (x=1 \wedge y=1 \wedge z=0)\} \\
S_1'\colon \ \textbf{await}\ true \rightarrow x := x+1; & \| & S_2'\colon \ \textbf{await}\ true \rightarrow x := x+1; \\
\quad y := 1\ \textbf{end} & & \quad z := 1\ \textbf{end} \\
\{q_1\colon (x=1 \wedge y=1 \wedge z=0) \vee & & \{q_2\colon (x=1 \wedge y=0 \wedge z=1) \vee \\
\quad (x=2 \wedge y=1 \wedge z=1)\} & & \quad (x=2 \wedge y=1 \wedge z=1)\}]
\end{array}$$

Figure 7.4 Correct interference-free proof outlines.

Note that the assignments to the new variables are placed inside the conditional delay statements. Applying (SCONC), we get

$$\begin{array}{l}
\{((x=0 \wedge y=0 \wedge z=0) \vee (x=1 \wedge y=0 \wedge z=1)) \wedge \\
\quad ((x=0 \wedge y=0 \wedge z=0) \vee (x=1 \wedge y=1 \wedge z=0))\} \\
\{P_1' \| P_2'\} \\
\{((x=1 \wedge y=1 \wedge z=0) \vee (x=2 \wedge y=1 \wedge z=1) \wedge \\
\quad ((x=1 \wedge y=0 \wedge z=1) \vee (x=2 \wedge y=1 \wedge z=1))\}
\end{array}$$

from which (by (CONS)) we obtain

$$\{x=0 \wedge y=0 \wedge z=0\}\,[P_1' \| P_2']\,\{x=2 \wedge y=1 \wedge z=1\}$$

If we now 'forget' about y and z, (and their assignments), we get $\{x = 0\}$ $[P_1 \| P_2]\{x = 2\}$, which we were really after.

This example is not accidental. There is an inherent incompleteness of the approach if state assertions have to be expressed strictly by means of the proper state. The solution using auxiliary variables *is* complete, as is shown in the next section. The auxiliary variables are incorporated into **O** by means of the rule (AUX).

Definition: A collection of variables AX is said to be **auxiliary** w.r.t. a program $P \in SVL$ and state predicate q iff the following conditions hold:

(1) $AX \cap free\,(q) = \varnothing$.

(2) Variables in AX appear in P only in assignments.

(3) For every assignment $x := e \in P$, if e refers to a variable in AX, then $x \in AX$.

□

Definition: For any program $P \in SVL$, assertion q, and a collection of variables AX auxiliary w.r.t. P and q, let $P_{|AX}$ be the program obtained by deleting from P all the variables in AX and all the assignments to them. (If by this deletion an empty program is obtained, it is replaced by '*skip*'.)

□

Auxiliary variables rule:

For AX auxiliary for S and q,

$$\frac{\{p\}\,S\,\{q\}}{\{p\}\,S_{|AX}\,\{q\}} \tag{AUX}$$

□

From the definition of AX being auxiliary w.r.t. S it is clear that the removal of the variables of AX and the assignments to them cannot affect the flow of control. Such variables cannot directly appear in tests and their values cannot be copied to other variables appearing in tests. Hence, they can only record some intermediate state. Therefore, the final state restricted to its 'proper' part is the same in P and $P_{|AX}$.

EXERCISE:

Find a counter example showing the need for the assumption about the disjointness of AX from *free* (q). Why can AX intersect *free* (p)? (Hint: regard $AX \cap$ *free* (p) as specification variables.)

□

EXAMPLE:

Returning to bounded buffer example P_{buf}, we prove the partial correctness of [*producer* ‖ *consumer*] w.r.t. the specification $\phi = \langle p, q \rangle$, where

$$p \stackrel{df.}{=} (n = N \geqslant 0 \wedge b > 0 \wedge in = 0 \wedge out = 0 \wedge i = 1 \wedge j = 1)$$

$$q \stackrel{df.}{=} (\bigwedge_{k=1,N} B[k] = A[k])$$

Note that the effect of the initialization in P_{buf} is accounted for by the precondition p. Let I be the following assertion

$$I \stackrel{df.}{=} \begin{cases} buffer[(k-1) \ \mathbf{mod} \ b] = A[k],\ out < k \leqslant in \\ \wedge\, 0 \leqslant in - out \leqslant b \wedge b > 0 \\ \wedge\, 1 \leqslant i \leqslant n+1 \wedge 1 \leqslant j \leqslant n+1 \end{cases}$$

The proof outline for P_{buf} is presented in Figure 7.5.

$\{I \wedge i = in+1\}$

producer: **while** $i \leqslant n$ **do**

$\{I \wedge i = in+1 \wedge i \leqslant n\}$
$x := A[i]$;
$\{I \wedge i = in+1 \wedge i \leqslant n \wedge x = A[i]\}$
await $in - out < b \rightarrow$ *skip* **end**;
$\{I \wedge i = in+1 \wedge i \leqslant n \wedge x = A[i] \wedge in - out < b\}$
buffer [*in* **mod** *b*] := x;
$\{I \wedge i = in+1 \wedge i \leqslant n \wedge buffer[in \bmod b] = A[i] \wedge in - out < b\}$
$in := in + 1$;
$\{I \wedge i = in \wedge i \leqslant n\}$
$i := i+1$ **od**
$\{I \wedge i = in+1 \wedge i > n\}$
$\{I \wedge i = in+1 = n+1\}$
$\{I \wedge IC \wedge j = out+1\}$

consumer: **while** $j \leqslant n$ **do**

$\{I \wedge IC \wedge j = out+1 \wedge j \leqslant n\}$
await $in - out > 0 \rightarrow$ *skip* **end**;
$\{I \wedge IC \wedge j = out+1 \wedge j \leqslant n \wedge in - out > 0\}$
$y :=$ *buffer* [*out* **mod** *b*];
$\{I \wedge IC \wedge j = out+1 \wedge j \leqslant n \wedge in - out > 0 \wedge y = A[j]\}$
$out := out + 1$;
$\{I \wedge IC \wedge j = out \wedge j \leqslant n \wedge y = A[j]\}$
$B[j] := y$;
$\{I \wedge IC \wedge j = out \wedge j \leqslant n \wedge B[j] = A[j]\}$
$j := j+1$ **od**
$\{I \wedge IC \wedge j = out+1 \wedge j > n\}$
$\{I \wedge IC \wedge j = out+1 = n+1\}$
$\{I \wedge (B[k] = A[k], 1 \leqslant k \leqslant n)\}$

where $IC \stackrel{df.}{=} \{B[k] = A[k], 1 \leqslant k < j\}$.

Figure 7.5 Proof outline for the bounded buffer.

Omitting the details of the sequential proofs, we check for interference freedom. The only assertion in the *producer* process which may be interfered with is $in - out < b$. The only statement in the consumer process that may potentially interfere with that assertion is the *producer* process $out := out + 1$ which clearly leaves $in - out < b$ holding (independently of its own precondition). Similarly, the only 'sensitive' assertion in the *producer* process is $in - out > 0$, and it is easy to see its immunity against the *consumer* process' assignment $in := in+1$. Thus, by the concurrent composition rule (and (CONS)) the final required outcome is obtained.

We return to this example later and discuss some more of its properties. □

EXAMPLE:

In order to see that the failure of the attempt to prove

$$\{x = 0\} \; [\textbf{await } true \rightarrow x := x+1 \textbf{ end} \parallel \textbf{await } true \rightarrow x := x+1 \textbf{ end}] \; \{x = 2\}$$

without using shared variables is not accidental, we now show that there does not exist such a proof outline for this program.

Suppose, by way of contradiction, that such a proof outline does exist. Thus, there are state predicates p_1, p_2, q_1, q_2 satisfying:

$$x = 0 \Rightarrow p_1 \wedge p_2 \quad \textbf{(1)}$$
$$q_1 \wedge q_2 \Rightarrow x = 2 \quad \textbf{(2)}$$
$$\{p_1\} \; x := x+1 \; \{q_1\} \quad \textbf{(3)}$$
$$\{p_2\} \; x := x+1 \; \{q_2\} \quad \textbf{(4)}$$

as well as the interference-freedom tests

$$\{p_1 \wedge p_2\} \; x := x+1 \; \{p_1\} \quad \textbf{(5)}$$
$$\{p_1 \wedge p_2\} \; x := x+1 \; \{p_2\} \quad \textbf{(6)}$$

and two more, regarding preservation of q_i, $i = 1, 2$, which we do not need in order to derive a contradiction.

From (3) and (4) we get

$$p_1 \wedge p_2 \Rightarrow (q_1 \wedge q_2)^x_{x+1} \quad \textbf{(7)}$$

From (5) and (6) we get

$$(p_1 \wedge p_2) \supset (p_1 \wedge p_2)^x_{x+1} \quad \textbf{(8)}$$

Intuitively, (8) reflects the inability to 'remember' how many times x can be incremented. Indeed, by induction we get from (8)

$$p_1 \wedge p_2 \Rightarrow \forall x \geqslant 0 \colon p_1 \wedge p_2 \quad \textbf{(9)}$$

Combining (7) with (9) yields

$$p_1 \wedge p_2 \Rightarrow \forall x \geqslant 1 \colon q_1 \wedge q_2 \quad \textbf{(10)}$$

Finally, combining (10) with (1) and (2), we get

$$x = 0 \Rightarrow \forall x \geqslant 1: x = 2 \tag{11}$$

which is false.

Thus, no p_i, q_i, $i = 1, 2$ satisfying the required properties may exist.

□

7.4 Soundness and completeness of O

In this section we consider the soundness and completeness of the two-leveled proof system **O** for *SVL*.

Theorem (strong soundness of O):

For every interpretation **I**, if $Tr_I \vdash_{\mathbf{O}} \{\bigwedge_{i=1,n} p_i\}[\, \|_{i=1,n} P_i]\{\bigwedge_{i=1,n} q_i\}$, then $\models_{\mathbf{I}} \{\bigwedge_{i=1,n} p_i\}[\, \|_{i=1,n} P_i]\{\bigwedge_{i=1,n} q_i\}$.

Proof: The only interesting case is the concurrent composition meta-rule (SCONC). Suppose interference-free proofs $\{p_i\} P_i \{q_i\}$, $1 \leqslant i \leqslant n$, are given (presented as proof outlines). Consider any computation π of $[\, \|_{i=1,n} P_i]$ starting in an initial state σ_0, such that $\sigma_0 \models_{\mathbf{I}} \bigwedge_{i=1,n} p_i$. If π is infinite or deadlocked then there is nothing to prove. Thus, assume π is properly terminating, ending in a state σ^*. We have to show that $\sigma^* \models_{\mathbf{I}} \bigwedge_{i=1,n} q_i$. The claim follows from the concurrent preservation lemma, since, in the final configuration in π, say $C^* = \langle [E \| \cdots \| E], \sigma^* \rangle$, we have $\sigma^* \models_{\mathbf{I}} \bigwedge_{i=1,n} post(P_i)$ concluding the soundness proof.

EXERCISE:

Provide a detailed proof of the soundness of the AUX rule.

□

Note, however, that the soundness of the auxiliary variables rule (AUX), though obvious, depends on the assumption (carried over from the sequential languages) about the value of an expression in the r.h.s. of an assignment statement being always defined. Otherwise, this rule could be used to derive $\{true\}$ *skip* $\{false\}$, which does not hold semantically, from $\{true\}\ x := 1/0;\ skip\ \{false\}$, which does hold semantically because of the improper termination of the assignment.

□

We now turn to the other direction. Again arithmetic interpretations are used, this time using their ability to code sequences representing histories of computations.

Theorem (arithmetic completeness of O):

For any arithmetic interpretation $\mathbf{I}^+$, if $\models_{\mathbf{I}^+}\{\bigwedge_{i=1,n} p_i\}[\ \|_{i=1,n}\ P_i]\{\bigwedge_{i=1,n} q_i\}$ then $Tr_{\mathbf{I}^+}\vdash_{\mathbf{O}}\{\bigwedge_{i=1,n} p_i\}[\ \|_{i=1,n}\ P_i]\{\bigwedge_{i=1,n} q_i\}$.

Proof: Again, we consider only the concurrent composition. Suppose that $\models_{\mathbf{I}^+}\{\bigwedge_{i=l,n} p_i\}[\ \|_{i=1,n}\ P_i]\ \{\bigwedge_{i=1,n} q_i\}$ holds. We need to construct proof outlines for $\{p_i\}\ P_i\ \{q_i\}$, $1 \leqslant i \leqslant n$, which are interference free. To this end, we introduce a *new* variable z, not appearing in P, p_i or q_i, $1 \leqslant i \leqslant n$. This is going to be an auxiliary variable, recording the history of the computation. Suppose that $\bar{x}$ is the list of variables in P. We replace each P_i by P_i' according to the following rules.

(1) Each assignment $x := e$, which is a normal subprogram of P_i, is replaced by **await** $true \rightarrow z := z\hat{}\langle i, \bar{x}\rangle;\ x := e$ **end**.

(2) Each **await** $B \rightarrow S$ **end** statement which is a normal subprogram of P_i is replaced by **await** $B \rightarrow z := z\hat{}\langle i, \bar{x}\rangle;\ S$ **end**.

We use a list notation for history values of z, which can be coded as natural numbers in arithmetical interpretations. Recall that '^' denotes list concatenation, and $\langle\rangle$ the empty list.

We first establish

$$Tr_{\mathbf{I}^+}\vdash_{\mathbf{O}}\{\bigwedge_{i=1,n} p_i\}\ z := \langle\rangle;\ P'\ \{\bigwedge_{i=1,n} q_i\} \qquad \textbf{(7.1)}$$

and then obtain the final result by applying (AUX) with $AX = \{z\}$. We call a (partial) computation $\langle P', \sigma\rangle \xrightarrow{h} \langle P'', \sigma''\rangle$ z-**compatible** iff in each intermediate configuration the value of z in the corresponding state equals the code of the prefix h' of h immediately leading to that configuration. A simple argument shows that the merging lemma holds also if we replace a computation with a z-compatible computation, adding the requirement that the initial state satisfies $\sigma_0 \models p_i \wedge z = \langle\rangle$. We assume the latter version here.

Let S be any normal subprogram of P_i'. We define *pre* (S) and *post* (S) for the ith proof outlines as follows.

$\sigma \models_{I^+} pre(S)$ iff there exist a history h, $h = h_1 h_2$, a state σ_0, and (possibly empty) programs S_i, $1 \leqslant i \leqslant n$, such that

(1) $\sigma_0 \models_{I^+} \bigwedge_{i=l,n} p_i \wedge z = \langle\,\rangle$, and

(2) $\langle [\,\|_{i=1,n} P_i'], \sigma_0\rangle \overset{h}{\rightarrow} \langle [S_1 \| \cdots \| S; S_i \| \cdots \| S_n], \sigma\rangle$ is a z-compatible (partial) computation.

$\sigma \models_{I^+} post(S)$ iff there exist a history $h = h_1 h_2$, a state σ_0 and programs S_i, S_i', $1 \leqslant i \leqslant n$, such that

(1) is as above, and

(2) $\langle [\,\|_{i=1,n} P_i'], \sigma_0\rangle \overset{h_1}{\rightarrow} \langle [S_1' \| \cdots \| S; S_i' \| \cdots \| S_n'], \sigma'\rangle$

$\overset{h_2}{\rightarrow} \langle [S_1 \| \cdots \| S_i' \| \cdots \| S_n], \sigma\rangle$

is a z-compatible (partial) computation. This latter condition captures all possible situations where P_i' is just after S, the other processes being anywhere.

One can easily recognize the minimal invariants once again. Again, by our assumption that $\mathbf{I}^+$ is an arithmetical interpretation, *pre* (S) and *post* (S) are expressible as state assertions.

A similar argument to the one used in the sequential case shows that $\{pre(P_i')\}\, P_i' \{post(P_i')\}$ is a valid proof outline in $\mathbf{H}^a$. The more interesting part is proving their interference freedom. Consider first condition (1) in the definition. Let σ be a state where $\sigma \models pre(S') \wedge pre(S'')$, for S' a normal substatement in P_i' and S'' an **await** $B \rightarrow T$ **end** substatement in P_j', $j \neq i$.

By the definition of preconditions and by the merging lemma, there exist programs $T_1, \ldots, T_n$ with $T_i = S'; T_i'$ for some T_i' and $T_j' =$ **await** $B \rightarrow T$ **end**; T_j' for some T_j', and there exists a state σ_0 with $\sigma_0 \models_{I^+} \bigwedge_{i=1,n} p_i \wedge z = \langle\,\rangle$ such that $\langle P', \sigma_0\rangle \overset{h}{\rightarrow} \langle [\,\|_{i=1,n} T_i], \sigma\rangle$ is a z-compatible computation.

Suppose that $\sigma \models_{I^+} B$ holds, and $\langle T, \sigma\rangle \overset{*}{\rightarrow} \langle E, \sigma^*\rangle$. From the definition of '$\rightarrow$', we have that

$$\langle [\,\|_{i=1,n} T_i], \sigma\rangle \overset{\langle j,\sigma\rangle}{\rightarrow} \langle [T_1 \| \cdots \| T_{j-1} \| T_j' \| \cdots \| T_n], \sigma^*\rangle$$

By the definition of the transformation P' of P, T is of the form $z := z\hat{\ }\langle j, \bar{x}\rangle;\ \hat{T}$, for some $\hat{T}$. Hence $\sigma^* \models_{I^+} z = \sigma[z]\hat{\ }\langle j, \sigma[\bar{x}]\rangle$, and hence, $\langle P', \sigma_0\rangle \overset{h\hat{\ }\langle j,\sigma\rangle}{\rightarrow} \langle [T_1 \| \cdots \| T_{j-1} \| T_j' \| \cdots \| T_n], \sigma^*\rangle$ is also a z-compatible computation. Since $T_i = S'; T'_i$ still holds (P_i did not move) we get that $\sigma^* \models_{I^+} pre(S')$ remains true. Hence, we established

$$\models_{I^+} \{pre(S') \wedge pre(S'') \wedge B\}\, T\, \{pre(S')\}.$$

EXERCISE:

Prove (in a similar way) the second condition (2) of the definition of interference freedom, namely $\{post(S') \wedge pre(S'') \wedge B\}\, T\, \{post(S')\}$.

□

By the relative completeness of $\mathbf{H^a}$, we deduce

$$Tr_{I^+} \vdash_{\mathbf{H^a}} \{pre(S') \wedge pre(S'') \wedge B\}\, T\, \{pre(S')\}$$

and

$$Tr_{I^+} \vdash_{\mathbf{H^a}} \{post(S') \wedge pre(S'') \wedge B\}\, T\, \{post(S')\}$$

Since $S'' =$ **await** $B \rightarrow T$ **end** by assumption, we may apply the (AWAIT) rule and obtain

$$Tr_{I^+} \vdash_{\mathbf{H^a}} \{pre(S') \wedge pre(S'')\}\, S''\, \{pre(S')\}$$

and

$$Tr_{I^+} \vdash_{\mathbf{H^a}} \{post(S') \wedge pre(S'')\}\, S''\, \{post(S')\}$$

Since by the construction *all* normal subprograms of P' are **awaits** (all assignments were transformed to accommodate the atomic update of z), this establishes the interference freedom of the outline so constructed. By applying (SCONC), we obtain $Tr_{I^+} \vdash_{\mathbf{O}} \{\bigwedge_{i=l,n} pre(P'_i)\}\, P'\, \{\bigwedge_{i=l,n} post(P'_i)\}$. By a simple use of the consequence rule and finally an application of (AUX), we obtain

$$Tr_{I^+} \vdash_{\mathbf{O}} \{\bigwedge_{i=1,n} p_i\}\, P\, \{\bigwedge_{i=1,n} q_i\}$$

concluding the completeness proof.

□

EXERCISE:

Show that the definition of interference freedom may be weakened by requiring the second condition to apply only to $post(P_i)$, the final postcondition, instead of $post(S)$ for every normal subprogram S.

□

7.5 Synchronization primitives

In the previous section we have seen the crucial role of the interference freedom of the local proof outlines. The origin of the complexity is the unrestricted structure of reference and updates of the shared variables. Clearly, this is an obstacle both to ease of verification and to the ease of programming.

In this section, we consider (somewhat) more structured synchronization primitives, which protect the shared variables by forcing implicit mutual exclusion of program sections that access or modify them.

As a by-product, we also obtain a more structured sharing of variables, instead of the monolithic sharing employed by *SVL*, by which different collections of variables may be shared by different collections of processes. We consider here only a simple version of such primitives, just to get the spirit of the approach. More elaborate synchronization primitives have been proposed and used with a similar approach.

The synchronization construct we consider is the so-called **conditional critical section** (*ccs*), the sole function of which is to handle the mutual exclusion mentioned above. Another construct is generically referred to as a **monitor**, which refines the atomicity of the body of a *ccs* by permitting the temporary release of the resource by waiting for an explicit signal by some other process. This way, more elaborate synchronization and resource allocation strategies may be implemented. The original form of the monitor construct involved also the modularity of data abstraction. Hence, the operations on the shared data were structured as procedures, encapsulating the details of the representation. See the suggestions for further reading for references to work on verification of monitor programs.

7.5.1 Conditional critical sections

The main idea is to introduce collections of variables called **resources**, which are declared outside the scope of a concurrent composition. Whenever a process needs access to shared variables contained in a resource *r*, it executes a statement of the form

with *r* **when** *B* **do** *S* **endwith**

where *B* is a Boolean condition† and *S* a statement using the variables in *r*. Informally, the executing process is delayed until the resource *r* is not used by any other process (*r* is *free*) and the condition *B* holds. When this happens, the

† If the Boolean condition is 'true', one sometimes omits the '**when**' clause altogether: **with** *r* **do** *S* **endwith**.

executing process may gain control over the resource r (the resource becoming **occupied**) and execute the statement S uninterrupted. If and when S terminates the executing process **releases** the resource r (which again becomes free). No assumptions are made about the resolution of conflicts between different processes attempting to gain control for the same resource, which is nondeterministic.

Thus, syntactic form directs the usage of shared variables, allowing the text of the program to determine the sharing structure that had to be deduced in the case of *SVL*.

We now turn to a formal definition of the simple minilanguage *RVL* (resource variables language).

The *RVL* language:

A **program** has the form

$$P :: \textbf{resource } r_1\,(\textit{var-list}_1); \ldots; \textbf{resource } r_m\,(\textit{var-list}_m);\ P_0;\ [\ \underset{i=1,n}{\|}\ P_i]$$

Here $\textit{var-list}_j$, $1 \leqslant j \leqslant m$, are pairwise disjoint lists of program variables. □

The initial program P_0 is a *PLW* statement. A **process** P_i, $1 \leqslant i \leqslant n$, consists of a statement S. Statements are those in *PLW* with the additional *ccs* statement S:: **with** r_j **when** B **do** S' **endwith**$_j$, with $1 \leqslant j \leqslant m$. Here B is an arbitrary Boolean expression and the substatement S' does not contain a nested *ccs* statement for the (same) resource r_j. Note that we index the terminator **endwith** with the corresponding resource, for aiding the definition of the semantics. Again, no nested concurrency is assumed at this point.

To ensure the intended behavior of programs, the following two syntactic conditions on variables usage are imposed.

(1) A variable v belonging to a resource r_j, $1 \leqslant j \leqslant m$, cannot appear in any P_i, $1 \leqslant i \leqslant n$, except in a *ccs* statement.

(2) A variable $v \in \textit{change}(P_i)$, $1 \leqslant i \leqslant n$, cannot appear in $\textit{free}(P_j), j \neq i$, unless it belongs to some resource r_k, $1 \leqslant k \leqslant m$.

This way, the resources cover any reference to a variable shared among different processes and any such reference is protected as far as exclusive access is concerned.

We now present a semantics for *RVL*, again based on a transition relation among suitably defined configurations.

Let P:: **resource** $r_1; \ldots;$ **resource** $r_m; P_0; [\ \underset{i=1,n}{\|}\ P_i]$, where for simplicity we omit the actual variable lists, assuming that restrictions (1) and (2) apply.

A **concurrent configuration** $C \stackrel{df.}{=} \langle [\ \|_{i=1,n}\ S_i], \rho[1\,..\,m], \sigma\rangle$ for *RVL* consists of the syntactic continuation and visible state as before, with the addition of the **resource availability** vector $\rho[j], i \leqslant j \leqslant m$, which is 0–1 valued. We interpret $\rho[j] = 0$ holding in configuration C to mean that the resource r_j is available in configuration C. We abbreviate $\rho[1], .. , \rho[m]$ to just ρ. Note that ρ is an invisible state component of a configuration.

Once again, we assume the transition relation '$\rightarrow$' among sequential configurations as for *PLW*. We extend it to concurrent configurations by adding the following transition rules.

(1) For S_i not a *ccs* statement,

if $\langle S_i, \sigma\rangle \rightarrow \langle S_i', \sigma'\rangle$, then

$$\langle [\ \|_{i=1,n}\ S_i], \rho, \sigma\rangle \stackrel{<i,\sigma>}{\rightarrow} \langle [S_1 \| \cdots \| S_i' \| \cdots S_n], \rho, \sigma'\rangle$$

(2) If for some $1 \leqslant j \leqslant m$ $\rho[j] = 0$ and $\sigma \models B$, then

$$\langle [S_1 \| \cdots \| \textbf{with } r_j \textbf{ when } B \textbf{ do } S_i \textbf{ endwith}_j \| \cdots \| S_n], \rho, \sigma\rangle \stackrel{<i,\sigma>}{\rightarrow}$$
$$\langle [S_1 \| \cdots \| S_i ; \textbf{endwith}_j \| \cdots \| S_n], \rho', \sigma\rangle$$

where $\rho'[j] = 1$ and $\rho'[k] = \rho[k]$ for $k \neq j$.

(3) $\langle [S_1 \| \cdots \| \textbf{endwith}_j \| \cdots \| S_n, \rho, \sigma\rangle \stackrel{<i,\sigma>}{\rightarrow} \langle [S_1 \| \cdots \| E \| \cdots \| S_n], \rho', \sigma\rangle$

where $\rho'[j] = 0$ and $\rho'[k] = \rho[k]$ for $k \neq j$.

The extension to '$\stackrel{h}{\rightarrow}$' is as before. Similarly, a concurrent computation is again a maximal '$\stackrel{h}{\rightarrow}$'-sequence, where the initial configuration C_0 satisfies $\rho[j] = 0, 1 \leqslant j \leqslant m$, (that is, initially all resources are available). We transfer the definitions of termination, divergence, and deadlock from the *SVL* context. Also, the definitions of *val* and **M** are similarly adapted.

EXERCISE:

Prove that in a terminal configuration $\rho[j] = 0, 1 \leqslant j \leqslant m$.

□

From the definition of '$\rightarrow$' it is clear that **mutual exclusion** is guaranteed for usage of resource variables. In other words, no computation contains a configuration of the form $\langle [S_1 \| \cdots \| S_i \| \cdots \| S_j \| \cdots \| S_n], \rho, \sigma\rangle$, $i \neq j$, with S_i a

$$PSORT :: \textbf{resource}\ r(a, rdy)[1 \ldots n];\ [SEND \,\|\, \mathop{\|}_{i=1,n} COMP_i]$$

where

$SEND :: j = 1;$ **while** $j \leqslant n$ **do**
  with $r[1]$ **when** $rdy[1]$ **do** $a[1] := in[j];\ rdy[1] := false$ **endwith**;
  $j := j + 1$ **od**
$COMP_i ::$ **with** $r[i]$ **when** $\neg rdy[i]$ **do** $b[i] := a[i];\ rdy[i] := true$ **endwith**;
  $k[i] := 1;$
  while $k[i] \leqslant n - i$ **do with** $r[i], r[i+1]$ **when** $\neg rdy[i] \wedge rdy[i+1]$ **do**
    $a[i+1] := min(a[i], b[i]);$
    $b[i] := max(a[i], b[i]);$
    $rdy[i] := true;\ rdy[i+1] := false$ **endwith**;
  $k[i] := k[i] + 1$ **od**

Figure 7.6 The parallel sorting example.

substatement of a *ccs* for some r_k in P_i and S_j a substatement of a *ccs* for the same r_k in P_j.

As an example of a program in *RVL* consider the *PSORT* program for parallel sorting shown in Figure 7.6. This is a parallel version of the bubble sort algorithm. Its functioning is explained in the next section, where its correctness proof is presented. Basically, it 'pushes' elements as far right as possible along the COMP$_i$ pipeline, generating a descending order.

7.5.2 A proof system S for partial correctness

In this section we present a proof system for proving the partial correctness of *RVL* programs. As mentioned before, the synchronization primitives prevent interference, as they control the interleavings to guarantee mutual exclusion among *ccs* bodies. To simplify the notation, we assume that there is only one resource $r(\bar{v})$.

The main new idea is to associate with the resource $r(\bar{v})$ a **resource invariant** $I_r(\bar{v})$, which characterizes the permissible states of the resource. The invariant $I_r(\bar{v})$ should be satisfied by the resource state, and should hold whenever a process gains (the exclusive) control over the resource r. It need not hold during the execution of a *ccs* associated with r, as the variables $\bar{v}$ of the resource r may be modified during the execution of that *ccs*. However, these intermediate states become 'invisible' to all other processes until the execution of the *ccs* is terminated and another process may gain control over r. The invariant has, however, to be re-established upon the completion of the body of the *ccs*, so that the next process gaining control over r again finds

$I_r(\bar{v})$ holding. Thus, the invariant always holds when the resource r is free, and in particular upon the termination of the whole program.

We now turn to formalizing these ideas.

ccs rule:

$$\frac{\{I_r \wedge p \wedge B\}\, S\, \{I_r \wedge q\}}{\{p\}\ \textbf{with}\ r\ \textbf{when}\ B\ \textbf{do}\ S\ \textbf{endwith}\ \{q\}} \qquad \text{(CCS)}$$

□

EXERCISE:

Why can I_r not be asserted upon the termination of the *ccs*, together with the post condition q?

□

Concurrent composition rule:

$$\frac{\{p_i\}\, P_i\, \{q_i\},\ i = 1, n,\ \text{using}\ I_r}{\{I_r \wedge \bigwedge_{i=1,n} p_i\}\ \textbf{resource}\ r; [\ \|_{i=1,n}\ P_i]\ \{I_r \wedge \bigwedge_{i=1,n} q_i\}}$$

where for both rules $free(p_i, q_i) \cap change(P_j) = \varnothing$ for $i \neq j$ and $free(I_r) \subseteq r$. The condition 'using I_r' means that I_r is the resource invariant used by the *ccs* rule within the process bodies' proofs.

□

We also include in **S** the (AUX) rule which facilitates the use of auxiliary variables. These are needed here for the same reasons as they were needed in *SVL*, namely for reasoning about the history of the computation and the values in configurations which are not represented in the visible state.

EXAMPLE:

We demonstrate the use of the system **S** by providing parts of the partial correctness proof for the parallel sorting program *PSORT* from Figure 7.6. As the specification, we consider the following pair of state assertions p and q.

$$p \equiv \bigwedge_{i=1,n} rdy[i] = tt$$

$$q \equiv \bigwedge_{i=2,n} (b[i] \leqslant b[i-1]) \wedge perm(in, b)$$

We could refrain from including a claim on the *rdy* values in the precondition by prefixing the program with a P_0 properly initializing these variables to *tt*.

$SEND :: \{np_0 = 0 \wedge rdy[1]\}$
$j = 1$; **while** $j \leqslant n$ **do**
  with $r[1]$ **when** $rdy[1]$ **do** $\{I_r \wedge rdy[1] \wedge np_0 = j-1 \wedge 1 \leqslant j \leqslant n\}$
    $a[1] := in[j]$; $rdy[1] := false$; $np_0 := np_0 + 1$ **endwith**; $\{np_0 = j\}$
  $j := j+1$
od; $\{np_0 = n\}$

$COMP_i :: \{np_i = 0\}$
with $r[i]$ **when** $\neg\, rdy[i]$ **do** $\{I_r \wedge \neg\, rdy[i] \wedge np_i = 0\}\, b[i] := a[i]$;
    $rdy[i] := tt$; $np_i := 1$ **endwith**; $\{np_i = 1\}$
$k[i] := 1$;
while $k[i] \leqslant n-i$ **do with** $r[i], r[i+1]$ **when** $\neg\, rdy[i] \wedge rdy[i+1]$ **do**
    $\{I_r \wedge \neg\, rdy[i] \wedge rdy[i+1] \wedge np_i = k[i] \bigwedge_{i=1,n} 1 \leqslant k[i] \leqslant n-i\}$
  $a[i+1] := min(a[i], b[i])$;
  $b[i] := max(a[i], b[i])$;
  $rdy[i] := true$; $rdy[i+1] := false$;
  $np_i := np_i + 1$ **endwith**; $\{np_i = k[i]+1\}$
$k[i] := k[i]+1$ **od** $\{np_i = n-i+1\}$

Figure 7.7 The proof outline for the parallel sorting example.

We completely omit the easier part of the proof which establishes the second conjunct of q, as it is easy to see that $perm(a, b)$ is left invariant by using *min* and *max* effectively as an exchange operation; we concentrate on establishing the first and more interesting conjunct of q.

We augment the program with an auxiliary variable np_i in each $COMP_i$, which counts the number of values received by $COMP_i$. Similarly, an auxiliary counter np_0 is added to *SEND*. The skeleton of the proof outline of the augmented program is shown in Figure 7.7.

The resource invariant I_r expresses the following four basic facts:

(1) The (indices of) processes for which the $b[i]$ elements are already sorted form a contiguous initial segment of $[1 \ldots n]$, and this segment contains all and only processes that received input elements.
(2) A process passes an element to its (right) neighbor only if it is not larger than the value it currently holds.
(3) The termination of processes propagates properly from right to left.
(4) The processes *SEND* and $COMP_1$ are coordinated.

For proving the full postcondition, yet another clause, asserting the preservation of input values, would be needed.

These conditions are captured by the following formal definition.

$I_r \stackrel{df.}{=}$

(1) $\bigvee_{j=1,n} \bigwedge_{i=1,n} (j < i \Leftrightarrow np_i = 0) \wedge (1 \leqslant i \leqslant j-1 \Rightarrow b[i] \geqslant b[i+1])$

$\wedge$

(2) $\bigwedge_{i=2,n} (\neg\, rdy[i] \Rightarrow a[i] \leqslant b[i-1])$

$\wedge$

(3) $\bigwedge_{i=1,n-1} (np_i = n-i+1 \wedge rdy[i] \wedge rdy[i+1] \Rightarrow np_{i+1} = n-i)$

$\wedge$

(4) $rdy[1] \Rightarrow np_0 = np_1 \wedge \neg\, rdy[1] \Rightarrow np_0 = np_1 + 1$

We present some of the main parts of the proof. First, suppose that $\{p_i\}\, COMP_i\, \{q_i\}$, $1 \leqslant i \leqslant n$, as well as $\{p_0\}\, SEND\, \{q_0\}$ have all been established using I_r. By the concurrent composition rule we obtain $I_r \wedge \bigwedge_{i=1,n} q_i$, provided that $I_r \wedge \bigwedge_{i=1,n} p_i$, holds initially. The following argument can be formalized as an application of the consequence rule (CONS). The conjunction $\bigwedge_{i=1,n} q_i$ implies $\bigwedge_{i=1,n} np_i > 0$. Therefore, from clause (1) of I_r holding in the final state it follows that $j = n$. Hence, the second part of (1) yields $\bigwedge_{1 \leqslant i \leqslant n-1} b[i] \geqslant b[i+1]$, which is the required postcondition.

To see that I_r holds initially, we inspect each conjunct separately.

(1) Since $\bigwedge_{i=1,n} p_i$ implies $\bigwedge_{i=1,n} np_i = 0$, this conjunct can be satisfied by choosing $j = 0$.

(2) This conjunct is satisfied vacuously, as $rdy[i] = tt$ for $1 \leqslant i \leqslant n$.

(3) This conjunct is also satisfied vacuously, since $np_i = 0$ for $1 \leqslant i \leqslant n$, and hence $np_i \neq n-i+1$ for $1 \leqslant i \leqslant n$.

(4) Initially, $rdy[i] = tt$ and $np_0 = np_1 = 0$, so this conjunct is also satisfied.

We now have to show that for $1 \leqslant i \leqslant n$, the proof outlines of $COMP_i$, as well as that of *SEND*, are sequentially valid. We leave out the purely sequential reasoning and focus on the applications of the *ccs* rule.

First, consider the application of the rule within the proof outline of *SEND*. We have to show

$$\{I_r \wedge 1 \leqslant j \leqslant n \wedge np_j = j-1 \wedge rdy[1]\}\, a[1] := in[j]; rdy[1] := ff;$$
$$np_0 := np_0 + 1\, \{I_r \wedge np_0 = j\}$$

The second conjunct in the postcondition, namely $np_0 = j$, follows immediately by (ASS) and (CONS) from the conjunct $np_0 = j-1$ in the precondition and the assignment $np_0 := np_0 - 1$.

The first two conjuncts of I_r were true in the precondition by assumption and remain true in the postcondition since none of the variables on which they depend is being modified by the body of the *ccs*. The third conjunct of I_r holds vacuously in the postcondition for $i = 1$, since $rdy[1] = ff$ is the case. For $2 \leqslant i \leqslant n-1$ it remains true again since the variables np_i have not changed. Finally, since the fourth conjunct held in the precondition while $rdy[1] = tt$, we have $np_0 = j-1 = np_1$. However, in the final state we have $rdy[1] = ff$ and $np_0 = j \neq j-1 = np_1$, establishing the fourth conjunct.

A very similar argument establishes the correctness of the first *ccs* in $COMP_i$. We turn to the second *ccs* in $COMP_i$. We have to show

$$\{I_r \wedge 1 \leqslant k[i] \leqslant n-i \wedge np_i = k[i] \wedge \neg rdy[i] \wedge rdy[i+1]\}$$
$$a[i+1] := min(a[i], b[i]);\ b[i] := max(a[i], b[i]);$$
$$rdy[i] := tt;\ rdy[i+1] := ff;\ np_i := np_i + 1$$
$$\{I_r \wedge np_i = k[i]+1\}$$

Again, the second conjunct $np_i = k[i]+1$ follows immediately by (ASS) and (CONS) from $np_i = k[i]$ and the assignment $np_i := np_i + 1$. The fourth conjunct is unaffected by the body of the *ccs* for $i \neq 1$ and thus remains true. For $i = 1$ its truth is re-established too. Consider the second conjunct. Because of the assignment $rdy[i+1] := ff$, we have to establish that $a[i+1] \leqslant b[i]$. This follows immediately, since $min(x, y) \leqslant max(x, y)$ is always true. Finally, consider the third conjunct, and fix some $1 \leqslant i \leqslant n-1$. One way of I_r holding initially for i, is, as seen by the precondition, having $\neg rdy[i] \wedge rdy[i+1]$, satisfying the implication vacuously. In this case, after executing the body of the *ccs* ((ASS) and (CONS) rules), we get $rdy[i] = tt$, but $rdy[i+1] = ff$, again satisfying the implication vacuously. The other thing to consider is the effect of the execution of the ith *ccs* body on the $(i-1)$th conjunct, which held initially by having $rdy[i-1] \wedge \neg rdy[i]$, that is vacuously. After the assignment $rdy[i] := tt$ and $np_{i-1} = n-i$ the antecedent of the $(i-1)$th implication becomes true. By considering the condition $np_i = k[i]$ the result follows.

This ends the proof of the example.

□

Finally, we consider the issues of soundness and arithmetical completeness of **S**. Both hold, and the considerations and arguments for establishing them are rather similar to the corresponding ones for **O** and are not presented in detail. The only essential difference is in having to take care also of the resource invariant while merging computations. In the bibliographic notes the references to the literature are given, where the missing details can be found.

7.6 Proving safety and liveness properties

Until this section, we have considered only the two most basic correctness properties of programs, namely partial correctness and termination (the latter identified with the absence of infinite computations). In this section we turn to other properties, which are characteristic only of concurrent programs. The presentation is in terms of representative properties, namely **deadlock freedom** and **mutual exclusion** for safety, and **nonstarvation** for liveness, not covering the whole spectrum of additional properties. These properties are defined in terms of configurations (involving control locations) and not merely (visible) states. As already mentioned, more powerful logics are needed to express the additional properties. Our aim here is to show that we can make use of the proof techniques developed so far, namely invariants and well-founded decreasing variants, in order to handle additional properties. The safety family of properties, in our context, is characterized by being provable by computational induction, using invariants. Liveness properties are provable by decreasing, well-founded variants. Thus, we avoid here any consideration of intrinsic characterizations of such properties, independently of their proof methods. The suggestions for further reading point out further literature dealing with intrinsic characterizations.

The main need for these additional properties stems from the nature of many concurrent programs, which are not meant to terminate. Rather, their correctness criteria are expressed in terms of their continuous behavior. We saw some simple means of relating to such infinite behaviors in Chapter 3, using intermittent assertions. Temporal logic is one powerful specification language, in which such specifications can be expressed. However, a full treatment of these issues within temporal logic is beyond the scope of this book. Thus, we leave the definition of the extra properties proof on an *ad hoc* basis, and satisfy our needs by showing that the proof techniques used extend to these properties too.

7.6.1 Safety: deadlock freedom and mutual exclusion

We start by presenting a general method for establishing the absence of deadlock in a given program P, relative to a precondition p. We apply the method both to SVL and to RVL programs. In the next chapter, the method is adapted also to distributed programs expressed by means of message-passing concurrency.

Recall that semantically a computation reaches a deadlock in case it reaches a nonterminal configuration from which no '$\rightarrow$' transition exists. This means that every concurrent component (process) in the syntactic continuation of that configuration which is not empty has the form of a **delaying** statement, where the condition for the delay is satisfied by the state (including its invisible parts) of the considered configuration. The actual details of the delay depend on the semantics of the language constructs at hand. The proof obligation is to establish that no such configuration is ever reached in any computation of a given program.

The point of departure is a valid proof outline for $\{p\}\,P\,\{q\}$. We stress already at this point the strong dependence of the method on an appropriate choice of proof outline. Not every proof outline that is strong enough to establish partial correctness is also strong enough to establish deadlock freedom. The method involves two steps.

(1) Identify (syntactically) all blocked situations in P.

(2) Show that their semantic image (under the given proof outline) is a contradiction.

We now describe the above notions in more detail. A **blocked situation** is an n-tuple of **blocked residence points** (*brps*), one for each process P_i in P, such that the corresponding next statement in each such blocked residence point is a statement the meaning of which implies a (potential) delay, or is the end of that process. Since we want to distinguish between deadlock and proper termination, an n-tuple in which all the *brps* for the respective processes are their ends is never taken to be blocked, as it reflects a terminal configuration.

However, we are not interested in the *brps* themselves, but in the fact that during a computation all processes are simultaneously at their corresponding *brps*. In order to be able to express this fact by means of state assertions (possibly using auxiliary variables), we make use of the concurrent preservation lemma applied to the given proof outline. We express the fact that control of a process P_i is at its respective *brp* by an assertion α_i associated with the statement S at that point: α_i is *pre* (S) if S is a blocking statement and is *post* (P_i) if P_i has terminated. In addition, another component δ_i is conjoined, expressing the condition for delay. The latter depends on the exact primitive used. These are the **semantic images** of the *brps*. The semantic image of the blocked situation is taken as $\delta \stackrel{df.}{\equiv} \bigwedge_{i=1,n} \alpha_i \wedge \delta_i$.

From the definition it is clear that, once the semantic image δ of every blocked situation is shown to be contradictory, no deadlock can occur. This is an immediate consequence of the concurrent structured preservation lemma. Clearly, this condition is only sufficient because of its dependence on the initially selected proof outline.

We now turn to study the application of this method both to *SVL* and *RVL* programs.

A. Deadlock freedom in *SVL*

In *SVL*, the delaying operations are the **await** statements (recall the exclusion of nested concurrency from our consideration). Thus, in a blocked situation in $P :: [\ \underset{i=1,n}{\|}\ P_i]$ some (but not all) processes have terminated, while the others are about to execute a delaying **await** statement, finding the delaying condition B false. Thus, for S:: **await** $B \rightarrow S'$ **end,** we define $\delta_i \overset{df.}{=} \neg B$.

EXERCISE:

Why is not a blocked situation concerned about competition over the ability to evaluate the delaying condition?

□

As an example of a deadlock freedom proof, we return to the bounded buffer example.

EXAMPLE:

Consider again the bounded buffer program P_{buf} from a previous section and its partial correctness proof presented before. We show that P_{buf} is deadlock free. It has three blocked situations:

(1) The *producer* process has terminated and the *consumer* process is blocked in its **await** delaying statement. The semantic image of this blocked situation is $in = n \wedge I \wedge in - out \leqslant 0$ (the first conjunct coming from *post* (*producer*), the second from *pre* (**await**) and the third is the negation of the delaying predicate). From $I \wedge in - out \leqslant 0$ we get $in - out = 0$. Together with $in = n$, we get $out = n$. Then, from I we have $j = out + 1 = n + 1 \leqslant n$, a contradiction.

(2) The *consumer* process has terminated and the *producer* process is blocked in its **await.** The semantic image is $out = n \wedge I \wedge in - out \geqslant b$.

EXERCISE:

Derive the contradiction in case (2).

□

(3) Both the *producer* process and the *consumer* process are blocked at their respective conditional delaying statements. The semantic image is $I \wedge in < n \wedge in - out \geqslant b \wedge out < n \wedge in - out \leqslant 0$. We get $0 = in - out = b \wedge b > 0$, a clear contradiction.

□

B. Deadlock freedom in *RVL*

Again, as a simple consequence of the operational semantics of *RVL*, we see that a blocked situation occurs when some (but not all) of the processes have terminated, while all the other processes are delayed in front of *ccs*, with the continuation condition false. The semantic image is constructed in a similar way as for *SVL*, with the difference that the resource invariant I_r is conjoined, since no process resides in a *ccs* in a blocked situation.

EXAMPLE:

Consider again the sorting program *PSORT* and its proof outline in Figure 7.7. We shall attempt to prove its deadlock freedom using the same outline. We consider some of the blocked situations.

(1) The process *SEND* is blocked in front of its first *ccs* and *all* the $COMP_i$ processes have terminated. The semantic image is

$$I_r \wedge np_0 = j-1 \wedge 1 \leqslant j \leqslant n \wedge \bigwedge_{i=1,n} np_i = n-i+1 \wedge \neg\, rdy[1].$$

From the fourth conjunct of I_r, together with $\neg\, rdy[1]$, we get $np_0 = np_1+1$. From the fourth conjunct of the semantic image (for $i = 1$), we get $np_1 = n$. Combining the two equalities yields $np_0 = n+1$. From the second conjunct of the semantic image we get $np_0 = j-1$. Combining again, we get $j-1 = n+1$, which implies $j = n+2$. This contradicts the conjunct $1 \leqslant j \leqslant n$ of the semantic image.

(2) Suppose, for some $1 \leqslant i < n$, that $COMP_i$ is blocked at its first *ccs* while P_k and $COMP_k, i < k \leqslant n$ have already terminated. Then, $COMP_i$ contributes $np_i = 0$ (from its precondition) to the semantic image, while P_k contributes $np_k = n-k+1 > 0$. Together, the first conjnct I_r is contradicted.

□

EXERCISE:

Identify the rest of the blocked situations of the *PSORT* program and derive the contradiction from their respective semantic images.

□

As is seen from the above example, proofs of deadlock freedom can become quite tedious and sensitive to fine details. However, the approach presented provides a systematic way of proof, reducing the possibility of error due to negligence of some blocked situation.

Note again the global nature of the reasoning involved in deadlock freedom proofs. They enforce a clever design of the local outlines, that have to anticipate this global reasoning.

In case of the availability of a theorem prover, all the semantic images can be disjunctively combined into one formula, the negation of which is then presented to the theorem prover for the automatic derivation of a contradiction.

C. Proof of mutual exclusion

Mutual exclusion among **critical sections** is another safety property, which makes sense for perpetual concurrent programs. We formulate the explanation in terms of the *RVL* language. The semantics of the language guarantees 'low-level' exclusion between *ccs*s. However, the latter are language-defined units. In many cases, a specification requires exclusion among program-defined critical sections, where the exclusion is programmed by some exclusion algorithm. A typical application of this concept is in scheduling the use of a resource, for example in an operating system.

As it turns out, this property can be also proved based on a given proof outline (using some unimportant postcondition). The method is similar to that of deadlock freedom, again constituting a sufficient condition only.

(1) Identify (syntactically) all non-exclusive situations in P.

(2) Show that their semantic image (under the given proof outline) is contradictory.

Thus, the same idea of identifying the residence of a process in a residence point with the assertion attached to that point, by the given proof outline is used again. However, since we deal with program sections and not single residence points, the semantic image is more complicated.

Note that in contrast to deadlock freedom, the absence of which (that is, the occurrence of a deadlock) is reflected in the meaning of P (by the **f** value), the semantics we defined provides no reflection of exclusion or its absence. Thus, for a given program $P::[\underset{i=1,n}{\|} P_i]$ and a proof outline for $\{p\}\,P\,\{q\}$ (for any q), and for statements $S^{(i)}$ in P_i, $S^{(j)}$ in P_j, (both not within a *ccs* of r), we have to show the inconsistency of $\eta\,(S^{(i)}) \wedge \eta\,(S^{(j)}) \wedge I_r$.

Here $\eta\,(S)$ is a state assertion representing residence in S.

Definition: A representing assertion $\eta\,(S)$ for a program section S satisfies $pre\,(S') \Rightarrow \eta\,(S)$ for every substatement S' of S.

□

Thus, $\eta\,(S)$ holds the execution of S, or, in other words, is an invariant of S.

A natural question at this point is the following: Why can I_r be *dining philosophers*:

$f := 2$; **resource** *forks* (f); $[\ \|_{i=0,4}\ DP_i]$, where:

DP_i :: **while** *true* **do**

with *forks* **when** $f[i] = 2$ **do**

$f[i-1] := f[i-1]-1; f[i+1] := f[i+1]-1$ **endwith**;

eat_i: '*eat*';

with *forks* **do**

$f[i-1] := f[i-1]+1; f[i+1] := f[i+1]+1$ **endwith**;

$think_i$: '*think*' **od**

Figure 7.8 The dining philosophers program.

assumed at the semantic image of a non-exclusive situation? What if some P_k, $k \neq i$ and $k \neq j$, happens to reside within a *ccs* ? The answer follows from the exclusion lemma.

Lemma (exclusion):

If P has a non-exclusive computation (starting in state σ) s.t. some process is within a *ccs* at the non-exclusion point, then P has an equivalent non-exclusive computation where no process resides in a *ccs* at the non-exclusion point.

□

Here the equivalence relation among computations is the one obtained by commuting independent actions of different processes. This equivalence relation occurs quite often in the study of concurrency.

EXERCISE:

Prove the exclusion lemma based on the definition of '$\rightarrow$'.

□

EXAMPLE (dining philosophers):

As an example of an exclusion proof, we consider a simple solution to the famous dining philosophers problem, no treatment of concurrency being adequate without relating to this problem. Five philosophers sit around a circular table, alternately *thinking* and *eating* spaghetti. The spaghetti is so long and tangled that a philosopher needs two forks to eat it, but unfortunately there are only five forks on the table. The only

$\{true\}$
dining philosophers:
$f := 2;\ eating := 0;$
$\{I_{forks} \wedge \bigwedge_{i=0,4} eating[i] = 0\}$
resource *forks* (f); $[\ \|_{i=0,4}\ DP_i]$, where:
$\{I_{forks} \wedge \bigwedge_{i=0,4} eating[i] = 0\}$

$\{eating[i] = 0\}$
DP_i:: **while** *true* **do**
$\{eating[i] = 0\}$
with *forks* **when** $f[i] = 2$ **do**
$\{eating[i] = 0 \wedge f[i] = 2 \wedge I_{forks}\}$
$f[i-1] := f[i-1]-1;\ f[i+1] := f[i+1]-1;$
$eating[i] := 1$ **endwith**;
$\{eating[i] = 1 \wedge I_{forks}\}$
$\{eating[i] = 1\}$
eat_i: '*eat*';
$\{eating[i] = 1\}$
with *forks* **do**
$\{eating[i] = 1 \wedge I_{forks}\}$
$f[i-1] := f[i-1]+1;\ f[i+1] := f[i+1]+1;$
$eating[i] := 0$ **endwith**;
$\{eating[i] = 0 \wedge I_{forks}\}$
$\{eating[i] = 0\}$
$think_i$: '*think*' **od**
$\{eating[i] = 0\}$

where

$$I_{forks} = \bigwedge_{i=0,4} [0 \leqslant eating[i] \leqslant 1 \wedge (eating[i] = 1 \Rightarrow f[i] = 2) \wedge f[i] = 2 - (eating[i-1] + eating[i+1])]$$

Figure 7.9 Proof outline for the dining philosophers program.

forks which a philosopher can use are the ones to his immediate right and left. Obviously two neighbors cannot eat at the same time. The problem is to write a program for each philosopher to provide this synchronization. A solution is presented in Figure 7.8.

The array $f[0\,..\,4]$ records the number of forks available to each philosopher. In order to eat, a philosopher must wait until two forks are available; he then takes the forks and reduces the number available to each of his neighbors. All the arithmetic on indices is in modulo 5.

Assignments like $f := 2$ are abbreviations for a sequence $f[1] := 2; \cdots;$ $f[5] := 2$.

We are interested in proving the mutual exclusion of the '*eat*' sections (the details of which are not shown). It is assumed that '*eat*' and '*think*' do not modify f. In Figure 7.9, a proof outline for the dining philosophers program is presented, using the auxiliary array *eating* [0 . . 4], representing residence in the eating section.

We use this proof outline to prove that mutual exclusion is accomplished, that is two neighbors do not eat at the same time. Consider the semantic image of a non-exclusion point for P_i and P_{i+1}. At this point $eating[i] = 1$ and $eating[i+1] = 1$, from the preconditions for 'eat_i' and 'eat_{i+1}'. Since it can be assumed (by the exclusion lemma) that I_{forks} is also true at this point we have the desired contradiction, for $eating[i] = 1 \wedge eating[i+1] = 1 \wedge I_{forks}$ implies $f[i] = 2 \wedge f[i] < 2$. This ends the proof of exclusion and the example.

□

7.6.2 Liveness: termination and nonstarvation

In this section we consider the extension of the proof systems for shared-variable concurrency to handle also proofs of termination and total correctness. Furthermore, similarly to the extension of partial correctness to the more general safety properties, we consider here another kind of properties, referred to as **liveness** properties, of which termination and total correctness are special cases.

There is a very strong dependence of liveness properties of programs on the specific liveness properties embedded in the semantic definition of the language. The influence of the basic liveness assumptions is stronger than the corresponding ones in sequential programs due to the much larger number of possible such assumptions in the concurrent case, in contrast to an almost standard possibility in the sequential case. Recall that for *SVL*, for example, only the fundamental liveness property was assumed (directly following from the maximality of a computation). Thus, the program in Figure 7.10 need not terminate. It will terminate under a slightly stronger assumption, constituting a very limited form of fairness, stating that every enabled local atomic statement (assignments or **await**s in the case of *SVL*) is eventually executed. Under this variant of the semantics, the condition $x = 1$ will eventually become false (after the transition involving P_2) and P_1 will exit its local loop. Stronger liveness requirements made by the semantics will induce stronger liveness properties of programs. In particular, programs may terminate under such liveness requirements, whereas they do not terminate without this assumption.

Liveness conditions are a generalization of termination, requiring the eventual reachability of a certain program state (or, sometimes, of a certain

$P :: [P_1 \| P_2]$, where
$P_1 :: x := 1$; **while** $x = 1$ **do** *skip* **od**
$P_2 :: x := 0$

Figure 7.10 A concurrent program not terminating under the fundamental liveness assumption.

event or action in the program). They may be expressed by means of the *leads_to* operator from Chapter 3, or by other means mentioned in the suggestions for further reading. Similarly to termination, very few liveness properties can be guaranteed without incorporating some fairness assumptions into the semantics of the programming language. For example, consider again the solution to the dining philosophers problem in Figure 7.9. A typical liveness condition for this program, known metaphorically speaking as *nonstarvation*, requires that for each DP_i, if (in any computation) the condition $f[i] = 2$ holds infinitely often with DP_i in front of its *ccs*, then eventually $eating[i] = 1$ should hold (hence, it should hold infinitely often too). Informally, this means that 'every hungry philosopher will eventually eat'. This property is not satisfied (and hence cannot be proven) by the solution program in Figure 7.9, in the absence of fairness assumptions in the semantics as stated. For example, an infinite computation in which DP_{i-1} and DP_{i+1} eat alternately, while DP_i never eats, is possible, and certainly violates the above-stated liveness condition. The phenomenon exhibited by such a computation is sometimes referred to as a **conspiracy** (of DP_{i-1} and DP_{i+1} against DP_i). Clearly, imposing certain fairness assumptions with respect to access to the *ccs* might eliminate this undesirable behavior.

Since there was not an elaborate treatment of fairness for shared variables languages, we defer further discussion of this issue to the next chapter. Some references are given in the suggestions for further reading. Fairness for distributed programs was studied more extensively.

A. Termination proofs for *SVL* programs

The way to prove termination of *SVL* programs under the given semantics is a natural extension of the two-staged proof approach. For each local **while** statement, a parametrized invariant is constructed, satisfying the same requirements as in the corresponding rule for *PLW* programs, and, in addition, noninterference w.r.t. all companion local proofs is established. However, the value of the variant need not remain the same after a transition by another process – it only should not increase. Note that, strictly speaking, what we are proving by using this method is the absence of infinite computation. This is equivalent to (proper) termination only when deadlock freedom is also established. A deadlock computation also halts within finite time, though we want to distinguish it from proper termination. In this section, we assume that deadlock freedom has been shown independently.

Denote by $\mathbf{H}^{a+}$ the augmentation of $\mathbf{H}^{a}$ with the parametrized invariant rule for **while** statement, with the provision that all the assertions used in establishing the decrease of the well-founded variant are interference free. The above is captured by the following definition.

Definition: A collection of local $\mathbf{H}^{a+}$ proof outlines for $\langle p_i \rangle S_i \langle q_i \rangle$, $1 \leqslant i \leqslant n$, is **strongly interference free** iff we have the following.

(1) For every parametrized invariant $pi(w)$ of a **while** statement in S_i (not within an **await** statement) and every normal substatement S' of $S_j, j \neq i$, which is either an assignment or an **await** statement, the following holds:

$$\langle pi(w) \wedge pre(S') \rangle S' \langle \exists v \leqslant w : pi(v) \rangle$$

(2) All the assertions used in establishing the decrease of w (within the $\mathbf{H}^{a+}$ system) are interference free.

□

Denote by $\mathbf{O}^*$ the resulting proof system for proving total correctness of *SVL* programs. The arithmetical soundness and completeness theorems are established in a similar way to previous cases. We turn to examples of a termination proof.

EXAMPLE:

Consider the factorial example of Section 7.1. We show $\vdash_{\mathbf{O}^*} \langle N > 0 \rangle [P_1 \| P_2] \langle true \rangle$. For P_1, we choose as the parametrized invariant $pi_1(w)$, where

$$pi_1(w, i, j, c1) \overset{df.}{=} 1 \leqslant i \leqslant j \leqslant N \wedge (c1 \wedge w = N - i \wedge c1 \vee \neg c1 \wedge w = 0)$$

First, we show that requirements for local termination of the **while** statement are satisfied. This amounts to showing that the body of the **await** statement decreases the variant. Suppose $c1 \wedge pi_1(w, i, j, c1)$ holds before the **await**. Thus, $w = N - i > 0$. If $i+1 < j$, i is increased by 1, so $pi_1(w-1, i, j, true)$ holds after the **await**. Otherwise, $c1$ becomes false, and $pi_1(0, i, j, false)$ holds. Both cases cause a decrease in w.

As for the strong noninterference test, we note that P_2 does not modify i at all. The conjunct $1 \leqslant i \leqslant j \leqslant N$ is immediate.

Similarly, for P_2, we choose

$$pi_2(u, i, j, c2) \overset{df.}{=} 1 \leqslant i \leqslant j \leqslant N \wedge (c2 \wedge u = j \vee \neg c2 \wedge u = 0).$$

□

$P :: [P_1 \| P_2]$, where

$P_1 ::$ **while** $x > 0$ **do** $y := 0$;
  if $y = 0$ **then** $x := x - 1$ **else** $y := 0$ **fi od**

$P_2 ::$ **while** $x > 0$ **do** $y := 1$;
  if $y = 1$ **then** $x := x - 1$ **else** $y := 1$ **fi od**

Figure 7.11 Nontermination due to the absence of strong noninterference.

EXERCISE:

Show that pi_2 satisfies the requirements.

□

EXAMPLE:

Consider again the bounded buffer example of Section 7.2. Recalling the invariants $1 \leqslant i \leqslant n+1$ and $1 \leqslant j \leqslant n+1$ from the partial correctness proof, we can immediately see that

$$pi_{producer}(w, i) \overset{df.}{=} 1 \leqslant i \leqslant n+1 \wedge w = n+1-i$$

and

$$pi_{consumer}(w, j) \overset{df.}{=} 1 \leqslant j \leqslant n \wedge w = n+1-j$$

satisfy the decrease condition. Strong interference freedom is trivial, since *producer* does not modify j and *consumer* does not modify i.

In order to see the need for the second clause in the definition of the strong noninterference, consider the program in Figure 7.11.

Clearly, $pi(x, n) \overset{df.}{=} (x = n \geqslant 0)$ satisfies the decrease condition on n, and also the first clause in the definition of strong interference freedom. However, the second clause in the latter definition is not satisfied. The assertion $y = 0$, needed in front of the **if** in P_1 to guarantee decrease of x, is clearly not preserved by the assignment $y := 1$ in P_2. Similarly, $y = 1$ in the proof of P_2 is not preserved by the assignment $y := 0$ in P_1. Indeed, if the actions of the two processes are interleaved in such a way that the 'destructive' assignments are always performed when the other process is about to test the condition of its **if** statement, x never changes and the computation never terminates.

□

EXERCISE:

Reconstruct a nonterminating computation of the above program.

□

7.7 Conclusions

In this chapter, we extended the verification method for the correctness assertions to concurrent programs, and in addition have considered additional correctness criteria, such as deadlock freedom, mutual exclusion and nonstarvation. We saw that the main verification techniques, namely invariants and well-founded decreasing variants, are still applicable, but we lost the compositionality property of proof systems, because of the need to consider claims about intermediate states, not captured by the kind of specifications we have considered. We had to resort to an approximation, which is not purely compositional, but still uses syntax directedness. These are the two-staged proof methods, in which first-stage proof outlines of separate processes are confronted in the second stage to check a consistency among them, as expressed by the noninterference property. In order to do that, auxiliary variables may be needed, recording in the state some information about the history of the computation.

Interference freedom is a structured, systematic way of capturing the behavior of all interleaved computations and the mutual effect atomic actions in the various processes have. By introducing a higher-level synchronization mechanism, easier control of possible interference is obtained, easing also the proof obligations.

As for other safety properties, the main tool for their verification is by providing assertions characterizing control positions violating the required property, and showing the inconsistency of such assertions with information obtained from (appropriately strengthened) partial correctness proofs.

As for liveness, we realized the strong dependency of program liveness properties on the corresponding language constructs' liveness assumptions. Under the weak progress properties assumed here, very weak liveness conditions in programs are provable. Stronger liveness properties of constructs, for example various forms of fairness, are needed to prove the required program properties.

Bibliographic notes and suggestions for further reading

Bibliographic notes The language *SVL* and the proof system **O** are taken from [132], which together with [133] were the first two-leveled proof systems presented for concurrent programs and the source of the notion of noninterference. The term **normal** substatement and the specific formulation of **O** used here are from [134]. A similar system was independently developed in [35]. Auxiliary variables were first introduced into proof systems by Clint [135], in the context of verifying programs using coroutines for pseudo-concurrency. The examples motivating their use here are from [132]. The totality of expressions condition for the soundness of the auxiliary variables rule was first pointed out in [136]. The relative completeness proof of **O** presented here was first presented in [134], based on Owicki's original proof for *RVL* presented in [137]. The formulation of the merging lemma presented here is due to Apt [134]. A more complicated merging lemma, related to an interpreter-based operational semantics, is presented in [137]. A detailed discussion of the role of the merging lemma in completeness proofs, as well as its various forms, is presented in an unpublished manuscript by Eike Best,

October 1983. The *RVL* language and its associated proof method were introduced in [132]. The *PSORT* program and its proof are from [130], where a comprehensive survey of various approaches to the verification of concurrent and distributed programs is presented. The approach presented here to proofs of deadlock freedom originates from [132] and [133]. The dining philosophers problem was first stated by Dijkstra [138]. The solution presented, using conditional critical sections, is due to Hoare [139]. The proof of mutual exclusion in this solution is from [133]. The extension **O*** to a total correctness proof system is implicit in [137], which also presents a completeness proof for **S**, albeit w.r.t. a more low-level operational semantics. The second clause in the definition of strong interference freedom was not included in the original definition. The need for it was noted in [140], which is the source of the example in Figure 7.11 also.

Suggestions for further reading In [134] the effect of using bounded auxiliary variables (essentially equivalent to location counters) is studied. The verification of pseudo-concurrent programs using coroutines can be found in [135]. A more formal definition of liveness properties, formulated as properties of computation sequences, can be found in [141]. Shared-variables languages with structured synchronization primitives were further developed to include the *monitor* construct, encapsulating both data and its concurrent manipulation [142], [143]. The issue of their verification created a heated debate. The first proposal for proof rules for partial correctness of monitor programs appears in [144]. Subsequently, [145], [146], [147], [148], and [149] are stages in this debate. The last one is the only one to present an actual (though indirect) semantics for monitors. To date, there is no satisfactory treatment of this issue. A reduction of fairness in shared variables languages to nondeterminism with random assignments can be found in [172] and [169]. A different semantics for concurrency, allowing simultaneous progress of maximal independent sets of processes (known as 'maximal concurrency' semantics) was described in several papers, for example [173].

EXERCISES

7.1 Disjoint concurrency [150]: Prove the validity of the naive concurrent composition rule

$$\frac{\{p_i\}\,S_i\,\{q_i\},\ 1 \leqslant i \leqslant n}{\{\bigwedge_{i=1,n} p_i\}[\ \|_{i=1,n}\ S_i]\{\bigwedge_{i=1,n} q_i\}}$$

under the assumption $(\mathit{free}(S_i) \cap \bigcup_{j \neq i} \mathit{change}(S_j)) = \varnothing$ for every $1 \leqslant i \leqslant n$. Interpret informally this assumption.

7.2 **Weakest local proof outlines:** A collection of proof outlines in $\mathbf{H}^{\mathrm{a}}$ with all the intermediate assertions equal to *true* is obviously interference free. Why cannot proofs always use such outlines?

7.3 **(AUX) converse rule:** For AX auxiliary for $S \in SVL$ and q, prove the soundness of the converse of the (AUX) rule, namely

$$\frac{\{p\}\, S_{|AX}\, \{q\}}{\{p\}\, S\, \{q\}}$$

7.4 **Multiple resources:** Extend the proof system **S** to handle an arbitrary number of resources. Show that your extension preserves soundness and completeness.

7.5 **Semaphores [132]:** Define the following two semaphore operations in terms of conditionally-delaying statements.

$\mathbf{p}\,(s) ::$ **await** $s > 0 \rightarrow s := s - 1$ **end**
$\mathbf{v}\,(s) ::$ **await** $true \rightarrow s := s + 1$ **end**

Consider the following solution to the critical section problem:

$CS :: s := 1;\ [\ \underset{i=1,n}{\|}\ P_i]$, where
$P_i ::$ **while** *true* **do** *non-critical section*;
  p (s);
  critical section;
  v (s) **od**.

Find a proof outline for CS in **O** and use it to establish the mutual exclusion and deadlock freedom of CS.

7.6 State and prove the theorems of arithmetical soundness and completeness for **O***.

7.7 **Array lookup [137], [151]:** Consider the following program, intended to find the least index k such that $a[k] > 0$ (if such a k exists), for an array $a[1\,..\,m]$.

$FINDPOS :: i := 2; j := 1; etop := m+1; otop := m+1;$
$[EVEN ::$ **while** $i < min(etop, otop)$ **do**
  if $a[i] > 0$ **then** $etop := i$ **else** $i := i+2$ **fi od**
$\|$
$ODD ::$ **while** $j < min(etop, otop)$ **do**
  if $a[j] > 0$ **then** $etop := j$ **else** $j := j+2$ **fi od**$]$

Formulate the appropriate formal specification (for k dependent on state variables), and show its satisfaction using the appropriate proof system.

7.8 **Bounded nondeterminism:** Show that both *SVL* and *RVL* exhibit bounded nondeterminism (cf. Chapter 5).

7.9 Can the following partial correctness assertion be proved in **O** *without* using auxiliary variables?

$$\{true\}\,[x := 0 \parallel x := x + 1]\,\{0 \leqslant x \leqslant 1\}$$

7.10 Give an example of a program S and AX auxiliary for S such that $S_{|AX}$ is empty (and hence replaced by '*skip*').

7.11 Prove the correctness assertion about the program in Figure 7.3 using a single auxiliary variable.

7.12 Consider the program P:: *cdone* := *true*; *pdone* := *false*; $[P_1 \parallel P_2]$, where:

```
P1:: while true do
        await cdone → cdone := false end;
        A1;
        await ¬ pdone → pdone := true end;
        await cdone → cdone := false end;
        B1;
        await ¬ pdone → pdone := true end
                od

P2:: while true do
        await pdone → pdone := false end;
        A2;
        await ¬ cdone → cdone := true end;
        await pdone → pdone := false end;
        B2;
        await ¬ cdone → cdone := true end
                od
```

A_1, A_2, B_1, B_2 do not modify any of the variables *cdone* and *pdone*.

(1) Show that P_1 and P_2 are never simultaneously inside their respective A-sections or B-sections.

(2) Show that P is deadlock free.

CHAPTER 8
VERIFYING DISTRIBUTED PROGRAMS

8.1 Introduction

In this chapter, we consider an alternative model of concurrent computation and present its verification theory. We refer to programs expressed by the primitives of this model as **distributed** programs, having the following main characteristic: processes are **disjoint** in their state space (that is, do not share any variables), and communicate and synchronize via **message passing**. We consider several variants of this model.

The first model assumes **synchronous** interprocess communication (referred to also as **handshaking** or **rendezvous**). According to this variant, the two local actions of sending a message by one process and receiving that message by another process coincide in time. Thus, the respective commands delay the process executing one of them until the enabledness of the other. An important feature in this variant is the usage of communication primitives as guards with a synchronization effect and a possible side effect, in addition to their conventional truth value. This variant is then extended to synchronous communication involving an arbitrary number of participants (referred to as an **interaction**). Thus, a notion of joint action emerges, as discussed in this chapter.

There are several interesting issues involved in the language conventions of **partner naming** for communication. We shall concentrate on one simple naming convention and leave others to the exercises.

The second variant assumes asynchronous interprocess communication, in which the **send** operation is a local, nonblocking operation, while the **receive** operation remains blocking until the availability of a message. No bound on arrival time of messages is assumed, while several alternatives regarding the order of arrival have been considered in the literature. We deal only with the case where messages arrive according to the order sent.

Regarding specifications and correctness properties treated, we again focus our attention on partial and total correctness and deadlock freedom, briefly sketching the more general liveness and safety families of properties.

The proof methodology remains that of noncompositional, two-leveled proofs. However, the consistency criterion between local proofs changes. Instead of interference freedom we have the notion of **cooperation** among proofs. Basically, whenever a process is engaged in a communication action, it may locally assume an assumption about its partners (most often an assumption about an input valued received). During the cooperation phase, all these assumptions are contrasted with the local proofs of the environment (the other processes) in order to justify and discharge them.

8.2 The *CSP* language for distributed (handshaked) programs

In this section we present a fragment of the *CSP* language originally introduced by C.A.R. Hoare for the study of distributed programs.

A *distributed* program $[P_1 \| \cdots \| P_n]$ is a parallel composition of **processes** (also abbreviated as before to $[\underset{i=1,n}{\|} P_i]$). A major difference w.r.t. *SVL* is that processes are disjoint in their state space, that is, they do not share variables. This is captured by the following restriction. Each process P_i, $1 \leqslant i \leqslant n$, consists of a statement, thereby also excluding nested concurrency. The atomic statements are here the assignment $x := e$, the *skip* statement and I/O (that is, input and output, respectively) statements $P_j?x$, $P_j!e$, for some $j \neq i$ (statements also referred to as **communication** statements). We use α, β to denote I/O statements.

We say that an input statement $P_j?x$, or an output statement $P_j!e$ (appearing in some process P_i) **refers** to P_j, the jth process (or **addresses** P_j). We say that two I/O statements α and β **syntactically match** if for some $1 \leqslant i, j \leqslant n$, $i \neq j$, α is taken from P_i, β from P_j, α refers to P_j, β refers to P_i, and one of α, β is an input and the other an output statement. In addition, they have the same **message type**, where types are indicated by explicit **tags** whenever the type is not the simple **integer** (or **Boolean** type). In particular, it is convenient to consider **tuple communication** of the form $P_i!(\bar{e})$, $P_i?(\bar{x})$. Syntactically matching pairs of communication commands are indicated by using α, $\bar{\alpha}$. Thus, an explicit partner-naming convention for communication is employed. In particular, names are statically determined (that is, do not depend on the state and, hence, are constants). In the exercises, a more dynamic naming convention is considered. For an input statement $P_j?x$ (in process P_i), the variable x is **local** to P_i. Similarly, for an output statement $P_j!e$ (in P_i), the term e is over the local variables of P_i. In some examples, concurrent composition of processes with identical statements is considered. In such cases, state variables are indexed by the process index, for distinction. Thus, x_i is P_i's x. We say that a state assertion is **local** to a process if it refers only to variables of that process.

Statements are composed using the sequential composition operation ';' and by forming **selection commands** $[\underset{j\in\Delta}{\Box} B_j; \alpha_j \rightarrow R_j]$ and **repetition commands** $*[\underset{j\in\Delta}{\Box} B_j; \alpha_j \rightarrow R_j]$, for $\Delta \overset{df.}{=} \{1,\ldots,m\}$ for some $m \geqslant 0$. The case $m = 0$ reduces to '*skip*'.

A variable x local to a process P_i is **subject to change** if it occurs on a left-hand side of an assignment within P_i or in an input statement in P_i. A parallel composition $[P_1 \| \cdots \| P_n]$ is considered as syntactically correct only if for $1 \leqslant i, j \leqslant n$ no variable subject to change in P_i occurs in $P_j (i \neq j)$. Furthermore, only other processes of the same concurrent composition (that is, $P_j, j = 1, n, j \neq i$) are referred to in I/O statements of P_i.

Before turning to a formal definition of the operational semantics, we first briefly present an informal description of it, and consider some of the novel issues raised by this model of distributed computations.

(1) The concurrent composition $[P_1 \| \cdots \| P_n]$ expressing concurrent execution of processes $P_1, \ldots, P_n$, is again interpreted as the interleaving of atomic statements. However, some atomic statements, namely I/O statements, are jointly executed by two partners. This synchronized, joint execution is commonly known as a **handshake** (or **rendezvous** in its Ada version) between the parties involved.

(2) Communication between P_i and $P_j (i \neq j)$ is expressed by the **receive** and **send** primitives $P_j?x$ and $P_i!e$, respectively. The input command $P_j?x$ (in P_i) expresses a request by P_i to P_j to assign a value to the (local) variable x of P_i. The output command $P_i!e$ (in P_j) expresses a request to P_i to receive the value of the expression e from P_j. Execution of $P_j?x$ in P_i and $P_i!e$ in P_j is **synchronized** where P_i is delayed at $P_j?x$ until P_j is ready (explained below) for $P_i!e$, and vice versa. The end result of a communication is assigning the value of e to x. In the case of tuple communication, the effect is that of the corresponding multiple assignment.

(3) *Guarded commands:* A novel feature of *CSP* is using I/O statements as guards, having a side effect in addition to a Boolean value.

- A guard is a Boolean expression, an I/O statement, or a combination of both. Usually, identically true Boolean guards are omitted. A guard is **open** in a state if its Boolean part evaluates to *true* in that state.
- A guarded selection **fails** in the case in which all guards are false.
- Guarded repetition continues as long as there exists an open guard and terminates when no guards are open.

Guarded commands introduce the possibility that more than one matching pair of I/O commands occurs. A process P_i is **ready** for a communication α if either α is its next command, or α is a part of an open guard in the next command. The communication $(\alpha, \bar{\alpha})$ is **enabled** whenever it is readied by both partners. Note that both readiness and enabledness are time dependent (that is, should be evaluated in a configuration during computation). Jointly enabled joint actions sharing a participant process are said to be in **conflict**, and the choice of the action, among the enabled conflicting actions, to be executed next is called **conflict resolution**.

Below we present some typical combinations of I/O guarded commands and explain their meanings and some of their implications.

Local compared with global nondeterminism This is a new distinction, derived from the possibility of having joint actions (I/O commands in the current context) as guards. Consider the following two 'versions' of a process P_1 which, informally, chooses between input from P_2 and output (of the value 0) to P_2.

$$P_1' :: [P_2?x \rightarrow skip \,[]\, P_2!0 \rightarrow skip]$$
$$P_1'' :: [true \rightarrow P_2?x \,[]\, true \rightarrow P_2!0]$$

There is a major difference between these two processes. The second one, P_1'', chooses **locally** (on its own, so to speak) which communication to **ready** and participate in, and only then is a handshake attempted. On the other hand, P_1' readies simultaneously both communications, and will choose one (and 'pass the corresponding arrow') only if the operation is also readied by the corresponding partner P_2, that is, the communication is enabled. We refer to the first kind of nondeterministic choice (exemplified by P_1'') as **local nondeterminism** (which is the same as in *GC*), while the second one is **global nondeterminism**.

As it turns out, this difference has no bearing on partial correctness, but is crucial for deadlock freedom. To see the difference, consider the following two concurrent compositions.

$$P' :: [P_1' \| P_2],\ P'' :: [P_1'' \| P_2],\ where\ P_2 :: P_1!0$$

The first one, P', successfully terminates, since P_1' finds its first guard ready and P_2 readies the dual command. There is exactly one possible computation, in which the communication occurs. On the other hand, P''

$P :: [P_1 \| P_2 \| P_3]$, where:
$P_1 :: [P_3 ? x \rightarrow skip \, [] \, P_2 ! 0 \rightarrow skip]$
$P_2 :: [P_1 ? y \rightarrow skip \, [] \, P_3 ! 0 \rightarrow skip]$
$P_3 :: [P_2 ? z \rightarrow skip \, [] \, P_1 ! 0 \rightarrow skip]$

Figure 8.1 Symmetry breaking.

need not terminate and may deadlock. It has two possible computations. In the first one, P_1' chooses its first direction, at which stage both parties ready the communication between them, which takes place, leading to termination. In the second computation, P_1'' chooses its second direction, leading to a situation where both processes are waiting for outputting each other, a deadlock.

Symmetry breaking A consequence of the presence of joint actions as guards, that is, of global nondeterminism, is that some global symmetry breaking is implied by the semantics. Consider the program P in Figure 8.1, obtained by concurrently composing three processes P_1, P_2, and P_3 arranged in a cycle. Each process is ready to communicate with either one of its 'neighbors'. Clearly, no process could locally decide upon a choice, as such noncoordinated choices might lead to a deadlock (for example, each one choosing its left neighbor), while the semantics (as stated informally so far) implies that one of the enabled communications must occur. Thus, implementations of *CSP* have to resort to symmetry-breaking algorithms, an issue extensively studied in the theory of distributed computing. Such algorithms use at least a linear (in n, the number of processes) number of control messages. To avoid this overhead, languages such as Ada abolish the possibility of such symmetric constructs from the language. Any symmetry breaking is explicit on the program level. However, program verification becomes more complicated in that case. We retain here the implicit symmetry breaking.

Operational semantics

We now turn to a formal presentation of the operational semantics as a transition relation among configurations. A **distributed configuration** $C = \langle [\, \|_{i=1,n} \, S_i], \sigma \rangle$ consists again of a concurrent composition of n statements, where S_i represents the syntactic continuation of process P_i, and the state is the current global state. Note that a global state consists of a collection of variable disjoint local states. We also refer to this semantics as **serialized**. Another semantics might be formulated, referred to as the **overlapping** semantics, in which atomic actions have duration and the execution of independent actions (acting on different state components) may overlap in time. The two are equivalent with respect to partial correctness, but induce different liveness properties on programs.

We use the notation σ/i, $1 \leqslant i \leqslant n$, to stand for P_i's **local** state, the projection of σ on the variables of P_i. The **history** (needed for the completeness proof) is defined as a sequence of **records of communication** (*roc*) of the form $[v,i,j]$, $1 \leqslant i,j \leqslant n, i \neq j$, recording the communicated value and the identities of the sender and the receiver, respectively. The empty history is denoted by $\in$.

The following rules define the transition relation '$\rightarrow$' among *CSP* distributed configurations.

$$\langle [S_1 \| \cdots \| S_i \| \cdots \| S_n], \sigma \rangle \stackrel{\in}{\rightarrow} \langle [S_1 \| \cdots \| E \| \cdots \| S_n], \sigma \rangle \tag{1}$$

for any $1 \leqslant i \leqslant n$, iff $S_i = skip$, or $S_i = {*}[\underset{j=1,n_i}{\square} B_j;\ \alpha_j \rightarrow T_j]$ and $\sigma \models \neg \bigvee_{j=1,n_i} B_j$.

$$\langle [S_1 \| \cdots \| S_i \| \cdots \| S_n], \sigma \rangle \stackrel{\in}{\rightarrow} \langle [S_1 \| \cdots \| E \| \cdots \| S_n], \sigma[\sigma[\![e]\!] | x] \rangle \tag{2}$$

for any $1 \leqslant i \leqslant n$, iff $S_i = (x := e)$.

$$\begin{array}{l}\langle [S_1 \| \cdots \| S_{i-1} \| S_i \| S_{i+1} \| \cdots \| S_{j-1} \| S_j \| S_{j+1} \| \cdots \| S_n], \sigma \rangle \stackrel{[\sigma[\![e]\!],i,j]}{\rightarrow} \\ \langle [S_1 \| \cdots \| S_{i-1} \| S'_i \| S_{i+1} \| \cdots \| S_{j-1} \| S'_j \| S_{j+1} \| \cdots \| S_n], \sigma' \rangle \end{array} \tag{3}$$

iff for $1 \leqslant i, j \leqslant n$, $i \neq j$,

(1) $S_i = P_j!e$, and $S'_i = E$, or

(2) $S_i = [\underset{k=1,n_i}{\square} B_k; \alpha_k \rightarrow T_k]$ and there exists some k, $1 \leqslant k \leqslant n_i$, s.t. $\sigma \models B_k$, $\alpha_k = P_j!e$, and $S'_i = T_k$, or

(3) $S_i = {*}[\underset{k=1,n_i}{\square} B_k; \alpha_k \rightarrow T_k]$ and there exists some k, $1 \leqslant k \leqslant n_i$, s.t. $\sigma \models B_k$, $\alpha_k = P_j!e$, and $S'_i = T_k; S_i$.

Similar rules apply for S_j with j replacing i and with $P_i?v$ replacing $P_j!e$.

Finally, for all these cases, $\sigma' = \sigma[\sigma[\![e]\!] | v]$.

For any $1 \leqslant i, j \leqslant n$, $i \neq j$, if **(4)**

$$\langle [S_1 \| \cdots \| S_i \| \cdots \| S_j \| \cdots \| S_n], \sigma \rangle \stackrel{h}{\rightarrow} \langle [S_1 \| \cdots \| S'_i \| \cdots \| S'_j \| \cdots \| S_n], \sigma' \rangle$$

then for any T_i and T_j

$$\begin{array}{l}\langle [S_1 \| \cdots \| S_i; T_i \| \cdots \| S_j; T_j \cdots \| S_n], \sigma \rangle \stackrel{h}{\rightarrow} \\ \quad \langle [S_1 \| \cdots \| S'_i; T_i \| \cdots \| S'_j; T_j \cdots \| S_n], \sigma' \rangle\end{array}$$

and, in addition, if for any $1 \leqslant i \leqslant n$

$$\langle [S_1 \| \cdots \| S_i \| \cdots \| S_n], \sigma \rangle \stackrel{h}{\rightarrow} \langle [S_1 \| \cdots \| S'_i \| \cdots \| S_n], \sigma' \rangle$$

$P :: [\ \underset{i=1,n}{\|}\ P_i \| U]$, where:

$P_i :: (my\_min_i, my\_size_i) := (a_i, 1);$

$*[\ \underset{j \in \Delta_i}{[]}\ 0 < my\_size_i < n;\ P_j!(my\_min_i, my\_size_i) \rightarrow my\_size_i := 0$

$\underset{j \in \Delta_i}{[]}\ 0 < my\_size_i < n;\ P_j?(their\_min_i, their\_size_i) \rightarrow$

$(my\_min_i, my\_size_i) := (min(my\_min_i, their\_min_i), my\_size_i + their\_size_i)$

$];$

$[my\_size_i := 0 \rightarrow skip$

$[]$

$my\_size_i = n \rightarrow U!my\_min_i$

$],$

$U :: [\ \underset{i=1,n}{[]}\ P_i?u\_min \rightarrow skip]$

Figure 8.2 Distributed minimum computation.

then for any T_i

$$\langle [S_1 \| \cdots \| S_i; T_i \| \cdots \| S_n], \sigma \rangle \overset{h}{\rightarrow} \langle [S_1 \| \cdots \| S_i'; T_i \| \cdots \| S_n], \sigma' \rangle$$

A distributed computation here is again a maximal '$\rightarrow$'-sequence of distributed configurations. Hence, once again the only liveness assumption is that of **fundamental liveness**, here guaranteeing the eventual execution of some atomic action, which possibly is a joint action. The merging lemma is satisfied here also (to be used in the completeness proof). Similarly, the definitions of termination, deadlock, and divergence also carry over from the *SVL* case.

EXERCISE:

Give an explicit description of the form of the final configuration in a deadlocked computation.

□

Following is an example of a *CSP* program, to the verification of which we turn after presenting the appropriate proof rules.

EXAMPLE:

The distributed program in Figure 8.2 computes the minimum of a set of (pairwise different) numbers $\{a_i | 1 \leqslant i \leqslant n\}$, where a_i 'belongs' to P_i as the initial value of the local variable my_min_i. The minimum is sent to a user process U upon completion of the computation. For $1 \leqslant i \leqslant n$, let $\Delta_i \overset{df.}{=} \{j | 1 \leqslant j \leqslant n, j \neq i\}$.

The way this program operates is by building dynamically a spanning forest of trees of processes, based on the conflict resolution implied by the semantics. In each tree, each root process is responsible for maintaining the minimum of all the local values of the processes in the subtree rooted in it. The number of trees keeps decreasing until one spanning tree remains.

Initially, each process P_i is a separate tree, responsible for the minimum of the set $A_i = \{a_i\}$. Invariably during the execution, each nonterminated process P_i is responsible for the minimum of a set A_i, keeping its size locally, and is ready to participate (globally) in one of two alternative communications.

(1) Sending the minimal value $min(A_i)$ to some other process P_j and terminate, making itself a descendant of P_j in P_j's tree. Doing so is recorded by assigning 0 to the local size variable.

(2) Receiving the minimal value of some other process P_j, together with the size of A_j, updating its local minimum to reflect $min(A_i \cup A_j)$ and resuming activity.

Whenever two processes agree and execute such a communication and its follow-up local action the number of trees decreases by 1. Eventually, one tree is left, the root of which has $my\_size = n$, thereby terminating its main repetition and reaching the output command to U.

□

EXERCISE:

Provide a detailed description of a computation of P for $n = 3$, where $a_i = i$, $1 \leqslant i \leqslant 3$. Which spanning tree is this computation defining?

□

8.3 A deductive system AFR for partial correctness

In this section we present a proof system for proving partial correctness of *CSP* distributed programs. As already mentioned, the **AFR** system, similarly to the **O** system, is a two-leveled system. We start by presenting the local proof rules for the first stage, in which each process is verified separately. The core of the local part is the system **D** for sequential guarded commands, adapted to I/O guards. We start by presenting axioms for the communication primitives, namely *input* and *output*.

Input axiom:

For *arbitrary* local assertions p and q,

$$\{p\}\, P_i?x\, \{q\} \qquad \text{(IN)}$$

□

While the arbitrariness of the precondition–postcondition relationship induced by an input command may look surprising at a first sight, it has a rather simple explanation. Methodologically, it expresses an assumption made in the local proof in the process containing the input command about its communication partner P_i. This assumption is then verified when the local proof outline from which it is taken is confronted with the local proof outline of P_i during the cooperation test at the second stage of the proof.

In general, such assumptions can be classified into two kinds. One kind of assumption is about the input value assigned to x. The second kind is assumptions about the control behavior of P_i and its readiness to execute a matching output command.

Output axiom:

For arbitrary local assertions p and q,

$$\{p\}\, P_i!\, e\, \{q\} \qquad \text{(OUT)}$$

□

The output axiom may also look surprising at first sight. As output has no local side effect, one might expect the simpler axiom $\{p\}\, P_i!\, e\, \{p\}$ for any local p. However, it turns out, as will be seen soon in examples, that the output command also involves an assumption about the control of P_i, namely its readiness for a matching input command. Again, this assumption is verified during the cooperation test.

Next, we modify the proof rules for nondeterministic selection and repetition to handle also I/O guards.

Nondeterministic I/O guarded selection:

$$\frac{\{p \wedge B_j\}\, \alpha_j;\, S_j\, \{q\},\ j \in \Delta}{\{p\}\, [\, \underset{j\in\Delta}{[]}\, B_j;\, \alpha_j \rightarrow S_j]\, \{q\}} \qquad \text{(COM-SEL)}$$

□

Nondeterministic I/O guarded repetition:

$$\frac{\{p \wedge B_j\}\, \alpha_j;\, S_j\, \{p\},\ j \in \Delta}{\{p\}\, {*}[\, \underset{j\in\Delta}{[]}\, B_j;\, \alpha_j \rightarrow S_j]\, \{p \wedge \bigwedge_{j\in\Delta} \neg B_j\}} \qquad \text{(COM-NDREP)}$$

□

Based on these proof rules of the first, local, stage, a corresponding notion of local proof outlines for *CSP* processes is induced.

EXERCISE:

Define the notion of a local proof outline of a *CSP* process.

□

We now pass to the second stage of a partial correctness proof, in which local proof outlines have to be confronted with each other, to verify the consistency of all the mutual assumptions made by them. Towards that end, we first present an axiom, known as the communication axiom, capturing the semantic contents of a synchronous execution of two (syntactically) matching communication commands. It is not surprising that the axiom resembles the standard assignment axiom, as synchronous (handshaked) communication is often viewed as a 'remote assignment'.

Communication axiom:

For two syntactically matching I/O commands $P_i?x$ (in P_j) and $P_j!e$ (in P_i),

$$\{p^x_e\}\ P_i?x \parallel P_j!e\ \{p\} \qquad \text{(COM)}$$

□

This axiom is only used in validating the cooperation test among local proof outlines, to be described first in a preliminary version, overlooking a major concern, to be added afterwards.

> **Definition:** Local proof outlines $\{p_i\}\ P_i\ \{q_i\}$, $1 \leqslant i \leqslant n$, *cooperate* iff for every pair of syntactically matching communication commands $\{pre_1\}\ P_j?x\ \{post_1\}$ (in P_i) and $\{pre_2\}\ P_i!e\ \{post_2\}$ (in P_j), we have
>
> $$\{pre_1 \wedge pre_2\}\ P_j? \parallel P_i!e\ \{post_1 \wedge post_2\} \qquad \text{(COOP)}$$
>
> □

We retain the name **satisfaction** for this preliminary version of cooperation, and return to it in the next subsection. The meaning of this definition is that the mutual assumptions of P_i and P_j are confronted and established. Once this is done for all possible pairs of syntactically matching communication commands, all assumptions in the program P have been justified, and the following (naive version) of a concurrent composition rule is applicable.

Concurrent composition rule:

$$\frac{\text{proof outlines } \{p_i\}\ P_i\ \{q_i\},\ 1 \leqslant i \leqslant n, \text{cooperate}}{\{\bigwedge_{i=1,n} p_i\}\ [\ \|_{i=1,n}\ P_i]\ \{\bigwedge_{i=1,n} q_i\}} \qquad \text{(D-CONC)}$$

□

$P :: [\ \underset{i=1,n}{\|}\ P_i]$, where
$P_1 :: P_2 ! y_1$
$P_i :: P_{i-1} ? y_i;\ P_{i+1} ! y_i, (1 < i < n)$
$P_n :: P_{n-1} ? y_n$

Figure 8.3 A pipeline example.

$P_1 :: \{y_1 = z\}\ P_2 ! y_1 \{y_1 = z\}$
$P_i :: \{true\}\ P_{i-1} ? y_i \{y_i = z\};\ P_{i+1} ! y_i \{y_i = z\}, (1 < i < n)$
$P_n :: \{true\}\ P_{n-1} \{y_n = z\}$

Figure 8.4 The pipeline local proof outlines.

$P :: [P_1 \| P_2]$, where
$P_1 :: x := 0;\ P_2 ! x;\ x := x + 1;\ P_2 ! x$
$P_2 :: P_1 ? y;\ P_1 ? y$

Figure 8.5 A disturbing example.

EXAMPLE:

Consider a very simple distributed program (in Figure 8.3), that describes a **pipeline**, propagating a value from P_1 to P_n.

We would like to prove $\{true\}\ P \{y_n = y_1\}$. The local proof outlines are shown in Figure 8.4, where z is a new variable, not mentioned in P. The validity of the above as local proof outlines is established in a simple way by means of the input and output axioms and the sequential composition rule.

We now turn to establish cooperation among all these local proof outlines. The pairs of syntactically matching communication commands are $P_{i+1} ! y_i$ (in P_i, $1 \leqslant i < n$), and $P_{i-1} ? y_i$ (in P_i, $1 < i \leqslant n$). Hence, we have to derive, for $1 \leqslant i < n$,

$$\{y_i = z \wedge true\}\ P_{i+1} ! y_i \| P_i ? y_{i+1} \{y_i = z \wedge y_{i+1} = z\}$$

which follows immediately from the communication axiom (and the consequence rule). Thus, the above proof outlines cooperate. By applying the concurrent composition rule, the premiss of which has just been established, we obtain $\{y_1 = z \wedge \bigwedge_{1 < i \leqslant n} true\}\ P \{\bigwedge_{1 \leqslant i \leqslant n} y_i = z\}$. By the consequence rule, we can 'forget' about intermediate y_i, and get $\{y_1 = z\}\ P \{y_1 = y_n\}$, and by substituting y_1 for z (which is a specification variable) we get the required conclusion.

□

$$P_1 :: \{true\}\, x := 0\, x = 0;\ P_2!x\, \{x = 0\};\ x := x+1\, \{x = 1\}\, P_2!x\, [x = 1\}$$
$$P_2 :: [true\}\, P_1?y\, \{y = 0];\ P_2?x\, \{y = 1\}$$

Figure 8.6 Local proof outlines for the disturbing example.

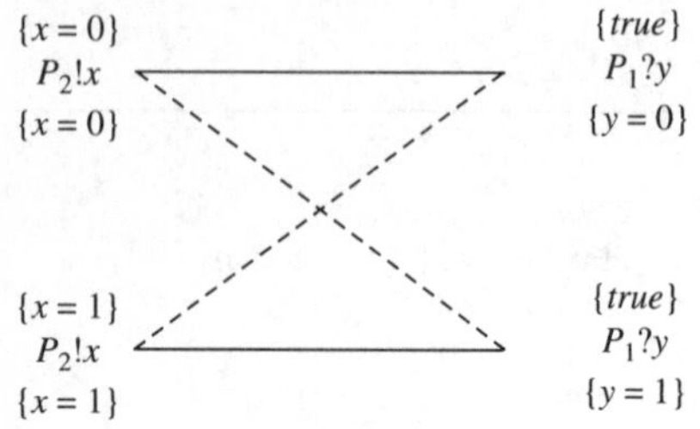

Figure 8.7 Improper syntactic matches.

So far, everything seems to work properly. However, consider the program P in Figure 8.5. Clearly, $\{true\}\, P\, \{y = 1\}$ holds. The natural proof outlines corresponding for P are in Figure 8.6, the local correctness of which is easy to verify.

We now turn to the cooperation test. The two input commands in P_2 make two respective assumptions $y = 0$ and $y = 1$. Both assumptions are justified when the first input command in P_2 is confronted with the first output command $P_2!x$ in P_1 (at which point $x = 0$ holds), and the second input command in P_2 is confronted with the second output command $P_1!x$ in P_2 (at which point $x = 1$ holds). However, the formal definition requires *every* pair of syntactically matching communication commands to be confronted. Hence, the definition forces us to confront also the first input command $P_2!x$ in P_1 with the second input command $P_1?y$ in P_2, as well as the second output command $P_2!x$ in P_1 with the first input command $P_1?y$ in P_2. Clearly, both these extra confrontations fail to satisfy the mutual assumptions (see Figure 8.7, where solid lines represent proper matches, while broken lines represent improper ones). It is not hard to realize that no valid local proof outlines could pass the cooperation test in its strict formulation. The problem arises because some syntactic matches do not semantically match, that is, there will never be a stage in an execution when these two commands are synchronized (handshaked). Recall a similar situation in the last example in Section 7.3 (p. 204), for *SVL* programs.

The conclusion is that we have to refine the cooperation test to cope with this distinction of syntactic matching and semantic matching. The refined rule should enforce only the confrontation of semantically matching communication commands, that reflect real communication events during execution. Mismatches should succeed in their cooperation test vacuously. How can this distinction, involving a full tracing of the computation, be incorporated into a static proof system? As before, the solution is obtained by using auxiliary variables, abstracting relevant parts of the history of the computation.

We first show how to overcome the specific problem in the previous example, and then show how to generalize the amendment of the cooperation test for the general case.

We add two auxiliary variables c_1 and c_2 to P_1 and P_2, respectively, whose role is to count locally the number of communications of P_1 and P_2, respectively. Thus, both variables are initialized to zero at the beginning of each process, and incremented by one after every communication command (see Figure 8.8).

Assume further that every auxiliary assignment is always executed jointly with the communication command which it follows (that is, there is no intermediate state between their executions). Then it follows that the value of $c_i, i = 1, 2$, is indeed the number of communication commands executed by P_i, $i = 1, 2$, respectively. Furthermore, since both processes count (independently) the *same* communication events, because of the semantics of synchronous communication, $c_1 = c_2$ holds before and after each communication event.

We now can take advantage of this invariant by incorporating it into the cooperation, and require

$$\{c_1 = c_2 \wedge pre_1 \wedge pre_2\}$$
$$[\langle P_2!x;\ c_1 := c_1 + 1\rangle \parallel \langle P_1?y;\ c_2 := c_2 + 1\rangle]$$
$$\{c_1 = c_2 \wedge post_1 \wedge post_2\}$$

to hold. The angle brackets group together the communication command and its counting into one *atomic* step, deviating somewhat from the standard semantics. We account later for this deviation.

For those pairs of semantically matching communications, the new test will indeed succeed. For example, for the first output command in P_1 and the first input command in P_2, this test yields

$$\{c_1 = c_2 \wedge c_1 = 0 \wedge c_2 = 0 \wedge x = 0\}$$
$$[\langle P_2!x;\ c_1 := c_1 + 1\rangle \parallel \langle P_1?y;\ c_2 := c_2 + 1\rangle]$$
$$\{c_1 = c_2 \wedge c_1 = 1 \wedge c_2 = 1 \wedge x = 0 \wedge y = 0\}$$

which can be derived by the communication axiom and sequential rules, and similarly for the other proper pair.

However, when attempting an improper confrontation, between syntactically matching communication commands which do not match semantically, the new cooperation test degenerates to a vacuous success. For example, if we confront the first output command in P_1 with the second input command in P_2, we get the following precondition for the cooperation test:

$$c_1 = c_2 \wedge c_1 = 0 \wedge c_2 = 1 \wedge x = 0 \wedge y = 1$$

$$
\begin{aligned}
&P_1::x:=0;\ c_1:=0\{x=0\wedge c_1=0\};\\
&\quad P_2!x;\ c_1:=c_1+1\ \{x=0\wedge c_1=1\};\\
&\quad x:=x+1\ \{x=1\wedge c_1=1\};\\
&\quad P_2!x;\ c_1:=c_1+1\ \{x=1\wedge c_1=2\};\\
&P_2::c_2:=0\{c_2=0\};\\
&\quad P_1?y;\ c_2:=c_2+1\ \{y=0\wedge c_2=1\};\\
&\quad P_1?y;c_2:=c_2+1\ \{y=1\wedge c_2=2\};
\end{aligned}
$$

Figure 8.8 Augmented local proof outlines.

which is contradictory. Hence, the whole partial correctness assertion holds vacuously.

Thus, by incorporating an additional invariant (at communication points), which contradicts situations representing improper confrontations, we force the cooperation test to succeed vacuously, leaving the 'real' confrontations to be properly checked.

We now generalize the treatment of this example to a general proof method. The main problem we have to overcome is the inadequacy of satisfaction to eliminate syntactic matches which are not semantic matchings.

The main idea of the extension is to introduce a **global invariant**, denoted *GI*, which may refer to all the variables in all processes and to local auxiliary variables. This invariant has to hold initially and to be preserved by every communication. Its role is to eliminate syntactically matching communications which do not match semantically. However, as we have seen in the example, the communications have to be regarded as executed together with local updating of auxiliary variables. For that, we introduce a bracketing, which delimits program sections regarded as if they were atomically executed.

Definition: A process is **bracketed** if the brackets '$\langle$' and '$\rangle$' are interspersed in its statement, so that the following holds.

- In each **bracketed section** $\langle S\rangle$, the statement S has one of the forms $S_1;\ \alpha;\ S_2$ or $\alpha\rightarrow S_1$, where S_1 and S_2 do not contain communication commands. We refer to α as the **core** of the bracketed section.
- Each communication command is encapsulated in some bracketed section.

□

Definition: Two bracketed sections **syntactically match** iff their respective cores syntactically match.

□

We now revise the definition of cooperation among proof outlines to account also for the global invariant.

Definition: The proof outlines of $\{p_i\} P_i \{q_i\}, i = 1, \ldots, n$, **cooperate** w.r.t. a global invariant GI iff

(1) every process P_i is bracketed,

(2) the assertions used in $\{p_i\} P_i \{q_i\}$ have no free variables subject to changes in $P_j (i \neq j)$, and

(3) $\{pre(S_1) \wedge pre(S_2) \wedge GI\}\ S_1 \parallel S_2 \{post(S_1) \wedge post(S_2) \wedge GI\}$ is provable for all syntactically matching pairs of bracketed sections $\langle S_1 \rangle$ and $\langle S_2 \rangle$.

□

In order to prove the partial correctness assertion needed for cooperation, some extra rules are introduced, reducing its conclusion to premisses of a sequential nature.

Rule of formation 1:

$$\frac{\{p\}\, S_1;\, S_3 \{p_1\}, \{p_1\}\, \alpha \parallel \bar{\alpha}\, \{p_2\}, \{p_2\}\, S_2;\, S_4\, \{q\}}{\{p\}\, (S_1;\, \alpha;\, S_2) \parallel (S_3;\, \bar{\alpha};\, S_4) \{q\}} \qquad \text{(FORM1)}$$

provided that α and $\bar{\alpha}$ syntactically match, and S_1, S_2, S_3, and S_4 do not contain I/O commands.

□

Rule of formation 2:

$$\frac{\{p\}\, (\alpha;\, S_1) \parallel S_2 \{q\}}{\{p\}\, (\alpha \rightarrow S_1) \parallel S_2\, \{q\}} \qquad \text{(FORM2)}$$

provided S_1 and S_2 do not contain I/O commands.

□

We may now introduce the concurrent composition rule in its full version, accounting for the new definition of cooperation.

Concurrent composition rule:

$$\frac{\text{proof outlines } \{p_i\}\, P_i \{q_i\}, i = 1, \ldots, n, \text{ cooperate w.r.t. } GI}{\{\bigwedge_{i=1,n} p_i \wedge GI\}[\ \parallel_{i=1,n} P_i]\{\bigwedge_{i=1,n} q_i \wedge GI\}} \qquad \text{(D-CONC)}$$

provided that no variable free in GI is subject to change outside any bracketed section.

Finally, the rule of auxiliary variables is retained too.

As before, we are now able to define the notion of a proof outline for a complete program.

Definition: A **proof outline** for $\{p\} P \{q\}$, where $P:: [\, \underset{i=1,n}{\|} \, P_i] \in CSP$, is a collection of local proof outlines $\{p_i\} P_i \{q_i\}$, $1 \leqslant i \leqslant n$, cooperating w.r.t. some global invariant GI, with the additional property that $p \Rightarrow \bigwedge_{i=1,n} p_i \wedge GI$, $\bigwedge_{i=1,n} q_i \wedge GI \Rightarrow q$.

□

The main property of interest satisfied by a proof outline for a *CSP* program P is yet another version of a preservation lemma, referred to as a **distributed preservation**. Before formulating it, we remind the reader that the cooperation test is always applied to matching bracketed sections, which constitute larger computation 'steps' than the atomic steps prescribed by the operational semantics. The gap between the two grains of atomicity has to be bridged somewhere in the theory. We assume an obvious extension of the operational semantics, where brackets in the original program are propagated to syntactic continuation in the natural way.

Let a *CSP* program P be given, together with a proof outline for $\{p\} P \{q\}$.

Next, we introduce a way of referring to **relative** syntactic continuations. Thus, $after(S, P_i)$, for some process P_i and a substatement† S of P_i, is the syntactic continuation of P_i immediately after the execution of S. It is defined by induction on the statement structure.

(1) For $S = P_i$, we let $after(S, P_i) \overset{df.}{=} E$.

(2) For $P_i = [\, \underset{j \in \Delta}{[]} \, B_j;\, \alpha_j \rightarrow S_j]$, and S a substatement of S_j, $j \in \Delta$, we let $after(S, P_i) \overset{df.}{=} after(S, S_j)$.

(3) For $P_i = *[\, \underset{j \in \Delta}{[]} \, B_j;\, \alpha_j \rightarrow S_j]$, and S a substatement of $S_j, j \in \Delta$, we let $after(S, P_i) \overset{df.}{=} after(S, S_j);\, P_i$.

(4) For $P_i = S_1;\, S_2$, if S is in S_1, we let $after(S, P_i) \overset{df.}{=} after(S, S_1);\, S_2$; otherwise, that is if S is in S_2, we let $after(S, P_i) \overset{df.}{=} after(S, S_2)$.

In addition, we define $before(S, P_i) \overset{df.}{=} S;\, after(S, P_i)$, with the meaning that S is the next statement to be executed by P_i.

Definition: A distributed configuration $C = \langle [\, \underset{i=1,n}{\|} \, S_i],\ \sigma \rangle$ is a

† Again, for simplicity we ignore the distinction between different occurrences of the same statement.

bracketing frontier (*bf*) iff for every S_i, $1 \leqslant i \leqslant n$, either $S_i = E$, or the leftmost brackets in S_i are '$\langle$' (that is, not '$\rangle$'). □

Thus, if a *bf* occurs during a computation, the control of every process either is terminated, or is outside a bracketed section.

Lemma (distributed preservation):

In any computation of P starting in an initial configuration $C = \langle P, \sigma_0 \rangle$ s.t. $\sigma_0 \models_I p$,
if an intermediate configuration $C_k = \langle [\underset{i=1,n}{\|} S_i^{(k)}], \sigma_k \rangle$, $k \geqslant 0$, is a bracketing frontier, then $\sigma_k \models \bigwedge_{i=1,n} pre(T_i^{(k)}) \wedge GI$, where
$T_i^{(k)} \overset{df.}{=} before(S_i^{(k)}, P_i)$,
and $pre(T_i^{(k)})$ is the precondition of $T_i^{(k)}$ from the given proof outline.
Recall that $pre(E)$ is taken as $post(P_i)$.

Proof: The proof is by induction on k. The basis for $k = 0$ is already given. So suppose that C_k, for some $k > 0$, is a *bf*. Let $C_{k-1} = \langle [\underset{i=1,n}{\|} S_i^{(k-1)}], \sigma_{k-1} \rangle$.

We distinguish between two cases:

(1) C_{k-1} is itself a *bf*. In this case, there are two possibilities for the transition $C_{k-1} \rightarrow C_k$.

(a) The transition did not involve a communication, and hence involved an action outside a bracketed section. By the induction hypothesis, $\sigma_{k-1} \models \bigwedge_{i=1,n} pre(T_i^{(k-1)}) \wedge GI$.
The local move, say by P_{i_0}, certainly leaves $\sigma_k \models \bigwedge_{j \neq i_0} pre(T_j^{(k)})$ holding, since $T_j^{(k-1)} = T_j^{(k)}$ for $j \neq i_0$, and processes have disjoint states. Furthermore, $pre(T_{i_0}^{(k)})$ is established as a result of the properties of the local proof outline for P_{i_0}. Finally, $\sigma_k \models GI$, since GI, by construction, does not refer to variables modified outside bracketed sections.

(b) The transition was a communication, say involving (the syntactically matching pairs) α in P_i and $\bar{\alpha}$ in P_j, for some $1 \leqslant i \neq j \leqslant n$. By the assumption that both C_{k-1} and C_k are *bf*s, both α and $\bar{\alpha}$ must constitute bracketed sections. From the induction assumption we obtain that $\sigma_{k-1} \models pre(\alpha) \wedge pre(\bar{\alpha}) \wedge GI$. By the assumption of cooperation, we have that

$$\{pre(\alpha) \wedge pre(\bar{\alpha}) \wedge GI\}\ \alpha \| \bar{\alpha}\ \{post(\alpha) \wedge post(\bar{\alpha}) \wedge GI\}$$

and hence $\sigma_k \models post(\alpha) \wedge post(\bar{\alpha}) \wedge GI$, as required.

(2) C_{k-1} is not a *bf*. This is a more complicated case, and here the particular view of advancing the computation in units of bracketed sections has to be justified.

From the assumption that C_{k-1} is not a *bf* while C_k is a *bf*, it follows that the transition $C_{k-1} \rightarrow C_k$ is the last action of some process, say P_{i_0}, within a bracketed section. Thus, in the partial computation $C_0 \overset{*}{\rightarrow} C_{k-1}$ at least one communication has taken place, and P_{i_0} is involved in the *last* communication within that partial computation. Suppose, w.l.o.g., that this communication matched $\alpha = P_j!e$ in P_i with $\bar{\alpha} = P_i?x$ in P_j, with the value e at that state being, say, a. Hence, in C_k both P_i and P_j are just after the execution of some bracketed sections, say R and R', respectively. Therefore, there exists an intermediate configuration $C_{k'} = \langle [\underset{i=1,n}{\|} S_i^{(k')}], \sigma_{k'} \rangle$, $0 \leqslant k' < k$, with $S_i^{(k')} = R; T$ and $S_j^{(k')} = R', T'$, for some T and T'. Furthermore, $C_{k'}$ is a *bf*. Thus, in the last $k-k'$ transitions, that is, those of the sequence $C_{k'} \overset{*}{\rightarrow} C_{k-1}$, the moves of P_i and P_j were confined to commands within the bracketed sections R and R', respectively. The main observation here is that by **commuting independent actions** the above actions of P_i and P_j can be shifted to be the last $k-k'$ actions in an equivalent computation $C_{k'} \overset{*}{\rightarrow} C_{k-1}$.

Independent actions here are local actions in different processes (due to state disjointness), and communications among disjoint pairs of processes.

Now, by the induction hypothesis $\sigma_{k'} \models pre(R) \wedge pre(R') \wedge GI$.

By using now the cooperation test between α and $\bar{\alpha}$, and the usual argument about local steps, the result follows.

□

We now present a detailed partial correctness proof of the distributed minimum computation program presented earlier. In the next subsection, another proof of this program, using another variant of this proof theory, is considered. The partial correctness assertion to be established is

$$\{\bigwedge_{1 \leqslant i \neq j \leqslant n} a_i \neq a_j\} P \{u\_min = \min_{i=1,n} a_i\}.$$

We first try to formulate a global invariant. Each P_i keeps the minimum of a set of values. We introduce the auxiliary variable set_i which records the indices of the actual elements that have been considered so far to obtain my_min_i as the ith process' minimum. The process U has an auxiliary variable set_U with a similar meaning. The global invariant (which holds outside the bracketed sections) should imply that the sets set_i and set_U exactly cover $\{1, \ldots, n\}$.

The global invariant is thus:

$P::[\ \underset{i=1,n}{\|}\ P_i \| U]$, where:

$$
\begin{array}{l}
P_i::(my\_min_i, my\_size_i, set_i) := (a_i, 1, \{i\}); \{li_i\} \\
\quad *[\{li\}\ \underset{j\in\Delta_i}{\Box}\ 0 < my\_size_i < n; \{li_i \wedge 0 < my\_size_i < n\} \\
\qquad\qquad \langle P_j!(my\_min_i, my\_size_i, set_i) \rightarrow my\_size_i := 0; set_i := \emptyset\rangle \{li_i\} \\
\qquad \underset{j\in\Delta_i}{\Box}\ 0 < my\_size_i < n; \{li_i \wedge 0 < my\_size_i < n\} \\
\qquad\qquad \langle P_j?(their\_min_i, their\_size_i, their\_set_i) \rightarrow \\
\qquad \{M(min(my\_min_i, their\_min_i), my\_size_i + their\_size_i, \\
\qquad set_i \cup their\_set_i)\} \\
\qquad (my\_min_i, my\_size_i, set_i) := (min(my\_min_i, their\_min_i), \\
\qquad my\_size_i + their\_size_i, set_i \cup their\_set_i)\rangle \{li_i\} \\
\qquad]; \{li_i \wedge (my\_size_i = 0 \vee my\_size_i = n)\} \\
\qquad [my\_size_i = 0 \rightarrow skip\ \{M(my\_min_i, 0, \emptyset)\} \\
\qquad \Box \\
\qquad my\_size_i = n \rightarrow \langle U!my\_min_i\rangle \{M(my\_min_i, n, \{1, \ldots, n\})\} \\
\qquad], \\
U::\{true\}[\ \underset{i=1,n}{\Box}\ \langle P_i?u\_min \rightarrow skip\rangle]\{M(u\_min, n, \{1, \ldots, n\})\}
\end{array}
$$

Figure 8.9 Proof outline for distributed minimum computation.

$$
\begin{array}{l}
GI \overset{df.}{\equiv} (\bigcup_{i=1\ldots n} set_i \cup set_U) = \{1, \ldots, n\} \wedge \\
\qquad \forall i, j \in \{1, \ldots, n\}: ((i \neq j \Rightarrow set_i \cap set_j = \emptyset) \wedge set_i \cap set_U = \emptyset)
\end{array}
$$

The bracketing and local proof outline for P_i and U are shown in Figure 8.9, where the auxiliary predicate M is defined as

$$M(m, sz, s) \overset{df.}{=} [sz = |s| \leqslant n \wedge (sz \neq 0 \Rightarrow m = min(\{a_i \mid i \in s\}))]$$

and the loop invariant of P_i is

$$li_i \overset{df.}{=} M(my\_min_i, my\_size_i, set_i)$$

We omit the details of the sequential proofs and consider the cooperation proofs. We present two such proofs in some detail, that of P_i sending a message to P_j; the others are similar.

Consider the bracketed sections

$$
\begin{array}{l}
S_i::\langle P_j!(my\_min_i, my\_size_i, set_i) \rightarrow my\_size_i := 0; set_i := \emptyset\rangle \\
S_j::\langle P_i?(their\_min_j, their\_size_j, their\_set_j) \rightarrow \\
\qquad\qquad\qquad my\_min_j := min(my\_min_j, their\_min_j); \\
\qquad\qquad\qquad my\_size_j := my\_size_j + their\_size_j; \\
\qquad\qquad\qquad set_j := set_j \cup their\_set_j\rangle
\end{array}
$$

For cooperation, we must establish

$$\{GI \wedge pre(S_i) \wedge pre(S_j)\}\ S_i \parallel S_j\ \{GI \wedge post(S_i) \wedge post(S_j)\}$$

By the communication axiom,

$$\begin{array}{l}\{true\}\\ P_j!(my\_min_i, my\_size_i, set_i) \parallel P_i?(their\_min_j, their\_size_j, their\_set_j)\\ \{their\_min_j = my\_min_i \wedge their\_size_j = my\_size_i \wedge their\_set_j = set_i\}\end{array} \qquad \textbf{(1)}$$

By preservation we get

$$\begin{array}{l}\{GI \wedge M(my\_min_i, my\_size_i, set_i) \wedge M(my\_min_j, my\_size_j, set_j)\}\\ P_j!(my\_min_i, my\_size_i, set_i) \parallel P_i?(their\_min_j, their\_size_j, their\_set_j)\\ \{GI \wedge M(my\_min_i, my\_size_i, set_i) \wedge M(my\_min_j, my\_size_j, set_j) \wedge\\ their\_min_j = my\_min_i \wedge their\_size_j = my\_size_i \wedge their\_set_j = set_i\}\end{array} \qquad \textbf{(2)}$$

Hence, by consequence,

$$\begin{array}{l}\{GI \wedge M(my\_min_i, my\_size_i, set_i) \wedge M(my\_min_j, my\_size_j, set_j)\}\\ P_j!(my\_min_i, my\_size_i, set_i) \parallel P_i?(their\_min_j, their\_size_j, their\_set_j)\\ \{GI \wedge M(my\_min_i, my\_size_i, set_i) \wedge M(my\_min_j, my\_size_j, set_j) \wedge\\ their\_min_j = my\_min_i \wedge their\_size_j = my\_size_i \wedge their\_set_j = set_i \wedge\\ M(their\_min_j, their\_size_j, their\_set_j)\}\end{array} \qquad \textbf{(3)}$$

Considering now the inner parts of the bracketed section, we must prove the following according to the formation rule:

$$\begin{array}{l}\{GI \wedge M(my\_min_i, my\_size_i, set_i) \wedge M(my\_min_j, my\_size_j, set_j) \wedge\\ their\_min_j = my\_min_i \wedge their\_size_j = my\_size_i \wedge their\_set_j = set_i \wedge\\ M(their\_min_j, their\_size_j, their\_set_j)\}\\ my\_size_i := 0;\ set_i := \varnothing;\\ my\_min_j := min(my\_min_j, their\_min_j);\ my\_size_j := my\_size_j + their\_size_j;\\ set_j := set_j \cup their\_set_j\\ \{GI \wedge M(my\_min_i, my\_size_i, set_i)) \wedge M(my\_min_j, my\_size_j, set_j)\}\end{array}$$

The above can indeed be deduced by the assignment and consequence rules. set_j is increased by $their\_set_j$, which is set_i, and therefore setting set_i as the empty set does not affect GI. Furthermore, both $M(\ldots)$ terms clearly hold. So the considered matching pair does cooperate.

EXERCISE:

Complete the rest of the cases of the cooperation proofs.

□

$\{z=0\}$ $x:=0$ $\{x=0 \wedge z=0\}$ $P_2!(x, z+1)$ $\{x=0 \wedge z=1\}$ $z:=1$ $\{x=0 \wedge z=1\}$ $x:=x+1$ $\{x=1 \wedge z=1\}$ $P_2!(x, z+1)$ $\{x=1 \wedge z=2\}$ $z:=2$	$\{z=0\}$ $P_1?(y, z)$ $\{y=0 \wedge z=1\}$ $P_1?(y, z)$ $\{y=1 \wedge z=2\}$

Figure 8.10 An alternative satisfaction proof outline.

8.3.1 The LG variant

In this subsection we briefly present an alternative remedy to the problem with the satisfaction relation. The main idea is to allow for local assertions within the proofs of the separate processes to refer to global auxiliary variables. By using such variables the need for the global invariant *GI* is eliminated, since local conditions can be made strong enough to rule out semantic mismatches of communication commands. However, this does not come for free. The price to pay is the revival of the need for a noninterference proof, since a local assertion in P_i may be invalidated by an assignment in $P_j, j \neq i$, to a global auxiliary variable referred to in that assertion.

The proof system thus obtained, to which we refer as **LG**, contains the following components.

For sequential proofs, all the axioms and rules of **AFR** are retained, with the provision that local assertions may refer to global (that is, shared) auxiliary variables.

For the required consistency criterion, we use both satisfaction (as stated above), and noninterference. Both are added as antecedents to the concurrent composition (meta-) rule.

To see how this alternative formulation solves the same problem, consider again the 'disturbing' example in the previous section. The new proof outline, using shared auxiliary variables, is presented in Figure 8.10. For the proper match of the respective first communication commands, we have to show, for satisfaction,

$$\{x=0 \wedge z=0 \wedge z=0\}$$
$$P_2!(x, z+1) \parallel P_1?(y, z)$$
$$\{x=0 \wedge z=1 \wedge y=0 \wedge z=1\}$$

which is easily obtained from the communication axiom (for tuple communication). As for the improper match of the first output in P_1 with the second input in P_2, the precondition for satisfaction is $x=0 \wedge z=0 \wedge y=0 \wedge z=1$, which is trivially contradictory. The other cases are similar.

As for the noninterference, it degenerates in this example, since the only modification of the shared auxiliary variable z is within communications. Such an auxiliary variable, called **synchronously altered**, can only change in company with the progress of the process referring to it, so noninterference is guaranteed. Many programs admit the usage of such auxiliary variables, saving effort in the burden of proof.

In particular, returning to the distributed minimum computation example, it is possible to use $li \wedge GI$ (where li is the loop invariant) as the local assertions, with the admissible reference to the nonlocal auxiliary variable set_j. The previous cooperation test serves here to establish satisfaction, while noninterference is again guaranteed by using set_i as synchronously altered variables.

In conclusion, we see that both systems, though differing in their formulation, are able to capture the same informal insight which ultimately leads to a correctness proof.

8.3.2 Proofs of deadlock freedom of distributed programs

In this section we treat proofs of deadlock freedom in distributed programs, applying a similar approach to that of the shared-variables proof method. Recall that according to this approach, all (syntactically determinable) blocked situations have to be identified, and their semantic image under a given proof outline for partial correctness has to be shown to be contradictory.

What does a blocked situation of a *CSP* program look like?

Some, but not all, of the processes may have terminated, while all the other, nonterminated processes are delayed, their control residing in front of a communication command for which the partner is not ready. In other words, no pair of matching I/O commands may be present in a blocked situation. Remember that such commands may appear also in guard positions, and the associated Boolean part of the guard has to be taken into account too. In view of the bracketing induced by the given partial correctness proof, it can be assumed that processes are located in front of bracketed sections, the cores of which satisfy the above description.

An important point to remember here is that deadlock freedom means the impossibility of a deadlock in any computation (starting in a state satisfying the given precondition). Thus, a program such as the one considered in Section 8.2, where the distinction between global and local nondeterminism was made, is not deadlock free.

The next question is, what is the semantic image of a blocked situation of a *CSP* program?

First, as in the case of shared variables, each blocked residence point within process P_i contributes an assertion to the image, as follows:

(1) $post(P_i)$ – in case P_i has terminated.

(2) $pre(S)$ – in case S is a bracketed section of the form $S_1; \alpha; S_2$.

(3) $pre(S) \wedge \bigwedge_{k \in O} B_k \wedge \bigwedge_{j \in (\Delta - O)} \neg B_j$ – in case S is a repetition statement or selection statement, and $\emptyset \neq O \subseteq \Delta$ is the set of **open** alternatives.

Recall that if no explicit Boolean part occurs in some guard, it is taken as '*true*'.

However, as with the cooperation test, we have to make sure that such a blocked situation is indeed jointly unreachable by all processes. This is represented by conjoining the global invariant GI to the semantic image.

In contrast to the situation in the shared-variables case, there is no *explicit* delaying condition. The delay of a member P_i in some *brp* is represented by the absence of a matching communication command in some $P_j, j \neq i$, in that blocked situation.

Again, from these definitions it is clear that if the semantic image of every blocked situation is contradictory, then the program is deadlock free.

EXAMPLE:

Consider again the pipeline program in Figure 8.3, which we want to show is deadlock free. First, observe that using the proof outline in Figure 8.4 leads nowhere (recall that no nontrivial global invariant was needed there for the partial correctness proof). Even the 'obviously impossible' blocked situation, in which P_1 has terminated, while $P_i, 2 \leqslant i \leqslant n$, have not started yet, is not ruled out. Its semantic image is $y_1 = z \wedge \bigwedge_{i=2,n} true$, which is not contradictory.

Thus, a stronger proof outline is needed, supporting a global invariant that characterizes the 'wave propagation' behavior of this program. To that end, we augment each process P_i with an auxiliary 'wave variable' w_i. The intended interpretation of $w_i = 0$ is that process P_i is ready to input y_i (from P_{i-1}), and $w_i = 1$ means that process P_i is ready to output y_i (to P_{i+1}); moreover, $w_i = 2$ signals the termination of process P_i. Initially, $w_1 = 1 \wedge \bigwedge_{i=2,n} w_i = 0$ holds. When $P_i, i < n$ sends y_i to P_{i+1} (and P_{i+1} receives y_{i+1}), w_i is set to 2, while w_{i+1} is set to 1. For P_n, w_n becomes directly 2 after the input (joint) action, reflecting the end of the wave. The augmented proof outline is presented in Figure 8.11.

We now may define as the global invariant the following assertion:

$$P_1 :: \{w_1 = 1\} \langle P_2 ! y_1;\ w_1 := 2\rangle \{w_1 = 2\}$$
$$P_i :: \{w_i = 0\} \langle p_{i-1} ? y_i;\ w_i := 1\rangle; \{w_i = 1\} \langle P_{i+1} ! y_i;\ w_i := 2\rangle \{w_i = 2\}, \quad (1 < i < n)$$
$$P_n :: \{w_n = 0\} \langle P_{n-1} ? y_n;\ w_n := 2\rangle \{w_n = 2\}$$

Figure 8.11 The augmented pipeline local proof outlines.

$$\Big(\bigwedge_{i=1,n} w_i = 2\Big) \vee \Big(\bigvee_{i=2,n} \Big[\bigwedge_{1 \leqslant j \leqslant i-1} w_j = 2 \wedge w_i = 1 \wedge \bigwedge_{i<k\leqslant n} w_i = 0\Big]\Big)$$

The cooperation test for this invariant actually shows a shift of 1 in the value of i (that satisfies the second disjunct) after every communication action.

EXERCISE:

Complete the details of the cooperation test.

□

Since in every blocked situation no two matching neighbors occur, in no such situation will $w_i = 1 \wedge w_{i+1} = 0$ hold, contradicting the above global invariant. For example, suppose that both P_i and P_{i+1} (for some $i < n$) are in front of their second output, while all other processes have terminated. In this case, the semantic image will contain $w_i = 1 \wedge w_{i+1} = 1 \wedge \bigwedge_{\substack{j \neq i \\ j \neq i+1}} w_j = 2$, which contradicts the global invariant, as claimed. This concludes the deadlock freedom proof.

□

EXERCISE:

Make an exhaustive list of all blocked situations in the pipeline program, and show that their semantic image is contradictory.

□

8.4 Soundness and completeness of AFR

In this section we turn to the soundness and arithmetic completeness of the **AFR** system. We need arithmetical structures here in order to code sequences representing communication histories, as values of auxiliary variables.

Theorem (strong soundness of AFR):

The **AFR** system is strongly sound.

Proof: Consider an interpretation **I** such that $Tr_{\mathbf{I}} \vdash_{\mathbf{AFR}} \{p\} P \{q\}$. By the way the operational semantics was defined, and in contrast to the shared variables case, there is no meaning associated with a *single* process (except for the degenerate case of a concurrent composition among noncommunicating processes). Thus, the 'strange' I/O axioms and all the proof rules for local transitions are sound in a vacuous sense. The main task is to account for the meta-rule of concurrent composition. Here, the harder part has already been done in proving the distributed preservation lemma.

Thus, suppose $\{p_i\} P_i \{q_i\}$, $1 \leqslant i \leqslant n$, are cooperating local proof outlines. Let $\sigma_0 \models \bigwedge_{I\, i=1,n} p_i \wedge GI$, and suppose P terminates with σ'. From the distributed preservation lemma applied to the terminal configuration $\langle [E \| \cdots \| E], \sigma' \rangle$, we have that $\sigma' \models \bigwedge_{I\, i=1,n} q_i \wedge GI$, which is the desired property.

□

Theorem (Arithmetical completeness of AFR):

The **AFR** system is arithmetically complete.

Proof: Let $\mathbf{I}^+$ be an arithmetical structure and suppose $\models_{\mathbf{I}^+} \{p\} P \{q\}$. We have to show how to construct cooperating proof outlines for the processes P_i, $1 \leqslant i \leqslant n$, of P.

Let h_i, $1 \leqslant i \leqslant n$, be new variables, not appearing in P, p or q. These variables are intended to serve as auxiliary variables, recording the respective histories of communication.

First, we transform every process P_i, into P'_i, $1 \leqslant i \leqslant n$. By this transformation, each sequential input command $P_j?x$ is transformed into $\langle P_j?x;\, h_i := h_i\hat{\ }[x, j, i] \rangle$, and each sequential output command is transformed into $\langle P_j!e_j;\, h_i := h_i\hat{\ }[e, i, j] \rangle$. Furthermore, for I/O guards, we transform $B;\, P_i?x \rightarrow S$ into $B;\, \langle P_j?x \rightarrow h_i := h_i\hat{\ }[x, j, i] \rangle;\, S$, and similarly for output guards. Let $P' :: [\, \|_{i=1,n}\, P'_i]$. This transformation also determines the bracketing to be used for the cooperation test.

Suppose $\bar{x}$ is the list of all variables in P. Let $\bar{X}$ be a list of logical variables in bijection with $\bar{x}$. We first show how to establish $Tr_{\mathbf{I}^+} \vdash_{\mathbf{AFR}} \{p'\} P' \{q\}$, where

$$p' \stackrel{df.}{\equiv} p \wedge \bigvee_{i=1,n} h_i = \epsilon \wedge \bar{x} = \bar{X}$$

We denote by Aux_P the collection of variables h_i, $1 \leqslant i \leqslant n$, and $\bar{X}$. For a history of communications h, let $[h]_i$ denote its projection on process i, $1 \leqslant i \leqslant n$, that is the subsequence of all the *rocs* $[a, k, l]$, such that $k = i$ or $l = i$. Thus, $[h]_i$ represents the sequence of all the communications in which P_i participated during h.

We now define three predicates (over global states).

First, $I(\sigma)$ holds iff there exist states σ_0, σ', syntactic continuations S'_i, $1 \leqslant i \leqslant n$, and a history h, such that:

(G1) $\sigma_0 \models_{I^+} p'$

(G2) $C_0 = \langle [\underset{i=1,n}{\|} P'_i], \sigma_0 \rangle \xrightarrow{h} C' = \langle [\underset{i=1,n}{\|} S'_i], \sigma' \rangle$

(G3) C' is a *bf*

(G4) $\sigma'[\![v]\!] = \sigma[\![v]\!]$ for $v \in Aux_P$

(G5) $\sigma[\![h_i]\!] = [h]_i$, $1 \leqslant i \leqslant n$

Let $GI(\bar{h}, \bar{X})$ express I, that is $\sigma \models_{I^+} GI(\bar{h}, \bar{X})$ iff $I(\sigma)$.

Next, we define the local proof outlines for P'_i, $1 \leqslant i \leqslant n$. Let S be any statement within P'_i. We define two predicates, $PRE(S)(\sigma)$ and $POST(S)(\sigma)$.

$PRE(S)(\sigma)$ holds iff there exist states σ_0, σ', syntactic continuations S'_i, $1 \leqslant i \leqslant n$, and a history h, such that

(PR1) $\sigma_0 \models_{I^+} p'$

(PR2) $C_0 = \langle [\underset{i=1,n}{\|} P'_i], \sigma_0 \rangle \xrightarrow{h} C' = \langle [\underset{i=1,n}{\|} S'_i], \sigma' \rangle$

(PR3) $S'_i = before\,(S, P'_i)$

(PR4) $\sigma' / i = \sigma / i$

(PR5) $\sigma[\![h_i]\!] = [h]_i$

For $POST(S)(\sigma)$ a similar definition is used, by which clause (PR3) is replaced by

(PO3) $S'_i = after\,(S, P_i)$

Let *pre* (S) and *post* (S) be the respective formulas expressing those predicates (using only free variables local to P'_i).

The meanings of GI, *pre* (S), and *post* (S) are the expected ones. GI asserts the reachability of a configuration which is a *bf* and has the current state σ. Similarly, *pre* (S) asserts the reachability of a configuration in which P_i is about to execute S in a current state σ. Finally, *post* (S) asserts a similar claim about a configuration just after the termination of S. In all cases, the reaching computation starts from an initial state satisfying the precondition.

We now have to show that the local proof outlines and global invariant (w.r.t. the indicated bracketing) satisfy all the requirements of the **AFR** rules. The validity of the local proof outlines is obtained by a simple extension of the argument in the completeness proof of **H**. We present in detail the process of establishing the cooperation test.

Let S_1 and S_2 be two matching bracketed sections, say in P'_{i_1} and P'_{i_2}, respectively. Suppose S_1 contains an input core, while S_2 contains a syntactically matching output core. We first consider the semantic validity of the cooperation test. Thus, we want to show that

$$\models_{I^+} \{pre(S_1) \wedge pre(S_2) \wedge GI\}\, S_1 \,\|\, S_2\, \{post(S_1) \wedge post(S_1) \wedge GI\} \qquad (*)$$

holds. Assume $\sigma \models_{I^+} pre(S_1) \wedge pre(S_2) \wedge GI$ holds. We have to show that $\sigma^* \models_{I^+} post(S_1) \wedge post(S_2) \wedge GI$ holds for any state σ^* resulting by executing $S_1 \,\|\, S_2$ on σ.

By the definition of the $pre(S_i)$ assertions, and by the merging lemma (reformulated to fit the current setup; see Exercise 8.11), there exist states σ_0, σ', a history h and syntactic continuations S_i', $1 \leqslant i \leqslant n$, such that

$$C_0 = \langle [\ \underset{i=1,n}{\|}\ P_i'], \sigma_0] \rangle \overset{h}{\rightarrow} C' = \langle [\ \underset{i=1,n}{\|}\ S_i'], \sigma' \rangle$$

and (G1)–(G5), (PR1)–(PR5) are satisfied. Suppose that σ^* is a state resulting from σ by executing $S_1 \,\|\, S_2$. Let $\hat{\sigma}$ be a state s.t. $\hat{\sigma}[\![v]\!] = \sigma^*[\![v]\!]$ for v local to P_i or P_j, or $v \in Aux_p$, and $\sigma[\![v]\!] = \sigma'[\![v]\!]$ for any other variable v. Then, σ is a state resulting by the execution of $S_2 \,\|\, S_2$ on σ'. Hence

$$C' = \langle [\ \underset{i=1,n}{\|}\ S_i'], \sigma' \rangle \overset{[a,j,i]}{\rightarrow} \hat{C} = \langle [\ \underset{i=1,n}{\|}\ \hat{S}_i], \hat{\sigma} \rangle$$

for some value a, where $\hat{S}_{i_1} = after(S_1'\, P_{i_1})$ and $\hat{S}_{i_2} = after(S_2', P_{i_2})$, and $\hat{S}_i = S_i'$ for $i \neq i_1$, $i \neq i_2$. Combining the two derivations, we obtain that $C_0 \overset{\hat{h}[a,j,i]}{\rightarrow} \hat{C}$. By the definition of $post(S)$ and GI, we have that $\hat{\sigma} \models post(S_1) \wedge post(S_2) \wedge GI$, as required.

The next step is to show that the semantically valid assertion (*) above is derivable in **AFR**. Thus, we have to show that

$$\text{If} \models_{I^+} \{p\}\, S_1 \,\|\, S_2 \{q\}, \text{ then } Tr_{I^+} \vdash_{\mathbf{AFR}} \{p\}\, S_1 \,\|\, S_2 \{q\} \qquad \textbf{(1)}$$

Suppose $\models_{I^+} \{p\}\, S_1 \,\|\, S_2 \{q\}$ holds. There are several cases to consider, depending on the structure of the bracketed sections S_1 and S_2. We consider one case in more detail. What we have to do is prepare the ground for an application of a formation rule. Suppose that $S_1 :: S_1'; \alpha; S_1'$ and $S_2 :: S_2'; \bar{\alpha}; S_2''$, with α and $\bar{\alpha}$ matching cores. By the disjointness of local states, we have that

$$\models_{I^+} \{p\}\, S_1'; S_2' \{post_{I^+}(p, S_1'; S_2')\} \qquad \textbf{(2)}$$

and

$$\models_{I^+} \{pre_{I^+}(S_1''; S_2'', q)\}\, S_1''; S_2''\{q\} \qquad \textbf{(3)}$$

Since S_1', S_2', S_1'', S_2'' are communication free, by the completeness of **D**, which is 'embedded' in **AFR**, we obtain

$$Tr_{\mathrm{I}^+} \vdash_{\mathbf{AFR}} \{p\}\, S_1';\, S_2' \{post_{\mathrm{I}^+}(p, S_1';\, S_2')\} \tag{4}$$

and

$$Tr_{\mathrm{I}^+} \vdash_{\mathbf{AFR}} \{pre_{\mathrm{I}^+}(S_1'';\, S_2'', q)\}\, S_1'';\, S_2'' \{q\} \tag{5}$$

Finally, we show that

$$\models_{\mathrm{I}^+} post_{\mathrm{I}^+}(p, S_1';\, S_2')\}\, \alpha \,\|\, \bar{\alpha} \{pre_{\mathrm{I}^+}(S_1'';\, S_2'', q)\} \tag{6}$$

However, it is immediate from the semantics of communication that any violation of (6), together with (2) and (3), implies a violation of $\models_{\mathrm{I}^+} \{p\}\, S_1 \,\|\, S_2 \{q\}$, which was assumed to hold.

By the communication axiom (and the consequence rule), we get

$$Tr_{\mathrm{I}^+} \vdash_{\mathbf{AFR}} \{post_{\mathrm{I}^+}(p, S_1';\, S_2')\}\, \alpha \,\|\, \bar{\alpha} \{pre_{\mathrm{I}^+}(S_1'';\, S_2'', q)\} \tag{7}$$

Now the formation rule (FORM1) is applicable to (4), (5) and (7) to yield the required outcome.

The other forms of bracketed sections are handled similarly.

□

EXERCISE:

Fill the details for another possibility of bracketed sections.

□

8.5 Termination and fair termination proofs of distributed programs

In this section we consider augmentations of the **AFR** proof system to prove termination and fair termination of distributed *CSP* programs. Recall that such rules establish the absence of infinite (or fair infinite, respectively) computations. Thus, deadlock is a kind of termination, and its absence has to be proven separately, as described previously. As might be expected by now, the augmentations appeal to the usage of a parametrized loop invariant with a well-founded variant, decreasing under all (or under helpful only, for fairness) directions.

An extra complication arises because termination of an I/O-guarded repetition local to some process is not a local property of that process. For example, the termination of

$P:: [P_1 \| P_2]$, where:
$P_1:: *[x \geqslant 0; \langle P_2!x \rightarrow x := x-1 \rangle]$
$P_2:: z := 0; *[y \neq 0; \langle P_1?y \rightarrow skip; z := 1 \rangle]$

Figure 8.12 A terminating distributed program.

$$P_i:: *[x \neq 0; P_j?x \rightarrow skip]$$

depends on P_i eventually receiving an input value 0 from P_j. Thus, the decrease of the local variant has to be made into an assumption, to be established during the corresponding cooperation test. The initialization of the parametrized invariant adds another difficulty, since the bound on the length of the computation of a local repetition may depend on global information. We elaborate more on these difficulties in the discussion of the examples following the modified rule.

8.5.1 Termination proofs

We now present the augmented system **AFR*** for proving termination (and thereby total correctness) assertions for distributed *CSP* programs. The system is obtained from **AFR** by replacing the (COM–NDREP) rule by its following counterpart. Let m be a fresh variable, ranging over natural numbers.

I/O-guarded nondeterministic repetition rule: (COM–NDREP*)

(INIT): $p \Rightarrow \exists m: pi(m)$
(CONT): $pi(m+1) \Rightarrow \bigvee_{j \in \Delta} B_j$
(DEC): $\langle pi(m) \wedge m > 0 \wedge B_j \rangle\, \alpha_j;\ S_j \langle \exists k: k < m \wedge pi(k) \rangle, j \in \Delta$
(TERM): $pi(0) \Rightarrow \bigwedge_{j \in \Delta} \neg B_j$

$$\frac{}{\langle p \rangle * [\ \square_{j \in \Delta} B_j;\ \alpha_j\ S_j] \langle pi(0) \rangle}$$

□

EXAMPLE:

Consider the distributed program in Figure 8.12. Here z is an auxiliary variable, used to distinguish the states before and after the first iteration of P_2's loop. We first show how to establish the following, simplified, termination assertion: $\langle 0 \leqslant x \leqslant 10 \wedge y \neq 0 \rangle P \langle true \rangle$. The oversimplification here is having a constant bound (10) on the repetition of P_1.

To prove the termination of P_1, we take as the parametrized invariant $pi(x, n) \overset{df.}{\equiv} (x \geqslant -1 \wedge n = x)$. The details of the application of the (COM–NDREP*) rule involve purely sequential reasoning and are omitted.

EXERCISE:

Complete the details of the above claim.

□

As for P_2, the parametrized invariant is defined as follows:

$$pi(y, z, m,) \overset{df.}{\equiv} (z = 0 \Rightarrow (m = 11 \wedge y \neq 0) \wedge (z \neq 0 \Rightarrow m = y \wedge y \geqslant 0))$$

(INIT): Since initially $z = 0$, $m = 11$ can be chosen to establish the invariant initially.

(CONT), (TERM): Immediate.

(DEC): Here we have to show that

$$\langle pi(y, z, m) \wedge m > 0 \wedge y \neq 0\rangle$$
$$P_1?y; skip; z := 1$$
$$\langle \exists m' : m' < m \wedge pi(y, z, m)\rangle$$

This claim is established by the input axiom (a 'guess' about the value of y) and sequential reasoning.

Next, the cooperation test has to be applied, to verify the 'guesses'. As the global invariant we take $GI \overset{df.}{\equiv} 0 \leqslant z \leqslant 1 \wedge [z = 1 \Rightarrow y = x + 1]$. We have to show that

$$\{[x \geqslant -1 \wedge n = x] \wedge [(z = 0 \Rightarrow (m = 11 \wedge y \neq 0)) \wedge$$
$$((z \neq 0 \Rightarrow m = y \wedge y \geqslant 0))] \wedge [x \geqslant 0] \wedge [y \neq 0] \wedge GI\}$$
$$P_2!x; x := x - 1 \parallel P_1?y; skip; z := 1$$
$$\{[x \geqslant -1 \wedge n = x] \wedge [(z = 0 \Rightarrow (m = 11 \wedge y \neq 0) \wedge$$
$$(z \neq 0 \Rightarrow m = y \wedge y \geqslant 0))] \wedge GI\}$$

This also involves a simple sequential reasoning, that can be summarized semantically as follows. If $z = 0$ holds initially, then $m = 11$. In the postcondition, we have $z = 1$ (by assignment), and hence $m = y$. Since by GI $y = x + 1 < 10$, the decrease is established. In the other case, namely $z = 1$ both in the pre- and postconditions, y decreases since x decreases.

To see the other subtlety involved, consider the establishment of the following termination assertion (for the same program): $\langle 0 \leqslant x \wedge y \neq 0\rangle\, P\, \langle true\rangle$. Here we do not have the constant bound on the initial value of x. Still, clause (INIT) for P_1 can be establishable by choosing as the value of n the initial value of x. The problem is, how to satisfy (INIT) for P_2, the loop invariant of which cannot refer to x, a variable subject to change in another process. The solution once again is to introduce logical variables. We add $x = X$ to the precondition of P, and use X as the initial value for m in the loop invariant of P_2. Note that X is not a program variable and not subject to change anywhere. The rest of the proof is similar, where X plays the role of 10 in the previous proof.

□

8.5.2 Fair termination proofs

When passing to *CSP*-like languages for distributed programming, endowed with a much richer structure, two new aspects of fairness emerge.

A. Choice levels

There are more possibilities for the attribution of fairness. We indicate here the main three levels. For each of them, one can consider the orthogonal subdivision into the unconditional, weak, and strong versions, where for explanatory reasons, we formulate everything in terms of the strong case.

(1) *Process fairness:* In an infinite execution each process which is infinitely often enabled will eventually progress. In the absence of enabled local actions, this means that each process will infinitely often communicate (without imposing restrictions on its partners for communication) if it is infinitely often able to communicate.

(2) *Channel fairness:* Each pair of processes which infinitely often are able to communicate mutually with each other will infinitely often do so.

(3) *Communication fairness:* This is similar to case (2) but regarding two specific matching communication commands within the two processes.

We treat here case (3) only. The treatment of cases (1) and (2), though different in details, is similar in essence.

Following are some example programs showing the impact of the different levels of fairness on fair termination of communicating processes.

EXAMPLE (unbounded chattering):

In the program in Figure 8.13 P_1 and P_2 may communicate for any number of times via their respective first alternatives. Once the communication between P_2 and P_3 occurs P_3 terminates and the value of *go_on* in P_2 is set to *false*. In the next iteration of P_2's body this *false*

$P:: [P_1 \| P_2 \| P_3]$, where
$P_1:: b := true;$
$\quad *[1: b;\ P_2 ? b \rightarrow skip]$

$P_2:: go\_on := true;\ c := true;$
$\quad *[1: c;\ P_1 ! go\_on \rightarrow [go\_on \rightarrow skip \,[]\, \neg go\_on \rightarrow c := false]$
$\quad []$
$\quad 2: c;\ P_3 ? go\_on \rightarrow skip]$

$P_3:: P_2 ! false$

Figure 8.13 Communicating processes – unbounded chattering.

$P:: [P_1 \| P_2 \| P_3]$, where
$P_1:: a2 := true;\ a3 := true;$
$\quad *[1: a2;\ P_2 ? a2 \rightarrow skip$
$\quad []$
$\quad 2: a3;\ P_3 ? a3 \rightarrow skip]$

$P_2:: b := true;\ go\_on\_2 := true;\ x := 0;$
$\quad *[1: b;\ P_1 ! go\_on\_2 \rightarrow [\neg go\_on\_2 \rightarrow b := false \,[]\, go\_on\_2 \rightarrow skip]$
$\quad []$
$\quad 2: b;\ P_3 ! x \rightarrow go\_on\_2 := false]$

$P_3:: c := true;\ go\_on\_3 := true;\ y = 0;$
$\quad *[1: c;\ P_1 ! go\_on\_3 \rightarrow [\neg go\_on\_3 \rightarrow c := false \,[]\, go\_on\_3 \rightarrow skip]$
$\quad []$
$\quad 2: c;\ P_2 ? y \rightarrow go\_on\_3 := false]$

Figure 8.14 Communicating processes – neglected channel.

value of *go_on* is propagated to P_1, and in their respective next iterations P_1 and P_2 set *b* and *c*, respectively, to *false*, and all processes terminate.

Process fairness suffices to terminate this program, since its termination depends on P_3 eventually getting its chance to communicate. Note that P_3 is loop free and communicates once only before terminating.

□

EXAMPLE (neglected channel):

This is a program (see Figure 8.14) which does not terminate under the assumption of process fairness but does terminate under the channel fairness assumption. In this example, P_1 is willing to communicate

```
P::[P1 || P2], where

P1::b := true;
    *[1:b; P2?b→skip]

P2::c := true;
    *[1:c; P1!true→skip
       □
      2:c; P1!false→c := false]
```

Figure 8.15 Communicating processes – neglected communication,

indefinitely both with P_2 and with P_3. Once, however, the communication between P_2 and P_3 occurs, both *go_on* variables become false and the program terminates eventually. Thus, channel fairness is needed to prevent neglecting indefinitely the channel (P_2, P_3).

□

Finally, we present an example program the termination of which is not guaranteed even by channel fairness, and communication fairness is needed.

EXAMPLE (neglected communication):

This time (see Figure 8.15), two processes suffice to illustrate the problem. As there are only two processes (forming one channel) both process fairness and channel fairness are guaranteed. However, P_1 and P_2 may communicate indefinitely along P_2's first direction. As soon as the second direction is chosen the program terminates.

□

Thus, the various fairness levels form a hierarchy.

B. Simultaneity

Because of the presence of joint actions, **simultaneity** must be considered, whereby enabledness means simultaneous, joint-readying. Moreover, when a process is busy in one communication, it, of course, is not available to participate in others, even if their Boolean guards could be evaluated to true at that moment. If the definitions are not sensitive enough to this aspect, almost every infinite computation might be 'fair', and very few such programs will fairly terminate.

We now proceed to introduce a proof method for fair termination.

To prove RI: $\ll p \gg P \ll true \gg$:

Choose a well-founded, partially ordered, set $(W, \leqslant)$, and a parametrized invariant $pi(w)$, $w \in W$, and for each $w \in W$, $w > 0$, choose a decreasing matching pair of directions $d_w = (\langle i_w, k_w \rangle, \langle i'_w, k'_w \rangle)$, satisfying

(INIT) $p \Rightarrow \exists w : pi(w)$.

(CONT) $pi(w) \wedge w > 0 \Rightarrow \bigvee_{(\langle i,k \rangle, \langle i',k' \rangle)} B^{i,i'}_{k,k'}$ (Again for matching pairs.)

(DEC) $\ll pi(w) \wedge B^{i_w, i'_w}_{k_w, k'_w} \wedge w > 0 \gg$
$\alpha^{i_w}_{k_w} \rightarrow S^{i_w}_{k_w} \parallel \alpha^{i'_w}_{k'_w} \rightarrow S^{i'_w}_{k'_w}$
$\ll \exists v : v < w \wedge pi(v) \gg$.

(NOINC) $\ll pi(w) \wedge B^{i,i'}_{k,k'} \wedge w > 0 \gg$
$\alpha^i_k \rightarrow S^i_k \parallel \alpha^{i'}_{k'} \rightarrow S^{i'}_{k'}$
$\ll \exists v : v \leqslant w \wedge pi(v) \gg$ for every matching pair $(\langle i,k \rangle, \langle i',k' \rangle)$.

(TERM) $pi(0) \Rightarrow \bigwedge_{(\langle i,k \rangle, \langle i',k' \rangle)} \neg(B^{i,i'}_{k,k'}) \vee \neg RI$.

(IOE) RI': $\ll pi(w) \wedge w > 0 \gg P \ll true \gg$, for $RI' = RI \wedge \neg(B^{i_w, i'_w}_{k_w, k'_w})$, for the decreasing pair $(\langle i_w, k_w \rangle, \langle i'_w, k'_w \rangle)$.

Figure 8.16 The rule **RI-CFAIR** (relativized communication fairness).

Definitions:

(1) An infinite computation π of P is **strongly communication fair** (henceforth abbreviated to **fair**) iff every matching pair of communication commands which is infinitely often enabled (that is, infinitely often jointly readied) along π is infinitely often executed along π. A finite computation of P is always fair.

(2) A program P is **fairly terminating** iff all its fair computations are finite.

□

Next, we extend the helpful directions method to apply to communicating processes. In applying this method to nondeterministic (GC) programs the eventual enabledness of a helpful direction is expressed by means of a subproof establishing fair termination of a derived program the guards of which were augmented with the negation of the guard (the enabledness condition) of the decreasing direction.

This approach to establishing infinite enabledness is only possible if the programming language has some closure properties allowing the expression of the derived program. As it turns out, *CSP* does not have the required closure property. Since enabledness depends on the simultaneous holding of two (Boolean parts of) guards, taken from two different processes, the negation of such a conjunction cannot be added to any of the involved processes without violating the basic property of state disjointness of different processes. Therefore, another variant of the approach, appealing to relativizing invariants, which avoids the closure problem, is applied in the case of *CSP*. Let *RI* be a predicate over σ the (global) state, called the **relativizing invariant**.

> **Definition:** A concurrent program *P* is ***RI*-fairly terminating** iff each of its infinite executions is either unfair or contains a state σ such that $\sigma \models \neg RI$.
>
> □

This kind of fair termination is denoted by $RI\colon \ll p \gg P \ll q \gg$, where p and q are the pre- and postconditions, respectively, which here refer to the global state.

The rule, called **RI-CFAIR** (for **communication fairness**), is given in Figure 8.16. We use a self-explanatory notation for joint-directions, as $< i, k, i', k', >$ for the kth guard in P_i when matched with the k'th guard in $P_{i'}$. Similarly, $B^{i,\ i'}_{k,\ k'}$ denotes the conjunction of the two local Boolean parts of the respective guards.

Thus, infinite enabledness is established by considering (recursively) the same program, but with a different relativizing invariant *RI*. Basically, the negation of the enabledness condition of the decreasing move is added to the previous relativizing invariant. Obviously, for top-level proofs one takes *RI* as *true*.

Theorem (strong soundness of RI-CFAIR):

$$\text{if } Tr_{\mathrm{I}} \vdash_{\mathbf{RI\text{-}CFAIR}} RI\colon \ll p \gg P \ll true \gg, \text{ then } \models_{\mathrm{I}} RI\colon \ll p \gg P \ll true \gg$$

Proof: Similar to the nondeterministic case, generating an infinite decreasing sequence of elements of *W* if *P* does not *RI* terminate.

□

Theorem: (semantic completeness of RI-CFAIR):

$$\text{if } \models_{\mathrm{I}} RI\colon \ll p \gg P \ll true \gg, \text{ then } Tr_{\mathrm{I}} \vdash_{\mathbf{RI\text{-}CFAIR}} RI\colon \ll p \gg P \ll true \gg$$

Proof: The proof is an adaptation of the tree transformation construction to the context of communicating processes. The details are omitted and a reference for further reading is given at the end of the chapter.

□

EXAMPLE:

Fair termination is proven for the program Q presented in Figure 8.17, with four processes (that is, $n = 4$), and the initial condition

$$p \overset{df.}{\equiv} \bigwedge_{i=1,4} b_i \wedge xgo_1 \wedge ygo_1 \wedge \bigwedge_{j=2,4} (\neg xgo_j \wedge \neg ygo_j)$$

The proof depends on the facts that at each moment there is only one left communication which can occur anywhere on the ring, and also only one such right communication. This can be expressed in terms of the program variables by the invariant

$$IN:: \bigvee_{i=1,4} (ygo_i \wedge \bigwedge_{j \neq i} \neg ygo_j) \wedge \bigvee_{i=1,4} (xgo_i \wedge b_i \wedge \bigwedge_{1 \leqslant j < i} \neg b_j \wedge \bigwedge_{i < j \leqslant 4} (\neg xgo_j \wedge b_j))$$

The proof of the invariance of IN is easy and is omitted.

In order to prove $true: \ll p \gg Q \ll true \gg$ we choose $W = \{0, 1, 2, 3\}$ and $pi(w) \overset{df.}{\equiv} (IN \wedge xgo_{4-w} \wedge b_{4-w})$. For each $w > 0$, the decreasing move is $(\langle 4-w, 3\rangle, \langle 5-w, 1\rangle)$. We check that all the clauses of the rule apply.

(TERM) $pi(0) \Rightarrow xgo_4 \wedge b_4$

which, in turn, implies, using IN, $\neg b_1 \wedge \neg b_2 \wedge \neg b_3$, so that no move is possible.

(INIT) $p \Rightarrow pi(3)$

For each $w > 0$, we define $k = 4 - w$, so that the decreasing move is $(\langle k, 3\rangle, \langle k+1, 1\rangle)$, and then prove

(DEC) $\ll pi(w) \wedge xgo_k \wedge b_k \wedge b_{k+1} \gg$
$Q_{k+1}!x_k \rightarrow b_k := false \parallel Q_k?x_{k+1} \rightarrow xgo_{k+1} := true$
$\ll pi(w-1) \gg$

(NOINC) holds for every enabled nondecreasing move because no b_i changes its value from true to false.

(CONT) $pi(w) \wedge IN \Rightarrow xgo_k \wedge b_k \wedge b_{k+1}$

For (IOE) we have to show

$RI': \ll pi(w) \gg P \ll true \gg$,

where $RI' = \neg (b_k \wedge b_{k+1} \wedge xgo_k)$. We now choose $W' = \{0\}$, and the proof is immediate.

$$
\begin{aligned}
&Q :: [Q_1 \parallel \cdots \parallel Q_n], \text{ where}\\
&Q_i :: *[b_i;\ Q_{i-1}?x_i \rightarrow xgo_i := \mathit{true}\\
&\qquad \square\\
&\qquad b_i;\ Q_{i+1}?y_i \rightarrow ygo_i := \mathit{true}\\
&\qquad \square\\
&\qquad xgo_i \wedge b_i;\ Q_{i+1}!x_i \rightarrow b_i := \mathit{false}\\
&\qquad \square\\
&\qquad b_i \wedge ygo_i;\ Q_{i-1}!y_i \rightarrow ygo_i := \mathit{false}]
\end{aligned}
$$

Figure 8.17 A fairly terminating program.

Thus, we have proved the fair termination of Q.

□

8.6 Partial correctness proofs of multiparty interactions

In this section we extend the proof theoretical notion of **cooperating proofs** to synchronous interprocess communication involving an arbitrary number of participants, in contrast to the sender–receiver pair in the point-to-point *CSP* model. Such a primitive enjoys a higher level of abstraction, hiding a lot of low-level details and encouraging modular programming and design.

Proposals of constructs of this kind can be classified into **communication primitives** and **communication abstractions**. Here we focus on the former and consider a language *IP* (**Interacting Processes**) which uses the multiparty (synchronous) interaction as its sole interprocess communication and synchronization primitive.

It turns out that cooperating proofs can be very smoothly extended to the multiparty interactions, with some natural generalization of the concepts involved, but with no need for any essentially different proof-theoretic machinery.

8.6.1 The language *IP*

This is a language the core of which is an abstraction and simplification of languages having multiparty interaction as their interprocess communication and synchronization primitive (references are given at the end of the chapter), and is suitable for focusing on cooperating proofs for partial correctness. In particular, multiparty interactions can be used as guards, thereby generalizing both *GC*, which has only Boolean guards, and *CSP*, using synchronous binary communication as guards. This construct encapsulates **coordination algorithms**, one of the most important classes of distributed algorithms.

A program P:: $[P_1 \| \cdots \| P_n]$ consists (as before) of a **concurrent composition** of $n \geqslant 1$ (fixed n) **processes**, having **disjoint** local states (that is, no shared variables). A **process** P_i $1 \leqslant i \leqslant n$, consists of a statement S, where S may take one of the following forms:

Skip: The usual *skip* statement with no effect on the state.

Assignment $x := e$: Here x is a variable local to P_i and e is an expression over P_i's local state. Assignments have their usual meaning of state transformation.

Interaction $\alpha[\bar{v} := \bar{e}]$: Here α is the **interaction name** and $[\bar{v} := \bar{e}]$ is an optional parallel assignment constituting a **local interaction part** (where an empty part appears as $\alpha[\,]$). All variables in $\bar{v}$ are local to P_i and different from each other. The expressions $\bar{e}$ may involve variables not local to P_i (belonging to other participants of that interaction). The set of **participants** of an interaction α, denoted by PA_α, consists of all processes which syntactically refer to α in their program. When a process reaches (during execution) a local interaction part, it is said to **ready** the corresponding interaction. An interaction α is enabled only when all its participants have readied it, that is have arrived at an interaction point involving α, at which point the interaction can be executed. Its execution implies the execution of all the parallel assignments of all the local interaction parts of all participants. Every reference in the right-hand side of an assignment in one local interaction body to a variable belonging to another participating process always means using the initial value, that is the one determined by the state at the time the interaction started.

Thus, an interaction synchronizes all its participants, and all the parts are executed in parallel. Upon termination of all parts, each process resumes its local thread of control. Note that if a part is empty, its effect is pure synchronization.

Sequential composition $S_1; S_2$: First S_1 is executed; if and when it terminates, S_2 is executed. We freely use $S_1; \ldots; S_k$ for any $k \geqslant 2$.

Nondeterministic selection $[\underset{k=1,m}{\square} B_k; \alpha_k[\bar{v}_k := \bar{e}_k] \rightarrow S_k]$: Here $B_k; \alpha_k[\bar{v}_k := \bar{e}_k]$ is a **guard**, composed of two components. The component B_k is a Boolean expression over the local state of P_i, as for *CSP*. The interaction part component $\alpha_k[\bar{v}_k := \bar{e}_k]$ is an **interaction guard** extending *CSP*'s I/O guards. S_k is any *IP* statement. When a nondeterministic selection statement is evaluated in some state, the k'th guard is **open** if B_k is true in that state and its interaction is **readied** at that stage. In general, several interactions may be readied by such a statement and are said to be in **conflict**. Executing this kind of statement involves the following steps. Evaluate all Boolean parts to determine the collection of open guards. If this collection is empty the statement **fails**. Otherwise an open guard with an enabled interaction is passed (simultaneously with the execution of all the other parts in the other parties) and S_k is executed.

Nondeterministic iteration $*[\underset{k=1,m}{\square} B_k;\alpha_k[\bar{v}_k := \bar{e}_k]\rightarrow S_k]$: Similar to the choice, but execution terminates once no open guards exist, and the whole procedure is repeated after each execution of a guarded command.

In both the selection and iteration constructs, identically true guards may be omitted. Note that nested concurrency is again excluded by this definition.

We now turn to formal definitions of the operational semantics. Since we are interested here only in partial correctness, only the serialized semantics is presented. The central characteristic of the semantics is that actions and interactions take place one at a time. A **distributed configuration** $\langle[S_1 \| \cdots \| S_n],\sigma\rangle$ consists of a distributed program as its syntactic continuation, and a **global** state, assigning values to all variables. Again, a configuration $\langle[E \| \cdots \| E],\sigma\rangle$ is a **terminal** configuration.

We now define the **(serialized) transition** relation '$\rightarrow$' among configurations.

$$\langle[S_1 \| \cdots \| S_i \| \cdots \| S_n],\sigma\rangle \rightarrow \langle[S_1 \| \cdots \| E \| \cdots \| S_n],\sigma\rangle \tag{1}$$

for any $1 \leqslant i \leqslant n$ iff $S_i = skip$, or $S_i = *[\underset{j=1,n_i}{\square}; B_j;\alpha_j[\bar{v}_j := \bar{e}_j]\rightarrow T_j]$ and $\neg \bigvee_{j=1,n_i} B_j$ holds in σ.

$$\langle[S_1 \| \cdots \| S_i \| \cdots \| S_n],\sigma\rangle \rightarrow \langle[S_1 \| \cdots \| E \| \cdots \| S_n],\sigma[\sigma[\![e]\!]|x]\rangle \tag{2}$$

for any $1 \leqslant i \leqslant n$ iff $S_i = (x := e)$.

$$\begin{aligned}&\langle[S_1 \| \cdots \| S_{i_1-1} \| S_{i_1} \| S_{i_1+1} \| \cdots \| S_{i_k-1} \| S_{i_k} \| S_{i_k+1} \| \cdots \| S_n],\sigma\rangle \rightarrow\\ &\langle[S_1 \| \cdots \| S_{i_1-1} \| S'_{i_1} \| S_{i_1+1} \| \cdots \| S_{i_k-1} \| S'_{i_k} \| S_{i_k+1} \| \cdots \| S_n],\sigma'\rangle\end{aligned} \tag{3}$$

for some $1 \leqslant k \leqslant n$ and $1 \leqslant i_j \leqslant n$ for $1 \leqslant j \leqslant k$, iff the following holds. There is an interaction α with a set of participants $PA_\alpha = \{P_{i_1},\ldots,P_{i_k}\}$, and for every i s.t. $P_i \in PA_\alpha$ one of the following conditions holds:

(a) $S_i = \alpha[\bar{v}_i := \bar{e}_i]$ and $S'_i = E$;

(b) $S_i = [\underset{j=1,n_i}{\square} B_j;\alpha_j[\bar{v}_j := \bar{e}_j]\rightarrow T_j]$ and there exists some j, $1 \leqslant j \leqslant n_i$, s.t. B_j holds in σ, $\alpha_j = \alpha$ and $S'_i = T_j$;

(c) $S_i = *[\underset{j=1,n_i}{\square} B_j;\alpha_j[\bar{v}_j := \bar{e}_j]\rightarrow T_j]$ and there exists some j, $1 \leqslant j \leqslant n_i$, s.t. B_j holds in σ, $\alpha_j = \alpha$, $S'_i = T_j;\, S_i$.

Finally, for all these cases, $\sigma' = \sigma[\sigma[\bar{e}]|\bar{v}]$, with $\bar{v} = \bigcup_{P_i \in PA_\alpha} \bar{v}_i$ and $\bar{e} = \bigcup_{P_i \in PA_\alpha} \bar{e}_i$.

$$
\begin{aligned}
Q::[&P_1::[\alpha_1[x:=y]\rightarrow skip \,[]\, \alpha_2[x:=z]\rightarrow skip]\\
&\|\\
&P_2::y:=0;[true\rightarrow\alpha_1\,[]\,false\rightarrow\alpha_2]\\
&\|\\
&P_3::z:=1;[true\rightarrow\alpha_1\,[]\,false\rightarrow\alpha_2]\\
&]
\end{aligned}
$$

Figure 8.18 Example program Q.

If

$$\langle[S_1\|\cdots\|S_i\|\cdots\|S_n],\sigma\rangle\rightarrow\langle[S_1'\|\cdots\|S_i'\|\cdots\|S_n'],\sigma'\rangle \qquad \textbf{(4)}$$

then

$$
\begin{aligned}
&\langle[S_1;T_1\|\cdots\|S_i;T_i\|\cdots\|S_n;T_n],\sigma\rangle\rightarrow\\
&\quad\langle[S_1';T_1\|\cdots\|S_i';T_i\|\cdots\|S_n';T_n],\sigma'\rangle
\end{aligned}
$$

For this semantics, we again inherit the notions of (serialized) computation, termination, and deadlock.

An interaction α is **enabled** in a configuration C iff C has one of the forms in clause (3) of the definition of '$\rightarrow$' and all the conditions are satisfied for α.

Two interactions α_1 and α_2 are in **conflict** in a configuration C iff both interactions are enabled in C and they have nondisjoint set of participants, that is $PA_{\alpha_1}\cap PA_{\alpha_2}\neq\varnothing$.

EXERCISE:

Formulate and prove an appropriate computations lemma for *IP* (in analogy with previous languages).

□

We next present the extension of cooperating proofs to the language *IP*.

The basic components of a proof are again represented as proof outlines. These proof outlines satisfy the usual sequential partial correctness axioms and rules, and in addition the following axiom.

Interaction body axiom (*iba*):

$$\{p\}\,\alpha[\bar{v}:=\bar{e}]\,\{q\} \qquad \text{(IBA)}$$

for arbitrary local assertions p and q.

□

This axiom is the natural generalization of the I/O axioms in **AFR**. In so much as the I/O axioms constitute an assumption about the state of the communication partner (in some matching communication), the interaction body axiom may be considered to constitute a **joint-assumption** about the preinteraction states of all the participants of some collection of matching local interaction bodies. The collection of all such joint-assumptions made by all members of PA_α are confronted simultaneously in the cooperation test described below. This is the proof-theoretical counterpart of the synchronized nature of a multiparty interaction.

EXAMPLE:

As a simple example, we consider the following applications of the (IBA) axiom.

$$P:: [P_1:: \alpha[x := x+y+z] \parallel P_2:: \alpha[y := x+y+z] \parallel P_3:: \alpha[z := x+y+z]]$$

Each of the following is a valid proof outline:

$\{x \geqslant 0\}\,\alpha[x := x+y+z]\,\{x \geqslant 0\}$ for P_1
$\{y \geqslant 0\}\,\alpha[y := x+y+z]\,\{y \geqslant 0\}$ for P_2
$\{z \geqslant 0\}\,\alpha[z := x+y+z]\,\{z \geqslant 0\}$ for P_3

Thus, in the first one, we conclude locally for P_1 a postcondition $x \geqslant 0$ based on its own precondition and an assumption about the preconditions of P_2 and P_3, about the values of y and z. As it happens, the conjunction of the respective preconditions $y \geqslant 0$ and $z \geqslant 0$ indeed satisfies the assumption, as would be revealed during the cooperation test.

□

Another kind of an assumption made by a process is that a certain interaction will never occur. This can be seen in the following simple example.

EXAMPLE:

Consider the program Q in Figure 8.18. Note that $PA_{\alpha_2} = \{P_1, P_2, P_3\}$, in spite of the identically *false* guards (introduced for simplicity, to avoid local computation) of α_2 in P_2 and P_3.

As a part of a proof of $\{true\}\,Q\,\{x = y = 0\}$, we might have a proof outline for P_1 with a postcondition $\{x = 0\}$. However, since x is modified both in the body of α_1 and in the body of α_2, to preserve the sequential nondeterministic branching rule an assumption is needed

$P_1 :: \{true\}$
$[\alpha_1 [x := y] \{x = 0\} \rightarrow skip \{x = 0\}$
$\square$
$\alpha_2 [x := z] \{x = 0\} \rightarrow skip \{x = 0\}$
$] \{x = 0\}$

Figure 8.19 A proof outline for P_1.

also about the local interaction body $\alpha_2 [x := z]$, even though this interaction will never occur. We obtain the proof outline in Figure 8.19 for P_1. The interaction α_2 will pass the cooperation test **vacuously**, by having a *false* precondition in any matching collection of local interaction bodies.

$\square$

Definition: A collection of local interaction $\{\alpha_i [\bar{v}_i := \bar{e}_i] \mid i \in A\}$ **syntactically match** iff for some interaction α, $\bigwedge_{i \in A} \alpha_i = \alpha$ holds, where $\alpha_i [\bar{v}_i := \bar{e}_i]$ occurs in process P_i. Furthermore, $A = PA_\alpha$.

$\square$

Let P be an *IP* program and α be an interaction in P. Our most basic aim, after having separate proof outlines for each P_i in P, is to establish the satisfaction relation

$$(*)\ \{\bigwedge_{P_j \in PA_\alpha} pre_j\} \left[\alpha[\bar{v}_{i_1} := \bar{e}_{i_1}] \parallel \cdots \parallel \alpha[\bar{v}_{i_k} := \bar{e}_{i_k}]\right] \{\bigwedge_{P_j \in PA_\alpha} post_j\}$$

Here $\{pre_j\}\, \alpha[\bar{v}_j := \bar{e}_j]\, \{post_j\}$ is taken from the local proof outline of P_j, $P_j \in PA_\alpha$, for a syntactically matching collection of local interaction bodies. The correctness assertion (*) captures the operational synchronous nature of an interaction.

The first step is to introduce the **(global) interaction axiom** (gia), the natural generalization of the communication axiom of **AFR**.

(Global) interaction axiom (*gia*):

$$\{p_{\bar{e}}^{\bar{v}}\} [\ \parallel_{P_j \in PA_\alpha} \alpha[\bar{v}_j := \bar{e}_j]] \{p\}, \text{ where } \bar{v} = \bigcup_{P_j \in PA_\alpha} \bar{v}_j \text{ and } \bar{e} = \bigcup_{P_j \in PA_\alpha} \bar{e}_j \qquad \text{(GIA)}$$

$\square$

This axiom captures the operational semantics of an interaction as a parallel (atomic) execution of all the parallel assignments in the local interaction bodies. The syntactic constraint of all variables in $\bar{v}$ being different follows from the formation rules of local interaction bodies in *IP* and from process state disjointness.

EXAMPLE:

Returning to the program P in a previous example, an application of the interaction axiom and the rule of consequence immediately yield

$$(**)\{x \geqslant 0 \wedge y \geqslant 0 \wedge z \geqslant 0\}$$
$$\left[\alpha[x := x+y+z] \,\|\, \alpha[y := x+y+z] \,\|\, \alpha[z := x+y+z]\right]$$
$$\{x \geqslant 0 \wedge y \geqslant 0 \wedge z \geqslant 0\}.$$

We might also prove a stronger partial correctness assertion about P, with the same precondition and the postcondition $x = y = z \geqslant 0$. To obtain this proof, we have to appeal also to the substitution rule. The problem is that we need to 'freeze' initial values of variables, to which local interaction bodies have access, but local assertions do not. We modify the proof outlines for that example.

The stronger proof outlines for the program P above are as follows:

$\{x = a \geqslant 0\}\,\alpha[x := x+y+z]\,\{x = a+b+c \geqslant 0\}$ for P_1
$\{y = b \geqslant 0\}\,\alpha[y := x+y+z]\,\{y = a+b+c \geqslant 0\}$ for P_2
$\{z = c \geqslant 0\}\,\alpha[z := x+y+z]\,\{z = a+b+c \geqslant 0\}$ for P_3

Since

$$x = a \geqslant 0 \wedge y = b \geqslant 0 \wedge z = c \geqslant 0 \Rightarrow x+y+z = a+b+c \geqslant 0$$

an application of the global interaction axiom and the consequence rule yields

$$\{x = a \geqslant 0 \wedge y = b \geqslant 0 \wedge z = c \geqslant 0\}\,P\,\{x = a+b+c = y = z \geqslant 0\}$$

By weakening the postcondition, we get

$$\{x = a \geqslant 0 \wedge y = b \geqslant 0 \wedge z = c \geqslant 0\}\,P\,\{x = y = z \geqslant 0\}$$

Since none of a, b, and c is free either in P or in the postcondition, we can substitute $a|x$, $b|y$, $c|z$, to obtain

$$\{x \geqslant 0 \wedge y \geqslant 0 \wedge z \geqslant 0\}\,P\,\{x = y = z \geqslant 0\}$$

□

However, as in the case of *CSP*, things are a little more complicated. The main problem is again the identification of semantically matching interactions. So, similarly to the communicating processes case, we introduce auxiliary variables that carry the additional information needed to express the conditions for such a semantic matching, which happen not to be present in the state. In addition, we introduce a global invariant and bracketed sections, where the invariant has to hold before and after every execution of a semantically matching tuple of bracketed sections. The global invariant may refer to the variable in all processes. While its main role is the one stated above, in actual proofs it can be used to propagate any global information.

We now slightly extend the bracketing notion of *CSP*.

Definition:

(1) A process P_i is **bracketed** iff the brackets '$\langle$' and '$\rangle$' are interspersed in its body in such a way that each **bracketed section** $\langle S\rangle$ is of the form $S_1;\ \alpha[\bar{v}:=\bar{e}];\ S_2$, for some local S_1 and S_2 (that is, without interaction bodies, possibly empty). Again, we refer to $\alpha[\bar{v}:=\bar{e}]$ as the core of the bracketed section.

(2) A collection $\langle S_i\rangle$, $i\in A$, of bracketed sections **syntactically match** iff the collection of respective cores syntactically match.

(3) An **outline section** $\{p\}\langle S\rangle\{q\}$ is a bracketed section with its precondition and postcondition taken from a local proof outline of some process. Outline sections syntactically match when their respective bracketed sections match.

□

As for *CSP*, the bracketing suggests a slightly different operational semantics, where the grain of atomicity is a semantically matching pair of bracketed sections. As far as partial correctness is concerned, this is equivalent to the original semantics, and enables updating auxiliary variables together with visible effects in an interaction. This approach extends to *IP* as well, taking as atomic steps semantically matching collections of local interaction bodies.

We now reintroduce a global invariant *GI*, to be preserved by a program *P* when executed with this coarser grain of interleaving, induced by the bracketed sections. The invariant has free variables whose values are modifiable only within bracketed sections.

Definition:

(1) A syntactically matching collection of outline sections $\{pre_i\}\langle S_i\rangle$ $\{post_i\}$, $1\leqslant i\leqslant n$, **cooperates** w.r.t. the invariant *GI* iff

$$\{\bigwedge_{i=1,n} pre_i \wedge GI\}\ [S_1\parallel\cdots\parallel S_n]\ \{\bigwedge_{i=1,n} post_i \wedge GI\}$$

can be proved.

$L :: [P_1 \parallel \cdots \parallel P_n]$, where

$P_i :: \{id_i = id_i^0\}$

$minid_i := id_i;\ round_i := 1;$

$*[\{id_i = id_i^0 \wedge 1 \leqslant round_i \leqslant n \wedge minid_i = \min_{i+1-round_i \leqslant j \leqslant i} id_j^0\}$

$\langle round_i < n; pass\,[minid_i := min\,(minid_{i-1}, minid_i)] \rightarrow$
$round_i := round_i + 1\rangle];$

$\{id_i = id_i^0 \wedge minid_i = \min_{0 \leqslant j < n} id_j^0\}$

$leader_i := (id_i = minid_i)$

$\{leader_i \equiv (id_i = \min_{0 \leqslant j < n} id_i^0)\}$

Figure 8.20 Local proof outline for the ring leader election program.

(2) For an *IP* program $P :: [\ \parallel_{i=1,n} P_i]$, proof outlines $\{p_i\}\, P_i\, \{q_i\}$, $1 \leqslant i \leqslant n$, **cooperate** w.r.t. *GI* iff every syntactically matching collection of outline sections cooperate w.r.t. *GI*.

□

To establish the condition in (1), one can use the global interaction axiom and formation rules similar to the ones in **AFR**.

We now can introduce the usual **concurrent composition** meta-rule, which is the same as for communicating processes, but with the extended definition of cooperation among proofs.

Let $P :: [P_1 \parallel \cdots \parallel P_n]$ be an *IP* program and let $\{p_i\}\, P_i\, \{q_i\}$, $1 \leqslant i \leqslant n$, be valid local proof outlines.

$$\frac{\{p_i\}\, P_i\, \{q_i\},\ 1 \leqslant i \leqslant n, \text{ cooperate w.r.t. } GI}{\{\bigwedge_{i=1,n} p_i \wedge GI\}\ P\ \{\bigwedge_{i=1,n} q_i \wedge GI\}}$$

Finally, one uses the usual auxiliary variables rule to eliminate the auxiliary variables and assignments introduced for the sake of the proof only.

EXAMPLE (Leader election on a ring):

We show how cooperating proofs are applied to a leader election program *L*, employing a unidirectional ring arrangement of processes. In terms of *IP*, the ring arrangement may be interpreted so that only pairs of neighboring processes (that is, of the form $\langle P_i, P_{i+1}\rangle$) can exchange values (in the specified direction) in interactions. (See exercise for a 'stronger' interpretation of the ring arrangement, using binary interactions only.)

Initially, each process has an identifier *id*, and the identifiers are pairwise distinct. In this solution, the processes interact in *rounds*, attempting to compute the index of the process with the minimal *id* value, to be selected as the leader. In each round, every process passes its local minimal value (the contents of the $minid_i$ variable) to its left neighbor, the latter updating its local minimum value. After n rounds, each process obtains the global minimum value as the value of its $minid_i$ variable, and is able to determine whether it is the leader or not, updating $leader_i$ accordingly.

The local proof outlines are presented in Figure 8.20. They can be shown valid using the sequential rule and the (IBA) axiom.

We turn to the cooperation proof. As a global invariant, we take

$$I \stackrel{df.}{=} distinct(\overline{id}) \wedge \bigwedge_{0 \leqslant j < n} \bigwedge_{0 \leqslant k < n} round_j = round_k$$

Thus, we have to show

$$\{distinct(\overline{id}) \wedge \bigwedge_{0 \leqslant j < n} \bigwedge_{0 \leqslant k < n} round_j = round_k \wedge \bigwedge_{0 \leqslant i < n} id_i = id_i^0 \wedge$$
$$\bigwedge_{0 \leqslant i < n} 1 \leqslant round_i < n \wedge \bigwedge_{0 \leqslant i < n} minid_i = \min_{i+1-round_i \leqslant j \leqslant i} id_j^0\}$$
$$\|_{0 \leqslant i < n} \langle round_i < n; pass\,[minid_i := min\,(minid_{i-1}, minid_i)]$$
$$\rightarrow round_i := round_i + 1 \rangle$$
$$\{distinct(\overline{id}) \wedge \bigwedge_{0 \leqslant j < n} \bigwedge_{0 \leqslant k < n} round_j = round_k \wedge \bigwedge_{0 \leqslant i < n} id_i = id_i^0 \wedge$$
$$\bigwedge_{0 \leqslant i < n} 1 \leqslant round_i \leqslant n \wedge \bigwedge_{0 \leqslant i < n} minid_i = \min_{i+1-round_i \leqslant j \leqslant i} id_j^0\}$$

This follows directly by the (GIA) axiom. The required partial correctness assertion is now obtained via the concurrent composition rule.

□

8.7 Asynchronous message passing

In this section we return to the point-to-point model of interprocess communication and consider another variant thereof. According to this variant, the *send* operation does not block (delay) the sending process. The *receive* operation does delay the receiving process until a time when a message is available. The total asynchrony is reflected in the absence of any bound on the transit time of messages, though this time is always finite. Among the various subvariants of this model, we concentrate here on one satisfying an additional property: messages arrive in their destination in the same order in which they were sent (FIFO regime). No message loss or corruption is considered.

We also adhere to a different naming convention for communication: we equip the model with **named channels**, on which messages are sent by processes and from which messages are received by processes. To simplify the treatment, we impose the syntactic restriction that each channel connects exactly two processes, a sender and a receiver.

We now present *ACSP*, a variant of *CSP* with asynchronous interprocess communication. The basic communication commands are as follows:

$c!!e$: The current value of the expression e (where e is local to the sending process) is sent on channel c.

$c??x$: If there is a pending message on channel c, it is received and assigned to the (local to the receiving process) variable x; otherwise, the receiving process is delayed until the arrival of such a message on channel c (possibly forever, in case no such message ever arrives).

The structure of all other commands remains as in *CSP*, except that output guards are excluded. Two communication commands are **syntactically matching** in this context iff one is an output and the other is an input command, both referring to the same channel.

Operational semantics

In order to define the operational semantics, we again have to augment the configuration with an invisible state component that records 'messages in transit', that is, messages sent (along some channel c), but not yet received. We refer to this component as the **communication state**, a mapping γ from the set of channels to sequences of messages. The interpretation of $\gamma[\![c]\!]$ is the sequence of all messages sent on channel c and not yet received. We use the usual operations on sequences (lists) to handle channels.

Thus, an asynchronous distributed configuration for *ACSP* has the form $C = \langle [\ \|_{i=1,n}\ S_i], \gamma, \sigma\rangle$, where the first and last components are the usual syntactic continuation and global state, respectively, and γ is the communication state.

The transition relation '$\rightarrow$' is again defined as the least relation among configurations satisfying the following clauses.

$$\langle [S_1 \| \cdots \| S_i \| \cdots \| S_n], \gamma, \sigma\rangle \rightarrow \langle [S_1 \| \cdots \| E \| \cdots \| S_n], \gamma, \sigma\rangle \tag{1}$$

for any $1 \leqslant i \leqslant n$, iff $S_i = skip$, or $S_i = *[\ \square_{j=1,n_i}\ B_j;\ \alpha_j \rightarrow T_j]$ and $\sigma \models \neg \bigvee_{j=1,n_i} B_j$.

$$\langle [S_1 \| \cdots \| S_i \| \cdots \| S_n], \gamma, \sigma\rangle \rightarrow \langle [S_1 \| \cdots \| E \| \cdots \| S_n], \gamma, \sigma[e|x]\rangle \tag{2}$$

$$P::[\underset{i=1,n}{\|} P_i], \text{ where}$$

$$\begin{aligned}
&P_i::z_i := 0; y_i := 0; c_i!!x_i;\\
&\quad *[y_i \neq \infty \rightarrow c_{i-1}??y_i;\\
&\qquad\qquad [x_i = y_i \rightarrow z_i := 1; y_i := \infty; c_i!!\infty\\
&\qquad\qquad \square\\
&\qquad\qquad x_i > y_i \rightarrow skip\\
&\qquad\qquad \square\\
&\qquad\qquad x_i < y_i \rightarrow c_i!!y_i]\\
&\quad]
\end{aligned}$$

Figure 8.21 Distributed leader election.

for any $1 \leqslant i \leqslant n$, iff $S_i = (x := e)$.

$$\langle [S_1 \| \cdots \| S_i \| \cdots \| S_n], \gamma, \sigma \rangle \rightarrow$$
$$\langle [S_1 \| \cdots \| E \| \cdots \| S_n], \gamma[enqueue(\sigma[\![e]\!], \gamma[\![c]\!]) | c], \sigma \rangle \qquad \textbf{(3)}$$

for any $1 \leqslant i \leqslant n$, iff $S_i = (c!!e)$.

$$\langle [S_1 \| \cdots \| S_i \| \cdots \| S_n], \gamma, \sigma \rangle \rightarrow$$
$$\langle [S_1 \| \cdots \| E \| \cdots \| S_n], \gamma[dequeue(\gamma[\![c]\!]) | c], \sigma[first(\gamma[\![c]\!]) | x] \rangle \qquad \textbf{(4)}$$

for any $1 \leqslant i \leqslant n$, iff $S_i = (c??x)$, and $\gamma[\![c]\!] \neq \varepsilon$.

$$\langle [S_1 \| \cdots \| S_i \| \cdots \| S_n], \gamma, \sigma \rangle \rightarrow$$
$$\langle S_1 \| \cdots \| T_j; S_i \| \cdots S_n], \gamma[dequeue(\gamma[\![c]\!]) | c], \sigma[first(\gamma[\![c]\!]) | x] \rangle \qquad \textbf{(5)}$$

for any $1 \leqslant i \leqslant n$, iff $S_i = *[\underset{k=1,n_i}{\square} B_k;\, \alpha_\kappa \rightarrow T_k]$, $1 \leqslant j \leqslant n_i$, $\sigma \models B_j$, $\alpha_j = (c??x)$ and $\gamma[\![c]\!] \neq \varepsilon$.

If, for any $1 \leqslant i \leqslant n$

$$\langle S_1 \| \cdots \| S_i \| \cdots \| S_n], \gamma, \sigma \rangle \rightarrow \langle [S_1 \| \cdots \| S_i' \| \cdots \| S_n], \gamma', \sigma' \rangle \qquad \textbf{(7)}$$

then

$$\langle [S_1 \| \cdots \| S_i; T_i \| \cdots \| S_n], \gamma, \sigma \rangle \rightarrow \langle [S_1 \| \cdots \| S'_i; T_i \| \cdots \| S_n], \gamma', \sigma' \rangle$$

EXERCISE:

Provide clause (6) for the selection statement.

□

Since we are not going to deal with completeness issues for this model, we omit recording the relevant history on the transitions.

In an initial configuration, we require that $\gamma[\![c]\!] = \varepsilon$ for every channel c, that is, all channels are initially empty. A terminal configuration is again one with a syntactic continuation of the form $[\ \underset{i=1,n}{\|}\ E]$. An **asynchronous distributed computation** is a maximal '$\rightarrow$'-sequence of asynchronous distributed configurations, starting in an initial configuration. Again the only liveness assumption guaranteed is that of fundamental liveness. The definitions of termination, deadlock, and divergence carry over from the *CSP* case, with the appropriate modification to account for nonblocking output operation.

EXERCISE:

(1) Give an explicit description of the form of the final configuration in a deadlocked computation.

(2) Can a program terminate with some non-empty channel (that is, with $\gamma[\![c]\!] \neq \varepsilon$, for some channel c)?

□

EXAMPLE:

As a typical *ACSP* program, consider the solution in Figure 8.21 to the leader election problem.

In this program, there are $n > 2$ processes arranged in a ring, with channel c_i connecting P_i to P_{i+1}. Each process P_i has a local variable x_i (all indices are explicit, for readability), with pairwise distinct integer values. Here '∞' denotes a value larger than all integers (to avoid typing messages or multiple parallel channels). In addition, each process has a local variable z_i, initialized to 0. Upon termination, it is required that there exists exactly one index i_0, the 'leader', such that $z_{i_0} = 1$, and $z_j = 0$, $j \neq i_0$. The idea is to choose as the 'leader' P_{i_0} s.t. $x_{i_0} = \max_{1 \leqslant k \leqslant n} x_k$, the index of the process with the largest value of x_i. Each process sends its value x_i to the right, and propagates to the right any received value y larger than its own x. The maximal value is the only one to traverse the whole ring. When it arrives back to its origin, a '∞' message is sent around the ring, to terminate all other processes.

We return to a partial correctness proof of this program after the presentation of the proof rules.

□

We now turn to the formulation of a proof system for proving partial correctness of *ACSP* programs. The system is again two leveled. The first observation is that the communication state has to be represented in the proof system. To that end, we associate with every channel c two variables at the proof level: IN_c and OUT_c. The interpretation of these variables is enforced by the axioms and rules to be the intended one: the sequence of values received and the sequence of values sent (on the corresponding channel), respectively. Note that IN_c is local to the process receiving from c, while OUT_c is local to the process sending on c. Cooperation is again needed to verify 'guesses' about the input value and the state of the sender.

Output axiom:

$$\{p^{OUT_c}_{OUT_c \cdot e}\}\ c!!e\ \{p\}.$$

This axiom captures the effect of output as appending (shortened here to '.') the value of the expression e to the output history of channel c. Note that, in contrast to the analogous situation in *CSP*, no 'guess' about control is involved here. An output command is always executable, independently of the control of any receiver process.

□

Input axiom:

$\{p\}\ c??x\ \{q\}$, for arbitrary local state assertions p and q.

This axiom reflects the usual local 'guess' about the input value, and about the control of the sender (having sent yet another message). The fact that the channel c is indeed non-empty, as well as IN_c is properly updated, is tested at the second stage of the proof.

□

Fifo axiom:

$$\forall k: |IN_c| = k \Rightarrow |OUT_c| \geqslant k \wedge IN_c[k] = OUT_c[k].$$

This axiom reflects the fact that messages on every channel are received in the order sent. We abbreviate it to $IN_c \leqslant OUT_c$.

□

The proof rules for the sequential constructs remain as for *CSP*. We now turn to the description of the second stage, where mutual consistency among the local proof outlines is validated. Cooperation here reduces to a variant of satisfaction, with no need to appeal to a global invariant.

Definition: Two syntactically matching I/O commands (with their accompanying pre- and postconditions from the local proof outlines) $\{pre_1\}c!!e\{post_1\}$ and $\{pre_2\}c??x\{post_2\}$ **cooperate** iff $\{pre_1 \wedge pre_2 \wedge IN_c = OUT_c\}\langle c!!e;\ S_1\rangle \parallel \langle c??x;\ S_2\rangle\{post_2\}$, where S_1, S_2 do not contain communication commands. The role of the bracketing is as for *CSP*.

□

This cooperation test establishes, with the aid of the sender's precondition, the 'guess' of the receiver about the value of x. Note that this pair of syntactically matching I/O commands may not match semantically. This happens in case the input value was produced by some other output command (to the same channel) in the sender's program. In this case, the two preconditions should contradict each other under the assumption that the value received is the value sent, causing a vacuous cooperation. This assumption is the meaning of the extra conjunct $IN_c = OUT_c$ added to the precondition.

EXERCISE:

Why does not $post_1$ participate in the cooperation test?

□

In order to facilitate cooperation proofs, one more axiom is needed, handling the communication itself.

Communication axiom:

$$\{p^{x,IN_c}_{e,IN_c e}\}c!!e \parallel c??x\{p\} \qquad \text{(A-COM)}$$

We stress here that this axiom is confined to be used in cooperation proof only (see Exercise 8.13).

□

The above culminates in the asynchronous concurrent composition (meta-) rule, which also incorporates the initialization of channels to empty sequences before execution (reflecting the definition of an initial configuration in the semantics).

Asynchronous concurrent composition:

$$\frac{\text{proof outlines } \{p_i\}P_i\{q_i\},\ 1 \leqslant i \leqslant n, \text{ cooperate}}{\{\bigwedge_{i=1,n} p_i \wedge \bigwedge_{c} IN_c = OUT_c = \varepsilon\}[\ \|_{i=1,n}\ P_i]\{\bigwedge_{i=1,n} q_i\}} \qquad \text{(A-CONC)}$$

□

EXAMPLE:

We return now to the verification of the leader election program in Figure 8.21, and as an aid to the proof modify it as shown in Figure 8.22. Basically, a second element is added to the message representing its **hop**, namely the distance on the ring it has already traversed. It is represented in the program by the variable h_i. Note that this constitutes an auxiliary variable not affecting the computation. We also incorporate the bracketing for the cooperation proof.

The correctness assertion we want to establish is

$$\{\bigwedge_{1\leqslant i\leqslant n} (IN_i = OUT_i = \varepsilon \wedge x_i = X_i \neq \infty \wedge \bigwedge_{j\neq i} X_j \neq X_i)\}$$
$$P$$
$$\{\bigvee_{1\leqslant i\leqslant n} (z_i = 1 \wedge \bigwedge_{j\neq i} (z_j = 0 \wedge X_i > X_j))\}$$

Since all the channels here have the form $(i-1, i)$, we use the notation IN_i and OUT_i for $IN_{(i-1,i)}$ and $OUT_{(i,i+1)}$, respectively. The loop invariants I_i of P_i are shown below, each comprising a number of conjuncts, numbered for convenience.

(1) $x_i = X_i \neq \infty \wedge \bigwedge_{j\neq i} X_j \neq X_i \wedge (x_i, 0)\in OUT_i \wedge (z_i = 0 \vee z_i = 1)$
(2) $z_i = 1 \Rightarrow y_i = \infty$
(3) $y_i = \infty \Rightarrow \exists (x, h)\in IN_i\colon x_i \leqslant x$
(4) $(\exists h\colon (x_i, h)\in IN_i) \Leftrightarrow z_i = 1$
(5) $\forall (x, h)\in OUT_i\colon x \geqslant x_i$
(6) $\forall h\colon [(\infty, h)\in OUT_i \Rightarrow [h > 0 \wedge ((\infty, h-1)\in IN_i \vee (x_i, h-1)\in IN_i)]]$
(7) $\forall (x, h)\in OUT_i\colon x \neq \infty \Rightarrow (x = x_i \wedge h = 0) \vee ((x, h-1)\in IN_i \wedge h > 0)$
(8) $\forall (x, h)\in IN_i\colon x > x_i \wedge x \neq \infty \Rightarrow (x, h+1)\in OUT_i$

The establishment of the loop invariant is shown by the output axiom and the consequence rule, and assignment axiom plus sequential composition rule for the sequential part.

We show in some detail part of the proof of the invariance of I_i in P_i. First, we introduce the assertion ALT_i, holding prior to the branching point in P_i. It also comprises several numbered conjuncts. Conjuncts (1′), (3′), (5′), (6′), (7′) are like (1), (3), (5), (6), (7) in I_i, respectively.

(2′) $z_i = 0$
(4′) $\forall n, h\colon n < |IN_i| \Rightarrow (x_i, h) \neq IN_i[n]$
(8′) $\forall n, x, h\colon (n < |IN_i| \wedge (x, h) = IN_i[n] \wedge x > x_i \wedge x \neq \infty) \Rightarrow (x, h+1)\in OUT_i$

$P_i :: z_i := 0; y_i := 0; \langle c_i !!(x_i, 0)\rangle;$
$\quad * [y_i \neq \infty \rightarrow \langle c_{i-1} ??(y_i, h_i)\rangle;$
$\qquad [x_i = y_i \rightarrow z_i := 1; y_i := \infty; \langle c_i !!(\infty, h_i + 1); h_i := h_i + 1\rangle$
$\qquad \square$
$\qquad x_i > y_i \rightarrow skip$
$\qquad \square$
$\qquad x_i < y_i \rightarrow \langle c_i !!(y_i, h_i + 1); h_i := h_i + 1\rangle]$
$\quad]$

Figure 8.22 Distributed leader election – modified.

(9′) $IN_i \neq \varepsilon \wedge last(IN_i) = (y_i, h) \wedge h_i \geqslant 0$

We note that

$\{I_i \wedge y_i \neq \infty\}$
$c_{i-1} ?? y_i$
$\{ALT_i\}$

is obtained via the input axiom. We now consider the separate directions.

$\{ALT_i \wedge x_i = y_i\} z_i := 1 \{z_i = 1 \wedge (1) \wedge (3') \wedge (4') \wedge (5) \wedge (6) \wedge (7) \wedge (9')\}$

by the assignment axiom and the consequence rule. By similar means, we have

$\{z_i = 1 \wedge (1) \wedge (3') \wedge (4') \wedge (5) \wedge (6) \wedge (7) \wedge (9')\}$
$\qquad y_i := \infty$
$\{z_i = 1 \wedge y_i = \infty \wedge IN_i \neq \varepsilon \wedge last(IN_i) = (x_i, h_i) \wedge h_i \geqslant 0$
$\wedge (4') \wedge (5) \wedge (6) \wedge (7)\}$

From the latter postcondition, via the output axiom applied to $c_i!!(\infty, h_i + 1)$, we re-establish I_i.

The other directions are treated similarly.

□

EXERCISE:

Complete all other cases of the invariance proof.

□

By the iteration rule, we deduce that $q_i \equiv I_i \wedge y_i = \infty$ is the local postcondition for P_i.

Next, cooperation has to be established.

Again, we present only some detail of the proof, leaving the rest as exercises. Let us consider the case of the input command in P_i, matched against one output command in P_{i-1}, both on channel c_{i-1}.

We have to show

$$\{I_i \wedge y_i \neq \infty \wedge y_{i-1} = 0 \wedge z_{i-1} = 0 \wedge IN_{i-1} = OUT_{i-1} = \varepsilon$$
$$\wedge\, x_{i-1} = X_{i-1} \neq \infty \wedge \bigwedge_{j \neq i-1} X_i \neq X_j \wedge IN_i = OUT_{i-1}\}$$
$$c_{i-1}??(y_i, h_i) \parallel c_{i-1}!!(x_{i-1}, 0)$$
$$\{ALT_i\}$$

The conjuncts are as follows

(1′) $x_i = X_i \neq \infty \wedge \bigwedge_{j \neq i-1} X_i \neq X_j$ is carried from the precondition.
$(x_i, 0) \in OUT_i$ follows by the output axiom. Also, z_i was not changed.

(2′) $I_i \wedge y_i \neq \infty$ in the precondition imply $z_i = 0$, and it is not changed.

(3′) Holds vacuously, since $y_i \neq \infty$.

(4′) Suppose $n < |IN_i . (x_{i-1}, 0)|$. Since from the precondition we have $IN_i = OUT_{i-1} = \varepsilon$, we get that the implication holds vacuously.

(5′)–(8′) Skipped.

(9′) Follows from last $(IN_i . (x_{ij}, 0) = (x_{i-1}, 0)$.

Other cases are similar.

EXERCISE:

Identify and complete all other cases in the cooperation proof.

□

Finally, from the concurrent composition rule we deduce that

$$\bigwedge_{i=1,n} I_i \wedge y_i = \infty$$

holds. Denote this condition by F. We now have to derive the required postcondition from F.

First, by clause (3) of the invariants I_i, we get from F that

(8) $\bigwedge_{i=1,n} (\exists (x, h) \in IN_i : x \geqslant x_i)$

By weakening, we get from (8) that

$$(9) \quad \bigwedge_{i=1,n} (\exists (x,h) \in IN_i : x = x_i \vee (x = \infty \wedge x_i < x) \vee (x \neq \infty \wedge x_i < x)$$

From this, we now derive by *reductio ad absurdum* that

$$(*) \quad \bigvee_{i=1,n} \exists k : (x_i, k) \in IN_i$$

Suppose (*) is not the case. Then,

$$(10) \quad \bigwedge_{i=1,n} \forall k : (x_i, k) \notin IN_i$$

From steps (9) and (10) we get

$$(11) \quad \bigwedge_{i=1,n} \exists k : (x,k) \in IN_i \wedge (x_i < x \wedge x = \infty \vee x_i < x \wedge x \neq \infty)$$

By the Fifo axiom, we get

$$(12) \quad \bigwedge_{i=1,n} \exists k : (x,k) \in OUT_{i-1} \wedge (x_i < x \wedge x = \infty \vee x_i < x \wedge x \neq \infty)$$

By clauses (2), (3) and (4) of the invariant and step (*), we get

$$(13) \quad \exists k : (x, k-1) \in IN_{i-1} \wedge k-1 > 0 \wedge (x_i < x \wedge x = \infty \vee x_i < x \wedge x \neq \infty)$$

This way, we may generate an infinite decreasing sequence of natural numbers $k-j, j \geqslant 0$, which is a contradiction. This establishes (*).

We still have to show that there is no more than one such pair. Suppose that $z_{i_0} = 0$. By conjunct (4) of I_i,

$$(**) \quad \exists k : (x_{i_0}, k) \in IN_{i_0}$$

From (**) and the Fifo axiom of I_i, we get

$$(14) \quad \exists k : (x_{i_0}, k) \in OUT_{i_0 - 1}$$

and from step (14) and clauses (6) and (7) of the invariant we get

$$(15) \quad x_{i_0} > x_{i_0 - 1}$$

Continuing this way, we get

$$\exists k : (x_{i_0}, k) \in IN_{i_0} \Rightarrow \bigwedge_{1 \leqslant j \neq i \leqslant n} x_{i_0} > x_j$$

establishing the uniqueness of i_0.

□

8.8 Conclusions

In this chapter, we extended the verification method for the correctness assertions to distributed programs. We saw once again that the main verification techniques, namely invariants and well-founded variants, are applicable, but that compositionality has to be given up, approximated by a two-staged proof method.

A major problem in distributed programming is the lack of a global state and common knowledge about this state. To compensate for this lack joint-actions, performed simultaneously by several processes, are introduced. Hence, the second stage is expressed by the cooperation property, non-interference being obsolete because of disjointness of states. Cooperation tests have to use global invariants, to compensate for the absence of global states and common knowledge. The proof methodology known as **assume–guarantee** is used, where processes make assumptions about other processes, which are afterwards verified for mutual consistency.

We also saw that the fairness notions appropriate for joint-actions have a richer structure than the fairness of simple choice mechanisms, and have a crucial role in proving liveness properties of programs. Basically, the helpful directions method, under a proper notion of direction, extends to this model too.

As for asynchronous communication, the verification is even harder than for the synchronous case. This explains a tendency to prefer synchronous communication, which abstracts away some of the problems, in contexts dealing with verification. The modularity here is not clearly the right one, and more global approaches may be more intuitive. The subject of verifying asynchronous distributed programs has not been receiving the right attention in the literature.

Overall, one can see many advantages for program verification in using any of the models of distributed programs (or many others not described) instead of shared-variables concurrency. There are better prospects of finding disciplined programming methods in the distributed models, so that the verification methods will ultimately lead to a beneficial usage of *prima facie* correct design of concurrent programs.

Bibliographic notes and suggestions for further reading

Bibliographic notes The *CSP* language was introduced by C.A.R. Hoare in [152]. The **AFR** cooperating proofs system was first presented in [153]. An alternative formulation, using proofs from assumptions, is presented in [154], where one can find also the outline of the extension to termination proofs. Its soundness and relative completeness were shown in [155], though the current formulation is slightly different. A review of partial correctness proof systems for *CSP* appears in [156]. The proof of the distributed minimum computation in the **AFR** system is from [130]. The program itself is from [157], which is the source of the **LG** alternative proof system. The deadlock freedom proof method was presented in [153] and reviewed in [154]. The core of the language *IP* and extension of **AFR** to multiparty interaction are new [158]. The proof method for fair termination of *CSP* distributed programs was first presented in [159] and is reviewed also in [80]. The latter contains also a more detailed discussion of relativized fair termination proofs. The treatment of asynchronous communication is a variation on [160].

Suggestions for further reading In [156] extensions of **AFR** to nested concurrency and hiding are presented, for the channel-naming convention. Also, compositional proof systems for *CSP* based on trace assertions (in contrast to our state assertions) are discussed there, and further references are given. An extension of **AFR** for exception handling can be found in [161]. More information about the language *IP*, in particular its overlapping semantics, can be found in [162], [163], and in more detail in a forthcoming book [164]. A noninterleaving semantics for *CSP*, based on partial orders, is considered in [165].

EXERCISES

8.1 Proof outlines: Give an exact definition of a local proof outline for a *CSP* process, based on the proof rules of the local stage of **AFR**.

8.2 Extended naming conventions [166]: Extend the cooperating proofs system to a language with the following naming conventions for interprocess communication:

Dynamic target: $P_e?x, P_e!e'$: *receive* (respectively, *send*) from (to) the process whose identifier is the current value of *e*.

Unspecified target: $?x, !e'$: *receive* (respectively, *send*) from (to) any process readying a matching I/O command.

Provide also an operational semantics for the extended language and relate to the soundness and relative completeness of the extension you are proposing.

8.3 Alternative semantics for CSP: Consider the following transition rule instead of rule (2) in the text:

if $\langle S_i, \sigma / i\rangle \rightarrow \langle S_i', \sigma' / i\rangle$, then

$$\langle [S_1 \| \cdots \| S_i \| \cdots \| S_n], \sigma \rangle \stackrel{\varepsilon}{\rightarrow} \langle [S_1 \| \cdots \| E \| \cdots \| S_n], \sigma\rangle \qquad \textbf{(2')}$$

Explain the meaning of this replacement. Does it affect partial correctness properties?

8.4 Bracketing frontiers accessibility: Prove that by the definition of '$\rightarrow$', if a configuration C is not a *bf*, then there is a *bf* configuration C', s.t. $C \rightarrow C'$

8.5 Static verification [154], [167]: Assume some unique labeling of all I/O commands in a *CSP* program P. Define $\hat{P}$ to be obtained from P by replacing all its Boolean parts of guards by *true*, the identically true Boolean guard. Define a (finite) sequence of communication commands as **statically possible** iff it is a sequence arising from $\hat{P}$. Let $L[\![P]\!]$ be the set of all statically possible communication sequences of P.

Prove that for any *CSP* program $P, L[\![P]\!]$ is a **regular** language (in the sense of formal language theory).

8.6 Channel CSP [156]: Replace the naming convention of *CSP* communication by $\alpha!e$, $\alpha?x$, where α is a **channel name**. Impose the restriction that each channel name connects exactly two processes. Formulate the corresponding variant of **AFR** for the revised language. Provide also an *sos* operational semantics for the revised language and discuss the soundness and relative completeness of your extension of **AFR** w.r.t. the semantics proposed.

8.7 Bounded communication channels: Consider a variant of *ACSP* in which for each channel c there is a bound n_c, s.t. an output on c is enabled only if the current length of (the content of) c is less than the bound, and otherwise delays the sender. Formulate an operational semantics and proof rules for partial correctness for programs in this language.

8.8 Distributed termination convention ([152], [153]): Modify the **AFR** system presented here to accommodate the following change in the semantics of *CSP*, changing the conditions of loop exit. A guard is **closed** if either the Boolean part evaluates to *false*, or the process addressed in its communication part has terminated.

Which other correctness criteria, besides partial correctness, are affected by this change?

8.9 Leader election: Consider the following *IP* solution of the leader election problem (similar to one in [168]) in Figure 8.23. Prove, using **AFR** extended to *IP*, that it satisfies the specification of L in the corresponding example.

$LEADER :: [P_1 \| \cdots \| P_n]$, where
$P_i :: minid_i := id_i; round_i := 1; given_i := 0; last_i := 0;$
$*[\ round_i < n; pass_{i-1}, [minid_i := min(minid_{i-1}, minid_i)$
$round_i := min(round_{i-1} + 1, n)] \rightarrow skip$
$\square$
$given_i < round_i \wedge (last_i < minid_i \vee round_i = n); pass_i[]$
$\rightarrow given_i := round_i; last_i := minid_i];$
$leader_i := (id_i = minid_i)$

Figure 8.23 Binary interactions solution of the ring leader election problem in *IP*.

8.10 **Rotation [164]:** Consider the following *IP* program $P :: [\ \|_{i=1,n}\ P_i]$, where

$P_i :: s_i := false; r_i := false;$
$*[\neg s_i; a_{i+1}[] \rightarrow s_i := true \square \neg r_i; a_i[t_i := x_{i-1}] \rightarrow r_i := true];$
$x_i := t_i$

Show that P satisfies $\{\bigwedge_{i=1,n} x_i = X_i\}\ P\ \{\bigwedge_{i=1,n} x_i = X_{i-1}\}$, where all indices are cyclical.

8.11 **Merging lemma [155]:** Reformulate the merging lemma as needed for the completeness proof of **AFR**, and prove your reformulated lemma.

8.12 **Non-Fifo asynchronous communication:** Show how to weaken the Fifo axiom to reflect message arrival independently of sending order.

8.13 Show that using the communication axiom outside cooperation proofs leads to unsoundness (in the asynchronous communication case).

8.14 Give an explicit description of a deadlocking configuration in *ACSP*.

8.15 Provide another example of fair termination proof for *CSP*.

CONCLUSION

What did we achieve? Throughout this book, we presented a theory of program verification. We focused on some very simple properties of programs, namely partial correctness, total correctness (and termination), and for concurrent and distributed programs we also considered deadlock freedom and starvation freedom – special cases of the more general safety and liveness properties. On the other hand, restricting the theory to simple specifications had two advantages. First, we were able to formulate proof rules (for proving the satisfaction of such specifications) for a rich variety of programming language constructs. The reader will no doubt conclude that extension, along the lines considered, to more language constructs is a feasible task. In addition, we had the advantage of developing a comprehensive meta-theory, studying properties of the proof systems themselves.

Have we achieved our methodological goal? Well, not quite! Even more, at this point in time the actual industrial application of formal program verification does not look realizable in the near future. Extending the theory to 'real' specifications (in some well-chosen specification language) is a topic of intensive research, and has not yet produced immediately applicable results. Specification formalisms with very rich expressive power have been proposed, but then they do not enjoy a simple proof method. Important properties of programs such as performance issues, fault tolerance, security (in the cryptographic sense), device dependence, and many more do not yet have the right formalization to allow formal verification. In addition, many useful programs do not have a clear specification much different from the program itself. How would one specify a program implementing the tax rules? Or a medical expert system?

The notorious 'size' problem, that of verifying 'real' programs – in contrast to the 'toy programs' considered in the book – is a real obstacle, and scalability of proof methods is also still a research topic.

So, why bother about what was achieved? There are several reasons which may lead to more encouraging conclusions. First, while the book focused on what might be called *a posteriori* verification, namely the verification of programs after they have been designed, it is clear that the real industrial application of the formal method is in the reverse direction: use the available rules in the inverse direction in order to derive correct programs from their specifications. However, as mentioned already, a judicious use of the derivation methodology is enhanced by a deeper understanding of the theory involved (including the meta-theory). So far, the literature on program derivation concentrated on program refinement, a kind of an 'ideal' top-down design approach. Recently, the bottom-up approach has been getting the attention it deserves. This approach calls for the construction of building blocks that have been verified, and provides rules for their correct combination in various ways to obtain larger designs.

In addition, there is hope that with more elaborate machine assistance some of the scalability problems will disappear in the end. For small sections of critical importance in a program, even automatic verification is now a feasible solution.

A major benefit of mastering the theory presented is in creating awareness of the tools and techniques suggested by the theory. Becoming adjusted to thinking in terms of the concepts provided by this theory, even if not following the methodology to the letter, may lead to a less error-prone design method. The techniques and methods studied form one of the scientific foundations of this engineering discipline, and foundations, in the long run, always suggest a firm ground on which one could build.

REFERENCES

[1] DeMillo R. A., Lipton R. J. and Perlis A. J. (1979). Social processes and proof of theorems and programs. *Comm. ACM*, **22** (5), 271–80

[2] Fletzer J. H. (1989). Program verification: the very idea. *Comm. ACM*, **31** (9), 1048–63

[3] Barwise J. (1989). Mathematical proofs of computer systems correctness. *Notices American Mathematical Society*, **36** (7), 838–51

[4] Boyer R. S. and Moore J. S. (1981). *The Correctness Principle in Computer Science*. New York: Academic Press

[5] Biørner D. and Druffle L. (1990). Position statement: ICSE 12 workshop on industrial experience using formal methods. In *Proc. 12th Int. Conf. on Software Engineering*, Nice, March 1990

[6] Craigen D. (1990). Assessment of formal methods for trustworthy computer systems. In *Proc. 12th Int. Conf. on Software Engineering*, Nice, March 1990

[7] Hennessy M. C. B. and Plotkin G. D. (1979). Full abstraction for a simple programming language. In *Proc. 8th Sym. on the Mathematical Foundation of Computer Science*. Lecture Notes on Computer Science Vol. 74. Berlin: Springer

[8] Plotkin G. D. (1981). *A Structural Approach to Operational Semantics*. Technical Report DAIMI–FN 19, Computer Science Department, Aarhus University

[9] Floyd R. W. (1967). Assigning meaning to programs. In *Proc. American Mathematical Society Sym. on Applied Mathematics* Vol. 19

[10] Hoare C. A. R. (1969). An axiomatic basis for computer programming. *Comm. ACM*, **12** (10), 576–80

[11] Manna Z. (1974). *Mathematical Theory of Computation*. New York: McGraw-Hill

[12] Gerhart S. L. and Yelowitz L. (1976). Observations of fallibility in applications of modern programming methodologies. *IEEE Trans. Software Engineering*, **2** (3), 195–207

[13] Harel D., Pnueli A. and Stavi J. (1977). A complete axiomatic system for proving deductions about recursive programs. In *Proc. 9th ACM Sym. on Theory of Computation*, Boulder CO, May 1977

[14] Gries D. and Levin G. (1980). Assignment and procedure call proof rules. *ACM Trans. Programming Languages Systems*, **2** (4), 564–79

[15] Constable R. and O'Donnel M. (1978). *A Programming Logic*. Wintrop

[16] Ernst G. W. (1977). Rules of inference for procedure calls. *Acta Informatica*, **8**, 145–52

[17] de Bakker J. W. (1980). *Mathematical Theory of Program Correctness*. Englewood Cliffs NJ: Prentice-Hall

[18] Schmidt D. A. (1986). *Denotational Semantics*. Boston MA: Allyn and Bacon

[19] Loecks J. and Sieber K. (1987). *The Foundations of Program Verification* 2nd edn. New York: Wiley

[20] Jones C. B. (1980). *Software Development, a Rigorous Approach*. Englewood Cliffs NJ: Prentice-Hall

[21] Jones C. B. (1986). *Developing Software using VDM*. Englewood Cliffs NJ: Prentice-Hall

[22] Turski W. M. and Maibaum T. S. E. (1987). *The Specification of Computer Programs*. Reading MA: Addison-Wesley

[23] Dijkstra E. W. (1976). *A Discipline of Programming*. Englewood Cliffs NJ: Prentice-Hall

[24] Gries D. (1981). *The Science of Programming*. Berlin: Springer

[25] Backhouse R. C. (1986). *Program Construction and Verification*. Englewood Cliffs NJ: Prentice-Hall

[26] Baber R. L. (1987). *The Spine of Software, Designing Provably Correct Software – Theory and Practice*. New York: Wiley

[27] Ehrig H. and Mahr B. (1985). *Fundamentals of Algebraic Specifications 1: Equations and Initial Semantics*. European Association for Theoretical Computer Science Monographs on Theoretical Computer Sciences Vol. 6. Berlin: Springer

[28] Tucker J. V. and Zucker J. I. (1988). *Program Correctness Over Data Types with Error-state Semantics*. Centrum voor Wiskunde en Informatica Monograph 6. Amsterdam: North-Holland

[29] Goldstine H.H. and von Neumann J. (1963). Planning and coding problems for an electronic computer. In *Collected Works of John von Neumann* Vol. 5 (Traub A. H., ed.), pp. 80–235. Oxford: Pergamon

[30] Turing A. (1950). Checking a large routine. In *Proc. Conf. on High Speed Automatic Calculating Machines*, McLennan Laboratory, University of Toronto

[31] Naur P. (1966). Proof of algorithms by general snapshots. *BIT*, **6**, 310–16

[32] Gorn S. (1959). *Common Programming Language Task* Part 1, Section 5. Final Report AD59UR1, US Army Signal Corps, Moore School of Electrical Engineering

[33] Burstall R. M. (1974). Program proving as hand simulation with a little induction. In *Proc. IFIP 74*, pp. 308–12. Amsterdam: North-Holland

[34] Manna Z. and Waldinger R. (1978). Is 'sometime' better than 'always'? Intermittent assertions in proving programs correct. *Comm. ACM*, **21** (2), 159–171

[35] Lamport L. (1977). Proving the correctness of multiprocess programs. *IEEE Trans. Software Engineering*, **3** (2), 125–43

[36] Francez N. (1976). The analysis of cyclic programs. *PhD Thesis*, Weizmann Institute of Science, Rehovot

[37] Francez N. and Pnueli A. (1978). A proof method for cyclic programs. *Acta Informatica*, **9**, 133–57

[38] Wang A. (1976). An axiomatic basis for proving total correctness of goto programs. *BIT*, **16**, 88–102

[39] Lauer P. E. (1971). *Consistent Formal Theories of the Semantics of Programming Languages*. Technical Report 25.121, IBM Laboratories, Vienna

[40] Cook S. A. (1978). Soundness and completeness of an axiom system for program verification. *SIAM J. Computing*, **7** (1), 70–90

[41] Morris J. H. Jr. and Wegbreit B. (1977). Subgoal induction. *Comm. ACM*, **20** (4), 209–22

[42] Schwartz J. (1976). Event based reasoning – a system for proving correct termination of programs. In *Proc. 1st Int. Colloq. on Automata, Languages and Programming* (European Assoc. for Theoretical Computer Science) Sym. (Nivat M., ed). Amsterdam: North-Holland

[43] Ashcroft E. (1976). *Intermittent Assertions in LUCID*. Technical Report CS–76–47, Computer Science Department, University of Waterloo, Canada

[44] Ashcroft E. A. and Wadge W. W. (1976). LUCID – a formal system for writing and proving programs. *SIAM J. Computing*, **5** (3), 336–354

[45] King J. C. (1980). Program correctness: on inductive assertions methods. *IEEE Trans. Software Engineering*, **6** (5), 465–79

[46] Cousot P. and Cousot R. (1987). Sometimes = always + recursion ≡ always – on the equivalence of the intermittent and invariant assertions methods for proving inevitability properties of programs. *Acta Informatica*, **24**, 1–31

[47] Manna Z. and Waldinger R. (1985). *The Logical Basis for Computer Programming* Vol. 1 *Deductive Reasoning*. Cambridge MA: Addison-Wesley

[48] Manna Z. (1969). The correctness of programs. *J. Computer System Sciences*, **3**, 119–27

[49] Katz S. M. and Manna Z. (1975). A closer look at termination. *Acta Informatica*, **5**, 333–532

[50] Katz S. M. and Manna Z. (1976). Logical analysis of programs. *Comm. ACM*, **19** (4), 188–206

[51] Basu S. K. and Yeh R. T. (1975). Strong verification of programs. *IEEE Trans. Software Engineering*, **1** (3), 339–45

[52] Sites R. L. (1974). Proving that computer programs terminate cleanly. *PhD Thesis*, Stanford University

[53] Hoare C. A. R. (1971). Proof of a program: FIND. *Comm. ACM*. **14**, 1: 39–45

[54] Apt K.R. (1981). Ten years of Hoare's logic: a survey – part I. *ACM Trans. Programming Languages Systems*, **3** (4), 431–83

[55] Manna Z. and Pnueli A. (1974). Axiomatic approach to total correctness of programs. *Acta Informatica*, **3**, 253–63

[56] Igarashi S., London R. L. and Luckham D. C. (1975). Automatic program verification I – a logical basis and its implementation. *Acta Informatica*, **4**, 145–82

[57] Harel D. (1979). *First Order Dynamic Logic*. Lecture Notes in Computer Science Vol. 36. Berlin: Springer

[58] Lifschitz W. (1984). On verification of programs with goto statements. *Information Processing Lett.*, **18**, 221–5

[59] Gumb R. D. (1989), *Programming Logics: An Introduction to Verification and Semantics*. John Wiley & Sons

[60] Manna Z. and Waldinger R. (1981). Problematic features in programming languages. *Acta Informatica*, **16**, 371–426

[61] Hoare C. A. R. and Wirth N. (1973). An axiomatic definition of the programming language PASCAL. *Acta Informatica*, **2**, 335–55

[62] Pratt V. R. (1976). Semantical considerations of Floyd–Hoare logics. In *Proc. 17th IEEE Sym. on Foundations of Computer Science*

[63] Harel D. (1984). Dynamic logic. In *Handbook of Philosophical Logic* Vol. 2 (Gabbay D. and Guenther F., eds.), Chapter II.10. Dordrecht: Reidel

[64] McCarthy J. (1962). Towards a mathematical science of computation. In *Proc. IFIP Congr. on Information Processing* (Popplewill C. M., ed.). Amsterdam: North-Holland

[65] Harel D. (1980). Proving the correctness of regular deterministic programs: a unifying survey using dynamic logic. *Theoretical Computer Science*, **12**, 61–81

[66] Clint M. and Hoare C. A. R. (1972). Program proving: jumps and functions. *Acta Informatica*, **1**, 214–44

[67] Sokolowski S. (1977). Axioms for total correctness. *Acta Informatica*, **9** (1), 61–71

[68] London R. L., Guttag J. V., Horning J. J., Lampson B. W., Mitchell J. G. and Popek G. J. (1978). Proof rules for the programming language Euclid. *Acta Informatica*, **10**, 1–26

[69] Jansen T. M. V. (1983). Foundations and applications of Montague grammar. *PhD Thesis*, University of Amsterdam

[70] Hoare C. A. R. (1971). Procedures and parameters: an axiomatic approach. In *Proc. Sym. on Semantics of Algorithmic Languages* (Engeler E., ed.). Lecture Notes in Mathematics Vol. 188. Berlin: Springer

[71] Francez N. (1983). Extended naming conventions for communicating processes. *Science of Computer Programming*, **3**, 101–14

[72] Ashcroft E. and Manna Z. (1971). The translation of 'GOTO' programs to 'WHILE' programs. In *Proc. IFIP Congress*, pp. 250–55. Amsterdam: North-Holland

[73] Greibach S. A. (1975). *Theory of Verification*. Lecture Notes in Computer Science Vol. 36. Berlin: Springer

[74] Enderton H. B. (1972). *A Mathematical Introduction to Logic*. New York: Academic Press

[75] Takaoka T. (1987). A decomposition rule for the Hoare logic. *Information Processing Lett.*, **26**, 205–8

[76] Dijkstra E. W. (1975). Guarded commands, nondeterminacy and formal derivation of programs. *Comm. ACM*, **18** (8), 453–7

[77] Apt K. R. (1984). Ten years of Hoare's logic: a survey – part II: nondeterminism. *Theoretical Computer Science*, **28**, 83–109

[78] Apt K. R. and Plotkin G. D. (1986). Countable nondeterminism and random assignment. *J. ACM*, **33** (4), 724–67

[79] Back R. J. (1984). Proving total correctness of non-deterministic programs in infinitary logic. *Acta Informatica*, **15**, 233–50

[80] Francez N. (1986) *Fairness*. Berlin: Springer

[81] Grumberg O. (1984). *PhD Thesis*, Computer Science Department, Technion, Haifa (in Hebrew)

[82] Grumberg O., Francez N., Makowsky J. A. and de Roever W.-P. (1985). A proof rule for fair termination of guarded commands. *Information and Control*, **66** (1/2), 83–102

[83] Lehmann D., Pnueli A. and Stavi J. (1981). Impartiality, justice and fairness: the ethics of concurrent termination. In *Proc. 8th Int. Colloq. on Automata,*

Languages and Programming (European Assoc. for Theoretical Computer Science), Acre, July 1981 (Kariv O. and Even S., eds.). Lecture Notes in Computer Science Vol. 115. Berlin: Springer

[84] Apt K. R. and Olderog E.-R. (1983). Proof rules and transformations dealing with fairness. *Science of Computer Programming*, **3**, 65–100

[85] Plotkin G. D. (1976). A power domain construction. *SIAM J. Computing*, **5** (3), 452–87

[86] Smyth M. (1978). Power domains. *J. Computer System Sciences*, **16** (1), 23–6

[87] Hitchcock P. and Park D. M. R. (1975). Induction rules and termination proofs. In *Proc. 1st Int. Colloq. on Automata, Languages and Programming* (European Assoc. for Theoretical Computer Science) Sym. (Nivat M., ed.). Amsterdam: North-Holland

[88] Stomp F. A., de Roever W.-P. and Gerth, R. T. (1989). The μ-calculus as an assertion language for fairness arguments. *Information and Computation*, **82** (3), 278–322

[89] Park D. M. R. (1979). On the semantics of fair parallelism. In *Proc. Abstract Software Specification* (Biørner D., ed.). Lecture Notes in Computer Science Vol. 86. Berlin: Springer

[90] Park D. M. R. (1981). A predicate transformer for weak fair iteration. In *Proc. 6th IBM Sym. on Mathematical Foundations of Computer Science,* Hakone

[91] Apt K. R., Pnueli A. and Stavi J. (1984). Fair termination revisited with delay. *Theoretical Computer Science*, **33**, 65–84

[92] Francez N. and Kozen D. (1984). Generalized fair termination. In *Proc. 14th ACM Annual Sym. on Principles of Programming Languages,* Salt Lake City UT, January 1984

[93] Harel D. (1986). Effective transformations on infinite trees, with applications to high undecidability, dominoes, and fairness. *J. ACM*, **33** (1), 224–48

[94] Francez N. (1977). A case for a forward predicate transformer. *Information Processing Lett.*, **6** (6), 196–8

[95] Kuiper R. Enforcing nondeterminism via linear temporal logic. In *Proc. Colloq. on Temporal Logic and Specification*, Altrincham, April 1987 (Banieqbal B., Barringer H. and Pnueli A., eds.). Lecture Notes in Computer Science Vol. 398. Berlin: Springer

[96] Spaan E., Torenvliet L. and van Emde Boas P. (1989). *Nondeterminism, Fairness and a Fundamental Analogy*. Technical Report CT–88–10, Institute for Language, Logic and Information, University of Amsterdam (also in: European Association for Theoretical Computer Science Bull. 37, February 1989)

[97] Jacobs D. and Gries D. (1985). General correctness; a unification of partial and total correctness. *Acta Informatica*, **22** (1), 67–83

[98] Dijkstra E. W. (1977). *A Sequel to EWD 592.* Report EWD 600, Burroughs, Nuenen, The Netherlands

[99] America P. and de Boer F. S. (1990). Proving total correctness of recursive programs. *Information and Computation*, **84** (2), 129–62

[100] Gorelik G. A. (1975). *A Complete Axiomatic System for Proving Assertions about Recursive and Non-recursive Programs*, TR75, Dept of CS, University of Toronto

[101] Sokolowski S. (1977). Total correctness for procedures. In *Proc. 6th Sym. on*

Mathematical Foundation of Computer Science. Lecture Notes in Computer Science Vol. 53. Berlin: Springer

[102] Bijlsma A., Matthews P. A. and Wittie J. G. (1989). A sharp proof rule for procedures in wp semantics. *Acta Informatica*, **26**, 409–19

[103] Olderog E.-R. (1983). On the notion of expressiveness and the rule of adaptation. *Theoretical Computer Science*, **24**, 337–47

[104] Cartright R. and Oppen D. C. (1978). Unrestricted procedure calls in Hoare's logic. In *Proc. 5th ACM Annual Sym. on Principles of Programming Languages*, Tucson AZ, January 1978

[105] Cartwright R. and Oppen D. C. (1981). The logic of aliasing. *Acta Informatica*, **15**, 368–84

[106] Clarke E. M. (1979). Programming languages for which it is impossible to obtain good Hoare axiom systems. *J. ACM*, **26** (1), 129–47

[107] Martin A. J. (1983). A general proof rule for procedures in predicate transformer semantics. *Acta Informatica*, **20**, 301–13

[108] Bijlsma A., Wittie J. G. and Matthews P. A. (1986). Equivalence of the Gries and Martin proof rules for procedure calls. *Acta Informatica*, **23** (4), 357–60

[109] Nielsen H. R. (1985). *A Hoare-like Proof System for Total Correctness of Nested Recursive Procedures*. Technical Report 85–4, Institute of Electronic Systems, Aalborg University

[110] Meyer A. R. and Mitchell J. C. (1983). Termination assertions for recursive programs: completeness and axiomatic definability. *Information and Control*, **56**, 112–38

[111] Ah-kee A. (1990). Proof obligations for blocks and procedures. *Formal Aspects of Computing*, **2** (4), 312–30

[112] Olderog E.-R. (1983). Hoare's logic for programs with procedures – what has been achieved? In *Proc. Logics of Programs Workshop*, Carnegie-Mellon University, Pittsburgh PA, June 1983 (Clarke E. M. and Kozen D., eds.). Lecture Notes in Computer Science Vol. 164. Berlin: Springer

[113] Clarke E. M. (1985). The characterization problem in Hoare logic. In *Mathematical Logic and Programming Languages* (Hoare C. A. R. and Shepherdson J. C., eds.), pp. 89–106. Englewood Cliffs NJ: Prentice-Hall

[114] Cherniavsky J. C. and Kamin S. N. (1979). A complete and consistent Hoare axiomatics for a simple programming language. *J. ACM*, **26** (1), 119–28

[115] Meyer A. R. and Mitchell J. C. (1982). Axiomatic definability and completeness for recursive programs. In *Proc. 9th ACM Annual Sym. on Principles of Programming Languages*, Albuquerque NM, January 1982

[116] de Bakker J. W. and Meertens L. G. L. T. (1975). On the completeness of the inductive assertions method. *J. Computer System Sciences*, **11** (3), 323–57

[117] Ashcroft E. (1975). Proving assertions about parallel programs. *J. Computer System Sciences*, **10** (1), 110–35

[118] Ashcroft E. and Manna Z. (1971). Formalization of properties of parallel programs. In *Machine Intelligence* Vol. 6, pp. 17–41. Edinburgh: Edinburgh University Press

[119] van Lamsweerde A. and Sintzoff M. (1979). Formal derivation of strongly correct concurrent programs. *Acta Informatica*, **12**, 1–31

[120] Flon L. and Suzuki N. (1981). The total correctness of parallel programs. *SIAM J. Computing*, **10** (1), 227–46

[121] Manna Z. and Pnueli A. (1991). The Temporal Logic of Reactive and Concurrent Systems: Specification. Berlin: Springer

[122] Lamport L. (1989). A simple approach to specifying concurrent systems. *Comm. ACM*, **32** (1), 32–45

[123] Hoare C. A. R. (1985). *Communicating Sequential Processes*. Englewood Cliffs NJ: Prentice-Hall

[124] Milner R. M. M. (1980). *A Calculus for Communicating Systems*. Lecture Notes in Computer Science Vol. 94. Berlin: Springer

[125] Milner R. M. M. (1989). *Communication and Concurrency*. Englewood Cliffs NJ: Prentice-Hall

[126] Bergstra J. A. and Klopp J. W. (1984). Process algebra for synchronous communication. *Information and Computation*, **60**, 109–37

[127] de Bakker J. W., de Roever W.-P. and Rozenberg G. (eds.) (1988). *Linear Time, Branching Time and Partial Order Logics and Models of Concurrency*. Lecture Notes in Computer Science Vol. 354. Berlin: Springer

[128] Petri C. A. (1977). *Non-sequential Processes*. Internal Report ISF–77–5, Gesellschaft für Mathematik und Datenverarbeitung

[129] Reisig W. (1985). *Petri Nets: an Introduction*. European Association for Theoretical Computer Science Monographs in Computer Science. Berlin: Springer

[130] Barringer H. (1985). *A Survey of Verification Techniques for Parallel Programs*. Lecture Notes in Computer Science Vol. 191. Berlin: Springer

[131] Schneider F. B. and Andrews G. R. (1986). Concepts for concurrent programming. In *Current Trends in Concurrency* (de Bakker J. W., de Roever W.-P. and Rozenberg G., eds.). Lecture Notes in Computer Science Vol. 224. Berlin: Springer

[132] Owicki S. and Gries D. (1976). An axiomatic proof technique for parallel programs. *Acta Informatica*, **6**, 319–40

[133] Owicki S. and Gries D. (1976). Verifying the properties of parallel programs: an axiomatic approach. *Comm. ACM*, **19** (5), 279–86

[134] Apt K. R. (1981). Recursive assertions and parallel programs. *Acta Informatica*, **15**, 219–32

[135] Clint M. (1973). Program proving: coroutines. *Acta Informatica*, **2** (1), 50–63

[136] McCurly E. R. (1989). Auxiliary variables in partial correctness programming logics. *Information Processing Lett.*, **33**, 131–3

[137] Owicki S. (1976). A consistent and complete deductive system for the verification of parallel programs. In *Proc. 8th Sym on Theory of Computation*, Houston TX, October 1976

[138] Dijkstra E. W. (1971). Hierarchical ordering of sequential processes. *Acta Informatica*, **1** (2), 115–38

[139] Hoare C. A. R. (1972). Towards a theory of parallel programming. In *Operating Systems Techniques* (Hoare C. A. R. and Perrot R. H., eds.). New York: Academic Press

[140] Apt K. R., de Boer F. S. and Olderog E.-R. (1990). *Proving Termination of Parallel Programs*. Technical Report CS – R9016, Centrum voor Wiskunde en Informatica, Amsterdam

[141] Alpern B. and Schneider F. B. (1985). Defining liveness. *Information Processing Lett.*, **21** (4), 181–5

[142] Brinch-Hansen P. (1973). *Operating Systems Principles*. Englewood Cliffs NJ: Prentice-Hall

[143] Hoare C. A. R. (1974). Monitors: an operating system structuring concept. *Comm. ACM*, **17** (10), 549–57

[144] Howard J. H. (1976). Proving monitors. *Comm. ACM*, **19** (5), 273–9

[145] Adams J. M. and Black A. P. (1982). On proof rules for monitors. *ACM SIGOPS Rev.*, **16** (2)

[146] Howard J. H. (1982). Signaling in monitors. In *Proc. IEEE Int. Conf. on Software Engineering*, 1976

[147] Howard J. H. (1982). Reply to 'On proof rules for monitors'. *ACM SIGOPS Rev.*, **16** (4)

[148] Adams J. M. and Black A. P. (1983). *ACM SIGOPS Rev.*, **17** (1)

[149] Nielsen L. S. and Black A. P. (1985). *Proving Monitor Proof Rules*. Technical Report 85–08–01, Department of Computer Science, University of Washington, Seattle WA

[150] Hoare C. A. R. (1975). Parallel programming: an axiomatic approach. *Computer Languages*, **1**, 151–60

[151] Rosen B. K. (1974). *Correctness of Parallel Programs: the Church–Rosser Approach*. Report RC5107, IBM T. J. Watson Research Center

[152] Hoare C. A. R. (1978). Communicating sequential processes. *Comm. ACM*, **21** (8), 666–77

[153] Apt K. R., Francez N. and de Roever W.-P. (1980). A proof system for communicating sequential processes. *ACM Trans. Programming Languages Systems*, **2** (3), 359–85

[154] Apt K. R. (1985). Proving the correctness of CSP programs – a tutorial. In *Proc. Int. Summer School*, Marktoberdorf, FRG. *Control Flow and Data Flow* (Broy M., ed.), pp. 441–75. NATO–ASI Series Vol. F14. Berlin: Springer

[155] Apt K. R. (1983). Formal justification of a proof system for communicating sequential processes. *J. ACM*, **30** (1), 197–216

[156] Hooman J. and de Roever W.-P. (1986). *The Quest Goes on – a Survey of Proofsystems for Partial Correctness of CSP*. EUT Report 80–wsk–01, Department of Mathematics and Computer Science, Eindhoven University

[157] Levin G. and Gries D. (1981). Proof techniques for communicating sequential processes. *Acta Informatica*, **15**, 281–302

[158] Francez N. (1989). Cooperating proofs for distributed programs with multiparty interactions. *Information Processing Lett.*, **32**, 235–42

[159] Grumberg O., Francez N. and Katz S. (1984). Fair termination of communicating processes. In *Proc. 3rd ACM Annual Sym. on Principles of Distributed Computing*, Vancouver, August 1984

[160] Schlichting R. D. and Schneider F. B. (1984). Message passing for distributed programming. *ACM Trans. Programming Languages Systems*, **6** (3), 402–31

[161] Lodaya K. and Shyamasundar R. K. (1990). Proof theory for exception handling in a tasking environment. *Acta Informatica*, **28** (1), 7–42

[162] Attie P., Francez N. and Grumberg O. (1990). Fairness and hyperfairness in multiparty interactions. In *Proc. 14th ACM Annual Sym. on Principles of Programming Languages*, San Francisco CA, January 1990

[163] Francez N. and Forman I. R. (1990). Conflict preparation. In *Proc. IEEE Int. Conf. on Computer Languages* (ICCL '90), New Orleans LA, March 1990

[164] Francez N. and Forman I. R. (1992). *Interacting Processes: Coordinated Distributed Programming*. Wokingham: Addison-Wesley (to be published)

[165] Reisig W. (1984). Partial order semantics versus interleaving semantics for CSP-like languages and its impact on fairness. In *Proc. Int. Colloq. on Automata, Languages and Programming* (European Assoc. for Theoretical Computer Science), Antwerp, July 1984

[166] Francez N. (1983). Product properties and their direct verification. *Acta Informatica*, **20**, 329–44.

[167] Apt K. R. (1984). A static analysis of CSP programs. In *Logics of Programs* (Clarke E. M. and Kozen D., eds.). Lecture Notes in Computer Science Vol. 164. Berlin: Springer

[168] Chang E. and Roberts R. (1979). An improved algorithm for decentralized extrema finding in circular configuration of processes. *Comm. ACM*, **22** (5), 281–3

[169] Apt K. R. and Olderog E.-R. (1991). *Verification of Sequential and Concurrent Programs*. Berlin: Springer

[170] Cousot P. and Cousot R. (1982). Induction principles for proving invariance properties of programs. In *Tools and Notions for Program Construction* (Néel D., ed.), pp. 75–119. Cambridge University Press

[171] Bergstra J. A. and Tucker J. V. (1981). Algebraically specified programming systems and Hoare's logic. Lecture Notes in Computer Science Vol. 115, 348–62

[172] Olderog E.-R. and Apt K. R. (1988). Fairness in parallel programs: the transformational approach. *ACM-Transactions on Programming Languages and Systems*, **10** (3), 420–55

[173] Salwicki A. and Müldner T. (1981). On the algorithmic properties of concurrent programs. In *Logics of Programs* (Engeler E., ed.). Lecture Notes in Computer Science Vol. 125. Berlin: Springer

Index